Left of the Color Line

The John Hope Franklin Series in African American History and Culture

Waldo E. Martin Jr. and Patricia Sullivan, editors

Left of the Color Line

Race, Radicalism, and Twentieth-Century Literature of the United States

Edited by
Bill V. Mullen and
James Smethurst

The University of
North Carolina Press

Chapel Hill & London

Designed by April Leidig-Higgins
Set in Monotype Garamond by Copperline Book Services, Inc.
Manufactured in the United States of America

The paper in this book meets the guidelines for permanence and durability of the Committee on Production Guidelines for Book Longevity of the Council on Library Resources.

Anthony Dawahare's essay, "The Specter of Radicalism in Alain Locke's *The New Negro*," was previously published, in somewhat different form, in Anthony Dawahare, *Nationalism, Marxism, and African American Literature between the Wars: A New Pandora's Box* (Jackson: University Press of Mississippi, 2002), and is reprinted here with permission.

Bill V. Mullen's essay, "W. E. B. Du Bois, *Dark Princess*, and the Afro-Asian International," was previously published in slightly different form in *positions: east asia culture critique* 11, no. 1 (Spring 2003): 217–40, and is reprinted here with permission from Duke University Press.

Alan Wald's essay, "Narrating Nationalisms: Black Marxism and Jewish Communists through the Eyes of Harold Cruse," was previously published in *Science and Society* 64, no. 4 (Winter 2000–2001): 400–423, and is reprinted here with permission.

Library of Congress Cataloging-in-Publication Data
Left of the color line: race, radicalism, and twentieth-century literature of the United States / edited by Bill V. Mullen and James Smethurst.
p. cm.—(The John Hope Franklin series in African American history and culture) Includes bibliographical references and index.
ISBN 0-8078-2799-1 (cloth: alk. paper)
ISBN 0-8078-5477-8 (pbk.: alk. paper)
1. American literature—20th century—History and criticism. 2. Race in literature. 3. Politics and literature—United States—History—20th century. 4. Race relations—United States—History—20th century. 5. Radicalism—United States—History—20th century. 6. Right and left (Political science) in literature. 7. African Americans in literature. 8. Race relations in literature. 9. Radicalism in literature. 10. Minorities in literature. I. Mullen, Bill, 1959– II. Smethurst, James Edward. III. Series.
PS228.R32 L44 2003 810.9'358—dc21 2003005015

cloth 07 06 05 04 03 5 4 3 2 1
paper 07 06 05 04 03 5 4 3 2 1

Contents

Abbreviations

ABB	African Blood Brotherhood
ABC	American Broadcasting Companies
AMSAC	American Society for African Culture
ANT	American Negro Theater
APA	Asian Pacific American
BARTS	Black Arts Repertory Theater and School
BBC	British Broadcasting Corporation
CAP	Congress of African Peoples
CAW	Congress of American Women
CIA	Central Intelligence Agency
CIO	Congress of Industrial Unions
Comintern	Communist International
CPUSA	Communist Party of the United States of America
FBI	Federal Bureau of Investigation
FDR	Franklin Delano Roosevelt
FWP	Federal Writers Project
HUAC	House Un-American Activities Committee
HWG	Harlem Writers Guild
INS	Immigration and Naturalization Service
IWW	Industrial Workers of the World
LULAC	League of United Latin American Citizens
NAACP	National Association for the Advancement of Colored People
NBA	National Book Award
NOI	Nation of Islam
PBS	Public Broadcasting Service
PLM	Mexican Liberal Party
PLP	Progressive Labor Party
SDS	Students for a Democratic Society
SNCC	Student Nonviolent Coordinating Committee
SNYC	Southern Negro Youth Congress
SWP	Socialist Workers Party
UNIA	Universal Negro Improvement Association
WP	Workers Party
WPA	Works Progress Administration

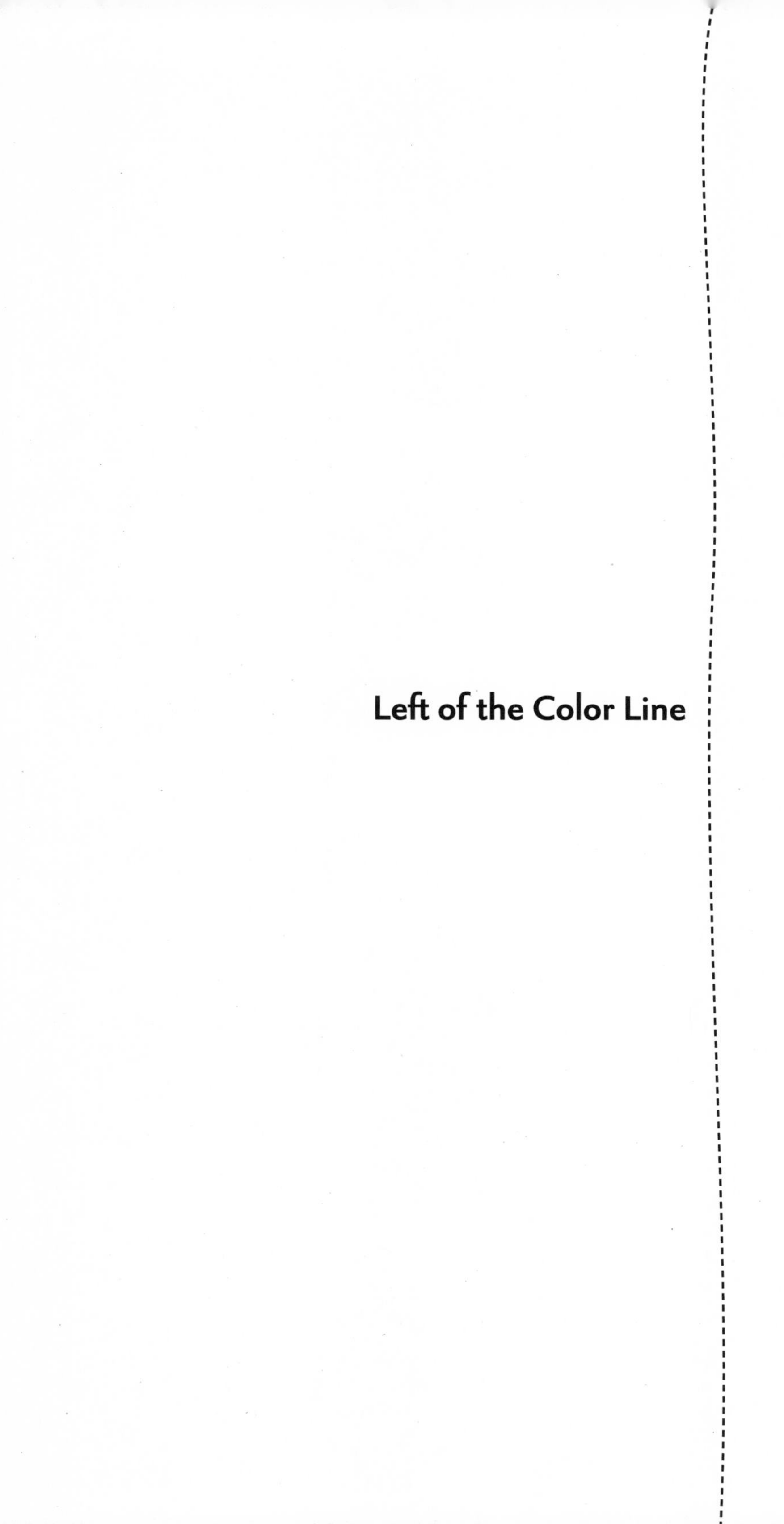

Left of the Color Line

Bill V. Mullen

James Smethurst

Introduction

The relation of the organized Left to the political and cultural life of the United States remains a vexed and contentious issue both inside and outside academia. The taxonomy of the Left, the nature of its parts, and the character and extent of its influence are debated with a ferocity that seems strangely discordant with the alleged end of the Cold War and the demise of existing socialism in Europe, especially in the precincts of the former Soviet Union. A new anti-Communist scholarship that sees the Communist Left in the United States as essentially a tool of Soviet foreign policy contends with "revisionist" historians and critics (and postrevisionist critics) who view the legacy of the Communist Party of the United States of America (CPUSA)—or at least its rank-and-file members—with various degrees of sympathy. This volume extends that cultural conversation. It could be considered to be in the revisionist camp but tries to go beyond a number of cultural and political assumptions about the Left and its influence frequently made by revisionist as well as new (and old) anti-Communist scholars, focusing particularly on how race and ethnicity have inflected the impact of the organized Left on literature and culture in the United States as well as on how the consideration (or lack of consideration) of these issues has structured scholarly responses to the subject of the Left and its influence.

One major assessment of the relationship of the Left to the culture(s) of the United States has been that the Left was (and is) insignificant except during relatively brief moments of social crisis or within certain "marginal" communities. This position is quite old, appearing throughout the twentieth century in various pamphlets, essays, monographs, and so on by European and U.S. scholars discussing why socialism never achieved mass currency—from Werner Sombart's *Why There Is No Socialism in the United States* (1906) to Richard Rorty's *Achieving Our Country: Leftist Thought in Twentieth-Century America* (1998). One still popular variant of this position is a story of a Left Eden (or a Left chance for redemption) and an ensuing fall into extremism, Bolshevism, Stalinism, opportunism, un-Americanism, and so on. In these accounts, the Left has the potential for mass influence but instead opts for a life on the periphery of U.S. culture. Often this story is couched in terms of an indigenous American radicalism—for example, the "Lyrical Left" of Greenwich Village and the *Masses* magazine, the Industrial Workers of the World (IWW), the Popular Front, the early incarnations of the Student Nonviolent Coordinating Committee (SNCC), and Students for a Democratic Society (SDS)—that is variously supplanted by a sectarian, often foreign and authoritarian, sometimes ideologically corrupt Left—for instance, the CPUSA, Stalinists, the Fosterites, Progressive Labor Party (PLP), Weathermen, and black nationalists. A somewhat less frequent Leftist version of this story involves the corruption of a militant political movement by reformists or "fake" Leftists (e.g., Lovestoneites, Trotskyites, Browderites, Schactmanites, New York Intellectuals, and accommodationists).

The point here is not to dismiss the valid, often valuable considerations of, say, the nature and legacy of Stalinism and its impact on the Leftist traditions of the United States. It is merely to point out that discussions of the Left in the United States often follow relatively unexamined narratives that emphasize rupture, fragmentation, heresy, futility, and failure. Even revisionist scholars are frequently constrained by these narratives in odd ways. Revisionist cultural archaeologists searching for the remains of a buried radical past too often limit their efforts to the Red Decade of the 1930s and the countercultural 1960s. The cultural moments of the thirties and sixties have long served as important elements of stories of Left possibility, failure, and marginalization. Both are seen as atypical periods of social crisis in which the Left had the opportunity to change the United States fundamentally but failed to seize that opportunity. These failures are attributed in no small part to the ultimate seduction of the Left by essentially foreign, un-American ideologies (and even foreign masters) resulting in betrayal (e.g., the Hitler-Stalin Pact) and sectarian extremism (reflected in the infighting that so damaged SDS and the Black Power movement). Although revisionists have generally contested more traditional scholarly anti-Communist and antiradical readings of those two decades, they have often seemed reluctant to look for a larger continuity of the Left and Leftist cultural activity outside and between those decades.

In recent years, a new examination of the Left and its influence in the United States has been undertaken by a diverse group of younger and of more established scholars, such as Michael Denning, Barbara Foley, Robin Kelley, Bill Maxwell, Cary Nelson, Ellen Schrecker, Alan Wald, and Mark Solomon. The ideological orientation of these scholars is generally Marxist but is not dominated by any single political stance, institution, or organization. Their work could be considered an extension of the revisionist studies that attempted to reclaim or reconsider the impact of left-wing grassroots activism, especially the CPUSA, on U.S. politics and culture but often left unexamined anti-Communist assumptions about periodization, institutional leadership, and long-term significance in place. There is, of course, considerable disagreement among many of these scholars. There is no consensus, for example, on the precise nature and long- and short-term impact of Stalinism. The relationship of modernism (and postmodernism) and the Left also remains a contentious issue.

What unites this work is a willingness to think about Left continuity as well as rupture and conflict. It is also marked by a much greater interest in race and ethnicity, particularly in the broad impact of the Left on African American culture and the equally profound influence of African American culture on the Left, an interest that was frequently missing in even such important, groundbreaking studies of U.S. literature and the Left as Daniel Aaron's *Writers on the Left: Episodes in American Literary Communism* (1961) and Richard H. Pell's *Radical Visions and American Dreams: Culture and Social Thought in the Depression Years* (1973).

This collection brings together the work of some of the most productive and interesting of these scholars without attempting to be encyclopedic or definitive. The authors themselves range considerably in their ideological stance, their institutional affiliation, and their degree of establishment within academia. The period covered by their essays runs from

LeFt

the early 1920s to the present. Our intention in assembling this collection is to take seriously Cary Nelson's question, "What happens when we put the Left at the center of literary and cultural studies?"[1] By the Left, we are not, for the most part, referring to the profound impact of such Leftist theorists as Antonio Gramsci and Louis Althusser on critical thought in the United States, but to the work of writers, artists, and intellectuals directly connected to and influenced by the institutions and ideologies of the organized Left of the United States. In other words, do the literatures of the United States look different when we use the Left as a starting point for the examination? Thus, the task undertaken here is not merely to excavate what was hidden or partially buried, but also to reorient or reframe what we thought we knew.

In our approach to this question, we also kept in mind Mary Helen Washington's variation, "What happens when we put African American Studies at the center?"[2] The issue of African American liberation, and of race and ethnicity generally, has been at the center of Leftist thought and practice in the United States since, at least, the Sixth Congress of the Communist International (Comintern) of 1928, which proclaimed African Americans in the South to be an "oppressed nation" and in the North to be a "national minority." The resulting focus on "Negro Liberation" in the work of the CPUSA also strongly influenced in various ways the Trotskyist, Socialist, Maoist, and other Leftist traditions in the United States. Militant antiracism and, often, pro–self-determination for African Americans, Chicana/os, and other "nationally oppressed" groups came to be a hallmark of an extremely wide spectrum of the Left in a way that would have seemed implausible before the late 1920s.

Strangely, until recently, African American writers, artists, and intellectuals were, with a few notable exceptions, extremely underconsidered in studies of Leftist influence on the literature and art of the United States; Chicana/o, Asian American, and Puerto Rican artists were more or less invisible. In some respects, the commonplace that the organized Left has been marginal to the cultural life of the United States has been facilitated by this exclusion. The impact of the Left on these communities has been persistent, and often more public than its influence on other U.S. communities, since at least the 1920s. It is our contention that these minorities are central to the story of the Left in the United States and to that of U.S. culture generally. Paying special attention to race, ethnicity, and the Left also challenges scholars to rethink periodization of Leftist influence that depends too heavily on the markers of the Crash of 1929 and the Hitler-Stalin Pact. For example, a quick perusal of Paul

Robeson's journal, *Freedom*, demonstrates that a vibrant, public, and significant African American Left subculture, including people like Robeson, W. E. B. Du Bois, Lorraine Hansberry, Alice Childress, Sidney Poitier, Harry Belafonte, John Henrik Clarke, Lloyd Brown, Julian Mayfield, John O. Killens, and Margaret Burroughs, still existed in the early 1950s —a Left that would be driven underground, but not completely destroyed, at the height of the McCarthy era. Thus, the essays in this volume are heavily concerned with issues of race and ethnicity as well as of gender and region.

These essays rethink notions of mainstream and margin that seem almost clichéd now, but that still retain much power in scholarly conversations and syllabi. Don West, a southern writer drawing much from Langston Hughes and other Leftist African American writers in his framing of a radical "Mountaineer" identity, published in many key left-wing journals and anthologies of the 1930s and 1940s and sold tens of thousands of volumes of poems almost entirely outside normal commercial distribution channels. Why is he virtually undetected on academic radar, including most studies of the literary Left of the 1930s and 1940s?

Similarly, the number of twentieth-century African American writers connected with some segment of the organized Left at a crucial moment of their careers is staggering (and not restricted to the 1930s). Yet this is not reflected in most examinations of twentieth-century African American literature other than studies of a few individuals, particularly Richard Wright and, to a lesser extent, Langston Hughes. If one believes African American literature and culture to be central to literature and culture in the United States, then so is the story of the Left and its influence on culture in the United States. Again, if we put the Left at the center, then we are forced to place issues of race and ethnicity at the center. Such a view forces us to rethink the fields of African American studies, Latina/o studies, multicultural studies, ethnic studies, and American studies as well as U.S. literature as it is typically taught in English Departments.

This collection's essays also generally share an interest in making connections and finding continuities between the Left in different historical eras rather than falling back on Red thirties and radical sixties exceptionalist arguments of lost Edens. This is not to say that the various arguments neglect to point out conflicts and contradictions within the Left over time. For example, a number of these essays point out that a public break with what came to be known as the Old Left was an important declaration of independence for many activists and institutions of the Black Power, Chicano, Nuyorican, and Asian American movements. But although it is important to note these gestures, the contributors argue explicitly or implicitly that it is also crucial to trace the connections of the new liberation movements with older movements.

Of course, this volume is intended to further the conversation on the cultural legacy of the Left, including its impact on current literature and culture (and the study of literature and culture), rather than define it. Though all of the scholars here are sympathetic to the Left to one degree or another, no single ideology animates the book. Seamless continuity or comprehensive coverage was not the editors' intention, especially given the space limitations of such a collection. Whereas we think that there is an organic integrity to the volume's focus on the organized Left and its influence since the Bolshevik Revolution, much more work could be done, say, to extend the pioneering studies of Paul Buhle and others on the importance of early-twentieth-century pre-Bolshevik socialist– and anarchist–influenced literary movements, in English, Yiddish, German, Russian, Polish, Finnish, Spanish, and so on, to the development of post–World War I literature in the United States and later Leftist cultural traditions. Similarly, there could have been more consideration of the impact of various expressions of the Trotskyist tradition on U.S. literature (a tradition not much considered beyond the influence of a relatively narrowly defined group of New York Intellectuals and of C. L. R. James outside of the work of Alan Wald). If the lack of such work is a shortcoming of this book, then we welcome corrections and additions.

The essays are arranged chronologically and topically. This structure is meant to suggest the historical continuities and, in places, detours that have marked Left relationships to the United States and other cultures of the Americas. Chronologically, the essays reconsider four general cultural moments from the twentieth century; modernism and literary internationalism, the Red Decade and its aftermath, the rise of ethnic nationalisms and ethnopoetics, and the contemporary period of cultural studies. The essays move from a close engagement with historical and material conditions relevant to the rise of Leftist culture to a more theoretical (and self-reflexive) consideration of current Leftist theory and practice in the academy. Throughout attention is paid to the relationship between Leftist theory and the aesthetic and formal concerns of writers working in varying ethnic traditions. Too, the essays are joined by questions of value and canonization: how texts and writers came to be included or excluded from either official or academic accounts of literary traditions because of (or in resistance to) questions of class struggle and representation.

Eric Schocket's essay, "Modernism and the Aesthetics of Management, or T. S. Eliot's Labor Literature," weds recent work on race and modernism with a rigorous original reading of what Schocket calls "class performativity" in the poetry of T. S. Eliot. Schocket challenges both critics of modernism and Marxist literary critics to apprehend the shift to industrial processes as the impetus toward an "aesthetics of engagement" in literary modernism meant to contain and control class struggle in the early century. Eliot's encounters with both African American and working-class referents, Schocket maintains, provided Eliot the basis for an "aesthetics of self-reference and materiality." Schocket dialectically reinterprets Eliot's famous "objective correlative" as the offspring of this encounter. The essay serves as a significant starting point for the collection by posing the specter of race and working-class presence as the engine driving modernist literary experiment.

Revisionist reading of the relationship between Leftist politics and modern aesthetics also informs William J. Maxwell's essay, "F. B. Eyes: The Bureau Reads Claude McKay." McKay, a more traditionally canonical Leftist author than Eliot, to be sure, forged in the 1920s what Maxwell calls a literary and political "double agency" meant to both announce and mask his sympathies for Bolshevism, on one hand, and to reveal his awareness of surveillance afforded his literary career by a young J. Edgar Hoover at the Federal Bureau of Investigation (FBI) on the other. Maxwell literally "reads" the FBI's readings of McKay's 1920s sonnets (via his FBI file) as both prescient of his Marxist outlook and formative of the poet's appreciation of the sonnet as a coded vehicle for representing black radicalism. Maxwell not only traces backward the century-long surveillance of African American writers to McKay but also argues that McKay's high seas battles with the FBI over and across the international "black Atlantic" offer new ways of thinking about the role of radical politics, internationalism, and political repression in describing routes and roots of the modern black diaspora.

Anthony Dawahare follows Maxwell closely on the topic of African American modernism and radicalism in his essay, "The Specter of Radicalism in Alain Locke's *The New Negro*." Dawahare carefully teases out the political meanings of Locke's defining Harlem Renaissance text as an ambiguous, ambivalent, but ultimately conservative attempt to mediate competing radical political discourses in 1920s black America, particularly Garveyism, socialism, and black nationalism. Locke, Dawahare argues, deployed a "progressive rhetoric of nationalism" in his introduction to *The New Negro* that was meant to conceal his identification with the black bourgeoisie and to suggest a black patriotic loyalty to capitalism that would undercut more radical claims to black identity and social action. Dawahare reads the arguments over the meaning of the New Negro in the collection as ultimately contained and resolved by Locke's assertion of a dual nationalism: both African and American. The book thus anticipates century-long debates about race and class variously held on the Left and within black communities, while enacting a black self-policing of radicalism that would falter within a few short years of *The New Negro*'s 1925 publication with the onset of the Great Depression's Red Decade.

Bill V. Mullen and B. V. Olguín follow with essays that stay within the circumference of the modern period but delve more deeply into literary internationalism as a creative pressure on African American and Chicana/o writers. Mullen's "W. E. B. Du Bois, *Dark Princess*, and the Afro-Asian International" examines Du Bois's neglected 1928 novel *Dark Princess* in the context of what Maxwell and Dawahare describe as a moment of remarkably fecund black engagement with U.S. and world revolutionary thought. He reads the novel as an allegory of Du Bois's own romantic internationalism wedding support for Indian socialism and revolution during World War I with the emergence of the U.S. black labor movement in the 1920s. Mullen demonstrates that Du Bois, encouraged by Bolshevism and the pioneering efforts of black Americans at the 1922 Comintern in Moscow, was also the first African American writer to finally perceive Orientalism and anti-Communism as direct threats against the racial fortunes of black Americans. He contends that Du Bois's prescient awareness of the need for Afro-Asian unity foreshadows not only the anticolonial movements of the 1940s and 1950s but also the author's own turn to Maoism and communism near the end of his life.

Olguín, in "*Barrios of the World Unite!*: Regionalism, Transnationalism, and Internationalism in Tejano War Poetry from the Mexican Revolution to World War II," uses Chicana/o war poetry written between the end of the U.S.-Mexican War and World War II to spell out how writers like Américo Paredes imagine a geopolitics of Chicano identity by grounding their poetic personas in the global material struggles that have shaped the twentieth century. Olguín demonstrates how the ideologically conflicted positions of Mexican and Mexican American soldiers fighting both for and against the United States helped to ignite themes of interracial and transnational solidarity, anticapitalism, and radical nationalism in Chicana/o poetry. He specifically examines how southwestern writers early in the century anticipated contemporary borderlands theory by imagining the contact zone between the United States and Mexico as a space and a metaphor for anticolonial struggles waged at home and around the world. Olguín is especially attentive to ways that gender in works by both male and female poets facilitates or undermines these paradigms of radical egalitarianism. The essay finally proposes that Chicana/o writers and war poets, because of their affiliations with the deterritorialized, colonized, and working class, became inevitable "soldiers" in the march of Left literary internationalisms in the early half of the twentieth century.

The next four essays reconsider the dimensions of the 1930s Red Decade particularly as it was experienced by and affected African American writers. Alan Wald, Barbara Foley, and Mary Helen Washington examine the respective relationships between Chester Himes, John O. Killens, Ralph Ellison, and Alice Childress and the American Left between the early 1930s and the 1950s. In "Narrating Nationalisms: Black Marxism and Jewish Communists through the Eyes of Harold Cruse," Wald carefully reads representations of Communism by 1940s and 1950s African American writers to rebut the now fairly notorious allegations by Harold Cruse that black writers generally were used and manipulated by Communists, especially Jewish Communists, before and after World War II. Wald uses novels by Himes (*The Lonely Crusade*, 1947) and Killens (*Youngblood*, 1954), for example, to show how sympathetic rather than hostile the blacks generally were to either the organized Left or the Leftist line on interracial unity during this period.

Meanwhile, Foley, in "From Communism to Brotherhood: The Drafts of *Invisible Man*," breaks new ground in Ralph Ellison scholarship. She carefully parses the unpublished drafts of Ralph Ellison's monumental novel *Invisible Man* (1952) to demonstrate how the author literally revised the book into an anti-Communist Cold War classic. Reminding us that the Ellison of the early 1940s was generally supportive of the Left and even published short stories in the CPUSA's journal *New Masses*, Foley demonstrates how between 1946, when he began composing *Invisible Man*, and its publication in 1952, Ellison consciously—if somewhat mysteriously—vilified and caricatured Leftist characters and thought. Indeed, she shows that early drafts portray the Brotherhood and minor characters like Mary Rambo if not as Communist heroes, at least as human and sympathetic antiracist Leftists. Foley asks us to consider Ellison's changes as demonstrative, if nothing else, of the "lower frequencies," as it were, at which he once heard and then erased the voices of the American Left, and to recall the finished text as something more than monologic.

Washington's "Alice Childress, Lorraine Hansberry, and Claudia Jones: Black Women Write the Popular Front" likewise recovers the Leftist organizational and literary ties of Childress as a case study in how black women shaped Leftist debate and cultural work in the 1950s. Washington describes Childress's activism in this period as an extension of a Popular Front ethos in which African Americans merged black nationalism and civil rights struggle with communist and socialist currents dating to the prewar period. Washington also describes Communist Claudia Jones and fellow traveler Lorraine Hansberry as participants with Childress in an informal circle of black women radicals who anticipated many struggles of the contemporary feminist movement.

Finally, Rachel Rubin's essay, "Voice of the Cracker: Don West Reinvents the Appalachian," interprets the case of West as emblematic of how a literary history blind to the role of the Left in U.S. culture literally cannot see the making of important regions of that culture. West, a cofounder with Myles Horton of the Highlander School, brought a seemingly homespun or native anticapitalism and antiracism to his 1930s and 1940s poems on Appalachia that Rubin sees as imbricated not only with Popular Front discourses on popular and mass culture, but also with the vernacular influences of African American Leftist poets like Langston Hughes. West, Rubin argues, worked adamantly in his poetry to reveal Appalachia's poor whites, or "crackers," as what might be called fruitful sites of either Americanist racism and false consciousness or potential revolutionary understanding. Her essay is significant, too, for showing how the South, and southern self-representation, is itself a larger part of twentieth-century American Leftist culture and theory understudied and underrepresented by traditional northern (and urban) concentrations.

The next four essays take up the relationship between the Left and significant post–World War II ethnic formation and social movement in the United States. As a group, they reveal the importance for contemporary cultural and ethnic studies of including Left history and influence in their own discursive descriptions. Michelle Stephens's "The First Negro Matinee Idol: Harry Belafonte and American Culture in the 1950s" uses the paradigms of Left cultural materialists like Michael Denning and Hazel Carby to revise and politicize the career of the popular West Indian singer. Belafonte's celebrity, Stephens notes, coincided with and helped to ameliorate the effects of U.S. imperialist expansion into the Caribbean. She reads Belafonte as one of a series of "black male bodies," including Marcus Garvey, Paul Robeson, and Bigger Thomas, to signify and measure the relative comfort or disease of the U.S. relationship to black oppositionality, be it without or within U.S. borders. This feminist essay also locates Belafonte's sexuality and sexual appeal to white female audiences in relation to his working-class Caribbean mother's otherness. "What we see in Belafonte's performances of his ethnicity throughout the 1950s" she writes, "is the transformation of his ethnic working-class story into the interracial romance of American integrationism." Stephens persuasively demonstrates that Belafonte is himself something of an index to U.S. twentieth-century dreams of empire.

Fred Ho's "Bamboo That Snaps Back! Resistance and Revolution in Asian Pacific American Working-Class and Left-Wing Expressive Culture" provides a dense survey of the political and cultural history of the Asian Pacific American (APA) movement in the United States. Using a materialist methodology, Ho delineates between nationalist, socialist, and other Leftist tendencies influencing the development of APA cultural forms since roughly the turn of the twentieth century. He ties these to the development of Asian Americans as immigrant workers in the United States and to the acute political consciousness and debate over APA identity in the 1960s and 1970s. Ho's essay also contains a cautionary examination of recent trends in Asian American studies within the academy, which be sees as invariably part of longer, less academic, more social forms of struggle for APAS.

James Smethurst's essay, "Poetry and Sympathy: New York, the Left, and the Rise of Black Arts," is one of the first studies to delineate the political and personal dimensions of New York's influential Black Arts scene. Smethurst gives a dense description of the figures and organizations that emerged in New York City and how they sustained and revised black radicalism. He pays special attention to key underrepresented periodicals like the *Liberator*, which published many of the seminal political and aesthetic essays that fueled the Black Arts Movement in New York and New Jersey and contributed to the national renaissance of 1960s black writing generally. This essay helps expand appreciation that the northeastern Black Arts scene has gone beyond the influence of prominent figures like Amiri Baraka and provides the most thorough description yet of the relationship between the scene and Leftist currents of thought in the 1960s.

Marcial González's "A Marxist Critique of Borderlands Postmodernism: Adorno's *Negative Dialectics* and Chicano Cultural Criticism" is a nuanced analysis of the "border" as a sign of both idealist and antimaterialist tendencies within contemporary Chicana/o studies and a plea for a more dialectical method of reading Chicano literature and identity. González notes that borderlands theory has tended to reinforce aspects of both Eurocentric and postmodern theory while positing a politics of Chicana/o identity that is tacitly oppositional to such paradigms. He posits instead a "negative" dialectical model of Chicana/o studies via Adorno's theory of commodity exchange abstraction. This essay is a bold challenge from within the field of Chicana/o cultural criticism—and by extension all ethnic studies—to reconsider the relationship between historical materialist methods of analysis and the larger political (and academic) projects of international liberation.

As a postscript that looks both backward and forward, Cary Nelson's "The Letters the Presidents Did Not Release: Radical Scholarship and the Legacy of the American Volunteers in Spain" examines the relationship of contemporary academic activism to the longer project of non-academic Leftist Americanisms, particularly those that transcend professional and political borders. Nelson uses an autobiographical scholarly anecdote about a decision to publish a letter from President Bill Clinton in support of American volunteers in the Spanish Civil War as the occasion for a meditation on the historical and cultural meanings of Leftist scholarship in the university. He finds the linkage vital to his own work, while exhorting those of us writing and rewriting the story of America's variegated Lefts to never substitute ideas for action. The essay provides a dialectical closing note, while opening up new questions about the relationship, for example, of the now notorious Yale graduate student strike with earlier watershed moments in U S. labor history. Indeed, by recalling the contributions of African Americans to the struggles at Yale (as graduate students) and in Spain (as volunteers) some seventy years apart, Nelson suggests fertile ways of excavating and rethinking the Left present for vestiges of its past and its past for foreshadowings of its present.

Notes

1. Cary Nelson, "What Happens When We Put the Left at the Center?," *American Literature* 66.4 (December 1994): 771–79.

2. Mary Helen Washington, "'Disturbing the Peace: What Happens to American Studies If You Put African American Studies at the Center?': Presidential Address to the American Studies Association, October 29, 1997," *American Quarterly* 50.1 (March 1998): 1–23.

Eric Schocket

Modernism and the Aesthetics of Management, or T. S. Eliot's Labor Literature

I have heard it said, in fact I believe that it's quite a current thought, that we have taken skill out of work. We have not. We have put a higher skill into planning, management, and the tool building, and the results of that skill are enjoyed by the man who is not skilled.
—Henry Ford, *My Life and Work*

It is wonderful how poor people love to take advice from people who are friendly and above them, from people who read in books and who are good.
—Gertrude Stein, *Three Lives*

The Cubist Vision and the Labor Process: A Prologue

When the Armory Show opened in New York on February 15, 1913, it was the first major presentation of postimpressionist art in the United States and thus rapidly came to represent the "moment at which the 'new' vanquished the 'old' in American culture with a single and stunning revolutionary blow."[1] The battle between old and new was most evident in the controversy surrounding Marcel Duchamp's infamous entry in the Cubist Room, *Nude Descending a Staircase, N. 2* (Fig. 1). Described variously as an "elevated railroad stairway in ruins after an earthquake," a "dynamited suit of Japanese armor," and "an explosion in a shingle factory,"[2] it became a lightning rod for popular opinion and a touchstone for the public's response to the disassociative stimuli of modernity. "To have looked at [the Cubist room] is to have passed through a pathological museum," summarized Kenyon Cox in *Harper's Weekly*. "One feels that one has seen not an exhibition, but an exposure."[3]

When cultural historians recount the inception of modernism in the United States, however, they usually dismiss such reactions in favor of an alternate story of Duchamp's genius, the Armory Show's success, and, in particular, modernism's rightful victory over Victorian gentility. If the 1950s version of this story depends on celebrations of modernism's formal complexities, and the 1970s version on its antibourgeois aestheticism, contemporary narratives increasingly draw connections between aesthetic and political "radicalisms" in the modernist era. The Armory Show thus appears, in J. M. Mancini's words, as part of a "wider struggle by workers, women, and others for liberation in the first decades of the twentieth century."[4] Once valorized for its purported transcendence of history and politics, modernism now maintains its centrality, paradoxically, through appeals to the historical conjunction of alliance politics. Pairing the Armory Show with the IWW's Paterson Strike Pageant in New York in 1913, Martin Green concludes: "The spirit of 1913 was an aspiration to transcend what most people accepted as ordinary and so inevitable. It was the ordinariness of capitalism and liberalism and class hierarchy, in the case of the IWW strike; and in the case of the Armory Show, it was old forms of art, appreciation and beauty."[5]

Though I will eventually turn my focus to literary modernism—to its epistemological links to labor management, to its roots in a reconceptualization of working-class forms, and to the early works of T. S. Eliot—I begin with the Armory Show, Duchamp's *Nude*, and their critical legacy to introduce a different story of modernism's relationship to class and labor in the 1910s. In this story, modernism neither evades history nor aids the working class through its ruptures, fractures, and quest for a new cultural totality. These aspects of the modernist project, I argue alternately, can be read as modernism's own technique for apprehending and containing the dissonances of class segmentation. They are not, therefore, an attempt to transcend "the limits of the individual self," as Green would have it, but a new way of configuring that self—not an aesthetics of liberation, but an aesthetics of management that was symptomatic of incipient configurations within the industrial labor process.[6] Understanding modernism in this manner is, I think, a crucial part of the radical reconstitution of U.S. culture undertaken in the present volume. For though we need to attend to authors and movements marginalized from the bourgeois canon, we need also to resist the easy essentialism that sees class, labor, and economic structures as the exclusive properties of radical and working-class cultural forms. For as Louis Fraina noted in his reply to Kenyon Cox, the "New Art" is not "pathologic" but "expresses

FIGURE 1. Marcel Duchamp, *Nude Descending a Staircase, N. 2.* (© 2002 Artists Rights Society [ARS], New York/ADAGP Paris Estate of Marcel Duchamp)

the vital urge of its age. . . . It is the art of capitalism. . . . Cubism transfers the technique of machinery, so to speak, to the canvas."[7]

We can measure Fraina's perceptiveness if we pair Duchamp's *Nude* with a quite different labor event of 1913–14, the implementation of modern line-production methods at Ford's Highland Park plant in Detroit.[8] Though not the only factory to apply Frederick Winslow Taylor's *Principles of Scientific Management* (1911)—observation, timing of each operation within the task, establishment of minimum unit times, and reconstruction of jobs with composite times as the standard—Highland Park was the first to combine these principles with uniform design specifications and the endless chain conveyer belt. As Stephen Meyer notes, the standardized design of the Model T enabled Ford's engineers to "specialize and routinize . . . work processes" in order to transfer skill from craft workers into "the design of sophisticated and complicated machines."[9] The conveyer belt then ensured that the repetitive and sequential nature of these processes would be enforced by the machines themselves, which now proscribed the pace and path of what had once been a series of complex operations completed by skilled craftsmen and their helpers. This constituted, in Harry Braverman words, a significant division of "the unity of thought and action. . . . The subjective factor of the labor process is removed to a place among its inanimate objective factors."[10]

The epistemological significance of this division can hardly be underestimated; it is here that we find the corollary to modernism's own aesthetic operations. For industrial engineers to design a mechanical process that would replicate the physical and cognitive skills of the craft worker, they needed to perform exactly the sort of objectification Braverman describes, comprehending the worker as a machine, whose motions could be traced and rationalized using precise chronological measures. For our purposes, the visual tracings of this objectification are the most immediately arresting since they so clearly prefigure Duchamp's *Nude*. Using a rapid-speed camera technique developed by Eadweard Muybridge and E. J. Marey, Frank Gilbreth (the inventor of time-motion studies) recorded "the paths of each of several motions made by various parts of the body and their exact distances, exact times, relative times, exact speeds, relative speeds, and directions."[11] Gilbreth's chronographs (Fig. 2), like Muybridge's examinations of the human figure (Fig. 3), thus give us a different way to connect Duchamp—and the cubist idiom generally—to the industrial culture of the 1910s. Such a comparison provides a visual record of both the aesthetic dimensions and the social permeation of management epistemology.

FIGURE 2. Gilbreth's chronograph for time-motion studies, 1919. (Reprinted from Frank R. Gilbreth and Lillian M. Gilbreth, *Fatigue Study: The Elimination of Humanity's Greatest Unnecessary Waste: A First Step in Motion Study* [London: George Routledge and Sons, 1919])

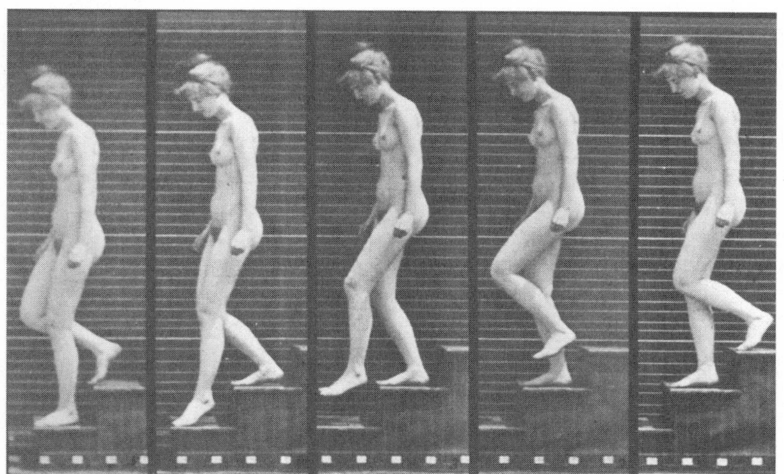

FIGURE 3. Eadweard Muybridge, "Descending Stairs and Turning Around," 1887. (Reprinted from *Animal Locomotion: An Electrophotographic Investigation of Consecutive Phases of Animal Movements* [Philadelphia: University of Pennsylvania Press, 1887])

For while it is generally known that chronophotography inspired Duchamp's cubism—that, in some general way, industrialism inspired modernism—this mode of figuration needs to be traced more specifically to changes in the labor process. Not only did new industrial technologies supply the tools to create atomized images, but also at a more fundamental level they supplied the problem that made such studies conceptually useful: How can the moving, working body be apprehended in a way that allows its most intimate physical knowledge—its knowledge of sensuous human labor—to be alienated from it and reinscribed in a process, a system, or a mode of representation? I think that Duchamp's *Nude*—and a good deal of early avant-garde modernism—

speaks to this problematic. Duchamp does not attempt to represent the moving body holistically, but rather to dissect movement as such, to reduce it to elemental static poses. By doing so, he makes a crucial transition from the norms of nineteenth-century portraiture to the analytic mood of avant-garde modernism. Rejecting the epistemology of realism, which grounds knowledge in the shared experience of the empirical, he instead vests the proprietary observer with a scientific comprehension of motion in the abstract. This shift is exemplative of what Anson Rabinbach sees as the "triumph of technology over sense perception" and predictive of other formally invested, self-referential modernist texts (which will exploit the spectacle of technical mastery along similar lines).[12] Importantly, the triumph of technology also links avant-garde modernism to the epistemological dictates of Taylorist production methods and the managerial systems that those methods underwrite: As Taylorism divides and separates each act of labor into conception and execution, Duchamp's *Nude* separates motion into cognitive and physical dimensions. As scientific management installs a system of administration that superintends these now disparate acts of labor, the *Nude* embodies a technical aesthetics that both fragments and links the divided object within its purview.

Modernism and Management

What avant-garde modernism and scientific management have in common, in other words, is a similar understanding of the way formal apparatuses can function to systematize bodies, labor, and the stresses and tensions of class conflict. In scientific management, this is explicit: "In the past the man has been first," writes Taylor, "in the future the system must be first." In other words, "What constitutes a fair day's work will be a question for scientific investigation, instead of a subject to be bargained and haggled over."[13] Most avant-garde modernist texts that can be read as instances of a managerial aesthetics are, in contrast, neither as obvious nor as unmediated in their connections. What these texts share, however, is a substructure that connects them to the social and economic processes of industrial modernization and to Taylor's mode of resolution through formal procedures. As with Duchamp's *Nude*, this substructure typically entails two main innovations: First, avant-garde modernists express a commitment to atomization and fragmentation, a desire to separate the object, scene, or theme into a set of disparate, elemental parts. Second, they reconnect these parts through an external system, logic, or, in more familiar terms, aesthetic technique. T. S. Eliot, who serves as the main example here, refines these moves further, subsuming the subjectivity of the poet and those whom he apprehends across the class divide within a system of coherences and affective relays that he will call the "objective correlative."

Eliot is also a significant example of modernism's imaginative affiliations with management since his early work so clearly reacts to urbanization and immigration, the two socioeconomic factors that largely prompted the management revolution. Taylorism and Fordism arose, in particular, as a response to the new concentration of unskilled foreign laborers who were willing to work outside of the traditional craft system. Though avant-garde modernism was, as one would expect, less baldly instrumental, it was often no less functionalist. Modernists such as Eliot registered urbanization and immigration as the simultaneous pressures of proximity and difference (a "swollen . . . stream of mixed immigration bringing . . . the danger of . . . a caste system"), which existent forms of literary representation could barely recognize, much less remediate.[14] For the early Eliot, before his turn to the unifying idea of Culture and much before his conversion to the Church of England, remediation could come through an aesthetic system that cushioned the shock of modernity by adding a measure of predictability and impersonality, a system of class management.

Of course, by referring to modernism as an aesthetic system, which along with other systems attempts to manage the economic and social pressures of modernization, I am proposing a substantially different method of reading class and labor in literature and, consequently, a different perspective on the literary history of the modernist movement. Most readings of "labor literature" implicitly proceed from an identitarian conception of class, where class denominators indicate a person's place within a social spectrum (lower class, middle class, upper class). Understandably, these readings then privilege realist fiction, which more "accurately" reveals these identities as they come into conflict. But as a result of this method, readers of labor literature, with a few conspicuous exceptions, have been unable to attend to nonrealist poetic and narrative forms. What I am suggesting, however, is that when Marxists look at modernism, we should look not for traditional class characters and characteristics, but for something one could call "class performativity": the manifestation of the forms or logic of the class process within the cultural text, moments in which the deep structures and processes that configure and are configured by economic forces surface and are visible. What this can give us is a historical understanding of modernism that is, as Perry Anderson puts it, "conjunctural," comprised of an "overdetermined configuration" of aesthetic forms and "key technologies or innovations of the second industrial revolution."[15] Placing modernism within this history—which is to say, within labor history—removes its aura of intellectual and aesthetic exclusiveness and grounds it in the lived history of its authors and readers. For though these authors and readers may not have understood the epistemological shifts of modernity as an "emptying of time-space," they could have hardly escaped the consequences of rudimentary shifts in the labor process that had fundamentally rationalized not only time and space, but also the human body.[16]

Modernism as Labor Literature

Another way to understand the connection between shifts in the labor process, managerial modes, and the rise of modernism is through the lens of literary history—and more specifically through an examination of the way in which literature's apprehension of workers and those marked as class "Other" changes at the "moment of modernism" in the 1910s. Although it is rarely treated to the sorts of thematic examinations that more typically embrace the 1930s, the literature of the 1910s is surprisingly flush with representations of labor. This is the decade of Jack London, Theodore Dreiser, and Upton Sinclair's prominence (if not their best fiction) and also the era of the *Masses*, which introduced readers to a more urban school of labor writing through the fiction and poetry of Floyd Dell, John Reed, and Max Eastman. The year 1913 not only encompassed the Armory Show and Ford's triumph in Highland Park, it was the year of Vachel Lindsay's poetic odes to industrial Springfield, Illinois, in *General William Booth Enters into Heaven and Other Poems*. Two years later Carl Sandburg followed Lindsay's lead by praising Chicago ("hog butcher for the world"), only to be echoed in 1918 by Sherwood Anderson's forgotten book of labor poetry, *Mid-American Chants*.[17] Even Robert Frost, whose fame has largely served to disarticulate him from his roots in early populism, was heavily reliant on class representation. *North of Boston* (1914), the book that established his reputation and solidified his poetic voice, stages a series of long dialogues between northeastern rural "folk." Finally, and perhaps most surprisingly (since it has gone entirely without critical note), this era finds a number of American modernists constituting their aesthetic principles through poetic and fictive interactions with the working class: T. S. Eliot, Gertrude Stein, William Carlos Williams, and Ezra Pound in the 1910s; John Dos Passos and William Faulkner in the 1920s.

Of course, ever since the romantic poets, formal innovations in literature have often been prompted by an apprehension of workers. William Wordsworth's movement toward a "natural language" in his interchanges with rural peasants, Émile Zola's attempt to ground naturalism in a taxonomic genealogy of the working-class family, Walt Whitman's expansive lines driven by a desire to encompass the "lowly," and even the urban expressionism of Stephen Crane—all conjoined literary experimentation with descriptions of work, workers, and the social divisions wrought by class. What distinguishes modernism's concern with the working class is, however, its distinct epistemological orientation. The motivational pressure does not arise, as it does in the nineteenth century and in the poetic populism of Carl Sandburg and Sherwood Anderson, from a greater desire to know, to reveal the sordidness of poverty, or to celebrate the (supposed) vital physicality of laborers. Modernism's propensity to make art from the experience of class has more to do with its drive to systematize and manage class referents that are already abundantly revealed. Indeed, as Walter Benjamin observes, the modernist responds to the urban masses with "fear, revulsion, and horror" rather than with anything like affective sentimentality. "The shock of experience," which, he suggests, "corresponds to what the worker 'experiences' at his machine," has "become the norm." And it is a norm from which one wants relief, not with which one wants greater intimacy.[18] Relief, at least for Benjamin's subject, Baudelaire, comes in a set of aesthetic tactics: transpositions, displacements, symbolisms. For American modernists who, I would argue, experience the shift toward machine processes as a more holistic cultural event, relief comes from articulating the aesthetic potential that lies within scientific management's formal system—in comprehending the way that the worker, once abstracted from a sentimental system of affect, can be used in a different, even more functionalist manner to vitalize new aesthetic structures.

The most obvious manifestation of this turn comes in modernism's different exploitation of the linguistic vernacular. As Elsa Nettels notes, by the late nineteenth century American realism represented vernacular voices both to record and to contain the cultural otherness of immigrants and African American migrants to the North.[19] Such representations were driven by a realist epistemology that tied discursive revelation to control through technologies of linguistic rearticulation (the way, for example, William Dean Howells frames foreign voices with orthographic marks). Most modernists were, on the other hand, only secondarily interested in exploring the vernacular for the purposes of verisimilitude. Modernism's utilization of the vernacular focuses rather on discourse itself, attempting to use the linguistic otherness of idiomatic speech to divest itself from the strictures of genteel English, and to propel itself toward more complex, self-referential linguistic systems. In other words, modernism looks to the speech of workers—which was thought to have a fluid vocabulary and non-normative syntactical patterns—to ground its own attempts to refunction literary forms. As Michael North writes of modernism's relationship to the African American vernacular, "The real attraction of the black voice to writers like Stein and Eliot was its technical distinction, its insurrectionary opposition to the known and familiar in language. . . . Modernism . . . mimicked the strategies of dialect and aspired to become a dialect itself."[20] Though North circumscribes his analysis of the "dialect of modernism" with metaphor of the "racial masquerade," the evidence suggests (indeed, his evidence suggests) that class, not race, structures modernism's interchange with the vernacular Other. Not only are Stein's and Eliot's racial Others from the working class (as are all of North's examples), their voices are interwoven with those of Irish and German immigrant workers, and are joined by the class-inflected vernacular experiments of Frost, Sandburg, Faulkner, Anderson, and others.

It is important to stress, however, that modernism's reliance on the linguistics of class otherness goes far beyond its utilization of the lexical fecundity of the vernacular. As Pound's poetry certainly shows, one need not venture into the music hall to explode the hermetic strictures of genteel literature. Non-Western poetic traditions and passages from Latin, Greek, and Sanskrit can similarly destabilize and denaturalize the sentimental pretensions of the Victorian lyric. Rather, modernists like Eliot —who literally discovered his aesthetic techniques as he moved through the working-class neighborhoods of North Cambridge, South Boston, and London—employ working-class forms (vernacular speech, artifacts, popular culture, and stereotyped characters) as tools in their efforts to shift from an aesthetics of reference to an aesthetics of self-reference and materiality. "Although there are many different accounts of literary modernism," explains Walter Benn Michaels, "probably all of them acknowledge its interest in the ontology of the sign—which is to say, in the materiality of the signifier, in the relation of signifier to signified, in the relation of sign to referent."[21] Put differently, modernism does not reject materiality (or indeed, in any a priori manner, materialism), it rather relocates materiality from the referent (the "real world" in realism) to the signifier (the materiality of language or of modernist linguistic practice). Working-class forms hence have functional utility because they carry with them an aura of a heightened materiality. They seem, in and of themselves, more "real"; thus their amplified reality (the vibrancy of working-class vernacular, the deep embodiment of the working-class subject, the hypermateriality of the smells and sounds of working-class neighborhoods) once transposed from referent to signifier can add a physicality to the linguistic operations of the modernist text. But once transposed, this working-class materiality is also more easily managed. The otherness that once seemed foreign and inassimilable is reconstituted as a material property of language itself.

"Dull Precipitates of Fact": Eliot's Working-Class Forms

If T. S. Eliot's poetry seems at first an unlikely example of the type of management aesthetics I have been discussing, that is in part due to the success of his tactics of self-censorship and self-fashioning. By all accounts a guarded person, Eliot defended himself against the invasions of modernity and the affronts of popularity by constructing early on a private persona for the public, a voice within his most confessional poems that could be taken as an authentic self. Thus conventional acceptance of Eliot as the poet of ennui, heroic failure, and the "refusal of assertion" is not so much incorrect as insufficiently probing; it fails to take into account how assertively Eliot produced this disposition.[22] Having now the benefit of *The Waste Land Facsimile* and especially the long-suppressed "notebook poems" of 1909–17 (published in 1996 under the title *Inventions of the March Hare*), we get a very different sense of the poet. If the initial sections of the standard *Complete Poems and Plays* present the poet as staid, restrained, and prematurely aged, these early notebook poems offer us what we would have otherwise missed: the young, tortured, and passionate Eliot who is repulsed by a working class he nonetheless must enact symbolic violence upon in order to construct his persona.

Indeed, the much-reported scandal of the notebook poems may only incidentally be the scandal of Eliot's misogyny and racism (which were, at any rate, famously "exposed" long before the publication of the notebook).[23] The more enduring scandal emerges from finding the poet of "ironic self-depreciation" practicing this pose against the backdrop of poverty, class stratification, and urban decay—the "waste land"—a trope that can now no longer be explained by reference to World War I or to Eliot's traumatic marriage (since these poems preceded both).[24] The fragments and waste that Eliot perpetually finds in his cityscapes are neither simply the objective renderings of postwar Europe nor the subjective expressions of the poet's mind. They are, more centrally, a mode of epistemological management (of disarticulation and totalization) that seeks to reconcile world and mind through a series of contextually resonant tactics. I want to argue, in particular, that the notebook poems stage a series of attempts to achieve personal and poetic coherence—attempts that reach fruition only as Eliot more completely systematizes his poetic method. Thus the "objective correlative," his most fully realized system of affective relays, marks the culmination of this process, a process of management that for Eliot is also a process of objectification and depersonalization.[25]

Although the working drafts, fragments, and prose segments that comprise the notebook are not organized in any rigid fashion, they do consistently orbit around two central motifs—slumming and music—which illustrate Eliot's continual attraction to class themes and efforts toward systematization. If the act of walking through the urban decay of North Cambridge, South Boston, and London presents the poet with disarticulate forms of class otherness, what Gregory Jay calls "the object world that dominates the lower classes," then the caprice, the interlude, the love song, and the ballad afford a continual attempt to circumscribe this otherness within the traditional structures of high culture.[26] Eliot would, in fact, later claim that such antipodal tensions were endemic to the poet's work, since "the contemplation of the horrid or sordid or disgusting by an artist, is the necessary and negative aspect of the impulse toward the pursuit of beauty."[27] Yet in the 1910s, Eliot's "pursuit of beauty" manifested itself mainly in ironic attempts to restrain the material and corporeal within a suggestion of the harmonic—a cloying and, indeed, jarring frame for the paratactic iterations of working-class forms. The more general problem—as Eliot would later both elucidate and "resolve" in *The Waste Land*—is that modernity is so rife with excess that there is a continual incommensurability between the objects of the world, its artifacts and realia, and the subjective, cognitive, and aesthetic systems that order them. It is not that these systems disappear at the moment of modernity, but rather that they come to seem extrinsic and thus incapable of fulfilling their totalizing role.

As James Buzard notes, Eliot tried in these slumming trips to surmount this problem through the borrowed paradigm of the ethnography, to gain "the privileged view of culture as a whole, a view denied to inhabitants."[28] But he was largely unprepared to relinquish either his fascination with materiality or his distancing mechanisms. The results, as in "First Caprice in North Cambridge," are telling:

A street-piano, garrulous and frail;
The yellow evening flung against the panes

Of dirty windows: and the distant strains
Of children's voices, ended in a wail. (13)

The problem here is not that these musical puns and motifs fail to knit the poem together. On the contrary, the doubled meaning of "Caprice" (a whimsical slumming journey through North Cambridge or a whimsical musical composition) rather precisely prefaces the condescension of the final line: "Oh, these minor considerations! . . ." (13). The "street-piano" (which recurs throughout the notebook as metonym for working-class culture) rattles nicely, but not discordantly. And the overworked meter and end rhymes serve to mimic, if not exactly the freedom of a caprice, at least the effect of musicality. The problem, rather, is that the method so thoroughly overreaches and underappreciates the material that the poem seems finally like a study in bourgeois arrogance. Such endeavors were not, of course, new in 1909 (Eliot's dating for the poem). Eliot would have known such elegant ditties as Baudelaire's "Bash the Poor!"[29] But Eliot is no Baudelaire, and the speaking voice is not substantiated enough to sustain the arrogance that the frame provides. In fact, the speaking voice is not substantiated at all. It is the rhyme and meter—and most particularly, the materiality of the objects themselves—that give this piece substantiality.

To put this somewhat differently, the objects in the poem stand in an ambiguous relationship to the poetic subject. They are, in one sense, maddeningly autonomous: Embodying the random violence of some past moment (through their brokenness) and insisting on passivity (through the passive voice), they exist, for Eliot, within a state of "sordid patience" (13), which is to say, sordid in their patience rather than patient of their sordidness. Yet they are also forcefully present, reverberating with the jagged physicality of the urban, interdependent, and coherent inasmuch as they renew a set of sentimental tropes of class otherness (wailing children, crowds, dirt) put into play by nineteenth-century industrial literature. If such tropes are more traditionally connected to the narrator and the reader through various apparatuses of affect, Eliot's goal is evidently otherwise. He attempts to disarticulate them—or to present them in their disarticulation—in order to push aside the weight of so much genteel sympathy and Victorian hand-wringing and to uncover the materiality of the words themselves. To give Eliot his due, there is a certain beauty within these urban pastoral rhymes ("broken barrows; / . . . tattered sparrows" [13] in the second stanza) that rises to the fore. Yet the beauty comes at the expense, one might say, of the children who wail rather than communicate their needs. Disconnected from such sensational designs, these wails can iterate the sounds of Eliot's urban caprice. But the ironic tone and arrogant stance required to sustain this form muffle, rather than amplify, the music.

We need the sonorousness of these working-class forms, Eliot insists regardless, because we need their vitality. Without the body (and for Eliot the working class always implies the bodily), "The pure Idea dies of inanition." It dies, he continues in "First Debate between the Body and Soul," through lack of incarnation—through the sterility of mental onanism:

> Imaginations
> Masturbations
> The withered leaves
> Of our sensations (64)

Our sensations are withered because we have cast them about unfruitfully ("imagination's / defecations" [65] in the final stanza). We should, rather, find a way to make them more effective, a way that transliterates the animate wails of children into the inspired voice of Culture. Toward these ends—which are, perhaps, the central ends for the early Eliot—he stages a number of contrapuntal "debates" between upper- and lower-class forms, encounters that are once again mediated through musical motifs, but that move us from the concert hall to the music hall. For instance, an untitled two-stanza poem fragment remediates the ennui of "torpid after-dinner drinks" (70) with the vitality of what would later be know as "low brow culture":

> What, you want action?
> Some attraction?
> . . . .
> Someone sings
> A lady of almost any age
> But chiefly breast and rings
> "Throw your arms around me—Aint you glad you found me"
> Still that's hardly enough—
> Here's a negro (teeth and smile)
> Has a dance that's quite worth while
> That's the stuff!
> (Here's your gin
> Now begin!) (70)

According to David Chinitz, the "music hall was Eliot's chief site of contact with popular culture."[30] His familiarity may explain why this fragment, despite its limitations, goes further than the "classical" selections toward enacting a dialogic relationship between "high" and "low" forms. As Chinitz notes, "the appropriate slang," "snappy rhymes," and "syncopated rhythms" of the second stanza are done with a verve that matches any similar experiments in Eliot's more mature poetry.[31] Yet like "First Caprice," the individual formal aspects are a good deal less problematic than the inner machinery that makes them work. For what gives relief to "the after dinner insolence" (70) (one of Eliot's stock metonyms for bourgeois culture) is not merely the action and attraction of the music hall, but the very particular form of miscegenation it allows.[32]

We would be wrong, in this regard, to ignore the structurally integral role that misogyny and racism play within this cross-class encounter. The musicality of the second stanza depends not just on the syncopated verbal cuts and chops, the quotational use of popular song, and the vernacular phraseology, but more fundamentally on the use of racial and sexual fetishism. Indeed, inasmuch as the fetish ("breast and rings," "teeth and smile") brings with it a specific system of signification—where parts not only stand for things but incarnate the things themselves—it serves as the poem's key figural form. In other words, the conspicuous materiality of the poem, its jazzy idiomatic mélange, reiterates and generalizes the fetish's ability to materialize and contain (to contain through materialization) larger social relations. If the identity of the singer is random ("a lady of almost any age") but her physicality specific ("chiefly breast and rings"), then so too, for instance, is the quoted song lyric—one of many, but for that fact, all the more evocative of the indiscriminate physicality of low cultural forms. The mélange is hence recuperative, but not because, as Chinitz would have it, "the music hall is a rare venue in which Eliot's modernist alienation is momentarily assuaged by a sense of genuine community."[33] Scopic dismemberment rather than imaginative communitas assuages the poet's alienation. "The avant-garde rejection of mimesis," writes Peter Nicholls, "is . . . clearly linked with a dismemberment of the body and its translation into inorganic form as a prerequisite of original aesthetic perception."[34] As in "First Caprice," the disarticulation of working-class forms from their previous symbolic systems permits their recuperative reintegration into modernist poetic forms.

Rather than the utopic space that Chinitz seems to imagine, for Eliot the working-class music hall is a threatening realm that repeatedly captures his attention only to engender consequent acts of violent intercession. The danger of the music hall is not the danger of cultural competition (of rising working-class configurations that threaten to supplant the oracular function of the poet), a familiar theory that Chinitz rightly disproves. The danger is decidedly more psychological; the music hall presents a community from which Eliot feels excluded, symbolically a community of the body, visceral in its exigency but repugnant to his sensibilities.[35] This explains the libidinal force of his disarticulations, the frequency with which the dismemberments of the class Other create fetishistic forms that energize the poem but exceed the poet's capacity to bring them into fruitful relationship with the poetic voice. This issue is somewhat circumvented by the strength of the second-person address in the fragment above, though not in "In the Department Store," a brief notebook poem from 1915. This poem begins with an image of working-class autonomy—

The lady of the porcelain department
Smiles at the world through a set of false teeth.
She is business-like and keeps a pencil in her hair (56)

—which eventually prompts the poet's reflection on his own ennui: "Man's life is powerless and brief and dark / It is not possible for me to make her happy" (56).

One of several notebook poems of failed sexual conquest, this text would be unremarkable if not for the conspicuous image of "false teeth" and the equally striking unlyricism of the final line. Throughout the 1910s and 1920s Eliot repeatedly returned to images of women's mouths, the gossiping mouths of bourgeois women who had too much to say and the decaying, odorous mouths of working-class women whose orality more explicitly stands in for their frightening sexuality (as Lil so famously exemplifies in *The Waste Land*, lines 139–73). In this case, the false teeth objectify not only the character's sexuality, but also her class pretensions, her desire to falsify the record of her life, to fill her own cavity with the marks of class mobility. The teeth that screen her smile hence serve as exteriorations of class otherness that simultaneously constitutes her disturbing autonomy and her otherwise unexplained desirability. In some sense, it is their pretension that permits the poet's own within the final line—not the Eliotic confession of sexual impotency, but the altogether unjustified supposition on which it depends: that the woman is in actuality not already happy. Indeed, her presupposed emotional impotence begets and validates his own, and propels the adolescent philosophy of the final couplet. If the last line were not so resolutely unpoetic, so clearly a demarcation of the limits of Eliot's lyric, it would stand as one of the more revealing moments in his early poetry. As it is, it most immediately reveals the strain put on the poetic voice as it stretches to encapsulate the Other—the boundaries of his managerial imagination.

The problem with these poems of sexual conquest, in other words, is not just that connections between the self and the class Other are troped as sexual, but that attachment itself is libidinized, a move that internalizes the chaos and anomie that Eliot sees in his surroundings. Connections between materiality and form, body and mind, alienated modernist and community rely thus on a sexual adhesiveness that Eliot, for whatever reason, is unable to enact. The objectifications of class (the false teeth, in this case) are not integrated into a whole, but stand, rather, outside of it—crystallizations of a powerlessness and an impossibility that verge into inconsequence. The pain of connection that prompted the distancing mechanisms of "First Caprice" and the fetishism of the music hall fragment give way to a corresponding pain of isolation, a state that threatens to silence forever the power of the poetic voice. For Eliot, two routes were possible given this impasse: He could work toward establishing identificatory bonds between the poetic voice and the working-class forms that surrounded it. Or he could establish a formal system whereby these bonds would be both displaced and rationalized, whereby the connections between the dualities that plagued him would be safely prefigured and prescribed. Though readers will likely know that Eliot took the second option, famously describing this poetic system of affect as the "objective correlative," the class dimensions of this decision have largely gone unnoticed. Alternately, too few celebrants of Eliot's "extinction of personality" have paused to examine his brief attempts to take the other route and explore cross-class identification.[36]

Toward the Objective Correlative

The notebook poems do, in fact, show several attempts at an alternative form of cross-class poetics. Yet these are halting and uncertain; they occur only in poem fragments and are typically contained within the conditional tense. In an undated fragment, for instance, the poet begins on an existential note, asking "Do I know how I feel? Do I know what I think?," before outlining two possible ways of answering these questions. The first entails taking up "ink and paper" presumably to capture the substance of the poet's mind. Alternately, the poet imagines asking his porter for a drink and, under that pretext, discovering from him "how I think and feel" (80). In essence, the poet imagines an alternative to the reality he simultaneously enacts. Even as he does indeed take ink and paper to try (unsuccessfully) to bridge ego, emotion, and cognition, he projects an external solution, a worker who can recognize his social being and, by doing so, grant him intrasubjective integrity. The problem, however, is that social interactions cannot so easily be prefigured. Relying on the Other for the essential connections of self means opening oneself to unforeseeable outcomes, the vicissitudes of alterity, a fact that Eliot finds social disabling:

If I questioned him with care, would he tell me what I think and feel
—Or only "You are the gentleman who has lived on the second floor
For a year or more"—
Yet I dread what a flash of madness might reveal
If he said "Sir we have seen so much beauty spilled on the open street
Or wasted in stately marriages or stained in railway carriages
Or left untasted in villages or stifled in darkened chambers
That if we are restless on winter nights, who can blame us?"

Do I know how I feel? Do I know how I think? (80)

As the near repetition of the opening questions might suggest, neither of the porter's imagined responses is suitable. If the first is merely the expected recognition of class difference, a propitious answer that politely recognizes the impropriety of such questions, the second ("a flash of madness") goes quite a bit further than the poet can comfortably contemplate. Everything in the second response circles around the meaning of "we," a crucial pronoun that either includes the poet in the porter's modernist denunciations of philistine culture or excludes the poet in a far more radical denunciation of bourgeois waste. The porter either robs the poet of the poem's best line or, more significantly, exposes the fraudulence of the poet's ennui and his poetic attempts at cultural recuperation. Whatever the case, the ambiguity is intolerable, and it leaves the poet contemplating (or perhaps committing) suicide in the fragment's final lines—an escape, one might say, not only from his own doubts, but also from the impossibility of having them assuaged by the class Other.

Through his work in the notebook, Eliot finally arrives at a different, more systematic approach to correlate emotions and objects, a methodology that allows him to integrate the aura of materiality that surrounds working-class forms, while predetermining the forms' relationship to the poetic subject. The "objective correlative," as he terms it, removes the need for sentimentality or the variances of social connection; these it replaces with the rationalized functionality of a linear relationship. "The only way of expressing emotion in the form of art," Eliot famously explains in 1919, "is by finding an 'objective correlative'; in other words, a set of objects, a situation, a chain of events which shall be the formula of that particular emotion; such that when the external facts, which must terminate in sensory experience, are given, the emotion is immediately evoked."[37] This definition is, of course, one of the mainstays of modernist criticism, often revisited in literary histories of the period. Yet I want to stress two aspects of this poetic method that have received little attention: that the objective correlative is, as Eliot defines it, practically a machine relation, and that Eliot fabricates it largely to rationalize his imaginative interactions across the class divide.

On the first point, it is probably enough to stress certain words in Eliot's definition, a definition that is as precise as it is, strictly speaking, unattainable. For what Eliot imagines for these correlatives is a system of specific equivalencies, a "formula," that matches objects, situations, and events to artistic affect without either friction or waste. Such correlatives are not only empirically substantiatable—"external facts" that meet the scientific criteria of replicability—but operate instantaneously, without the uncertain mediations of readerly interpretation. Merely to specify an object (the wail of a child, a set of false teeth) is to "immediately evoke" a specific emotion in all people, at all times, regardless of context. The objective correlative thus evades the painful Cartesian split between mind and body by fantasizing a world without the Cognito, where sensory experiences bear formulaic relation to emotion, skipping entirely the Sisyphean struggle to know how to "think and feel." Such sublime robotics are possible, though, not because of the poet's manipulative abilities, but because, for Eliot, humans are simply made this way. The artist must "find" the objective correlative just as the scientist must find the correct equation for the chemical reactions present in nature; such relations are understood to preexist and superintend their constitutive parts. In the terms I have been exploring, the objective correlative is thus a managerial epistemology, both in the simple sense that it works to manage otherwise chaotic sensory stimuli and in the more specific way that it denotes a totalizing relation that depends on the prior delineation and rationalization of all objects and events into subsequently systemizable parts. "In the achievement of the objective correlative," writes Terry Eagleton, "the poet passes beyond the encapsulating limits of private, poetic experience into an impersonally integrated objectivity."[38] But such a "passage," we might add, gives the poet the numb efficiency of the machine.

The objective correlative is, notwithstanding its precise definition, an impossible method to sustain. Human systems do not function so efficiently, a fact that Eliot certainly knew. Its invocation in 1919, at the end of the decade of the notebook and of Eliot's slumming trips, reflects the pain of cross-class effect and is aimed at aiding the modernist subject caught within the uncertainties of social causality. For though the objective correlative does not remove pain from life or from art—indeed, it builds pain into the affective system—it does make that pain predictable, measurable, and instrumental. By doing so, it thus constitutes the final rejection of middle-class sentimentality and all that this connective mode brings to representations of the working class. It is a significant step in Eliot's long struggle to refashion the relationship between the poetic subject and the social domain, a struggle that was part of modernism's larger process of resituating labor and the pressures of class within new epistemological systems of management.

One final way to understand this is to turn briefly to "The Love Song of J. Alfred Prufrock" and to note how the published version (1915 and 1917) uses some of Eliot's earliest experiments with the objective correlative to overwrite the markedly different class relations of the original notebook poem (written, probably, in 1911).[39] Prufrock is, of course, one of Eliot's more successful "characters," a cipher for the poet's sense of social impotence and the measured introspection of a certain kind of modernist masculinity. Insisting that—

There will be time, there will be time
To prepare a face to meet the faces that you meet;

—he is the manager par excellence, a role that, given the context of the notebook, seems not only caused by the pain of social interaction, but also erected to defend against it.[40] The published version of the poem, however, gives us little explanation for Prufrock's plight. Whereas this absence authorizes innumerable critical readings, along with the more general consecration of ambiguity as a chief modernist virtue, the poem did, in its earliest form, have a more substantial exploration of Prufrock's predicament.

In the published version, lines 70–74 encapsulate both Prufrock's attempt to sing his "love song" and its abrupt abandonment:

Shall I say, I have gone at dusk through narrow streets
And watched the smoke that rises from the pipes
Of lonely men in shirt-sleeves, leaning out of windows? . . .

I should have been a pair of ragged claws
Scuttling across the floors of silent seas.[41]

This gives us two disarticulated images that now, perforce, serve as correlatives (of class-inflected homosocial exclusion and of a consequent retreat to solipsism). But the original draft of the poem included, between these two correlatives, a separate section, "Prufrock's Pervigilium," that continues the abandoned "song." Comprising thirty-eight lines, it is too long to quote in full and, at any rate, recapitulates many of the themes already discussed here. During the night (a Pervigilium is a poem memorializing "a watching through the night"[42]), Prufrock hears the familiar "children whimpering in corners" and sees the familiar working-class forms: peeled oranges, newspapers, "evil houses leaning all together." But dawn ends the Pervigilium rather remarkably—

> I fumbled to the window to experience the world
> And to hear my Madness singing, sitting on the kerbstone
> [A blind old drunken man who sings and mutters,
> With broken boot heels stained in many gutters]
> And as he sang the world began to fall apart . . .

—before it returns us to the second objective correlative:

> I should have been a pair of ragged claws
> Scuttling across the floors of silent seas . . .[43]

Comparable in its effect to Pound's later, more noted, cuts to *The Waste Land*, the elision of these lines alters the poem considerably. The Pervigilium provides something of a back-story, a contextual apparatus through which to better comprehend what would become, in the published version, disparate figurative allusions to the working class: objective correlatives. In these final stanzas of the Pervigilium, the class Other, personified, empathetic, even empathic, is rather the apotheosis of a very different kind of cross-class association—one that amplifies rather than manages social pain. In a recent introduction to Eliot, Helen Vendler has called the displacement of this image into the singing mermaids ("I have heard the mermaids singing, each to each") the most "brilliant moment" in Eliot's development as a poet.[44] Yet surely, it is other than that: The deeply intersubjective moment in the Pervigilium is a road not taken, perhaps decisively, since it would have bonded the poetic subject not to the isolation of cultural retrospection, but with the possibility of the social. Eliot's preference for the mere artifacts of working-class life—these correlative forms—is, finally, a preference for the fragmentary over the connective. Or rather, to return to the model with which I began, it is a preference for the fragmentary as a way of removing the self from the social process, a way of situating the connective apart from the percept in a managerial role.

Conclusion

I have been arguing that one way to understand the rise of modernism, particularly its largely unanalyzed concern with the working-class, is to view it in the context of new labor processes and the new forms of managerial epistemology that arose concurrent with the avant-garde in the 1910s. But my claim throughout has not been that Duchamp's painting, Eliot's early poetry, or modernism generally either prompted or critiqued this political and epistemological shift. I argue rather that texts such as these have symptomatic value, permitting us to better understand the interrelationships between labor processes, management ideologies, and changing aesthetic principles in the cultural realm. More specifically, I have argued that some of the aesthetic tactics of high modernism—its simultaneous stress on fragmentation and totality, and the materiality of the signifier—can be understood as tactics of aesthetic management that are put into play to organize the disparate sensations of class-inflected urban space. This moves modernism decidedly away from earlier realist modes of labor representation, away from sentimental strategies that attempt to reconcile class difference and class struggle through imagined bonds of sympathy, and decidedly toward newer modes that replace reconciliation with management. However conservative and politically regressive this structure, it is important to note that modernism's rejection of the sentimental in favor of the systematic is not a rejection of the political, the material, or even of the existence of class. It is a recasting and a reorganization that regulates the pressure of class difference within new cultural models of modern efficiency.

This is, moreover, only one way to tell the story of high modernism and its early engagement with working-class forms. A similarly detailed account of Gertrude Stein's road to her working-class triptych, *Three Lives* (1909), or of William Carlos Williams's epiphantic discovery of his imagistic style as he first wrote of a working-class Paterson in "The Wanderer" (1914), would necessarily tell this story differently. Such differences would attest, in part, to the fact that the shifts in the labor process and in the epistemology of management were not simplistically determinant. They provided, rather, new dimensions to the class forces that have long troubled bourgeois writers and thus prompted new tactics of aesthetic representation and containment. That such tactics were, in the main, politically conservative rather than progressive has been the undercurrent of this argument throughout. Nevertheless, such tactics can neither be dismissed nor ignored. As radical critics of capitalist culture, we need to be attuned to the way in which such texts have worked to control class struggle—not, as one might think, by ignoring its presence in favor of some purely subjective flight into the imagination, but by constructing systems of the cultural imagination built out of disarticulated and fragmented working-class forms. To put the matter plainly, if more abstractly, bourgeois culture in the modernist moment seldom functions by simple refutations of the class struggle. Its most innovative texts work, rather, through a process of disarticulation and reintegration, a tactic I have interpreted here as the aesthetics of management.

Notes

Research for this article was generously funded by a Summer Stipend from the National Endowment for the Humanities.

1. J. M. Mancini, "'One Term Is as Fatuous as Another': Responses to the Armory Show Reconsidered," *American Quarterly* 51 (1999): 834.

2. Quoted in Milton Brown, *The Story of the Armory Show* (New York: Abbeville Press, 1988), 110. Jerrold Seigel also comments on these reactions in his valuable study, *The Private Worlds of Marcel Duchamp: Desire, Liberation, and the Self in Modern Culture* (Berkeley: University of California Press, 1995), 7.

3. Kenyon Cox, "The 'Modern' Spirit in Art: Some Reflections Inspired by the Recent International Exhibition," *Harper's Weekly*, March 15, 1913, 10.

4. Mancini, "Armory Show Reconsidered," 835.

5. Martin Green, *New York, 1913: The Armory Show and the Paterson Strike Pageant* (New York: Scribner, 1988), 4, 7. Green is not alone in seeing these events as a symbolic duo. See also Cary Nelson, *Repression and Recovery: Modern American Poetry and the Politics of Cultural Memory, 1910–1945* (Madison: University of Wisconsin Press, 1989) 77–78, and Daniel Aaron, *Writers on the Left: Episodes in Literary Communism* (1961; reprint, New York: Columbia University Press, 1992), 14.

6. Green, *New York, 1913*, 6.

7. Louis Fraina, *New Review*, December 1913, 964–65.

8. This pairing is not as random as it may seem. After the IWW lost the Paterson strike, it moved to Detroit to organize workers in the nascent auto industry. See Stephen Meyer III, *The Five Dollar Day: Labor Management and Social Control in the Ford Motor Company, 1908–1921* (Albany: State University of New York Press, 1981), 89–92, and Melvyn Dubofsky, *We Shall Be All: A History of the IWW* (Chicago: Quadrangle Books, 1969), 285–87.

9. Meyer, *Five Dollar Day*, 11.

10. Harry Braverman, *Labor and Monopoly Capital: The Degradation of Work in the Twentieth Century* (New York: Monthly Review Press, 1974), 171.

11. Frank R. Gilbreth and Lillian M. Gilbreth, *Fatigue Study: The Elimination of Humanity's Greatest Unnecessary Waste: A First Step in Motion Study* (London: George Routledge and Sons, 1919), 121.

12. Anson Rabinbach, *The Human Motor: Energy, Fatigue, and the Origins of Modernity* (New York: Basic Books, 1990), 93.

13. Frederick Winslow Taylor, *The Principles of Scientific Management* (New York: Harper and Row, 1911), 7, 142–43.

14. T. S. Eliot, *Notes toward the Definition of Culture* (London: Faber and Faber, 1948), 45.

15. Perry Anderson, "Modernity and Revolution," in *Marxism and the Interpretation of Culture*, ed. Cary Nelson and Lawrence Grossberg (Urbana: University of Illinois Press, 1988), 324.

16. Anthony Giddens, "Modernism and Postmodernism," *New German Critique* 22 (Winter 1981): 16.

17. Carl Sandburg, *Chicago Poems* (1915; reprint, New York: Dover Publications, 1994), 1. See also Sherwood Anderson, *Mid-American Chants* (Folcroft, Pa.: Folcroft Library Editions, 1978), and Robert Frost, *North of Boston* (1914; reprint, New York: Holt, 1915).

18. Walter Benjamin, *Illuminations* (New York: Schocken Books, 1969), 174, 176, 162.

19. Elsa Nettels, *Language, Race, and Social Class in Howells's America* (Lexington: University Press of Kentucky, 1988), 62–71. See also Kenneth Cmiel, *Democratic Eloquence: The Fight over Popular Speech in Nineteenth-Century America* (New York: William Morrow, 1990).

20. Michael North, *The Dialect of Modernism: Race, Language, and Twentieth-Century Literature* (New York: Oxford University Press, 1994), [v].

21. Walter Benn Michaels, *Our America: Nativism, Modernism, and Pluralism* (Durham, N.C.: Duke University Press, 1995), 2. "Nothing," he reiterates elsewhere, "is more characteristic of the literary ambition of modernism than its effort to overcome reference, its effort to make the words *be* the things rather than *refer* to them." "Response," *Modernism/Modernity* 3, no. 3 (1996): 125.

22. J. C. C. Mays, "Early Poems: From 'Prufrock' to 'Gerontion,'" in *The Cambridge Companion to T. S. Eliot*, ed. A. David Moody (Cambridge: Cambridge University Press, 1994), 110.

23. On the scandal caused by the publication of Eliot's early verse, especially the pornographic and racist poems he sent to Ezra Pound, see Vince Passaro, "A Flapping of the Scolds: The Literary Establishment Descends on T. S. Eliot," *Harper's*, January 1997, 62–68, and Richard Poirier, review of *Inventions of the March Hare*, ed. Christopher Ricks, *New Republic* 28 (April 1997): 36–45.

24. Mays, "Early Poems," 110.

25. Though Terry Eagleton apparently had no access to the notebook poems, he has also argued that Eliot's early poetry (in this case, his early *published* poetry) is a search for the objective correlative. See Eagleton, *Exiles and Émigrés: Studies in Modern Literature* (New York: Schocken Books, 1970), 138–78.

26. Gregory Jay, "Postmodernism in *The Waste Land*: Women, Mass Culture, and Others," in *Rereading the New: A Backward Glance at Modernism*, ed. Kevin Dettmar (Ann Arbor: University of Michigan Press, 1992), 237. Eliot's musical titles in the notebook include "First Caprice," "Second Caprice," "Fourth Caprice," "Interlude in London," "Opera," "Suite Clownesque," "Interlude: In a Bar," "The Little Passion," and "Airs of Palestine, No. 2." Christopher Ricks discusses this in his excellent notes to T. S. Eliot, *Inventions of the March Hare: Poems, 1909–1917*, ed. Ricks (New York: Harcourt Brace, 1996), 107. All notebook

poems refer to this edition; page numbers are included parenthetically in the text.

27. T. S. Eliot, *The Sacred Wood: Essays on Poetry and Criticism* (London: Methuen, 1920), 169.

28. James Buzard, "Eliot, Pound, and Expatriate Authority," *Raritan* 13, no. 3 (1994): 114.

29. Charles Baudelaire, *The Poems in Prose*, trans. Francis Scarfe (London: Anvil Press, 1989), 197.

30. David Chinitz, "T. S. Eliot and the Cultural Divide," *PMLA* 110 (1995): 239.

31. Ibid., 245.

32. North discusses Pound's and Eliot's "racial masquerade" in *Dialect of Modernism*, 77–99.

33. Chinitz, "Cultural Divide," 239.

34. Peter Nicholls, *Modernisms: A Literary Guide* (Berkeley: University of California Press, 1995), 115. Though Nicholls makes this observation in a discussion of Baudelaire's "Carion," his point has wider applicability.

35. Feminist Eliot scholars have made this point in a different context. See M. Teresa Gilbert-Maceda, "T. S. Eliot on Women: Women on T. S. Eliot" in *T. S. Eliot at the Turn of the Century*, ed. Marianne Thormählen (Lund, Sweden: Lund University Press, 1994), 105–19, and Carol Christ, "Gender, Voice, and Figuration in Eliot's Early Poetry," in *T. S. Eliot: The Modernist in History*, ed. Ronald Bush (Cambridge: Cambridge University Press, 1991), 23–37.

36. Eliot, *Sacred Wood*, 53.

37. T. S. Eliot, *The Selected Prose of T. S. Eliot*, ed. Frank Kermode (New York: Harcourt Brace Jovanovich, 1975), 48.

38. Eagleton, *Exiles and Émigrés*, 139.

39. Rick provides this date in Eliot, *Inventions*, xv.

40. T. S. Eliot, *The Waste Land and Other Poems*, selected and introduced by Helen Vendler (New York: Signet, 1998), 6.

41. Ibid., 8–9. Ellipsis in original.

42. Ricks in Eliot, *Inventions*, 177.

43. Eliot, *Waste Land*, 9. Ellipsis in original.

44. Vendler, introduction to Eliot, *Waste Land*, xviii. The quoted passage from *The Waste Land* occurs on p. 11.

I don't think we've ever held ourselves out as great book reviewers.
—Anonymous FBI agent

William J. Maxwell

F. B. Eyes: The Bureau Reads Claude McKay

Since the publication of Anthony Summers's sensational biography *Official and Confidential* (1993), J. Edgar Hoover's passion for black authorship has often been obscured by smirks over his supposed love of a quality evening gown. But Hoover's unshakable conviction that communism invented the U.S. civil rights movement was paired with an ardent dread of a radicalized black literary sphere, and recent Freedom of Information Act releases show that his arrival at the Federal Bureau of Investigation launched a fifty-year crusade to bully and savor African American writing, always presumed to be a type of communist sophistry. From the early 1920s through the early 1970s, Hoover's hard-line bureaucracy was also a major if inconspicuous consumer of black texts, a half-buried interpretive empire with aboveground effects on the creation of black modernism. Practically alone among publicly funded institutions of literary study, Hoover's FBI never treated African American writing as an ineffectual fad and never forgot its heavy traffic with the twentieth-century Left.

According to literary historian Hoover, named to head the bureau's Antiradical Division amid the Red Summer race riots of 1919, the Harlem Renaissance was notable for welcoming seditious bomb envy into black letters. A year before the publication of *The Weary Blues* (1925), Langston Hughes's role as a busboy volunteer for the All-American Anti-Imperialist League had thus earned him an FBI file of his own. Seasoned proletarian poems such as "Goodbye Christ" (1932) did nothing to relieve mistrust, winning Hughes the bureau tag of "Negro pornographic poet" (Robins 63). Richard Wright's file, opened three years before his first book, *Uncle Tom's Children* (1938), again displays a bureau with an exceptional ability to identify precocious literary talent—and a new capacity to kill it off, if there is truth in Addison Gayle Jr.'s theory of Wright's Hoover-induced hypertension (*Richard Wright*). As far away as *Paris noir*, and as late as 1960, the year of his death, Wright was still listed as a "possible subversive among US personnel in France" (Robins 285). In the unpublished poem "FB Eye Blues" (1949), Wright turned the tables on bureau note taking, filling classic blues stanzas with wry digs at the intimacy of spy-sight:

Woke up this morning
FB eye under my bed
Said I woke up this morning
FB eye under my bed
Told me all I dreamed last night,
  every word I said.

Defiant Wright pupil James Baldwin was shadowed by a whole gang of confidential FBI sources who intercepted his mail and photographed his daily rounds, not just in Harlem and France, but in Istanbul, where he began plotting retaliation through a never-completed bureau exposé entitled "The Blood Counters" (Campbell 153–67). In tune with a self-lacerating Hoover anxiety—"Isn't Baldwin a well-known pervert?" he wondered (Campbell 170)—the bureau's General Crimes Section combed Baldwin's novels for traces of sexual as well as political obscenity. Yet *Another Country* (1962) impressed one open-minded FBI reviewer, who was astonished to discover a book of genuine "literary merit . . . [that] may be of value to students of psychology and social behavior" (Robins 347). W. E. B. Du Bois's work was the beneficiary of no such dissenting raves, ensuring his high place on the bureau's Security Index of imminently arrestable Leftists from 1950 until his death in Ghana in 1963 (Keen 15). Chester Himes did not make the index, but his Harlem detective fiction was foreshadowed by FBI gumshoes who began investigating his prison time and anticolonial outlook in 1944, with the results itemized in a personal file marked "Internal Security-Sedition" (Walters

6–7). Paule Marshall and Ishmael Reed, for their part, escaped with relatively slim files for signing petitions in favor of civil rights legislation and against the Vietnam War, though Amiri Baraka's wider swath through Castro's Cuba, the American Communist Party, and the home base he rechristened "New Ark," New Jersey, was sufficient to generate two thousand pages of gossip, reconnaissance, and dirty tricks beginning in 1960 (Robins 411, 349–52). Years earlier, a bureau memo had wondered if William Carlos Williams's "very queer or possibly mental" objectivist poetry concealed revolutionary cryptograms (Robins 293). Given the FBI's intense concern for the best of African American modernism, we may soon discover that it judged Jean Toomer's *Cane* (1923) a work of both elusive imagist lyrics and secret Bolshevik code.

This essay explores the overlooked episode of bureau surveillance that installed the odd dialectic between black literary modernism and FBI literary espionage, the latter the domestic intelligence community's initial quasi-legal analog for modern practical criticism. Even before the bureau was looking for Langston, it was snooping on Claude McKay, the Jamaican-born poet, novelist, diehard bohemian, nomadic social radical, and self-described principled "son of a bitch" (Letter to Walter White) whom the State Department would denounce as a "notorious negro revolutionary" (U.S. Mar. 11, 1924). When he was not waiting tables, cultivating a mature standard English idiom, or helping to found the Harlem Renaissance, McKay spent his early New York years (1914–19) harmonizing Greenwich Village–, Harlem-, and Moscow-style Leftisms. Back in Manhattan in 1921 after a London stint, these political labors earned him posts of honor with downtown's soft-focus Marxist journal, the *Liberator*, and uptown's combative Left nationalist faction, the African Blood Brotherhood (ABB). But they also stationed him at dead center of the radical intersection that the FBI most feared, the crossroads where African American resistance bargained with the devil of world communism. At the peak of its suspicion, the bureau identified McKay as a clandestine Soviet agent, a slippery emissary whose travel plans were international incidents. As we will see, the paperwork surrounding this suspicion argues that the bureau was not simply hallucinating: McKay may have been recruited as an underground operative by the Communist International, and he certainly enjoyed writing as one. In the pages that follow, McKay's substantial FBI file will be tapped to shed fresh light on his shadowy career as a would-be "spy-writer" and on the ventures of the Harlem Renaissance, black Atlantic radicalism, and international black modernism his career helped to define.

While McKay was honing his black Bolshevism and his furiously elegant sonnets, U.S. federal intelligence gathering swelled to enforce legislation passed in the anxious climate of World War I and the Russian Revolution. One neglected but insistent tutor of McKay's full-grown, American voice, this is to say, was the birth of the modern U.S. security state. Theodore Kornweibel Jr. notes that the Espionage Act of 1917 and the Sedition Act of 1918 "granted broad power to the federal government to punish any appearance of disloyalty or interference with the draft; muzzle the dissenting press and censor other forms of communication; and, most ominously, punish writing or speech that *might* harm the country's war efforts, promote the cause of Germany, or discredit the American government, Constitution, or flag" (4–5; emphasis in original). The Alien Act, rushed into law just before the armistice of November 1918, echoed its eighteenth-century namesake in speeding mechanisms for the arrest and expulsion of immigrants with "anti-American" leanings. Modern, coordinated, professionalized U.S. political intelligence, Kornweibel shows, came of age to administer this trio of laws. Whatever their obstruction of free speech and free association, then, the new measures opened a boom market for spies. Empowered State and Justice Department agents initiated weekly meetings with army and navy intelligence heads on the state of draft resistance. New hires at the Post Office Department pored over publications for signs of treachery, burning material containing excerpts of an imported morale killer called *Ulysses* (Kornweibel 4).

But it was the Bureau of Investigation, renamed the FBI in 1935, that reaped the greatest war profits among the American intelligence apparatus. Only 300 bureau agents were on staff in early 1917. Thanks to the organization's unique powers of specialization, however, by war's end some "1,500 agents watched enemy aliens, domestic enemies, war dissenters, and pacifists, helped prepare Espionage and Sedition act prosecutions, and enforced selective service regulations" (Kornweibel 7). The postwar Red Scare and anti-Leftist Palmer Raids solidified the bureau's preeminence and placed its trendsetting countersubversive unit under J. Edgar Hoover, a fastidious attorney still in his twenties. Born in Washington, D.C., at the height of Jim Crow, an avowed racist troubled by rumors of his own black ancestry (Summers 349–50), Hoover reasoned that black protest was triggered by equal desires for Lenin and miscegenation. Bolshevism and civil rights sentiment replaced German sympathy on the most-wanted list of his more influential and ideologized bureau, while "political intelligence and subversion of due process and civil liberties [became its] hallmarks" (Kornweibel 7). Augmenting the rightward turn of bureau politics, Hoover's Red-busters quickly learned to please their demanding boss with higher production numbers. By late 1919 they had classified 60,000 "radically inclined" individuals and declared 471 radical periodicals worthy of close reading (Powers 68).

To Hoover and his own superiors, McKay had reason to seem the black Red most likely to violate all the new security acts at a single bound. As a writer alone, he joined a profession Hoover thought full of "Communist thought-control relays" (qtd. in Robins 50), simultaneously susceptible to and handy with Bolshevik propaganda. As a black poet favored by New York's dissenting press, in particular, he contributed almost exclusively to race-radical publications that the bureau hoped to silence. A. Philip Randolph's socialist review, the *Messenger*, struck Hoover as "the Russian organ of the Bolsheviki in the United States" (Kornweibel 23) and Attorney General A. Mitchell Palmer as the most subversive African American publication. The *Messenger* was also an early venue for "If We Must Die" and other fiery McKay sonnets, especially those touching on two of Palmer's most "unacceptable themes": "the right of blacks to arm for self-defense against lynchers and rioters" and the "demand for total social equality" (Kornweibel 21). The ABB journal the *Crusader*, another frequent reprinter of "If We Must Die," carried the bureau rating of "entirely radical" and unknowingly employed an undercover FBI informant as an advertising salesman (23, 92). The *Liberator*, the Village monthly whose staff McKay joined in 1921, inherited the stain of its predecessor, Max Eastman's dashing *Masses*, which closed shop after two prosecutions under the Espionage Act.

The prominence of McKay's sonnets in these hot-button magazines, personally inspected by Hoover and Palmer, might itself have given him FBI fame. But McKay's political attachments also put his money where his verse was. Bureau investigators witnessed him triangulating among memberships in the young Communist Party, the International Workers of the World, and the African Blood Brotherhood, lumping together diverse anticapitalisms nearly as energetically as Hoover. Evidence of his place in the subculture where such radicalisms met queer New York sent up further red flags. Like the gayness of James Baldwin after him, McKay's thinly cloaked bisexuality exposed him to Hoover's ironic association of Leftism and licentiousness. Decades before Senator Joseph McCarthy testified on the symmetry of "Communists and queers" (Savran 5), the closeted bureau leader had already conflated undercover sexual longings and secret desires against the U.S. government (and had thus begun paving the way to post-Stonewall debates on the political price of queer self-concealment [Dumm 79–83]). Topping the list of bureau apprehensions, however, was McKay's concentrated, flagrant foreignness. As an outspoken, unnaturalized black West Indian incomer, he was tainted with the immigrant guilt by association consecrated in the Alien Act and aggravated by the bureau's fierce pursuit of fellow Jamaican Marcus Garvey. It was little wonder, then, that by 1921 the FBI and the State Department had pronounced McKay the single strongest link between Harlem's ascendant race capital and Moscow's Vatican of global communism. Beginning in December, both federal agencies began stuffing an FBI file whose initial page tells of the subject's faith in the Communist Party and guilt over tardy IWW dues (U.S. Dec. 16, 1921). Months before *Harlem Shadows* (1922)—the Harlem Renaissance incitement that the bureau reckoned "a collection of radical poems"—the first poet of Harlem's rebirth had thus become an official enemy of his adopted country, a multiply suspect alien agent whose friendship was enough to win Harlemites their own bureau dossiers (U.S. Feb. 3, 1923; Kornweibel 177).

McKay's FBI file was the first that the bureau opened on an important black author, but remains perhaps the least known. Aside from Kornweibel's *"Seeing Red": Federal Campaigns against Black Militancy, 1919–1925* (1998), historical studies of the bureau's long war on African American protest highlight events and documents of the civil rights years, when Hoover actually approved a strategy to maneuver Martin Luther King Jr. toward suicide (Garrow; O'Reilly). McKay's file also goes unmentioned in the thick books by Herbert Mitgang and Natalie Robins that annotate the FBI's blanket scrutiny of hundreds of American authors. McKay criticism neglects his bureau renown no less, with the exception of biographer Tyrone Tillery, who generously lent me his copy of McKay's file until my own arrived, two and one-half years after an initial Freedom of Information Act request. To finally read McKay's FBI portrait, however, is to learn that neither his stateside poetry nor his internationalist commitments can accurately be viewed apart from the prying eyes of the Bureau of Investigation. McKay's far-flung intellectual itinerary, attacked by the bureau during his own lifetime, might therefore now be clarified by bureau criticism: namely, by his FBI file considered as a work of *literary criticism*, of collectively authored textual analysis and cultural history. The compatibility of the author and the intelligence agent has been remarked at least since the Renaissance (pre-Harlem edition). "A writer-spy like [Christopher] Marlowe," suggests John Michael Archer, knew that his work on both sides of the hyphen depended on "observation of men and manners [that] made their manipulation through spectacle possible" (75). But what of the figure and impact of the *critic-spy*, whose observation of authors and texts is enabled not only by decryption, identity theft, and hermeneutics of suspicion—techniques that almost every literary critic shares with the intelligence agent—but also by FBI manipulation?

Diligent, periodically illegal surveillance from this collective critic-spy likely hounded McKay. As with Baldwin, whose 1964 flight from the United States was promoted by FBI harassment (Campbell 172), McKay's separations from Harlem were probably scheduled with bureau assistance. He shipped himself out for London in the fall of 1919, in the nick of time to avoid the December deportation of Emma Goldman and other fellow "enemy aliens," shackled on a "Soviet Ark" bound for Finland. His much lengthier excursion through Western Europe and North Africa beginning in 1923 was something of a forced black Atlanticism, required if not defined by bureau stop orders at U.S. ports of entry (U.S. Jan. 23, 1923). More than McKay's self-made antibourgeois wanderlust fueled the "spiritual truancy" (Locke 82) from Harlem that was found decadent by both New Negro elders and early African American studies, similarly discomfited by "post-national" black identities. Regarded in the grimmest light, the FBI may have succeeded in evicting the most radical instigator of Harlem's renaissance from its New York metropolitan core. And with long-range consequences: McKay's removal authorized *New Negro* editor Alain Locke and other framers of the renaissance boom years to presume that black Bolshevism would abandon the Harlem scene. Still, however much Hoover's critic-spies undercut the First Amendment and, like G-men Dr. Bledsoes, kept the youthful McKay running, they also produced genuine insight into his career. In certain estimable ways, the bureau in fact stands with the best of McKay's critics and stands alone in detecting his taste for performing in the guise of an urbane spy.

The Hoover school's contribution to McKay studies is not a result of corrupt espionage giving way to flashes of interpretive lucidity, for its unscrupulousness and occasional confusions helped to make it clear-eyed. The bureau's gullible, sometimes lawless spycraft fed the paranoid hermeneutic that gave it access to McKay's poetics of double agency and helped it gauge wider Harlem debts to a cosmopolitan black radicalism extending beyond the Atlantic rim into the bolshevized Black Sea. McKay's own response to this spy-criticism, meanwhile, indicates that the bureau's murky interpretive community could be received as a school for literary refinement, as an inspiration for heightened expression rather than for self-throttling counterintelligence. FBI pressure has regularly been invoked to explain high-profile retreats from literary radicalism: Amiri Baraka, for example, fingered the bureau as one culprit behind Langston Hughes's de-Marxification, and Howard Fast saw Hoover's clout behind the very death of social realism in midcentury America (Robins 284, 399). In McKay's case, however, the "FB eye" seems to have sharpened a radical aesthetic even as it made a radical life more tentative. Without reading against the grain all the way into redemptive fantasy, McKay's file can thus be approached as a productive addition to Leftist literary history and as positively constitutive of McKay's influential American poetics. The burden of this approach is not to prove that ubiquitous disciplinary power activated and overwhelmed another would-be resister, but at last to use the Freedom of Information Act to yield information about literary freedom.

Admittedly, sections of McKay's FBI dossier substantiate Michel Foucault's bleak notion of the modern "police text," the vast literature "of a complex documentary organization," which, "unlike the methods of judicial or administrative writing, . . . register[s] attitudes, possibilities, suspicions—a permanent account of individuals' behavior" (214). All manner of attitudes, possibilities, and suspicions cohabit with stable biographical data in the file, enough to compose a thick rather than an obsessive description by the standards of bureau spy-criticism. McKay's 119 pages of bureau commentary are comparable to Wright's 181—weightier than Gertrude Stein's 11, for example, but far lighter than Hughes's 559-page opus, a monument of FBI critique not much shorter than his forty years of *Collected Poems* (Robins 284, 207, 63). Like most FBI files, McKay's is a miscellaneous bundle. An individual bureau dossier, Natalie Robins explains, usually "consists of separate pages of investigative reports, legal forms, interviews, memorandums, petitions, letters, articles and news clippings that have been collected and clipped together" (17). McKay's file, covering the period from 1921 to 1940, juxtaposes materials from many of these categories. There are field notes from bureau spies assigned to tail him around Manhattan; accounts of his foreign political speeches compiled by U.S. legations in Europe; cautionary letters from Hoover and then–bureau director William J. Burns to State Department officials, and vice versa; summarized articles from Soviet newspapers; even blurry reproductions of photographs of McKay with Max Eastman and other Communist company, as well as memoranda carefully transcribing his poetry and journalism. Unlike the publicly available files of the civil rights era, McKay's shows only minor evidence of FBI censorship (or what the bureau prefers to earmark as "[e]xcisions . . . made to protect information exempt from disclosure pursuant to [the Freedom of Information Act]" [Kelso]). A few names have been whited out expressly to protect personal privacy, as has one probable reference to McKay's love of men (U.S. Dec. 13, 1922).

Even in its unexpurgated passages, however, the file's interest in McKay's sexuality is distinct, of a piece with its tendency to criminalize temperament along with dissident creeds. As Foucault insinuates of police text in general, the file certifies the felony of an identity as much as any illegal political activity, McKay's heretical being as much as his revolutionary doing. For the special benefit of Hoover, who acted as the bureau's executive editor of police writing, throwing his weight around through abundant, puritanical marginalia (Robins 20), McKay's private conduct is thus confirmed to be as illicit as his political contacts. Stolen correspondence in which McKay complains of unsanitary Frenchmen and a bout of venereal disease is breathlessly submitted into the record (U.S. Feb. 29, 1924). So are accounts of his cash-starved begging to friends and his ambiguously "confidential" business with a white radical woman (U.S. Jan. 31, 1924, Dec. 13, 1922). Frozen to McKay's bureau reputation as a "notorious negro revolutionary" was a fixed identity as a bohemian reprobate.

More of the file's pages than not, however, display prurient police text ceding ground to what might be called "judicial text," reportage soberly detecting possible treason and preparing overt forms of state interference. Unsurprisingly, sheets accumulate furiously as McKay undertakes his 1922–23 pilgrimage to the Soviet Union, the citadel of the Marxist revolution he proclaimed "the greatest event in the history of humanity" (U.S. Jan. 26, 1924). Initially, the bureau was led to expect artistic expatriation on the standard American plan: an unnamed, "strictly confidential source" had dropped word that "the well known radical of New York City . . . contemplates going to Europe" (U.S. July 21, 1922). McKay's well-publicized arrival in Moscow in late October 1922, just before the Fourth Congress of the Comintern opened its doors, exposed a less comforting itinerary and confirmed his aura of alien allegiance. The bureau's capacity for (imperfect) transnational surveillance is demonstrated by the paper storm that followed. American diplomats in Riga, Latvia—then a nest of anti-Soviet espionage—extensively reported on McKay's part in Comintern deliberations on the "Negro Question" and translated his several contributions to the Soviet press (U.S. Dec. 7, 11, 1922). Director Burns conveyed the gist of the bad news to the State Department and asked that McKay and other black Comintern delegates be held for "appropriate attention" on attempting to reenter the United States (U.S. Dec. 12, 1922).

The reach and energy of the bureau's efforts to discover McKay's precise travel schedule are staggering. Newspaper accounts of Russian-bound shipping were screened; the wife of ABB principal Cyril Briggs was pressed for clues in her Harlem apartment; and the U.S. Passport Office scoured its records, concluding that McKay and his comrades would sail as merchant seamen, just as theorists of the black Atlantic would now have it (U.S. Dec. 16, 1922, Jan. 6, 11, 1923). The national priority of blocking McKay's return was made known to officials in every American port city. Immigration and customs officials readied themselves to confine man, "baggage, . . . and documents" in New York and Los Angeles, but also in Seattle and Portland, Charleston and Wilmington, New Orleans and Baltimore (U.S. Jan. 23, 1923). Bureau agents in this last city paraded their caution in a bulletin directly addressed to Hoover, which boasts of a clued-in "Local Police Department" on the "lookout" for one "Claude McKay (Colored)" (U.S. Mar. 23, 1923). At the same moment that the Harlem Renaissance revved its engines, bureau vigilance made McKay a young intellectual to watch in many more places than literary New York—a welcoming locale he could not freely reenter had he tried. Which other writers of American consequence have been subject to so thorough an intelligence manhunt, or so quickly made to follow a movement-building debut—*Harlem Shadows*—with such reduced freedom of movement?

Such questions are not meant to suggest that FBI wariness of McKay's Moscow trip was entirely delirious. While in the Soviet Union, he had impressed militants as well as literati, conferring with officers of the Red Army and prompting Trotsky to affirm that "the training of black propagandists is the most imperative . . . revolutionary task of the present time" (8). McKay had contributed high-level propaganda of his own to the Soviet state publishing house, counseling "as large a number of Negroes as possible that they should turn for the solution of their problem to the Third International" (*The Negroes* 5–6). He had gone from Communist partisanship in Harlem to Communist leadership in Moscow, becoming a New Negro ambassador of a worldwide movement promising revolution in the United States and other capitalist nations (Maxwell 63–93). In short, he had grown into someone almost as eagerly dangerous to American business as usual as the Soviet materials in his FBI file made him out to be. These pages, at least, contain spy-criticism with a rare approximation of estimated and actual threat.

The precise form of McKay's threat, however, the bureau's collective critic-spy never determined. Had McKay adopted the Russophilic alias of "Sasha" and decided "to remain in [the Soviet Union] as President of the Negro Section of the Executive Committee of the 3rd International" (U.S. Feb. 3, 1923)? Or had he "graduated from the Bolshevik school at Moscow" and "been especially delegated by the Soviet Government for propaganda among the North American Negroes" (U.S. Mar. 6, 1923)? Would he return to the United States carrying "instructions and documents from the Communist International to the Communists in this country, together with a considerable sum of money" (U.S. Mar. 10, 1923)? Or would his American errand demand heroic organizing skills: building "a colored Soviet," a black socialist society in embryo, in Dixie or Manhattan (U.S. Mar. 17, 1923)? Had a "Bolshevik agent" named "Claude Mackey" instead been "ordered to proceed to The Hague from Norway," avoiding both the United States and the Soviet Union, or would he stick to earlier commands and "attempt to enter the United States via [the] West Indies" (U.S. Mar. 26, 1923)? (See Fig. 1.) McKay's unnoticed relocation from Moscow to Germany in May 1923 left all these speculations hanging. As far as the bureau's collective critic ever deduced, McKay was the most determined sort of Comintern operative. Insofar as he intended to leave Russia, he would do so as a Soviet agent, outfitted with big plans, secret orders, or Moscow gold.

Given the clashing imprecision of these FBI findings, not to mention the various misspellings of McKay's surname, dismissing the lot may seem responsible. Tillery and Kornweibel, the file's previous scholarly readers, chose just this option, seconding McKay's own post-Communist memory that "I went into Russia as a writer and a free spirit and left the same" (qtd. in Tillery 71). Yet it must be conceded that McKay's Moscow profile is close to that of the typical foreign-born Soviet courier of the early 1920s. Less a hard-bitten professional than an impassioned revolutionary, this courier was usually recruited by the Comintern, a body suited to persuading non-Russian Communists fearful of Soviet "espionage services . . . that they were serving the international [cause]" (Klehr, Haynes, and Firsov 20). Like McKay's Greenwich Village colleague John Reed, arrested by the Finns in 1920 while carrying $14,000 in Russian diamonds, this courier might refuse long-term spying but agree to smuggle "a considerable sum of money" to the Communist Party in the home country (24). Too many American Communists, now as in the McCarthy era, have wrongly suffered from Hoover's insistence that "any member of the Communist Party is an active or potential Soviet espionage agent" (Schrecker 129). Nonetheless, McKay's résumé does not allow for easy dismissal of the possibility that he was one of a small, pioneering international cadre sporadically engaged in nonviolent covert action.

McKay's unpublished correspondence, among other documents, shows that his road before and after Moscow was clogged by spies and by the suggestion that he had joined his stalkers' business. In renaissance Harlem, rival New Negroes were not shy of labeling him a "bolshevik

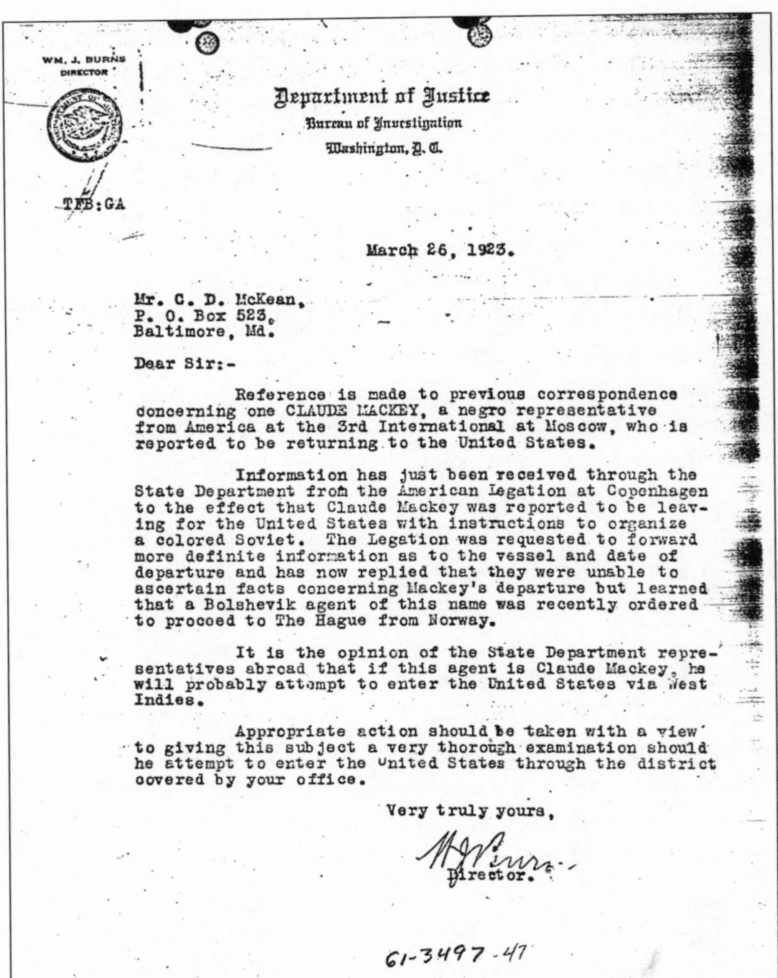

WM. J. BURNS
DIRECTOR

Department of Justice
Bureau of Investigation
Washington, D. C.

TFB:GA

March 26, 1923.

Mr. C. D. McKean,
P. O. Box 523,
Baltimore, Md.

Dear Sir:-

Reference is made to previous correspondence concerning one CLAUDE MACKEY, a negro representative from America at the 3rd International at Moscow, who is reported to be returning to the United States.

Information has just been received through the State Department from the American Legation at Copenhagen to the effect that Claude Mackey was reported to be leaving for the United States with instructions to organize a colored Soviet. The Legation was requested to forward more definite information as to the vessel and date of departure and has now replied that they were unable to ascertain facts concerning Mackey's departure but learned that a Bolshevik agent of this name was recently ordered to proceed to The Hague from Norway.

It is the opinion of the State Department representatives abroad that if this agent is Claude Mackey, he will probably attempt to enter the United States via West Indies.

Appropriate action should be taken with a view to giving this subject a very thorough examination should he attempt to enter the United States through the district covered by your office.

Very truly yours,

W J Burns
Director.

61-3497-47

IGURE 1. FBI director William J. Burns asks C. D. McKean of the Baltimore district office to keep eyes ɛeled for a Bolshevik agent who may be "Claude Mackey," larch 26, 1923. (From the Claude McKay file; courtesy of the U.S. Federal Bureau of Investigation)

agent" (McKay to Nancy Cunard). In radical London, he labored on the Communist *Workers' Dreadnought* shoulder to shoulder with a "Comrade Vie," eventually arrested by English police as a Bolshevik plant. McKay was, in turn, accused of betraying his coworker to Scotland Yard and replied to the allegation by rapidly departing England (Cooper 125–26). In Weimar Germany following his Soviet adventure, McKay himself claimed that he intended "to put over some propaganda . . . and send through things [local party plans and requests?] to Moscow" (McKay to Walter White). But he was forced to flee this sub-rosa "social revolutionary work" according to a familiar migratory pattern: "I had to get out of Berlin," he wrote Upton Sinclair, "before I was deported." In Tangier,

Morocco, he attributed a missing passport and a friend's Madrid arrest to British intelligence, and feared that American authorities would not "let me in with my Russian record without special intervention" (McKay to Max Eastman, Apr. 1933). His conviction that he was afflicted by spies, not "persecution mania" (McKay to Eastman), was braced by a frank letter from Her Majesty's Office of Works, which confirmed that British authorities at the Foreign Office retained "a full record of [his] political and other activities" and would bar "his admission to British Colonial or Protectorate territories" (Postgate). French intelligence, he learned, had kept abreast in caution: It "had reason . . . for objecting to [his] presence on French Protectorate soil" (Postgate). The antagonism of this last imperial power was perhaps sparked by clandestine anticolonial organizing: Sometime after 1934, McKay received a lightly coded note reminding him of his support for Moroccan independence and requesting his assistance to prevent the deportation of a "good friend" now "on the books" of the French police (Salem). When he returned to the United States for good in the mid-1930s, McKay's initial choice in literary agents was Maxim Lieber, whose moonlighting as a Soviet secret agent was dramatically unmasked during the Whittaker Chambers–Alger Hiss affair (Cooper 298). Everywhere that McKay went a spy was sure to follow. And most everywhere that spy assumed McKay was an opposite number.

This tangled trail of reciprocal distrust and confession, radical propaganda and imperial policing, affirms that McKay was the most audacious kind of postcolonial border intellectual. It also suggests that German, British, and French intelligence would not have been shocked by the FBI's charge of McKay's Soviet service. In no way, however, does this trail itself prove that McKay was a Bolshevik secret agent, an actual "writer-spy" to the left of confirmed British agents Graham Greene, Somerset Maugham, and Ian Fleming. Although McKay's roving revolutionary enthusiasm of the early 1920s fitted him for work as a nonprofessional Comintern courier, and 1924 saw him bluntly admitting plans to "send through things to Moscow" (McKay to Walter White), he thereafter denied that he was any kind of Soviet operative, especially after the elevation of Stalin, whom he had the foresight to denounce well before the Moscow Trials. Decommissioned Comintern papers may eventually tell a fuller tale of his role; until then, the intensity of FBI spy-reading alone permits several inferences otherwise absent from both McKay criticism and recent theories of black modernity. At its most basic, the FBI vigilance inscribed in McKay's file insists on the risky seriousness of his communism, habitually underestimated in renditions of the Harlem Renaissance. McKay's own contributions to the file confirm that the Harlem movement's vanguard poet conceived of the Soviet Union as one of the rebirth's closest satellites, as pressing as ancient Egypt, modern West Africa, the black Caribbean, and the Black Belt Southern countryside in its remapping of what Garveyism called the "Negro World." Despite the perplexity over McKay's job description—would he lead a global Negro Section or a black American Soviet?—FBI communiqués were sure of his importance to the Communist International, thus suggesting that he may well have been forcefully *recruited* as a full-time Comintern agent, a possibility that McKay now and then implied to Leftist colleagues. "Although the bolsheviks tried to *make* me represent the Negro race," he once signaled to Nancy Cunard, "I let them know I was a free spirit, a poet although *politically* my sympathies were communist" (emphases in original). The bureau's tense assessment of McKay's Soviet writing also usefully punctures his post-facto segregation of literary and political callings. In Moscow, as in New York, London, Berlin, and Tangier, McKay's favorite muse was revolutionary intrigue, and his taste for composing among conspirators made him a magnet for surveillant fantasies and escapades.

More abstractly, the vigilance of FBI spy-criticism offers valuable advice to now-leading models of black internationalism and the modernizing effects of racial discipline. Like other narratives of black transnational voyagers, McKay's bureau file spotlights themes often "erased by the universalizing of [middle-class] European travel" texts, including immigration and deportation (Grewal 2). But this file also accents erasures within the dominant template for describing the specifics of black wandering, the high-flown seas of Paul Gilroy's *The Black Atlantic: Modernity and Double Consciousness* (1993). As Sandra Gunning maintains, Gilroy's Atlantic world "of African diasporic hybridity enriched by cultural crossovers among peoples of African descent" has stimulated a "recent privileging of diaspora identification" among African Americanists (33). A "romanticizing [of] the revolutionary and subversive power of this identification," she argues, now "threatens to elide the very real impact of color, status, region, and gendered experience as sites of intra-racial difference within the context of the black diaspora" (33). The work of McKay's critic-spies, for its part, pleads for the inclusion of *political investment* on Gunning's list of unromantic, soon-to-be-unsung scenes of diasporan "intra-racial difference." For the left-wing Pan-Africanists who largely invented twentieth-century black diaspora identification, transnational crossings often led to involuntary experiences of banishment—paradoxically, their willful revisions and reversals of the Middle Passage brought unwilled returns. Think not only of McKay's informal extraditions from New York and Berlin, but also of Garvey's necessary remigration from Harlem to Kingston, Jamaica, after his conviction for mail fraud, or of C. L. R. James's deportation to England via the ironic docks of Ellis Island, where he took stock of Herman Melville's seafaring legacy to Communist prisoners by composing *Mariners, Renegades, and Castaways* (1953). McKay appears just once in Gilroy's *Black Atlantic*, in relation to his involvement with ships, what Peter Linebaugh calls "the most important conduit of Pan-African communication before the appearance of the long-playing record" (qtd. in Gilroy 13). Had McKay also entered for his costly involvement with those considered Leftist foreign agents—Hoover's candidates for the most important conduit of Pan-African communication—we might have a richer sense of the arrested and coerced motion that befell the black radicals most devoted to the subversive power of black Atlantic travel.

All the same, the vigilance of the bureau critic-spy equally clarifies an unnoticed chapter in the recognition of modern black mobility. The FBI's aspiration to airtight international surveillance both compelled certain directions in McKay's black Atlanticism and acknowledged that the black diasporan world was no longer readily subject to border patrols. The very application of this surveillance was a confession of local police inadequacy and one proof of the hollowness of FBI racism, forced to document the black agency produced in international circuits that threatened to exceed its intelligence. "Negroes are growing in global consciousness" (Robins 64), granted Hughes's dossier, and the bureau could only follow suit. Whatever the resemblance between elements of McKay's file and exemplary police text, the document thus also flags a novel, weighty failure in the imposition of disciplinary power onto American blacks, power that Foucault famously equates with the pervasive surveillance of post-Enlightenment society.

Saidiya Hartman's rigorously argued account of the racial subjugation of African Americans in the nineteenth century, *Scenes of Subjection* (1997), can help take stock of the break from correction. Emphasizing the even rhythm of subordination beneath Foucault's divided genealogy of punishment and observation, she traces a surprisingly smooth path from a slave plantation theater of cruelty to a post-Emancipation discipline of freedom, in which "dutiful submission" is continuously demanded "of black subjectivity, whether in the making and maintaining of chattel personal or in the fashioning of individuality, cultivation of conscience, and harnessing of free will" (7). Conceived as a work of historical interpretation, as much as a piece of literary criticism, McKay's file might answer Hartman with two postscripts: first, that the disciplinary cycle was humbled in the second decade of the twentieth century, thanks to the massive mobile evasion of the Great Migration to Harlem and other northern black city zones, locales proudly removed from the southern entanglement of slavery and freedom; and second, that this cycle was finally *seen* to be broken when black internationalists evaded and returned surveillance from abroad. It was the hyper-itinerant "Greater Migration" of black "spies" like McKay, the semblance of their international sightings, missions, and conspiracies, that required the bureau's leaky reapplication "of a state of conscious and permanent visibility" in its black targets (Foucault 201).

Discussing a related case of FBI blues, Maurice Wallace inventively reads Baldwin's bureau dossier as evidence of "the chronic effort to 'frame' the black male body . . . for the visual pleasures of whites" and of Baldwin's attempt to respond with an "eye-balling disposition of his own" (300, 303). In comparative light, McKay's file is distinguished by a younger bureau's agitated, first-wave *comprehension* of such reckless reverse eyeballing—many of its pages are explicitly provoked by McKay's counterdisciplinary sight. Unlike Foucault's eighteenth-century prisoners, prototypical citizens of his penitentiary modern state, or Hartman's unfree freedmen, veterans of a supposedly totalizing plantation system that predated Jeremy Bentham's panopticon, McKay is known to see as he is seen; he is recognized as a subject in communication with an international movement pledging liberation, even as he is an object of international police information. The somewhat paranoid compilation that is McKay's file thus doubles as insight into the official reception of a century of international black resistance, in which agency in the academically favored sense of autonomous power is first fathomed from without as agency in the sense of secret commerce with foreign powers.

It was flickers of double agency that the unexpectedly perceptive "FB eye" spotted in McKay's American poetry. One of the longest career summaries in McKay's file begins by questioning his lyrical bona fides: "Subject is apparently a poet," comments an anonymous bureau wit, "or at least he has written considerable verse" (U.S. Jan. 26, 1924). Yet the same document goes on to quote several poems in fascinated detail, from the unrelenting "Enslaved" to the well-known martyrology of "If We Must Die," the only Shakespearian sonnet ever to command equal attention in FBI spy-criticism, the wartime speeches of Winston Churchill, the Attica Prison uprising, and *The Norton Anthology of African-American Literature*. McKay's less circulated but likewise caustic sonnet "America" (1921) is quoted in full:

Although she feeds me bread of bitterness,
And sinks into my throat her tiger's tooth,
Stealing my breath of life, I will confess
I love this cultured hell that tests my youth!
Her vigor flows like tides into my blood,
Giving me strength erect against her hate.
Her bigness sweeps my being like a flood.
Yet as a rebel fronts a king in state,
I stand within her walls with not a shred
Of terror, malice, not a word of jeer.
Darkly I gaze into the days ahead[,]
And see her might and granite wonders there,
Beneath the touch of Time's unerring hand,
Like priceless treasures sinking in the sand.[1]

For critic-spies trained in modern literature departments, "America" is an invitation to old or new formalisms. Lushly allusive, semantically knotty, imagistically dense, hooked on conceptual tension, the sonnet's refusal to liquidate iambic pentameter and other high modernist enemies nonetheless begs for high modernist interpretive protocols. The first seven lines, an unbalanced, nonconforming unit of quatrain and virtual tercet, reach from the Harlem Renaissance to the English Renaissance to revive the sonnet motif of the cruel-fair mistress. In McKay's game hands, this motif tropes international (and interracial?) intimacy as sado-masochistic vampirism, with the "tiger's tooth" of feminine America both sapping the breath and inflating the potency of an erect but un-gendered lyric "I." Even the ostensibly anguished first line, feeding both gall and "bread" to the speaker, promises the final hydraulic equilibrium of the affair, its "vigor flow[ing] like tides" from America to her lover. McKay's imagery of troubled yet sustaining currents here dramatizes the traditional sonnet logic through which the cruel mistress fills out her victim, providing her lover with "effects . . . which, if distressing, are none the less manifestations of *him*" (Spiller 156; emphasis in original). The leading such effect in "America" is the speaker's astutely equivocal love for the hand that strangles and feeds him—or her. Anticipating Walter Benjamin's epigram on the proximity of civilization and barbarism, McKay's persona confesses affection for the nation's "cultured hell," where a body can learn that America's every document of grace, "vigor," and "bigness" is a document of thievery.

As Felipe Smith detects, the second seven-line unit in "America" expands the figure of the cruel national mistress into a mistress-mother with a phallic womb, at once "exploiting and nourishing the entrapped immigrant 'stand[ing] within her walls with not a shred / Of terror, malice, not a word of jeer'" (336). But this erotically charged standing also commends McKay's own discreet habitation within the walls of the sonnet form, its boxy fourteen lines often imaged, after John Donne, as a "pretty room [. . .]" (l. 32). The author as well as his persona accepts the theory of bottled resistance historically favored by sonneteers, the principle that the subject is essentially ensnared or confined but lives to undertake careful struggle within barriers, whether those of America or "America" the sonnet (Spiller 9). But in place of the sonneteer's recommended "paradigm / of straining forces harmonized sincerely" (Iain Smith ll. 13–14), McKay and his lyric "I" accommodate the strains of their confinement with avowed deceit. They move to treat their beloved enemies—America and the sonnet—to the polished insincerity of the courtly "rebel." The shift from queen's lover to king's traitor forecasts the concluding, vengeful dream of America-as-faded-empire: The final quatrain opens with the speaker's self-racializing biblical pun ("Darkly I gaze," a play on 1 Corinthians 13:12) and closes with the prophecy that monuments of national strength will collapse under Time's punishment. Through broad allusions to Shelley's sonnet on the ruined colossus of Ozymandias, the poem ultimately projects America's descent from vital mistress to antiquated wreck, from invigorating "cultured hell" to deathly Egyptian knock-off, its "granite wonders" turned derivative memorials of mighty collapse. To *The Waste Land*'s postwar string of morally sacked culture capitals—"Jerusalem Athens Alexandria / Vienna London" (Eliot ll. 378–79)—McKay's New Negro soothsayer would add Jazz Age Washington or New York City, or at least the granite-white stretch of Manhattan below 125th Street.

What is still lacking from this take on "America" is what is missing from most: adequate consideration of the crux at which the poem's drama breaks and pivots. The reference is to line eight, which through simile ties the way in which the speaker stands within America's walls to the style in which "a rebel fronts a king in state." The gravity of the line is secured by its place at the inner seam of the poem's irregular design: McKay sets a faithful English or Shakespearian sonnet rhyme scheme (*a b a b c d c d e f e f g g*) against customized Italian or Petrarchan sonnet stanzas (4 + 3 + 3 + 4 lines, with the first group of three tightly bound through a common subject, if not a common sentence). As a four-part Shakespearian tune flows from the end rhymes, "America" thus solders one seven-line conceptual sequence onto another, each composed of an ingenious half-Petrarchan block (stanzas of 4 + 3 rather than 8 + 6 lines, perhaps inspired by Baudelaire's sonnets in "enclosed form," which McKay learned to read in the original French). Joined at their shorter, three-line ends, the sequences together form a verbal mirror, with the syntax of the first half inversely reflected in the second. The overall effect of the sonnet's self-divided form—rhymes against stanzas, first block against the mirroring second—is fittingly discordant. Great expectations are placed on the "Yet" that launches both line eight and the turn into the second conceptual unit, but the line's announcement of reversal is muffled by a final rhyming link to the "hate" that comes before it (in line six, to be exact). Still, in this case McKay's ambivalence is relatively plainspoken. Line eight introduces an extended analogy between the persona's love for America and the ambivalent posture of the revolutionary secret agent.

In the inverting *camera obscura* of the poem's second half, McKay's speaker is reenvisioned as a covert renegade with unchallenged access to a head of government. Courtly political intrigue, rather than courtly love, has become the reigning enterprise. Like the knowing grandfather in Ralph Ellison's *Invisible Man* (1952), a kindred "spy in the enemy's country" made to "give up [the] gun back in the Reconstruction" (16), McKay's protagonist selects weapons of indirection, verbal cunning, and the silent collection of intelligence. Even so, through a mysterious channel of inside information, this secret agent knows of the violent future to be dealt by "Time's unerring hand"—through a whimper of fate, or perhaps a bang from a well-placed explosive, a humanly accessible motor of history much in the postwar news. Not far outside the walls of McKay's sonnet, thirty-eight U.S. politicians and industrialists were, in fact, sent mail bombs for May Day in 1919, and Attorney General Palmer's front porch was blown apart soon after, leading American intelligence to conclude that a violent takeover by Bolshevik agents was a legitimate threat (Kornweibel 5). The poem's thick layers of allusion and anachronism would appear to disallow the reference to these actual acts of sabotage, but McKay's revival of Elizabethan court discourse, at least, does not simply mask the possibility that his final lines exploit a vivid contemporary fear of underground Red violence. The Renaissance sonnets from which McKay draws were themselves products of a court culture of rebellious surveillance, in which aristocratic author-soldiers, Sir Philip Sidney among them, propelled early modern intelligence and the rise and fall of great powers (Archer 3). When the noble lover of the poem's first seven lines gazes darkly into the mirror of the second seven, he or she thus glimpses an apocalyptic but majestic reflection, a secret agent of political revenge who threatens presently (Palmer's house or the White House?) yet speaks with historical dignity (in the cadence of Elizabeth's courtly spy-writers, as well as Petrarch, Shakespeare, Shelley, and possibly Baudelaire).

When the "FB eye" gazed at "America," of course, it saw only portions of the interpretation above. A recognizably New Critical glance within U.S. intelligence would not emerge until World War II, when James Jesus Angleton—1941 Yale English B.A., admirer of William Empson and I. A. Richards, eventual chief of Counter-Intelligence at the Central Intelligence Agency (CIA)—began to develop a compelling theory of spycraft based on "the practical criticism of ambiguity" (Epstein 84). Fully formalist spy-reading, devoted to wrestling with subtle indeterminacies, might therefore be described as "CIA reading," the conquering method of the second Red Scare, when this intelligence agency exceeded the FBI in anti-Communist cachet and the New Criticism grew from southern agrarian dependent to national collegiate champion. "FBI reading," on the other hand, the master method of the first Red Scare of the late 1910s and 1920s, reflects both the bureau's place on top of an intelligence hierarchy free from Ivy League intruders, and the theoretical grounding of the biographical-historical literary criticism of its own day. McKay's file steadily exhibits the brusque, gossip-hungry diligence of such FBI reading—the infatuation with the independent literary artifact still imagined as an exotic confessional, the always close but never "New" criticism. Plucked from dozens of available McKay poems, "America" is found valuable enough for exacting transcription but is stripped of all internal traction. A one-note political meaning—support for America-hating enemy aliens—is thought clear enough: the sonnet directly precedes information that McKay "appeared . . . at Ellis Island, New York, as a witness in behalf of . . . a British Communist" within months of its publication (U.S. Jan. 26, 1924). The affected principle of FBI interpretive theory is proclaimed earlier in the same memorandum: "McKay's views, beliefs, principles, et cetera may properly be inferred from quotations from his writings." Avoidance of the "biographical fallacy" thus remains in the CIA–New Critical future, despite the heavy debt of McKay's sonnet persona to intertexts from Shelley to Shakespeare; the only thing New Critically "ambiguated" by the bureau's approach to his poem is its author's patriotism.

Like its understanding of McKay's international travels, however, the bureau's literal-mindedness allowed for unusual penetration into revealing aspects of his "America." This poem and the rest of McKay's "violent sonnets" are customarily honored for propelling dignified expressions of black rage, revenge, and active resistance into the main current of African American literature. For Addison Gayle Jr. and other nationalist Black Arts critics of the 1960s and 1970s, these lyrics indeed qualified McKay as the twentieth century's representative "Black poet at war," the modern elder in whose path all "Black poets who direct their art towards Black people . . . are sojourners" (Gayle, *Claude McKay* 40). The bureau critic-spy is notable not only for distinguishing this specific contribution to black letters before most of the non-Harlem public, but also for tying McKay's well-wrought violence to a precise scene of historical friction. The decorous curses that McKay launched at America's "cultured hell" flow not so much from a general postwar turn to New Negro militancy, as from a specific moment of black Bolshevik fencing with the FBI and other hostile intelligence services, nemeses on record in finding Communist deception behind almost any public statement of black discontent. The second movement of "America" politely flaunts the specter of obscure Bolshevik saboteurs, just as the first chivalrously revels in contact with Miss Liberty as well as Shakespeare's Dark Lady. Mixed with its clever argumentative turns, its learned redeployment of sonnet history, and its respectably classical moral on the fall of the mighty, this sonnet thus offered 1921 spy-critics a burnished, mocking confirmation of FBI nightmares over race and radicalism. The trained Communist, wrote Hoover, "is one on whom the party depends to commit espionage, derail a speeding train, and organize riots. If asked, gun in hand, to assault the Capitol of the United States, he will be expected to obey" (77). McKay, in turn, encouraged the trained bureau critic to discover such a Communist in the fallen capital of "America," its shattered "granite wonders" cursed by a rebel spy. Other McKay hymns to radical fury invite the same response, from the flammable sonnet threatening an emblematic building named "The White House" (1922), to the earlier sonnet "Enslaved" (1921), lines neatly reproduced in McKay's FBI file, which begs that "the white man's world of wonders utterly / . . . be swallowed up in earth's vast womb" (ll. 10–11). In such poems, all employing a candid-seeming lyric first person, McKay indulges his budding reputation as an evasive radical provocateur—no less often, in fact, than he plants metacritical hints of his own brave way with the sonnet form.

The claim here is not that the bureau critic-spy was correct in assuming that McKay's "violent sonnets" expressed the life and loves of their author, an actual Soviet operative-cum-Harlem shadow. Rather, the point is that the troubled literalism of the "FB eye" managed to catch a glimpse of McKay's self-referential American poetics of feigned double agency, an aesthetic built in the crush of combustible Leftist movement and intensive government counterintelligence. The bureau accepted McKay's U.S. lyrics as the work of a zealous black Bolshevik who volunteered anti-Communist testimony all the same. Like the double agent who agrees to spy for a former enemy while maintaining the basics of the original hidden service, their author both did the secret bidding of the Comintern and conveyed its designs to U.S. intelligence through the uncoerced confessional of the sonnet. This two-way service made McKay a rootless, committed foe and an intimate confidant of his second country, as "America" pleaded. Or so judged a bureau that took such poems as affidavits of McKay's intentions, "views, beliefs, principles," and so forth.

In McKay's corner, by contrast, double agency was a teasing enactment of such divided allegiance, and a wider stance and speaking position associated with improved sonnets, improved twitting of government snoops within narrowing provisions of free expression, and improved formulas for black duality. The double-sided spy persona offered a vehicle for rehearsing and ennobling a romantic, unprecedented New Negro type—the international black revolutionary—whose presence revivified a sonnet form forged by comparably equivocal, ambitious protagonists. It synthesized a relatively playful voice with which to frustrate countersubversive surveillance of black radicalism, tempting spy-readers with more or less notional accounts of dual loyalties (Epstein 74). It allowed a necessary modernization of African American masking texts and strategies, a respectful distance from Paul Laurence Dunbar's shaded plantation eyes—now not laughing to keep from crying, but collecting vanguard intelligence. Finally, in its stress on voluntarism and specifically political contradictions, it removed Du Boisian double consciousness from the region of given racial fate, disowning the state where blacks were imagined to be born self-divided by virtue of essential inheritance.

Among other objectives, McKay's version of double agency was thus designed to rebut that of the bureau critic-spy. Yet when it came to his sonnets' distinctive doubleness of form and content, the "FB eye" and the legal climate that endorsed it were inspirations demanding greater obedience. McKay was certainly aware that government intelligence composed one part of his small, well-placed American audience. He read the Harlem *Crusader* that reported on "Crackerized" bureau interference, and he noted with concern and pride that "If We Must Die" starred in the A. Mitchell Palmer production, *Investigation Activities of the Department of Justice* ("We 'Rile'"). McKay's curiously lofty, genteel, and ambivalent paeans to black hate and insurrection, perfected in the four years before

Harlem Shadows (1922), bait this known readership of intelligence gatherers with a confessional aura—but accept this readership's advice for staying clear of outright censorship. The Sedition Act of 1918, which energized the bureau just as McKay turned to verse of politicized formality, indeed resembles an instruction manual and a double dare for the average McKay violent sonnet. The act disallowed "profane, scurrilous, or abusive" language about the U.S. government, military, and flag during time of war (Washburn 13); so do the best-remembered of his poems, but only through elegant, equivocal verbal substitution at the last verge of law-breaking. The "foe" of "If We Must Die" is threatened with death but never specified (l. 9), while the "avenging angel" is beckoned to consume the "white man's world" in "Enslaved" (ll. 10–11), replacing the avenging "New Soldier and Worker" McKay felt able to summon in the London *Workers' Dreadnought*, an ocean away from U.S. sedition statutes ("Song"). There are many reasons why McKay's verse sidestepped most of the formal revolution of high modernism, from his early Jamaican training in the splendor of Keats, Pope, Milton, and the Elizabethan lyricists, to his post-Moscow conviction that the Poundian theater of modernist rebellion was nothing but formal, mere "bourgeois attitudinizing of the social revolutionary ferment" (McKay to Max Eastman, Apr. 25, 1932). The most insistent reason why his American poems retained an uncolloquial, sometimes misty high-romantic diction, however, was the need to elevate and obfuscate "anti-American" speech—thus ensuring that this speech would remain free. "America" and the like consciously excited bureau attention with their whispered promises of direct action, but their backward-looking anti-Imagism, their *in*direct treatment of the mutinous thing, successfully thwarted bureau-led prosecution by observing the letter of sedition law. In this sense, FBI "countermodernism," taking shape as an interdiction against profane or unreservedly critical political discourse, actually invigorated McKay's brightly torn brand of black poetic modernism, in which speaking as a fervent rebel but without "a word of jeer" is the highest prize ("America" l. 10).

The critic-spy responsible for McKay's FBI file thus ultimately prompts an unaccustomed speculation on the readership that shaped modern African American literature, in addition to illuminating McKay's seriously elusive political responsibilities, the bureau's patrolling of the black Atlantic, and the lyrical double agency collected in *Harlem Shadows*. Edgar Allan Poe scholar Terence Whalen sensibly observes that "writers necessarily have some notion of audience which, above and beyond [post-publication] feedback, guides them in the production of texts" (10). Like

Poe himself, McKay and the distinguished company of black authors pursued by the bureau were badgered by what Whalen calls the "Capital Reader," the personification of the logic of literature as commodity who "pre-reads" any text produced for a capitalist marketplace (10). As much criticism on African American literature appreciates, McKay and his peers were also preread by a racially divided, nominally progressive general audience that left binary traces before their books' release dates. McKay was not alone among black moderns, I suspect, in supposing that the next most powerful prereader of twentieth-century black letters was the school of J. Edgar Hoover. In the case of McKay's work—and perhaps that of Hughes, Wright, Baldwin, and so on—the wrongful but surprisingly tasteful connoisseurs of the FBI provoked defining previsions, not all regrettable, even when the manifest content wandered far from the "FB Eye Blues."

Notes

My thanks to the crew of prereaders who responded to an earlier draft of this essay: Nina Baym, Trish Loughran, Bill Mullen, Cary Nelson, Bob Parker, Jim Smethurst, Julia Walker, and the all-stars of the University of Illinois American Studies Reading Group.

1\. For those measuring the conscientiousness of the bureau's textual editing, the FBI critic-spy missed only the original comma after "ahead" in line 11.

Works Cited

Archer, John Michael. *Sovereignty and Intelligence: Spying and Court Culture in the English Renaissance*. Stanford: Stanford University Press, 1993.

Campbell, James. "I Heard It through the Grapevine." *Granta* 73 (Spring 2001): 151–82.

Cooper, Wayne F. *Claude McKay: Rebel Sojourner in the Harlem Renaissance: A Biography*. Baton Rouge: Louisiana State University Press, 1987.

Donne, John. "The Canonization." 1633. *The Complete English Poems*. Ed. A. J. Smith. New York: Penguin, 1981. 47–48.

Dumm, Thomas L. "The Trial of J. Edgar Hoover." Garber and Walkowitz 77–92.

Eliot, T. S. *The Waste Land*. 1922. *The Complete Poems and Plays, 1909–1950*. New York: Harcourt Brace, 1971. 37–55.

Ellison, Ralph. *Invisible Man*. 1952. New York: Vintage, 1989.

Epstein, William H. "Counter-Intelligence: Cold-War Criticism and Eighteenth-Century Studies." *ELH* 57.1 (Spring 1990): 63–99.

Foucault, Michel. *Discipline and Punish: The Birth of the Prison*. 1975. Trans. Alan Sheridan. New York: Vintage, 1979.

Garber, Marjorie, and Rebecca L. Walkowitz, eds. *Secret Agents: The Rosenberg Case, McCarthyism, and Fifties America.* New York: Routledge, 1995.

Garrow, David J. *The FBI and Martin Luther King, Jr.: From "Solo" to Memphis.* New York: W. W. Norton, 1981.

Gayle, Addison, Jr. *Claude McKay: The Black Poet at War.* Broadside Critics Ser. 2. Detroit: Broadside, 1972.

———. *Richard Wright: Ordeal of a Native Son.* New York: Doubleday, 1980.

Gilroy, Paul. *The Black Atlantic: Modernity and Double Consciousness.* Cambridge: Harvard University Press, 1993.

Grewal, Inderpal. *Home and Harem: Nation, Gender, Empire, and the Cultures of Travel.* Durham, N.C.: Duke University Press, 1996.

Gunning, Sandra. "Nancy Prince and the Politics of Mobility, Home, and Diasporic (Mis)Identification." *American Quarterly* 53.1 (March 2001): 32–69.

Hartman, Saidiya V. *Scenes of Subjection: Terror, Slavery, and Self-Making in Nineteenth-Century America.* New York: Oxford University Press, 1997.

Hoover, J. Edgar. *Masters of Deceit.* New York: Holt, 1959.

James, C. L. R. *Mariners, Renegades, and Castaways: The Story of Herman Melville and the World We Live In.* 1953. New York: Allison and Busby, 1985.

Keen, Mike Forrest. *Stalking the Sociological Imagination: J. Edgar Hoover's FBI Surveillance of American Sociology.* Westport, Conn.: Greenwood, 1999.

Kelso, John M., Jr. [Section Chief, Freedom of Information-Privacy Acts Section, Federal Bureau of Investigation]. Letter to the author. September 24, 1999.

Klehr, Harvey, John Earl Haynes, and Fridrikh Igorevich Firsov. *The Secret World of American Communism.* New Haven: Yale University Press, 1995.

Kornweibel, Theodore, Jr. *"Seeing Red": Federal Campaigns against Black Militancy, 1919–1925.* Bloomington: Indiana University Press, 1998.

Locke, Alain. "Spiritual Truancy." Rev. of *A Long Way from Home*, by Claude McKay. *New Challenge* 2.2 (Fall 1937): 81–85.

Maxwell, William J. *New Negro, Old Left: African-American Writing and Communism between the Wars.* New York: Columbia University Press, 1999.

McKay, Claude. "America." United States. Federal Bureau of Investigation. Claude McKay file. January 26, 1924. [Orig. pub. in *Liberator* 4 (December 1921): 9.]

———. "Enslaved." *Liberator* 4 (July 1921): 6.

———. *Harlem Shadows: The Poems of Claude McKay.* New York: Harcourt Brace, 1922.

———. "If We Must Die." *Liberator* 2 (July 1919): 21.

———. Letter to Nancy Cunard. September 18, 1932. Nancy Cunard Papers. Harry Ransom Humanities Research Center, Austin, Tex.

———. Letters to Max Eastman. April 25, 1932, April 1933 [?], September 21, 1933. Claude McKay Manuscripts. Lilly Library, Indiana University, Bloomington.

———. Letter to Upton Sinclair. June 16, 1924. Claude McKay Manuscripts. Lilly Library, Indiana University, Bloomington.

———. Letter to Walter White. July 5, 1923. National Association for the Advancement of Colored People Papers. Part 2, 1919–39. Personal Correspondence. Manuscript Division, Library of Congress, Washington, D.C.

———. *The Negroes in America.* 1923. Trans. Robert J. Winter. Ed. Alan L. McLeod. Port Washington, N.Y.: Kennikat, 1979.

———. "Song of the New Soldier and Worker." [Published under the pseudonym Hugh Hope.] *Workers' Dreadnought* (April 3, 1920): 4.

———. "The White House." *Liberator* 5 (May 1922): 16.

Mitgang, Herbert. *Dangerous Dossiers: Exposing the Secret War against America's Greatest Authors*. New York: Donald I. Fine, 1988.

O'Reilly, Kenneth. *Black Americans: The FBI Files*. Ed. David Gallen. New York: Carroll and Graf, 1994.

———. *"Racial Matters": The FBI's Secret War on Black America, 1960–1972*. New York: Free Press, 1989.

Postgate, Daisy. [Her Majesty's Office of Works]. Letter to Claude McKay. December 18, 1930. Claude McKay Collection. Yale Collection of American Literature, Beinecke Rare Book and Manuscript Library, New Haven.

Powers, Richard Gid. *Secrecy and Power: The Life of J. Edgar Hoover*. New York: Free Press, 1987.

Robins, Natalie. *Alien Ink: The FBI's War on Freedom of Expression*. New York: William Morrow, 1992.

Salem, Hanem. Letter to Claude McKay. September 3, 1937 [?]. Claude McKay Collection. Yale Collection of American Literature, Beinecke Rare Book and Manuscript Library, New Haven.

Savran, David. *Communists, Cowboys, and Queers: The Politics of Masculinity in the Work of Arthur Miller and Tennessee Williams*. Minneapolis: University of Minnesota Press, 1992.

Schrecker, Ellen. "Before the Rosenbergs: Espionage Scenarios in the Early Cold War." Garber and Walkowitz 127–41.

Shelley, Percy Bysshe. "Ozymandias." 1818. *Shelley's Poetry and Prose*. Ed. Donald H. Reiman and Sharon B. Powers. New York: W. W. Norton, 1977. 103.

Smith, Felipe. *American Body Politics: Race, Gender, and Black Literary Renaissance*. Athens: University of Georgia Press, 1998.

Smith, Iain Crichton. "Studies in Power (2)." *Selected Poems*. Chester Springs, Pa.: Dufour Editions, 1970. 22.

Spiller, Michael R. G. *The Development of the Sonnet: An Introduction*. New York: Routledge, 1992.

Summers, Anthony. *Official and Confidential: The Secret Life of J. Edgar Hoover*. New York: Putnam, 1993.

Tillery, Tyrone. *Claude McKay: A Black Poet's Struggle for Identity*. Amherst: University of Massachusetts Press, 1992.

Trotsky, Leon. "Letter to Comrade McKay." 1923. Reprinted in McKay, *The Negroes in America*. 7–8.

United States [U.S.]. Federal Bureau of Investigation. Claude McKay file obtained under provisions of the Freedom of Information Act. Assorted documents dated December 16, 1921, to May 31, 1940. File no. 61–3497.

Wallace, Maurice. "'I'm Not Entirely What I Look Like': Richard Wright, James Baldwin, and the Hegemony of Vision, or Jimmy's FBEye Blues." *James Baldwin Now*. Ed. Dwight A. McBride. New York: New York University Press, 1999. 289–306.

Walters, Wendy W. "Policing the Borders of the Text and the Body of the Writer: Chester Himes and the FBI." Paper presented at the American Studies Association Conference, Washington, D.C., November 2001.

Washburn, Patrick S. *A Question of Sedition: The Federal Government's Investigation of the Black Press during World War II*. New York: Oxford University Press, 1986.

"We 'Rile' the Crackerized Department of Justice." *Crusader* 2 (May 1920): 5–6.
Whalen, Terence. *Edgar Allan Poe and the Masses: The Political Economy of Literature in Antebellum America.* Princeton: Princeton University Press, 1999.
Wright, Richard. "FB Eye Blues." 1949. Manuscripts, Archives, and Rare Books Division, Schomburg Center for Research in Black Culture, New York Public Library, New York.

But fundamentally for the present the Negro is radical on race matters, conservative on others, in other words, a "forced radical," a social protestant rather than a genuine radical.—Alain Locke, The New Negro

Anthony Dawahare

The Specter of Radicalism in Alain Locke's The New Negro

In 1925 Alain Locke published what he hoped would be the founding anthology for the African American literary and cultural movement later called the "Harlem Renaissance." *The New Negro: An Interpretation* instantly established a literary canon bound by values and interests that, to this day, direct popular views toward African American literature and life. Locke firmly believed that the literary works composing *The New Negro* embodied "a renewed race-spirit that consciously and proudly sets itself apart" (xxvii). Unashamed of their race and culture, his black contributors stood as ideal representatives of the "New Negro," a postwar generation of black Americans whose cultural contributions, Locke claimed, would strengthen democracy in America. Recent anthologies of Harlem Renaissance literature continue to portray the movement as one devoted to racial expression, black pride, and American social reform. In this regard, *The New Negro* has been a tremendous success; its impact can still be felt.

But the popularity of Locke's conception of the New Negro is largely the effect of ignoring the many other voices intensely engaged in debates over black identity, culture, and politics during the 1920s. More precisely, *The New Negro* should be contextualized in terms of the important postwar ideological fight between advocates of black nationalism, socialism, and American capitalism who in different ways struggled to position themselves as leaders of working-class black Americans. Through their respective cultural fronts, each faction sought to define the politics of the New Negro. At stake was whether the black masses—many of whom were radicalized by the failed promises of World War I, the racist backlash of the Red Summer, and the political reverberations of the Bolshevik Revolution—would continue to support American capitalism or, conversely, embrace black nationalism or socialism as solutions to racism and class inequality in America.

Locke's introduction to and editing of *The New Negro* skillfully intervenes in this debate over the politics of postwar black Americans. He proves to be a wary navigator between what he must have viewed as the Scylla and Charybdis of socialism and black nationalism. Yet Locke appropriates the rhetoric of the Left and the black nationalists—indeed, at times representing himself as both an advocate of the rank and file and a national awakener—while he simultaneously excludes from his anthology virtually all of the writings published in radical black journals. Consequently, *The New Negro* narrowly comprises literary works that, taken as whole, confirm Locke's own desire that the New Negro possess a black "national" identity and a patriotic loyalty to American capitalism that transcend class differences and interests. In other words, it participates in the dominant anticommunist, nationalistic discourse following World War I that hoped to banish the specter of communism from the politics and culture of working-class blacks.

Locke was well aware that his anthology was an intervention in the postwar debates about the politics and culture of the new generation of black Americans; he justly subtitled the book *An Interpretation*. He premised his particular interpretation of the New Negro on his redefinition of the concept of race. Influenced by the anthropological studies of Franz Boas and his students, such as Melville Herskovits (whom he anthologizes in *The New Negro*), Locke argues against genetic or biological determinist notions of race. In an essay published shortly before *The New Negro*, entitled "The Concept of Race as Applied to Social Culture" (1924), he redefines race as a strictly social category. He views race—or what he terms "social race"—as historically determined, the result of "social heredity" (191), or inherited "cultural conditions," "stressed values" (194), and a "tradition, as preferred traits" (195). As Locke states, "Instead therefore of regarding culture as expressive of race, race by this interpretation is regarded as itself a culture product" (193). His view that race is social helps us to situate *The New Negro* as a symbolic political act in itself, since the anthology is an attempt to create a "tradition" of "stressed values" and "preferred traits" that will shape the way in which black Americans view themselves.

Significantly, the concept of "social race" squares nicely with the postwar ideologies of nationalism. In fact, Locke uses "social race" as a synonym for "nation," since integral to modern nationalist projects is the identification of common circumstances, traditions, cultural traits, and values that constitute nationhood. Locke consciously substituted the concept of race for nation as early as 1916, when, in a lecture at Howard University, he argued that "what men mean by 'race' when they are proud of race, is not blood race, but that kind of national unity and national type which belongs properly not to the race but to the nation" ("Racial Progress" 86). In this sense, Locke tells us that his own "race pride" is a kind of "national" pride, based on the unity he feels with other people of his "national type." As a project that aims to preserve, promote, and defend a black national culture, *The New Negro* represents Locke's desire to foster national pride among black Americans.

Locke's nationalist view of race is immediately apparent in his foreword to *The New Negro.* He conflates the terms "race" and "nation" in the key word "self-determination," which he uses to describe the political and cultural aspirations of the New Negro (xxv). The "racial awakening" of the New Negro, he explains, is similar to "those nascent movements of folk-expression and self determination which are playing a creative part in the world today. . . . As in India, in China, in Egypt, Ireland, Russia, Bohemia, Palestine and Mexico, we are witnessing the resurgence of a people" (xxvii). This comparison implies that black Americans are somehow a separate nation (like India, China, etc.) within the United States, suggesting the postwar view that "peoples" are more abundant than empires. Consequently, he later observes that black Americans are like those "emergent nationalities" (xxv) budding around the world after the breakup of the great, multinational empires.[1] Moreover, he uses the notion of "awakening" central to nationalist rhetoric, implying that the black nation-race, like other nations, has been dormant and, on awaking, will rise to reclaim its immemorial heritage and fulfill its historic destiny. Indeed, as David Levering Lewis notes, "Locke sought to graft abstractions for German, Irish, Italian, Jewish, and Slovakian nationalism to Afro-America" (117).

It is not surprising, then, that Locke would need to identify a capital for his imagined national/race community, since nationalist projects always speak of territory and lay claim to a geographic center for their realization. For Locke, Harlem "is—or promises at least to be—a race capital"; it has "the same role to play for the New Negro as Dublin has had for the New Ireland or Prague for the New Czechoslovakia." Harlem provided Locke with a dense black population and, more importantly, a center of cultural expression that would ethnicize internationally blacks whose consciousness and identity were not sufficiently racial. Harlem would lead to a greater "race-welding" by its "stressed values" and "tradition" requisite for the formation of a black social race. In this sense, Locke believed that he was witnessing the birth of the black American race, which has "been a race more in name than in fact" (*New Negro* 7)—his anthology would be a birth certificate of sorts for the race. Oddly, most of its contributors, including Locke, were from places other than Harlem, which thus rendered Harlem solely a symbolic place of birth for the literary-cultural nationalist movement.

Since Locke attempted to graft abstractions of other nationalisms onto the New Negro, the New Negro movement necessarily bears a striking resemblance to other traits of European nationalism. To Locke's messianism, one can add his view that, since black Americans represent an African advanced guard, they have a duty to enlighten African peoples and to rehabilitate "the race in world esteem" (14), as well as to help Africa in its future development (*New Negro* 15). Another defining trait of the nationalistic New Negro is his or her "folk" character and expression. Locke and other contributors such as Montgomery Gregory and Arthur Huff Fauset imbue their discussions of the New Negro with the notion of the folk; in "Negro Youth Speaks," Locke seems almost beside himself with the folk spirit he writes about. The young black writers, he asserts, "dig deep into the racy peasant undersoil of the race life" (51). Beneath their modernistic styles, he perceives "the instinctive gift of the folk spirit" evident in Jean Toomer's "folk-lilt" and "glamorous sensuous ecstasy," Claude McKay's "peasant irony" and "folk clarity," and Rudolph Fisher's "emotional raciness" (51)—concepts for the most part absent although implied in the *Survey Graphic* version of the book published earlier in the same year (1925). Locke's essay is in the vein of late-eighteenth- and early-nineteenth-century romantic nationalism, in spite of his claim that the writers, like "gifted pagans," "return to nature, not by the way of the forced and worn formula of Romanticism, but through the closeness of an imagination that has never broken kinship with nature" (52). How the young writers, who were not peasants by birth, residence, or occupation, have an unbroken "kinship with nature" is unexplained, and, in fact, cannot be explained except as a fantasy cultivated by an intellectual elite. The most "peasant" of Harlem Renaissance writers was McKay, who was raised on a farm in Jamaica, yet his family was literate, owned land, and belonged to the local elite. As Eric Hobsbawm observes in *Nations and Nationalism since 1780*:

> Since the later eighteenth century (and largely under German intellectual influence) Europe had been swept by the romantic passion for the pure, simple and uncorrupted peasantry, and for this folkloric rediscovery of "the people," the vernacular languages it spoke were crucial . . . more often than not the discovery of popular tradition and its transformation into the "national tradition" of some peasant people forgotten by history, was the work of enthusiasts from the (foreign) ruling class or elite. (103–4)

A student of German romanticism, Locke revives the romantic idealization of the folk and the poet's supposed relationship with that folk to establish a historical and natural precedent for his nationalistic conception of the New Negro cultural movement. Like other anti-Enlightenment philosophers of nationalism, he necessarily privileges "vitality," "feeling," and cultural specificity over notions of universality based in rationality.[2] The value of cultural specificity is important here, since Locke, as well as other contributors, expresses interest in recuperating black vernacular traditions as visible signs of the origins of the race-nation. For Locke, "the Spirituals are really the most characteristic product of the race genius as yet in America" ("Negro Spirituals" 199).

The political meaning of the nationalism of *The New Negro* emerges most clearly in Locke's attempt to distance himself from socialism. One indication that he considered socialists undesirable political contenders is that he fails to mention the existence of the African Blood Brotherhood, the Communist Workers Party (WP), or the black Socialists by name or organization. Yet the pressures of the black Left leave a trace on Locke's political characterization of the New Negro, which, like most discourses, must be read dialogically. He characterizes the New Negro as committed to "the ideals of American institutions and democracy" (10), namely to American capitalism. To postpone momentarily the question of whether or not he was right, I suggest that such a statement is intended to be not only sociological but also, as it relates to Locke's political goals, prescriptive. We sense the rhetorical force of a seemingly simple statement of fact when he follows it with a discussion of how the new "creed" of "race co-operation" among blacks arose spontaneously as a defense and offense against prejudice (11). But he assures us that the reaction to racism "is radical in tone, but not in purpose and only the most stupid forms of opposition, misunderstanding or persecution could make it other wise" (11). He goes on to dismiss the Left from his anthology of 446 pages (in the first edition) with the following few words: "Of course, *the thinking Negro* has shifted a little toward the left with the world-trend, and there is an increasing group who affiliate with radical and liberal movements. But fundamentally for the present the Negro is radical on race matters, conservative on others, in other words, a '*forced radical,*' a social protestant rather than a genuine radical" (11; emphases added).

Note that Locke begins by considering "the thinking Negro" and ends with a political assessment of black Americans in general. His earlier discussion about "the few" who "know that . . . the vital inner grip of prejudice has been broken" (4) suggests that the New Negro might actually encompass a rather small minority of the black population. In short, the New Negro anthology represents the New ("thinking") Negro and, logically, should also represent the new left-wing ("thinking") blacks who were, by Locke's own estimation, increasing in number in response to a world trend. Instead, he assures his reader that, as a "forced radical" on racial matters, the New Negro should be differentiated from the "genuine radical"; he is careful not to imply that the New Negro in any way agrees with socialist criticism of the capitalist basis of racism and class inequality in America. He concludes his point by characterizing left-wing blacks as fabricating "quixotic radicalism" (11), and he excludes the multitude of radical prose, fiction, and poetry that he could have culled from A. Philip Randolph and Chandler Owen's *Messenger*, the ABB's *Crusader*, or the CPUSA's *Daily Worker* published since the war. One could argue that the black Left constituted a minority, and Locke's goal was to be representative. However, the handful of black writers he champions (particularly Langston Hughes, Claude McKay, and Countee Cullen) were far from being representative, since, as scholars of the Harlem Renaissance have shown, they were part of an elite (in education, class, or affiliation) relative to the black masses (Huggins 305–6).

If we consider some of the ways that other black intellectuals interpreted the New Negro, we better appreciate the conservatism that informed Locke's definition and selection of material for his anthology. As one might expect, the black Socialists' interpretation of the political character of the New Negro greatly differs from that of Locke's. Locke would have agreed with the assertion of *Messenger* editors Owen and Randolph that the New Negro stands "for absolute and unequivocal '*social equality*'" ("The New Negro—What Is He?," 23); yet the gulf widens between the Socialists and Locke when we read that, for the former, the New Negro is primarily a worker who

> would repudiate and discard both of the old parties—Republican and Democrat. His knowledge of political science enables him to see that a political organization must have an economic foundation. . . . As workers, Negroes have nothing in common with their employers. The Negro wants high wages; the employer wants to pay low wages. The Negro wants to work short hours; the employer wants to work him long hours. Since this is true, it follows as a logical corollary that the Negro should not support the party of the employing class. (ibid., 74)

Owen and Randolph also shuttle between description and prescription, yet the conclusions of their argument are dramatically different from Locke's political assessment of black Americans. Implicit in their definition is the Socialist's critique of American and black nationalism: the workers' structural position under capitalism and their class identification fracture national identifications with the ruling class and produce instead an international, working-class identity. Consequently, the editors maintain that black nationalists are deluded because they believe that they can abolish the systemic evils of capitalism—such as unemployment, exploitation, and inequality—by restaffing capitalism with black bosses. "By making the question of unemployment an issue as between white and black men," Randolph argues, nationalists (like Marcus Garvey) miss the fact that unemployment "is a product of the capitalist system which brings about overproduction at certain cycles, and consequent unemployment of workers regardless of race, creed, nationality or color" ("Garveyism" 251). Because they comprehend their class positioning and interests, Owen and Randolph's New Negroes are much more politically savvy and left-wing than Locke's. Their class consciousness necessarily makes them radical on matters other than race.[3]

Similarly, Cyril Briggs, head of the nationalist-socialist ABB, defines the New Negro as militant and Leftist (particularly after the riots in Tulsa, Oklahoma, and elsewhere) when he writes: "The Old Negro and his futile methods must go. After fifty years of him the Race still suffers from lynching, disfranchisement, jim crowism, segregation and a hundred other ills. His abject crawling and pleading have availed the Cause nothing. He has sold his life and his people for vapid promises tinged with traitor gold. . . . The New Negro now takes the helm" ("The Old Negro Goes" 9). According to Briggs's definition, Locke would be classified as an Old Negro who plays it safe by dismissing the militant radicalism of the New Negro as quixotic, delusionally battling the industrial mills of capitalism as if they were dragons. And though Briggs is conservative in some ways on "race matters" (notably in his biological definition of race) and problematically advocates what he believes to be a revolutionary form of black nationalism, he does not share Locke's conservatism on the question of the New Negro's Americanism.[4] In fact, like Owen and Randolph, he argues that capitalism fosters nationalism among the working classes: "Capitalism . . . knows neither prejudice nor nationality, save the brands it seeks to foster for its own benefit among the workers" (Taylor 10), an opinion that obviously diverges from Locke's unproblematic presentation of the New Negro's patriotism.

We need not cite only left-wing intellectuals to better assess whether postwar black Americans were as conservative as Locke makes out for his rejection of socialism. For instance, in an article entitled "The New Negro" published in the *Oklahoma City Black Dispatch*, Roscoe Dunjee takes issue with claims circulating in the press at the time that black Americans who fight back against discrimination and persecution have been influenced by the IWW or the Bolsheviks. For Dunjee, the New Negro's radicalism has arisen spontaneously and, not simply confined to "race matters," extends to a critique of the racist U.S. legal system as a whole:

> I think you ought to know how the black man talks and feels at times when he knows that you are nowhere about, and I want to tell you, if you were to creep up to-night to a place where there are about 10,000 Negroes gathered, you would find no division on this one point, I know that they would all say, "WE HAVE NO CONFIDENCE IN WHITE POLICEMEN."
>
> Let there be one hundred or one hundred thousand, they would with one accord all say, WE HAVE NO CONFIDENCE IN THE WHITE MAN'S COURT. (66)

The famed World War I black lieutenant of the 367th U.S. infantry, William N. Colson, writes in a similar vein about black America's radicalism in an article he published in the *Messenger* entitled "The New Negro Patriotism" (1919). Like Locke, he begins with a seemingly exclusive category of the "thinking Negro" and ends by including most blacks, although, again, with different results: "Intelligent Negroes have all reached the point where their loyalty to the country is conditional. The patriotism of the mass of Negroes may now be called doubtful" (69). The articles by both Dunjee and Colson confirm the leftward shift among black intellectuals but contradict Locke's dismissive comment that the shift is only "radical in tone, but not in purpose" (69). There is no reason to believe that these and other radicalized black intellectuals did not mean what they said about the structural inequalities of postwar America and their lack of patriotism.

One lesson we learn from rehistoricizing Locke's pronouncements on the New Negro vis-à-vis some interpretations of the period is that Locke's progressive rhetoric of nationalism conceals (perhaps insufficiently) his identification with the bourgeoisie. Indeed, one of the greatest challenges the socialists presented to Locke and other bourgeois-identified black leaders was that the black working class (already radicalized by the war and postwar discrimination) would ally with white workers under the banner of socialism and act *by themselves* to limit (through reform) and eventually to destroy (through revolution) the American class system. Hence, Locke, as well as a number of the contributors to *The New Negro*, emphasizes the cultivation of a black elite (sufficiently trained with the principles of free enterprise and bourgeois democracy) who would ensure that the black working class continued to be "radical on race matters, conservative on others" (11). Arguments for the need of *multiracial, working-class unity*—popular among black socialists—are conspicuously absent. Instead, multiracial unity should only be cultivated among the elites (or a "Talented Tenth") of the country, for, as Locke warns, "the only safeguard for mass relations in the future must be provided in the carefully maintained contacts of the enlightened minorities of both race groups" (9). In other words, as Huggins aptly puts it, "there was nothing wrong with American society that interracial elitism could not cure" (115).

The names and employment of many of the contributors Locke chose for his anthology speak volumes: Charles S. Johnson, editor of the Urban League's *Opportunity*; James Weldon Johnson, executive secretary of the NAACP; Kelly Miller, dean of the College of Arts and Sciences at Howard University; Robert Russa Moton, president of Tuskegee and the Negro Business League; Walter White, assistant executive secretary of the NAACP; Elise McDougald, member of the Urban League and employee of the U.S. Department of Labor; W. E. B. Du Bois, a leader in the NAACP; Eric Walrond, business manager of *Opportunity*; and so forth. Moreover, their academic credentials are stunning, representing a host of private and Ivy League schools—among them, Harvard University, Brown University, Howard University, Cornell University, University of Chicago, Columbia University, and Fisk University. Trained by and affiliated with an intellectual elite, the contributors understandably were suspicious of those who promoted working-class leadership and self-determination, including the formally uneducated and "unrefined" Garvey.

A number of essays in Part II of *The New Negro* suggest that black Americans should be directed into predominantly black institutions of higher education (namely Howard and Hampton-Tuskegee) and black commercial and cultural communities (such as Durham, North Carolina, and Harlem) to safeguard the proper formation of their cultural nationalist and assimilationist identities. As Robert R. Moton writes in his contribution to the anthology, "the strongest recommendation that Hampton and Tuskegee have is the character and service of the men and women whom they have trained for the leadership of their people" (332). Or, as Kelley Miller writes of Howard University, "its essential objective from the beginning has been to develop a leadership for the reclamation and uplift of the Negro race through the influence of the higher culture" (313). (In Part I, Montgomery Gregory argues for the need of a "national Negro Theatre" for playwright, musician, actor, dancer, and artist [159]). Even Du Bois, in his powerful contribution on the relationship between colonial domination and the racist exploitation of "domestic" labor, does not call for a multiracial working-class movement, a position consistent with his well-intended but nonetheless paternalistic view of liberation. Du Bois, who gets the final word in *The New Negro*, is confident that the growing movement of Pan-Africanism against imperialism and colonial domination has its "main seat" of leadership in the United States (411)—in other words, in the leadership of the NAACP.

Yet Locke's adherence to bourgeois nationalism stops short of black nationalism proper; he straddles the fence between socialism and Garveyism. His adoption of the principles of postwar nationalism, particularly the notion of self-determination for the race-nation, is more rhetorical than substantive. Locke's grafting of the model of Dublin onto Harlem is meant to invoke, not provoke, a political movement among blacks for self-determination. Thus, his reference to "Harlem's quixotic radicalism" includes Garveyism, which he rejects for essentially the same reason he rejects socialism: it does not comprehend the allegiance blacks have or should have to America as an idealized democratic nation. He writes: "American nerves in sections unstrung with race hysteria are often fed the opiate that the trend of Negro advance is wholly separatist, and that the effect of its operation will be to encyst the Negro as a benign foreign body in the body politic. This cannot be—even if it were desirable. The racialism of the Negro [like his radicalism] is no limitation or reservation with respect to American life" (12). Just as he omits socialist literature, so he excludes overtly black nationalist literature from *The New Negro*. After all, plenty of writers were producing it at the time, especially in the pages of Marcus Garvey's *Negro World*. As Tony Martin tells us: "The writing of poetry was little short of an obsession with Garveyites. . . . Poetry was a regular feature of the *Negro World*" (43). Hence, the prolific black nationalist poets of the *Negro World*, such as Ethel Trew Dunlap, Leonard I. Brathwaite, and J. Ralph Casimir, whose poetry equals if not surpasses in form much of the poetry that Locke champions, find no place in the "national" community of *The New Negro*. Garvey's bourgeois-separatist Back to Africa program simply contests Locke's bourgeois-assimilationist desires.

Conceivably, Locke could have omitted any allusion to the socialists and Garveyites, thereby further insulating his interpretation against his ideological opponents. Yet his subtle allusions to socialists and Garveyites serve rhetorically to frame his desired interpretation of *The New Negro*: they function as threats to the white elite concerning their fortunes and the future of America. Thus, when he writes of the American "wants" and "ideas" of black Americans, he warns that "we cannot be undone without America's undoing" (12), suggesting that U.S. political and economic rulers must legally recognize the rights of blacks to be offered what American capitalism has to offer, or else they may face some form of revolution ("undoing"). We also find a threat in his warning that "Harlem's quixotic radicalisms call for their ounce of democracy to-day lest to-morrow they be beyond cure" (11). Locke offers his cultural nationalist-assimilationist program or else anarchy (spread by the "incurable disease" of radicalism). More precisely, we can say that strategically he raises the specters of Garveyism and socialism to frighten the bourgeoisie into making the main concessions he wants, which, to follow Charles S. Scruggs's argument, include a privileged place for him as one of the black political elite. Locke's postwar historical moment provided him with a prime opportunity to make such an argument, which, in another period (such as ours), would not have any of the rhetorical force.

Moreover, his adoption of the nationalist rhetoric so vital to the Garveyites can be understood as an attempt to co-opt the political sympathies of the movement, particularly among the younger generation of whom he was very fond, and to redirect the black nationalist impulses along safer paths. The texts of those contributors whom Garvey had influenced directly (such as Zora Neale Hurston, Eric Walrond, and J. A. Rogers) and indirectly (e.g., Langston Hughes in his Back-to-Africa sounding poem "Our Land"), are reinterpreted by Locke to suit his position in the debate. Like many petit-bourgeois nationalists, he creates a myth of a mighty movement of support behind him, composed of both southern peasants and urban intellectuals, to make his own pronouncements all the more authoritative and convincing.

As Jeffrey C. Stewart points out in his introduction to a collection of Locke's lectures given at Howard University in 1916, "Compared with the political nationalism advanced by Marcus Garvey in the early 1920s, Locke's New Negro arts movement must have seemed a relief to educated whites" (xlvi–xlvii). And, as I have argued, Locke's particular matrix of nationalism must have appeared much safer than the political programs of the WP, the ABB, and the black Socialists, notwithstanding the fact that the latter had moved to the political center by 1925 and, in truth, no longer presented an ideological threat to American capitalism. Locke was careful to exclude literary works of the two political movements that challenged his cultural nationalism and Americanism. Relative to Garveyism and socialism, the contributors all seem to suggest that blacks in the United States should identify themselves as "American," albeit perhaps of a "different shade" (Herskovits 353).

This model of an essentially unified black intellectual community in the pages of *The New Negro* does not come, however, without its share of internal debate. In fact, there are two extremes from Locke's position represented in "Negro Art and America" by Albert C. Barnes, the white millionaire collector of African art, and "The Negro's Americanism" by Melville Herskovits, the Boasian anthropologist. Simply put, Barnes represents blacks as "old Negroes" and Herskovits represents them as "no Negroes." Barnes regurgitates a host of racial stereotypes: black Americans are "a primitive race" possessing a "primitive nature"; they are "poet[s] by birth" (19); and, forever filled with joy and song, they live poetry "in the field, the shop, the factory" (20)—a fine lesson for those exploited white workers who complain about their prosaic lives! Herskovits rejects any notion that black Americans are innately or even culturally a different "race" from other Americans. Writing about his visit to Harlem, he notes that what he "was seeing was a community just like any other American community. The same pattern, only a different shade!" (353).

Perhaps it is puzzling why Locke would include essays that blatantly contradict his notion of "social race." But the racial characteristics Barnes praises and the Americanism on which Herskovits gloats are two sides of the same coin, tendered for the purposes of advancing Locke's goal of making the cultural movement safe for those from whom he asks recognition. In other words, the differences in the contributors' arguments are circumscribed by their adherence to a dual nationalism, best characterized by the current term "African American." The apparent diversity of perspectives reaches a consensus that "blacks" and "Americans" have together or separately the following criteria to constitute a race-nation: common ancestries, common experiences, common psychologies, and common cultures, all of which are conceived as equal to or better than other races-nations. Put differently, all agree that blacks in the United States constitute a separate race or are members (even if provisionally excluded) of the separate American nation.

We witness the dual nationalism at work throughout *The New Negro*. Other examples of the contributors' racial classification of black American identity and culture include William Stanley Braithwaite's identification of an "artistic temperament and psychology precious for itself" of black Americans (29); J. A. Rogers's claims about the "atavistically African" sources of jazz and ragtime (217); and James Weldon Johnson's assertions that the "unique characteristics" of "movement, color, gayety, singing, dancing, boisterous laughter and loud talk" are "typically Negro" (309).[5] The fiction and poetry support and supplement these observations, so that in the selections by Hurston, Toomer, and Fisher we find race portraits that (among other things) define blacks as different from white Americans. Or in the poetry of Cullen, Hughes, and Toomer we find references to an African soul ("The Negro Speaks of Rivers" 141), an African "dark blood" that courses through the New Negro's veins ("Heritage" 205), and African "race memories" ("Georgia Dusk" 136), respectively. Although these elements are not necessarily nationalistic (as in the case of Hurston, for instance), they function together (particularly because of Locke's framing) as criteria of nationalist identification; they are protonational elements that in the hands of Locke are transformed into a cultural nationalist appeal. Adapting Etienne Balibar's analysis of the characteristics of nationalism to black literature, we find narratives that posit the existence of an imaginary "invariant substance" (86)—soul or blood—and that represent the New Negro as the culmination of a long historical process of coming to consciousness of a special destiny. In nationalist fashion, black writers project their "individual existence into the weft of a collective narrative, on the recognition of a common name and on traditions lived as the trace of an immemorial past (even when they have been fabricated and inculcated in the recent past)" (Balibar 93). Even the decision to create racial/national narratives reflects the proliferation of so-called new nationalities with the breakup of the great prewar empires, as well as the influence of European anthropologists, such as Boas, who had an impact on Hurston's racial slice-of-life stories.

Aside from Herskovits, the other contributors who emphasize the

"Americanness" of blacks include Paul U. Kellogg, James Weldon Johnson, and Langston Hughes. In "The Negro Pioneers," Kellogg, the editor of the *Survey Graphic*, characterizes the Great Migration to the North as "an induction into the heritage of the national tradition, a baptism of the American spirit that slavery cheated him out of" (277). Similarly, Johnson writes that "Harlem talks American, reads American, thinks American" (309). But perhaps Hughes says it best when he writes, "I, too, am America" ("I Too" 145). Thus, virtually every contribution works to define blacks on this nationalistic/racial axis. Nationalism is the ideological limit beyond which Locke and his New Negro compatriots, as represented in the anthology, do not pass.

Locke could have chosen different works by a number of the same contributors, resulting in less of a nationalist and anticommunist consensus. Indeed, as Arnold Rampersad notes in the introduction, the disputes that various contributors had with Locke (especially McKay) illustrate that "the unity suggested by *The New Negro* was mainly a front presented to the world" (xxii). Locke's editorial practices thus function to reaffiliate politically some writers, making inconsequential their socialist and black nationalist affiliations. Aside from Eric Walrond, who frequently contributed to Garvey's *Negro World*, W. A. Domingo contributed to Owen and Randolph's *Messenger*, Langston Hughes to the Communists' *Workers Monthly* and the *Messenger*, and Claude McKay to virtually every radical magazine of the period. Domingo's socialist articles present a picture of him far different from the one Locke frames for his readers. Critical of racial or national loyalty, Domingo writes in the *Messenger*: "The owners of jobs have common interests and pay only as much wages as they are forced to pay. Their interests are opposed to those of their employees. And color or race makes no difference. Jews underpay Jews, and Negro employers rob their employees regardless of race or color. The interests of all workers are alike" ("A New Negro" 145). Similarly, various poems that Hughes published in socialist magazines, such as "Johannesburg Mines" and "Steel Mills," address, however inadequately, issues of class and exploitation under capitalism. In retrospect, given his aspirations, Locke was right to keep the debate in the pages of *The New Negro* within bourgeois-nationalist boundaries, since Charlotte Osgood Mason, one of his wealthy white patrons, did not tolerate any truck with radicalism, as evident in her withdrawal of patronage from Langston Hughes when he openly expressed his Communist sympathies in "Advertisement for the Waldorf-Astoria" in 1931.

From this perspective, *The New Negro* is symbolically a black convention—a kind of textual "Negro Sanhedrin." Locke does as good of a job controlling the debate over definitions of black Americans and the political options to overcome racism as had his anti-Communist and antilabor friend and colleague from Howard University, Kelly Miller, chairman of the Negro Sanhedrin or All-Race Assembly of 1924. Even though the purpose of the assembly was to create a program for civil rights in the United States, Miller shelved the labor issue, which was of utmost importance to the socialists present, until the last day of the conference and then had a committee "revise" (that is, distort) the original resolutions on labor that the Communists engineered. Perhaps Locke's well-publicized opposition to propagandistic poetry should be read in light of his own political agenda.[6] Unlike those socialist and black nationalist writings not represented in *The New Negro*, the literature Locke includes makes no reference to the politically explosive issues of the postwar period. Instead, we find labor and racial questions dealt with generally or fictionally at a distance. For example, none of the anthology's poetry is as sharply critical of the well-publicized murder of several black men in Jasper County, Georgia (killed by their employer for supposedly cooperating with a federal investigation into their debt-peonage) as is Dunlap's "The Peonage Horror" (1921), published in the *Negro World*. Jasper County, Dunlap bluntly writes, is "where the slave trade thrives as in the days of yore" (Martin 53).[7] Locke's most emblematic omission of labor issues is his replacement of Mahonri Young's striking drawing of "The Laborer" from the New Negro number of the *Survey Graphic* with a Winold Reiss portrait of Charles S. Johnson—suited, bespectacled, impeccably bourgeois.

Even when Locke allows entrance to a socialist poet like McKay, he carefully censors him so as not to offend the ruling classes, particularly those occupants of the White House who had an impressive record in the 1920s for simultaneously enacting racist legislation and crushing labor unions and the Left. Locke's revision of the title of McKay's "The White House" to "White Houses" greatly changes the meaning of the poem, a militant protest against the U.S. government's discriminatory laws.[8] (Braithwaite's essay seems to second Locke's move to silence radical poetry when he states his preference for the aestheticism of McKay's "The Harlem Dancer" over the propagandism of "If We Must Die" [40]). It is Miller's essay in *The New Negro* that sounds the keynote of the anthology: "Howard University must keep the race spirit courageous and firm, and direct it in harmony with ideals of God, country and truth" (322).

Undoubtedly, the contributors to *The New Negro* were profoundly committed to overcoming racism in America by supporting or developing a black culture that would challenge the racial stereotypes of the time. At question here are not their good intentions but rather the ways they define the New Negro and, by implication, their means and goals in creating a truly egalitarian society free from racism. As I have argued, the selected works that constitute *The New Negro* collectively elide many vital questions raised by black socialists, such as whether blacks could be defined primarily according to one of the postwar nationalisms, or whether they should identify themselves within any nationalistic framework whatsoever. Locke's editorial role in the making of *The New Negro* effectively turns a lively dialogue about the identity and political options of black Americans into a monological paean to a relatively conservative New Negro. Nationalism obscured the class character of the oppression of blacks under capitalism and the need to be able to choose one's allies irrespective of the color of skin or flags. But, then again, the political atmosphere in which they breathed was not of their own choosing either: their own ideological limitations were almost everyone's of the time, and it would take more than a handful of socialists to convince many of them otherwise. In short, it would take a Red Decade.

Notes

1. The nation-within-a-nation thesis finds expression in some of Cyril Briggs's and the ABB's articles published in the early 1920s. It is only systematically developed toward the decade's end by the Comintern, thus making Locke's implication more a product of the process of reasoning set going by postwar nationalistic discourses than his indebtedness to the ABB.

2. For an extended discussion of the nationalist trope of awakening and romantic nationalism, see Gellner 8–9, 66–71.

3. Owen and Randolph were two of the most critical black Leftists of nationalism in the early 1920s. At least until 1924, their insistence on viewing the "Negro Question" as a matter of class shielded them from framing the oppression of blacks as a racial or national issue. In other words, they did not adopt the quasi-nationalist Leninist view of African Americans—namely, that southern black Americans constituted an oppressed nation within the American nation—that came to dominate the Communist Left's theorization of black oppression and liberation in the 1930s. For fuller accounts of the black Socialists' critiques of nationalism, see Randolph's "Black Zionism" and "The Only Way to Redeem Africa."

4. For Briggs's defense of the concept of a superior black race and African nationalism, see ABB, "A Race Catechism" and "Program of the A.B.B.," respectively.

5. While Harlem Renaissance writers critiqued the chauvinist system of racial classification in America, they remained trapped within the ideology of race promoted by politicians, scientists, and writers of the period. For an informative

historical study and critique of the widespread currency of pseudoscientific racial classification in America, see Jacobson.

6. See Locke, "Our Little Renaissance" and "Art or Propaganda."

7. For the history and literarization of the murders, see Foley on Toomer.

8. For an informative study of the U.S. government's political repression of black socialists and labor leaders in the 1920s, see Kornweibel.

Works Cited

African Blood Brotherhood. "Program of the A.B.B." *Crusader* 5.2 (October 1921): 15–18.

———. "A Race Catechism." *Crusader* 1.1 (September 1918): 11.

Balibar, Etienne. "The Nation Form: History and Ideology." *Race, Nation, Class: Ambiguous Identities*. London: Verso, 1991. 86–106.

Barnes, Albert C. "Negro Art and America." Locke, *The New Negro* 19–25.

Braithwaite, William Stanley. "The Negro in American Literature." Locke, *The New Negro* 29–44.

Briggs, Cyril. "The Old Negro Goes: Let Him Go in Peace." *Crusader* 2.2 (October 1919): 9–10.

Colson, William N. "The New Negro Patriotism." 1919. *Voices of a Black Nation: Political Journalism in the Harlem Renaissance*. Ed. Theodore G. Vincent. Trenton, N.J.: Africa World Press, 1973. 67–69.

Cullen, Countee. "Heritage." Locke, *The New Negro* 250.

Domingo, W. A. "A New Negro and a New Day." *Messenger* 2.10 (November 1920): 144–45.

Du Bois, W. E. B. "The Negro Mind Reaches Out." Locke, *The New Negro* 385–414.

Dunjee, Roscoe. "The New Negro." *Voices of a Black Nation: Political Journalism in the Harlem Renaissance*. Ed. Theodore G. Vincent. Trenton, N.J.: Africa World Press, 1973. 65–66.

Foley, Barbara. "'In the Land of Cotton': Economics and Violence in Jean Toomer's *Cane*." *African American Review* 32.2 (1998): 181–98.

Gellner, Ernest. *Nationalism*. New York: New York University Press, 1997.

Gregory, Montgomery. "The Drama of Negro Life." Locke, *The New Negro* 153–60.

Herskovits, Melville J. "The Negro's Americanism." Locke, *The New Negro* 353–60.

Hobsbawm, Eric. *Nations and Nationalism since 1780: Programme, Myth, Reality*. Cambridge: Cambridge University Press, 1993.

Huggins, Nathan Irvin. *Harlem Renaissance*. London: Oxford University Press, 1971.

Hughes, Langston. "Advertisement for the Waldorf-Astoria." *The Collected Poems of Langston Hughes*. Ed. Arnold Rampersad. New York: Vintage, 1995. 143–46.

———. "I Too." Locke, *The New Negro* 145.

———. "Johannesburg Mines." *Collected Poems* 43.

———. "The Negro Speaks of Rivers." Locke, *The New Negro* 141.

———. "Our Land." Locke, *The New Negro* 144.

———. "Steel Mills." *Collected Poems* 43.

Jacobson, Matthew Frye. *Whiteness of a Different Color: European Immigrants and the Alchemy of Race.* Cambridge: Harvard University Press, 1998.

Johnson, James Weldon. "Harlem: The Culture Capital." Locke, *The New Negro* 301–11.

Kellogg, Paul U. "The Negro Pioneers." Locke, *The New Negro* 271–77.

Kornweibel, Theodore. *Seeing Red: Federal Campaigns against Black Militancy, 1919–1925.* Bloomington: Indiana University Press, 1998.

Lewis, David Levering. *When Harlem Was in Vogue.* 1979. New York: Oxford University Press, 1989.

Locke, Alain. "Art or Propaganda." 1928. *The Critical Temper of Alain Locke: A Selection of His Essays on Art and Culture.* Ed. Jeffrey C. Stewart. New York: Garland, 1983. 27–28.

———. "The Concept of Race as Applied to Social Culture." 1924. *The Philosophy of Alain Locke: Harlem Renaissance and Beyond.* Ed. Leonard Harris. Philadelphia: Temple University Press, 1989. 187–99.

———. "The Negro Spirituals." *The New Negro* 199–213.

———. "Negro Youth Speaks." *The New Negro* 47–53.

———. "The New Negro." *The New Negro* 3–16.

———. "Our Little Renaissance." 1927. *The Critical Temper of Alain Locke: A Selection of His Essays on Art and Culture.* Ed. Jeffrey C. Stewart. New York: Garland, 1983. 21–22.

———. "Racial Progress and Race Adjustment." 1915. *Race Contact and Interracial Relations: Lectures on the Theory and Practice of Race.* Ed. Jeffrey C. Stewart. Washington, D.C.: Howard University Press, 1992. 84–104.

———, ed. *The New Negro: An Interpretation.* 1925. Introduction by Arnold Rampersad. New York: Atheneum, 1992.

———, ed. *Survey Graphic: Harlem, Mecca of the New Negro.* 1925. Baltimore: Black Classic Press, 1980. (Report of *Survey Graphic: Harlem, Mecca of the New Negro* 6.6 [March 1925]).

Martin, Tony. *Literary Garveyism: Garvey, Black Arts, and the Harlem Renaissance.* Dover, Mass: Majority Press, 1983.

McKay, Claude. "White Houses." Locke, *The New Negro* 134.

Miller, Kelly. "Howard: The National Negro University." Locke, *The New Negro* 312–22.

Moton, Robert R. "Hampton-Tuskegee: Missioners of the Masses." Locke, *The New Negro* 323–32.

Owen, Chandler, and A. Philip Randolph. "The New Negro—What Is He?" *Messenger* 2.7 (August 1920): 73–74.

Rampersad, Arnold. Introduction. Locke, *The New Negro* ix–xxiii.

Randolph, A. Philip. "Black Zionism." *Messenger* 4.1 (January 1922): 330–35.

———. "Garveyism." *Messenger* 3.4 (September 1921): 248–52.

———. "The Only Way to Redeem Africa." *Messenger* 4.11 (November 1922): 522–24.

———. "The Only Way to Redeem Africa." *Messenger* 4.12 (December 1922): 540–42.

———. "The Only Way to Redeem Africa." *Messenger* 5.1 (January 1923): 568–70.

———. "The Only Way to Redeem Africa." *Messenger* 5.2 (February 1923): 612–14.

Rogers, J. A. "Jazz at Home." Locke, *The New Negro* 216–24.
Scruggs, Charles W. "Alain Locke and Walter White: Their Struggle for Control of the Harlem Renaissance." *Black American Literature Forum* 14.3 (Fall 1980): 91–99.
Stewart, Jeffrey Conrad. Introduction. *Race Contacts and Interracial Relations: Lectures on the Theory and Practice of Race.* By Alain LeRoy Locke. Washington, D.C.: Howard University Press, 1992. xix–lix.
Taylor, Theman Ray. "Cyril Briggs and the African Blood Brotherhood: Another Radical View of Race and Class during the 1920s." Diss. University of California, Santa Barbara, 1981.
Toomer, Jean. "Georgia Dusk." Locke, *The New Negro* 136.

Bill V. Mullen

W. E. B. Du Bois, Dark Princess, and the Afro-Asian International

At last India is rising again to that great and fateful moral leadership of the world which she exhibited so often in the past in the lives of Buddha, Mohammed and Jesus Christ, and now again in the life of Gandhi. . . . This mighty experiment, together with the eVort of Russia to organize work and distribute income according to some rule of reason, are the great events of the modern world. The black folk of America should look upon the present birth-pains of the Indian nation with reverence, hope and applause.
—W. E. B. Du Bois, Crisis

Hail, dark brethren
of mine,
Hail and farewell!
I die,
As you are born again,
bursting with new
life.
—W. E. B. Du Bois,
"I Sing to China"

W. E. B. Du Bois's lifelong advocacy for the liberation and independence of Asian countries is both the least appreciated aspect of his political career and the one most central to its Leftist trajectory. Between his support for Japan in its 1904 war with Russia and his second and final trip to Maoist China in 1959, Asia was for Du Bois a literal and figurative site of his intellectual evolution from "fabian socialist" to revolutionary Marxist.[1] Asia was the twin pole of Du Bois's black intellectual world: after 1900, he imagined the U.S. "color line" as the "world color line" extending into China, Japan, and India and considered Pan-Africanism and Pan-Asianism as mutually constituting global struggles. His support for radical Indian political movements near the turn of the century was likewise his first serious intellectual identification with Marxian politics. Thus it is not surprising that during and after World War I Du Bois found himself in the midst of a national and an international debate over the relationship of Asia and Asian national movements to the west, including Africa. Indeed, by 1921 he had become the target of and impetus for arguments in the United States over two vitally linked discourses enveloping this debate: Orientalism and Eurocentric race theory, on one hand, and Bolshevism and anticommunism on the other.

This essay will explore Du Bois's writings during this period as a means of measuring his role in and contribution to these debates. Specifically, it will examine his 1928 novel *Dark Princess* as a symbolic configuration of his political engagement with three central events of the interwar era: the rise of the Indian home rule and nationalist movements, the emergence of black radicalism in the United States, and the role of black and Asian radicals in revising Soviet policy on both "Negro" and Asian liberation during the formation of the Third International after 1919 and the crucial 1922 and 1928 Cominterns in Moscow. *Dark Princess*, I will argue, is Du Bois's attempt to synthesize these events as they unfolded in Moscow, Berlin, China, India, and the United States—the sites most prominent on the novel's geopolitical map. In addition, *Dark Princess* demonstrates Du Bois's transformation of his famous metaphor of "double consciousness" into a trope for the most hotly debated political questions for radicals of his time: proletarian internationalism and the role and function of the nation. Finally, it reveals how Du Bois's conception of Orientalism was wedded to a patriarchal or paternal ideology inflected by contemporary debates about female subalterns in the United States and India in particular, and by Du Bois's own romantic conceptions of the Asiatic.

The significance of Du Bois's political project in *Dark Princess* is thus severalfold. First, it marks a continuation and a departure in the history of African American intellectual engagement with the discourse of Orientalism, an engagement crucial for later generations of African American radicals and intellectuals. Second, it indicates the scope and depth of African American participation in internationalist political debates during and after World War I, a history recently beginning to be rerevealed. Third, it predicts a series of political decisions and maneuvers by black and Asian radicals away from the trajectory of an "American century" toward a deliberately miscegenated internationalist politics that anticipated, among other things, the shape of anticolonial movements of the 1930s, 1940s, and 1950s. Fourth, it centralizes the place of Marxism and Marxian views on internationalism for African Americans before the cataclysm of the Great Depression and thus foreshadows the wholesale turn by dozens of black intellectuals—Du Bois among them—toward a Marxism that would become by the end of World War II decidedly internationalist. *Dark Princess* thus stands as a central text in African American discursive engagement with the American, Asian, and international

Left in the twentieth century. It is also a key text for understanding how resistance especially to Eurocentric discourses of race led to the radical recasting of Afro-Asian relationships as central to twentieth-century world revolutionary struggles.

Dark Princess culminated nearly thirty years of Du Bois's active intellectual sympathy for the contemporary rise of Pan-African and Pan-Asian politics. Both earned his serious interest after the 1885 partition of Africa at the Berlin Conference and the formation of the Indian National Congress the same year. It was specifically the first Pan-African Congress in London in 1900, which Du Bois attended as secretary, that turned his attention to linkages between African and Asian liberation movements. His speech, "To the Nations of the World," announced his famous "color line" thesis by reference to "the question as to how far differences of race . . . are going to be made, hereafter, the basis of denying to over half the world the right of sharing to their utmost ability the opportunities and privileges of modern civilisation" (Aptheker, *Horizon* 513). Six years later, after Japan's 1904 victory over Russia, Du Bois concluded: "The Russo-Japanese war has marked an epoch. . . . The awakening of the yellow races is certain. That the awakening of the brown and black races will follow in time, no unprejudiced student of history can doubt" ("Color Line"). In 1907, in a column for *Horizon*, Du Bois declared that a militant speech at the Indian National Congress characterized the Asian uprising as a model for Pan-African and other "colored" rebellions: "The dark world awakens to life and articulate speech. Courage, Comrades!" Prior to World War I, he viewed the congress as India's (and one of the "colored" world's) best opportunities for the nonviolent overthrow of colonialism; the social democrat in him also admired its attempts at parliamentary inclusiveness—in 1937 he would cite it as a possible model for the National Negro Congress formed two years earlier. The Indian National Congress may also have inspired him to help organize the 1911 Universal Races Congress in London, attended by representatives of Pan-Asia and Pan-Africa. There Du Bois presented "The Negro Race in the United States of America," a statistical survey of black living conditions in the United States that were linked to those of the "darker races" around the world.

The Universal Races Congress likewise deepened Du Bois's support for Swaraj, or Indian home rule, a movement whose features also influenced the plot of *Dark Princess*. This interest grew with the creation of the Gadar (Arabic for revolution or mutiny) Party in San Francisco in

1913 by nationalist Indian émigrés to the United States. The same year the party formed the newspaper *Gadar* with Har Dayal serving as editor. The Gadar movement, as it came to be known, attempted to coordinate efforts with Indian nationals in Berlin to obtain German arms and ammunition to support independence struggles at home. These events would result in the Indo-German Conspiracy Trial conducted in San Francisco from November 1917 to April 1918 (Banerjee 79). In 1915 Lala Lajpat Rai, a founder of the Hindu reformist movement, Arya Samaj, began a five-year exile in the United States. Rai quickly became Du Bois's fast friend and mentor on Indian politics.[2] In 1917 Rai helped to found the Indian Home Rule League of the United States and organized the journal *Young India*.

In 1921 Du Bois reported favorably on the national convention of the Friends of Freedom for India in New York City (Kapur 26), and in 1922 he wrote his longest statement in support of Swaraj, entitled "Gandhi and India," for the *Crisis*. The article praised Gandhi's 1920 motion at the Indian National Congress (carried by the majority) calling for the rejection of all British titles and offices, the establishment of Indian national schools, and a boycott of British functions, British courts, and English-made goods. Gandhi's program of nonviolence was an "outstanding factor" in his proposal, Du Bois wrote. "It kills without striking its adversary." Gandhi was "a man who professes to love his enemies and who refuses to take advantage of or embarrass government in a crisis!" (207). Also in 1922 the Soviet Comintern hosted numerous Indian nationals, among them Bengali Brahmin M. N. Roy, at a Congress of East Peoples at Baku and held a vigorous debate on the "Eastern" question at the Comintern. Between 1914 and 1916 Roy had been active in the Indian Revolutionary Committee, linked to Gadar, in Berlin; he lived briefly on the campus of Stanford University before fleeing to Mexico after the outbreak of World War I. Roy posed a serious challenge to Lenin's thesis on nationalism at the 1922 Comintern, an event that would become part of the allegory of *Dark Princess*.

More immediately, this sequence of events, in combination with the outbreak of World War I, helped to ignite a fervor of Orientalist discourse in the United States in which Du Bois became immediately engaged. In fact, he was partially responsible for its emergence. In 1922, two years after World War I and four years after the Bolshevik Revolution, American historian Lothrop Stoddard published *The Rising Tide of Color against White World Supremacy*. Stoddard's book openly owed two debts: the first was to Count Arthur de Gobineau, a nineteenth-century eugenics theorist cited by Edward Said as a pioneer of European Orientalism. De Gobineau's 1853 *Essai sur l'inégalité des races humaines* (Essay on the Inequality of the Races) described a stark racial hierarchy of Aryan supremacy and Asian and Negro inferiority. In *Rising Tide of Color*, Stoddard evoked Gobineau in order to interpret the decimation of Western Europe in World War I as a tragic white holocaust. Ideologically, Stoddard's book was a sequel to fellow Gobineau disciple Madison Grant's 1916 eugenicist tome, *The Passing of the Great Race, or the Racial Basis of European History*. Stoddard's work primarily deviated from Grant's by basing its scientific racism hypothesis on events of 1917. In the introduction to *Rising Tide of Color*, the author linked the end of the war and the Bolshevik Revolution:

> Now that Asia, in the guise of Bolshevism with Semitic leadership and Chinese executioners, is organizing an assault upon western Europe, the new states—Slavic Alpine, with little Nordic blood—may prove to be not frontier guards of western Europe but vanguards of Asia in central Europe. Bolshevism is the renegade, the traitor within the gates, who would betray the citadel, degrade the very fibre of our being, and ultimately hurl a rebarbarized, racially impoverished world into the most debased and hopeless of mongrelizations. (qtd. in Aptheker, 6–7)

Stoddard's second debt complemented the first and is of even greater significance to this essay. *Rising Tide of Color* included an attack on Du Bois's 1915 *Atlantic Monthly* essay "The African Roots of the War," which had appeared one year earlier, in revised form, as "The Hands of Ethiopia" in *Darkwater*. "The African Roots of the War" revised Du Bois's 1903 color line thesis, viewing World War I as an exaggeration of the divide between white Western Europe and the "colored" world. European countries' support of colonialism drew Du Bois's condemnation and his call for "the trained man of darker blood" to organize against Europe (*Darkwater* 60). The revised essay also invoked biblical and nineteenth-century images of Ethiopia, with "hands of helplessness for an agonized God!" The resurrection of Africa was symbolized by the ascent to the throne of Queen Nefertiti, who "redeemed the world and her people" (74). In "The Damnation of Women," published for the first time in *Darkwater* in 1919, Du Bois returned to the image of defiant black womanhood in antiquity: "the primal black All-Mother of men down through the ghostly throng of mighty womanhood, who walked in the mysterious dawn of Asia and Africa" (165). The black mother is the progenitor of dark and dusky heroines of history—Cleopatra, Candace, Sojourner Truth. Du Bois names this figure as "Isis . . . the titlular goddess," whose spell still pervades the land of Africa. His final formulation is a global family tree descending from a primal moment of Afro-Asian commingling: "The father and his worship is Asia; Europe is the precocious, forward-striving child; but the land of the mother is and was Africa" (166).

As Alys Weinbaum has perceptively argued, the "primal black All-Mother" image in *Darkwater* bespoke Du Bois's efforts to critique both Orientalist eugenics theory and the specific U.S. cultural practice of denigrating or excluding black women from its "national genealogy."[3] *Dark Princess* would later signal these twin goals by ascribing images of "Black" maternity to both the biological mother of protagonist Matthew Towns and Princess Kautilya. Du Bois's attempt to revalue and reevaluate Afro-Asian maternity also reflected his critical engagement with Orientalist representations of India in books like Katherine Mayo's 1916 *Mother India*. Mayo, a liberal American feminist, offered a statistical indictment of reproductive risks, child-bride customs, and paternalism in Indian society; the book was patently essentialist and colonialist in its refusal to account for the role of imperialism in India's social development. Both Du Bois and Lajpat Rai responded separately and angrily to the book in their 1920s writings.[4] At the same time, Du Bois's romantic and biological essentializing of African and Asian maternity in *Darkwater* reflected his vulnerability to a tradition of what might be termed "Afro-Orientalism." It invoked what Wilson Moses calls Du Bois's "unilinear conception of progress" drawn from popular nineteenth-century Afrocentric notions that "the great civilizations of the past were Hamitic and therefore creations of the black Afro-Asiatic race" (97). With the notable exception of Anna Julia Cooper, this tradition generally depended on an exotic essentializing of Afro-Asian vitality, usually associated with the feminine and an uncritical glorification of black antiquity.[5] Variations on this theme appear in the works of nineteenth-century writers like Edward Wilmont Blyden and Alexander Crummell, as well as in the writings of Du Bois's contemporary Marcus Garvey. Also mediating Du Bois's tendency to romanticize African and Asian antiquity was the ever-competing influence of historical materialism and socialist ideology. As he would later write in *The World and Africa* (1947) on the same topic, "Africa saw the stars of god; Asia saw the soul of man; Europe saw and sees only man's body, which it feeds and polishes until it is fat, gross, and cruel" (149). Indeed, it was in *The World and Africa* that Du Bois, more committed to an anticolonialism rooted in historical materialist analysis, attempted to overcome and rebalance his own Orientalist tendency to diminish Africa's potential as its partner in world liberation: "Despite the crude and cruel motives behind her shame and exposure, her degradation and enchaining," he wrote, "the fire and freedom of black Africa, with the uncurbed might of her consort Asia, are indispensable to the fertilizing of the universal soil of mankind, which Europe alone would nor could give this aching earth" (260).

Interestingly, the supercharged rhetoric of the public response to *Darkwater* discloses each of these aspects of Du Bois's developing ideas on Asia and Africa: in addition to Stoddard's phlegmatic reaction to the book, the *Times Literary Supplement* of London maintained that *Darkwater* revealed "the dark depths of a passionate and fanatical mind" (Aptheker, Introduction to *Darkwater* 19). The Paris edition of the *New York Herald* devoted an editorial to the book entitled "Black Bolshevism": In *Darkwater*, the paper wrote, Du Bois is "intoxicated" by colonial self-determination which "partakes of frenzy" and "represents the spread of the Bolshevist madness" (19). In fact, in real political terms, his writings in *Darkwater* were by far his most militant to date. The just-concluded world war, he wrote in "The Souls of White Folk,"

> was primarily the jealous and avaricious struggle for the largest share in exploiting darker races. As such it is and must be but the prelude to the armed and indignant protest of these despised and raped peoples. Today Japan is hammering on the door of justice, China is raising her half-manacled hands to knock next, India is waiting for the freedom to knock, Egypt is suddenly muttering, the Negroes of South and West Africa, of the West Indies, and of the United States are just awakening to their shameful slavery. (*Darkwater* 49)

Typical of his color line formulations of this period, Du Bois perceived Asia as the probable forerunner to African and African American liberation. Yet *Darkwater* also featured a new characterization of black life in America that became gradually more central to Du Bois's long-term assessment of hemispheric struggle. In the essay "Of Work and Wealth," he described the ongoing black migration to the North and the horrific events of racist attacks in 1917 and 1919 as "the old world horror come to life again: all that Jews suffered in Spain and Poland; all that peasants suffering in France, and Indians in Calcutta" (95). His new conception of American blackness invoked a stagist view of material struggle that had deposited American Negroes in a vanguard position:

> There is not only the industrial unrest of war and revolutionized work, but there is the call for workers, the coming of black folk, and the deliberate effort to divert the thoughts of men, and particularly of workingmen, into channels of race hatred against blacks . . . the

> American Negroes stand today as the greatest strategic group in the world. Their services are indispensable, their temper and character are fine, and their souls have seen a vision more beautiful than any other mass of workers. They may win black culture to the world if their strength can be used with the forces of the world that make for justice and not against the hidden hates that fight for barbarism. (97)

Du Bois's largely unremarked-upon revision here of the "souls" of black folk as an untapped touchstone of internationalist race and labor consciousness was grounded in a new apprehension of black labor as a motive force in history. "Of Work and Wealth" posits black workers' "culture" as African America's most seductive offering to the world, a downward mobilizing of the "kingdom of culture" in his more famous 1903 formulation in *The Souls of Black Folk*. Too, the culture of black labor carries with it the blood message of ancient wounds suffered across the "colored" world, the stigmata of economic exploitation from Israel to Calcutta. That is, Du Bois's Pan-internationalism in *Darkwater* assumed an economist rhetoric absent from his prewar writings. This transformation of tropes and ideas in his works is most fully apprehended through a close reading of *Dark Princess*, a book that encapsulates and dramatizes the events between 1917 and 1928 that reconfigured both his later views on Afro-Asia and the color line as well as the color of his own political ideas.

Subtitled "*A Romance*," *Dark Princess*'s story line is both simple and complex. Matthew Towns, a twenty-five-year-old black American medical student, exiles himself from the United States in 1923 after being excluded by race from registering for obstetrics at the University of Manhattan in New York. He arrives in Berlin—where Du Bois himself attended university in 1892—and one day intervenes on behalf of a striking young Indian woman after a white American accosts her with a racist expletive. The woman is twenty-three-year-old Kautilya, Princess of Bwodpur, daughter of the maharaja, "the last of a line that had lived and ruled a thousand years" (228). Fresh from solidarity visits to China's Sun Yat-Sen, India's Gandhi, Japan, and Egypt, the princess invites Matthew to meet with a circle of international radicals coordinating the "darker" races against white world power. They include a Japanese, two Indians, two Chinese, an Egyptian and his wife, and a "cold and rather stiff Arab." The group represents "all the darker world except the darkest," the black American. One thrust of the group's deliberation is to unite "Pan-Africa . . . with Pan-Asia" as a response to "dominating Europe which has flung this challenge of the color line" (21). Another is to decide how to act on their recent collective education in the Soviet Union, sketchily referenced in the text, where the theater of Meyerhold and "reports on the American Negro" have left equally deep marks. "Their [the Negroes] education, their work, their property" and the "odds, the terrible, crushing odds against which, inch by inch, they have fought" have led some in the group, including the princess, to consider it essential to draw the Negro into the global "darker" sphere. For others, like the Egyptian, Moscow is "dangerous company" and like "leaning on broken reeds," while for the Japanese, "there is a deeper question—that of the ability, qualifications, and real possibilities of the black race in Africa or elsewhere." This remark elicits in Matthew one of a number of political epiphanies in the text, this one that "there loomed plain and clear the shadow of a color line within a color line, a prejudice within prejudice, and he and his again the sacrifice" (22). The shadow is not only of racial and national enmity (perhaps reflectimg Du Bois's ambivalence in 1927 about Japan's rising national ambitions) but also class distinction. Matthew, and by extension the laboring class he represents as a descendant of slaves, is the proletariat underdog in this aristocratic international, a point that foreshadows the princess's later downward mobility. The antiblack bias also likely signals Du Bois's awareness of caste prejudices that function as obstacles to successful international alliance with African Americans, an issue that Du Bois otherwise glosses over in the novel.

The princess then solicits Matthew to act as an agent of information on black Americans in the hope that it can orchestrate a U.S. uprising. Back home Matthew follows instructions and falls in with a man named Perigua, a West Indian (something like a Garveyite) who seeks to explode the "lynching belt" in the United States by persuading him to assist in the bombing of a passenger train carrying Ku Klux Klan members to Chicago. Matthew agrees, and the scheme is averted by happenstance when the princess ends up a passenger on the same train! When the plot and Matthew's part in it are exposed, he is sentenced to prison. He is released through the hard work of an ambitious black Chicago ward politician, Sammy Scott, who is persuaded by his mulatto assistant Sarah Andrews to use Matthew's case as political bait in his next election. On his release Matthew works for Sammy's office and enters a chilly political marriage with Sarah. Meanwhile, the princess is promised several times in marriage, including once to a British soldier, but her love for Matthew and fear that the marriages will abrogate the royal line and Indian home rule persuades her to evade them all. Instead, the partners descend together into the American working class: the princess in cognito as a house servant and union organizer, Matthew as a laborer and organizer among subway workers in Chicago. After consummating their affair, the princess travels to Prince County, Virginia, to meet Matthew's mother, a onetime sharecropper "who sold her forty acres" to pay for Matthew's education. The book ends at Matthew's Virginia homestead with a miraculous rendering of their marriage and Kautilya's surprise presentation of their newborn child, "Messenger and Messiah to all the Darker Races." The climactic scene takes place at sunrise, May 1, 1927.

Despite its 1923 dateline, the epigraph to *Dark Princess*, like its finale, suggests a more sweeping political, narrative, and biological cycle. "Earth is pregnant," writes Du Bois. "Life is big with pain and evil and hope. Summer in blue New York; summer in gray Berlin; summer in the red heart of the world!" Du Bois's color imagery and geography playfully evokes the Red Summer of 1919, the year of antiblack racial rioting in the United States resulting from the violent conflict of southern black migration and white northern labor, and the year, we are told, that Matthew Towns leaves Prince County for New York City. Relatedly, 1919 was the year of a split in the world socialist movement and the formation of the Third Communist International, events with immediate consequences for Du Bois's fictional political constituents. In the United States the split occasioned a break in the New York New Negro movement between opponents and supporters of the Bolshevik Revolution. The Third International was also noteworthy for its description of India as one of the "slaves" of colonialism following a 1919 visit to Moscow by Mahendra Pratep, a prominent émigré leader of the Berlin Provisional Government of India, established by the Indian Revolutionary Committee during World War I. Pratep was no communist, but he did present Lenin with a tract entitled the "Religion of Love," a nonmaterialist bid to force the Soviet leader to use the Provisional Government to establish links with revolutionary centers in Bengal and Punjab (Druhe 21). His example may well have given Du Bois the idea to use Towns and Kautilya's erotic romance as the test case of Afro-Asian solidarity.

Notwithstanding these suggestive historical roots, 1922 was most likely the year that crystallized the idea for *Dark Princess* in Du Bois's mind. That year the Fourth Congress of the Comintern in Moscow featured its first black representatives from America: West Indian–born Otto Huiswoud and Jamaican poet Claude McKay, pro-Bolshevik survivors of the 1919 New Negro split. Also present and a key player in debate was M. N. Roy, cofounder of the Mexican Communist Party. McKay and Roy both left the Comintern, and the triangular relations of the Soviet Union, American blacks, and Asia depicted in *Dark Princess* deeply changed. In a "Report on the Negro Question," McKay argued that the Great Migration, World War I, northern industrialization, and American racism, especially in the trade union movement, had made "the Negro question . . . at bottom a question of the working class" (Maxwell 81). By insisting that "the International bourgeoisie would use the Negro race as their trump card in their fight against world revolution," McKay's report helped give impetus to the congress's "Theses on the Negro Question" exhorting the Communist International to "use every instrument within its control to compel the trade unions to admit Negro workers to membership" (Maxwell 90). (Du Bois published McKay's subsequent essay on his Soviet visit, "Soviet Russia and the Negro," in the *Crisis* in 1924.) Indeed, Cedric Robinson, Harry Haywood, and most recently Bill Maxwell have demonstrated how McKay and Huiswoud's reports and influence at the 1922 Comintern contributed to Lenin, Zinoviev, and Stalin's pronouncements on the "National Question" and helped to formulate the "Black Belt thesis" of African Americans as a special "nation within a nation," which was debated hotly and heavily throughout the 1920s.[6] In his autobiography *Black Bolshevik*, Haywood summarized this shift in party line: "As the theory was put into practice, we learned that national cultures could be expressed with a proletarian (socialist) content and that there was no antagonistic contradictions, under socialism, between national cultures and proletarian internationalism. . . . Thus the Bolsheviks upheld the principle of 'proletarian in content, national in form'" (158).

Du Bois registers the impact of these events in *Dark Princess* in several ways. In the book's first pages the princess speaks of her recent study of the "Negro Question" in Moscow as impetus for inviting Matthew to join her "colored" circle of anticolonialists in Berlin. It is, she says, "a report I read there from America that astounded me and gave me great pleasure—for I almost alone have insisted that your group was worthy of cooperation." Elsewhere in the opening section she tells Matthew: "You American Negroes are not a mere amorphous handful. You are a nation!" (16). Still other events in the novel suggest black internationalists from contemporary real-world fiction as models: it was while working as a Pullman porter, for example, that young Claude McKay wrote the notorious 1919 sonnet, "If We Must Die," urging black compatriots to "nobly die" fighting antiblack, antilabor rioters in cities like Chicago. In the second part of *Dark Princess*, entitled "The Pullman Porter," Matthew joins the first all-black American trade union and commits to a plan of violent retaliation against the Ku Klux Klan after a failed strike. He justifies his participation by telling himself: "He was dying for Death. The world would know that black men dared to die" (85). The Pullman job also allows Matthew to see the Klan and white American labor as parallel organizations, using the threat of Filipino workers to break black strikes and trying to "pit the dark peoples against each other" (78). Du Bois thus presents both violent retaliation and all-black organizing as strategic local responses to attempts to divide the international proletariat by making "colored labor . . . the wage-hammering adjunct of white capital" (58). Indeed, parts two and three of *Dark Princess*, including a description of Chicago machine-style politics, are rendered as locus classicus reiterations of World War I's imperialist dimensions: "There was war in Chicago—silent, bitter war. It was part of the war throughout the whole nation; it was part of the World War. Money was bursting the coffers of the banks—poor people's savings, rich people's dividends. . . . So there was war in Chicago,—World War, and the Republican machine of Cook County was fighting in the van. And in the machine Sammy and Sara and Matthew were little cogs" (168).

Meanwhile, at the same 1922 Comintern that formulated the New Negro thesis, the Eastern Commission of the Fourth Congress, in direct response to Roy's pressuring of Lenin, drafted its "Theses on the Eastern Question" defining the goal of the Communist International to organize working and peasant masses and to 'fight for the most radical possible solution of the tasks of bourgeois-democratic revolution'" (Haithcox 33). John Haithcox has written that the Roy-Lenin debates in 1922 was the Comintern's first attempt to "formulate a policy which would successfully merge the revolutionary aspirations of nationalist anticolonialism and communist anticapitalism" (18). In his 1922 *Crisis* essay "Gandhi and India," Du Bois cited favorably the observation by a British Labour Party representative at the 1920 Indian National Congress that Gandhi was India's equivalent to Lenin. Indeed, Du Bois's 1922 support of the efforts of the Indian National Congress to achieve self-determination anticipates his epigraph to the 1922 essay offering Indians as a model for African Americans. In an attempt to fuse and sustain his evolving Marxist and anti-Orientalist agenda, then, Du Bois sought to literally make analogous what he called the "rising tide of new and popular thought" ("Gandhi and India" 206) in all corners of the "colored" world.

It is this complex moment of theoretical and geographic rapprochement that *Dark Princess* most astutely allegorizes. As Cedric Robinson has noted, Du Bois's hostility to narrow nationalism and Garveyism and his fabian socialism were romanced and wedded by the 1920s turn in the line of international Communism. In 1925 Du Bois gave one clear indication of this turn. His December column in the *Crisis*, "The Black Man and Labor," noted that "two significant moments have recently taken place among us," the organization of a Pullman Porters Union and a meeting of "colored Communists" in Chicago. The short-lived American Negro Labor Congress held in Chicago that year was a direct response by the American Communist Party to the new Soviet position on black labor and so registered by Du Bois: "If black men wish to meet and learn what laborers are doing in England or in Russia and sympathize with their movements they have a perfect right to do so. . . . *The Crisis* . . . asserts the right of any set of American Negroes to investigate and sympathize with any industrial reform whether it springs from Russia, China or the South Seas" (432). Matthew Towns's association with the Pullman Porters and the Chicago setting thus provided Du Bois a symbolic landscape and platform for Towns's blatant transformation to revolutionary consciousness: "If then in Chicago we can kill the thing that America stands for, we emancipate the world," writes Matthew to Princess Kautilya. "There must be developed here that world-tyranny which will impose by brute force a new heaven on this old and rotten earth" (*Dark Princess* 285).

Reciprocally, Matthew's new "theses" on black labor find parallel in Kautilya's work with the New York Box Makers Union, a fictitious rendering of the Paper Box Union in New York that Du Bois had also singled out for praise in the *Crisis* for accepting black workers. Indeed, at every turn of *Dark Princess* Du Bois sought to analogize the proletarian content of his protagonists' respective racial and national experiences: the princess suffers sexual harassment from a white overlord while working as an American domestic; Matthew's work as train car servant and subway digger not only evokes the important role of the All India Railway Federation in the organization of Indian trade unions after 1919, but also mirrors the extracurricular labor undertaken by Harry Haywood and his Egyptian, Chinese, and Indian colleagues at the Moscow University of Toilers of the East, a comrade training school opened with the support and instruction of M. N. Roy. Haywood, in fact, arrived for training at the university in 1926, the same year of Du Bois's first extensive six-week tour of the Soviet Union undertaken while writing *Dark Princess*. Du Bois's awareness of and support for such training was not so subtly referenced in the novel via Towns's experience of racism from an Italian worker aboard his steamship home: "They hated and despised most of their fellows," Towns declares, "and they fell like a pack of wolves on the weakest. Yet they all had the common bond of toil; their sweat and the sweat of toilers like them made one vast ocean around the world" (40).

Du Bois's image of "darkwater" as the amniotic fluid of proletarian internationalism also points to the complex configuration of the "feminine" in *Dark Princess*, particularly in light of Orientalist readings of global politics by his contemporaries. His representation of an essential maternal African nation in *Darkwater*, for example, was consistent with his early Pan-Africanist identification of the female as repository of national —and nationalist—culture. *Dark Princess* attempts to fuse Princess Kautilya and Matthew's black mother into a single image of this idea. Like Matthew and his mother, the princess emerges from the "black South in ancient days"; India is the "birthplace" and "black womb" of the ancient world; the princess's and Matthew's disparate lineage is fused by the image of Matthew's mother as "Kali, the Black One; wife of Siva, Mother of the World" (220). Kautilya's Bolshevik tough love not only evokes Kali's "double" aspect of destruction and compassion,[7] but also mirrors Du Bois's invocation of the black spirituals as cultural touchstones of Matthew's relationship to black earth, including his mother's experience of forty acres and a mule. At the same time, Kautilya's overwrought erotic charms—"She was a large woman—opulent and highly colored, and she lay there on her back looking straight up into his eyes" (76)—hint at a flattened Orientalist projection of exoticism that Du Bois baldly succumbs to while attempting to couple it to the twin forces of radical politics and love. Both of these aspects he found lacking in his famous 1926 attack on the Harlem Renaissance entitled "Criteria of Negro Art," as well as in his critique of touristic black sexuality in African American literature of the 1920s. As Claudia Tate aptly notes in her introduction to *Dark Princess*, Du Bois was "for most of his life a romantic who linked his revolutionary doctrine to his belief in providential history and thereby transformed social data into eroticized cultural metaphors" (xxxvi). Hence, Princess Kautilya's beauty is a "mongrel" miscegenation: her "colored" allies believe that her visit to Russia has "inoculated her with Bolshevism of a mild but dangerous type" (29). Du Bois's playful troping on the "one drop rule" is deepened by the semantic wedding of the princess and Matthew: both are called, at various points in the text, "Bolshevik" and "nigger," the equation of terms suggesting what might be seen as political catalysts for their fatal anti-imperialist attraction.

This complex and overdetermined doubling motif, as Paul Gilroy has noted, shows Du Bois struggling after "not the fusion of two purified essences but rather a meeting of two heterogeneous multiplicities that in yielding themselves up to each other create something durable and entirely appropriate to anti-colonial times" (144). More concretely, Du Bois is straining to release his own famous figure of "one dark body" in *The*

Souls of Black Folk from the "unreconciled strivings" of a single (and singular) double consciousness. In *The Souls of Black Folk*, Du Bois famously cast the Seventh Son as he who is "longing to attain self-conscious manhood, to merge his double self into a better and truer self" (11). This proto-Messianic figure is literally an heir to a cosmopolitan line of descent, "after the Egyptian and the Indian, the Greek and the Roman, the Teuton and Mongolian" (11). In *Dark Princess*, Kautilya trades her political inheritance as Indian royalty for an internationalist pedigree that includes collaboration with national revolutionary movements in China, Japan, and Egypt. She and Matthew's commitment to the international proletariat also adds the specter of class consciousness to "double" racial consciousness. "Can we accomplish this double end in one movement?" asks the princess of their joint efforts to liberate black workers and achieve Indian home rule. "Brain and Brawn must unite in one body. But where shall the work begin?" asks Matthew. The answer is in the physical and theoretical potential of their coupling: "Workers unite, men cry, while in truth always thinkers who do not work have tried to unite workers who do not think," writes the princess. "Only working thinkers can unite thinking workers" (286). Du Bois's conception is indeed immaculate: his recipe for the newborn messiah of "Dark Princess" must by necessity be proletarian in content, international in form!

Dark Princess was completed in 1927 and published in 1928. In February 1927 the Association of Oppressed Peoples (AOP)—founded in 1924 as the Anti-Imperialist League—met in Brussels. According to David Kimche, the AOP had "strong Communist leanings" but the support of many nationalists and radical non-Communists "centered mainly in Berlin" (4). Representation at the AOP included 175 delegates from thirty-seven countries and territories, including Nehru, Ho Chi Minh, Muhammad Hatta, Madame Sun Yat-sen, and Leopold Senghor. Kimche has described the 1927 meeting as "the father of Afro-Asian solidarity, the forerunner of the conference at Bandung" (4–5). In 1928 the Sixth Congress in Moscow formalized the Comintern's Black Belt thesis. The Congress consummated the hybrid work of Roy, Lenin, McKay, Huiswoud, and others before and after the 1922 Comintern. *Dark Princess* prophetically merged these contemporary historical plot lines. The book ends with the princess declaring that "the colored world goes free in 1952" and her declaration to Matthew of the need to center their global revolutionary work in the "womb" of his own world-historical experience: "Here in Virginia you are at the edge of a black world. The black belt of the Congo, the Nile, and the Ganges reaches up by way of Guiana, Haiti, and Jamaica, like a red arrow, up into the heart of white America. Thus I see a mighty synthesis: you can work in Africa and Asia right here in America if you work in the Black Belt" (286).

This culminating image of black penetration into the "heart of whiteness" bespeaks the tentative political formula for Du Bois's Afro-Asian internationale. It was his most pronounced, if veiled, statement of his interest in what he called in 1933 the "Russian experiment," while providing incontrovertible support for national liberation struggles motivated by the self-determinationist rhetoric of the World War I era, ranging from Woodrow Wilson, to Lajpat Rai, to the Comintern. By enacting Afro-Asian linkages amid world wars, colonialism, Orientalism, the Third International, and rising Pan-Africanism, *Dark Princess* also anticipated the roots and routes of a number of Afro-intellectuals who in its wake would take up the cause of both Asian independence and Afro-Asian solidarity. George Padmore, Aime Cesaire, Leopold Senghor, Paul Robeson, Stokely Carmichael, Martin Luther King Jr., Huey Newton, John Killens, Robert F. Williams, and the Black Panthers would all make the "Asian turn" during the anticolonial period. The princess's transnational migrations and circulations likewise resonated with the lives and political movements of Asian anticolonials from M. N. Roy to Ho Chi Minh, whose own roots and routes included passages from India and Vietnam through California, London, and New York City, respectively, and back into the crucible of revolutionary struggles. No other twentieth-century American novel provides a better fictional road map to these episodes. At the same time, *Dark Princess*'s melodramatic and sentimental climax offering a miscegenated messiah as the birth of a new international world order rendered visible the patrician paternalism of Du Bois's own Asian romance. "With its hallucination of Brahmin royalty, royal blood, and its vision of the golden child as the incarnation of a new interracial alliance," notes Weinbaum, "*Dark Princess* reinscribed the orientalism we might expect it to challenge, while simultaneously making what may be called a 'racial original mistake,' an essentializing argument about racial genealogy and belonging that is on a structural level a mere revamping of that made by advocates of racial nationalism in the U.S. context" (36–37)—notably his adversaries Stoddard and Grant.[8]

Finally, *Dark Princess*'s rendering of World War I Berlin, Moscow, New York, and Chicago as epicenters of Afro-Asian revolution anticipates most obviously and directly the seminal Afro-Asian moment of the twentieth century, the 1955 summit meeting of decolonizing African and

Asian internationalists at Bandung, Indonesia. In stunning prophecy of this period, Princess Kautilya declares near the novel's end, "The colored world goes free in 1952." Ironically, 1952 would see revocation of Du Bois's passport as American citizen—a revocation that prevented him from attending the Bandung conference. His lost passport may perhaps be seen as a final footnote on the discursive internationalisms predicted by *Dark Princess*. Among those it anticipated was Du Bois's own rebirth as a Communist Party member preceding his exile to Ghana. This moment is inscribed and foretold in *Dark Princess* on the occasion of his last visit to Maoist China. On May 1, 1959, thirty-two years to the day after the fictional birth of the "messiah of all the darker races," Du Bois dedicated the poem "I Sing to China." Its appeal to China to help wake a "sleeping" African continent carried the apocalyptic anger of a last judgment, the millennial hopes of liberation theology, and the utopian aspiration of a committed Marxist. It also conjured Asia one final time as the black world's significant Other, or as Matthew says of his love for Kautilya, "the rubbing of a kindred soul—the answering flash of another pole":

Help her China!
Help her, Dark People, who half-shared her slavery;
Who knows the depths of her sorrow and humiliation;
Help her, not in Charity,

But in glorious resurrection of that day to be,
When the black man lives again
And sings the Songs of the Ages!
Swing low, Sweet Chariot—
Good news! the Chariot's a' coming! . . .
. . . Communes, Communes, with the elect of Heaven
With Mother Earth, daughter of Sky and Sun
Born of Democracy, fertilized by Communism
Parents of Revolution, Makers of the World! . . .
. . . Shout, China!
Roar, Rock, roll River;
Sing, Sun and Moon and Sea!
Move Mountain, Lake and Land,
Exalt Mankind, Inspire!
For out of the East again, comes Salvation!
Leading all prophets of the Dead—
Osiris, Buddha, Christ and Mahmoud

Interning their ashes, cherishing their Good;
China save the World! Arise, China!

Notes

1. Reed ("fabian socialist"). Despite the pronouncement of his socialism and Marxist leanings as early as 1905, few of Du Bois's critics or biographers have taken seriously the task of discerning their finer points or influences particularly regarding *Dark Princess*. Manning Marable folds Du Bois's "radicalism" neatly into his "democratism." He reads *Dark Princess* primarily as emblematic of Du Bois polemics against Marcus Garvey's UNIA nationalism and literary debates with Alain Locke and younger Harlem Renaissance artists. Although these are certainly features of the novel, Marable does not, for example, link Du Bois's 1926 visit to the Soviet Union to the Bolshevik themes of the text. Likewise, Adolph Reed, claiming his own fabian socialist Du Bois against Marable, writes, "Throughout the interwar years Du Bois was hardly a radical democrat" (65). He notes Du Bois's "pro-Bolshevik rhetoric" of the 1920s but glosses over careful analysis of this rhetoric and the text of *Dark Princess*. Paul Gilroy's interpretation of the novel's "heterogeneous multiplicities" is consistent with his deployment of Du Bois's "double consciousness" as an aspect of diasporic hybridity but looks past the overt dialectical imagery and rhetoric of the novel—much less Du Bois's reactions to events like the Russian Revolution and Bolshevism (144). Claudia Tate, meanwhile, reads the novel's erotic politics as consistent with Du Bois's configuration of the maternal black mother with Pan-Africanism or black culture, drawing parallels between the Princess and the character Zora Cresswell from *The Quest of the Silver Fleece* (1911). Tate's argument does not account for the ethnic and national difference of the Princess in this formulation, nor for the possibility of Du Bois's "gendering" as a response to discourses like Orientalism. In general, these important, insightful analyses of Du Bois and the novel reflect a critical tendency to shy away from the historical details of his engagement with communism. For such an engagement one can look to the work of Aptheker, particularly his introduction to *Darkwater*, and Cedric Robinson's *Black Marxism*.

2. According to Arnold Rampersad (161–76), Du Bois sent Lai a draft of *Dark Princess* to review before its publication.

3. Weinbaum persuasively argues that Du Bois's articulation of political arguments about race through metaphors of reproduction is an understudied feature of his work.

4. In the spring of 1921, in *Crisis*, Du Bois tied the exploitation of women in India to the breakdown of industrialism under colonialism. See Kapur 26. Rai's 1928 book, *Unhappy India*, is in large part an attack on Mayo as imperialist stooge: "Miss Mayo's mentality is the mentality of the white race as a whole against the black or brown or yellow peoples of Asia. She is only the mouth-piece of the oppressors of the East" (xviii).

5. For a fuller account of Orientalism's relationship to Afrocentrism and nineteenth-century African American conceptions of Asia, see Moses. Cooper dissented from popular romantic readings of Asia by regarding footbinding and enforced domesticity of women in China as remnants of feudalism (see Moses 132).

6. See Haywood, *Black Bolshevik*, esp. 81–176. See also Robinson, *Black Marx-*

ism, 294–311, as well as Maxwell, *New Negro, Old Left*, esp. chap. 2, "Home to Moscow: Claude McKay's *The Negroes in America* and the Race of Marxist Theory," 63–94.

7. John Haithcox (*Communism and Nationalism in India*) has noted that early-twentieth-century Bengal revolutionary societies adopted Kali as a symbol of independent rebellion. Society newspapers described her as bloodthirsty and imploring of political sacrifice.

8. At the Chicago Coliseum on March 17, 1929, Du Bois debated Stoddard on the question, "Shall the Negro Be Encouraged to Seek Cultural Equality?" Du Bois's remarks appeared in a report published by the Chicago Forum, which sponsored the debate. In his remarks, Du Bois attacked Stoddard's theories of "Nordic" superiority as well as his racism and elitism.

Works Cited

Aptheker, Herbert. Introduction to *Darkwater: Voices From within the Veil.* W. E. B. Du Bois. 1921. Millwood, N.Y.: Kraus-Thomson Organization, Ltd., 1975.

Banerjee, Kalyan Kumar. *Indian Freedom Movement: Revolutionaries in America.* Calcutta: Sris Kuma Kunda, 1969.

Druhe, David N. *Soviet Russia and Indian Communism, 1917–1947.* New York: Bookman Associates, 1959.

Du Bois, W. E. B. "The Black Man and Labor." *Crisis* 31.2 (December 1925): 432.

———. "The Color Line Belts the World." *Collier's Weekly* October 20, 1906.

———. *Dark Princess: A Romance.* 1928. Jackson: University Press of Mississippi, 1995.

———. *Darkwater: Voices from within the Veil.* 1921. Millwood, N.Y.: Kraus-Thomson Organization, Ltd., 1975.

———. "Fact and Forum." *Pittsburgh Courier* February 29, 1937.

———. "Gandhi and India." *Crisis* 23 (March 1922): 203–7.

———. "*Horizon*, Vol. I, No. 2 (February 1907)." Annotated Bibliography of the Published Writings of W. E. B. Du Bois. Millwood, N.Y.: Kraus-Thomson Organization, Ltd., 1973.

———. "I Sing to China." *China Reconstructs* 8 (June 1959): 24–26.

———. "Marxism and the Negro Problem." *Crisis* 40.5 (1933): 103–4.

———. "Postscript." *Crisis* 37.7 (1930): 246.

———. *Selections from the Crisis, 1911–1925.* Vol. 1. Ed. Herbert Aptheker. Millwood, N.Y.: Kraus-Thomson Organization, Ltd., 1975.

———. *The Souls of Black Folk.* 1903. Ed. Henry Louis Gates Jr. and Terri Hume Oliver. New York: Norton Critical Edition, 1999.

———. *The World and Africa: An Inquiry into the Part Which Africa Has Played in World History.* 1947. Millwood, N.Y.: Kraus-Thomson Organization, Ltd., 1976.

Gilroy, Paul. *The Black Atlantic: Modernity and Double Consciousness.* Cambridge: Harvard University Press, 1993.

Grant, Madison. *The Passing of the Great Race.* 1916. New York: Arno Press, 1970.

Haithcox, John Patrick. *Communism and Nationalism in India: M. N. Roy and Comintern Policy, 1920–1939.* Princeton: Princeton University Press, 1971.

Haywood, Harry. *Black Bolshevik: Autobiography of an Afro-American Communist.* Chicago: Liberator Press, 1978.

Kapur, Sudarshan. *Raising Up a Prophet: The African-American Counter with Gandhi.* Boston: Beacon Press, 1992.

Kimche, David. *The Afro-Asian Movement: Ideology and Foreign Policy of the Third World.* New York: Halsted Press, 1973.

Marable, Manning. *W. E. B. Du Bois: Black Radical Democrat.* Boston: Twayne Publishers, 1986.

Maxwell, William J. *New Negro, Old Left: African-American Writing and Communism between the Wars.* New York: Columbia University Press, 1999.

Mayo, Katherine. *Mother India.* 1916. New York: Blue Ribbon Books, 1927.

Moses, Wilson Jeremiah. *Afrotopia: The Roots of African American Popular History.* Cambridge: Cambridge University Press, 1998.

Rai, Lajpat. *Unhappy India.* Calcutta: Banna Publishing Co., 1928.

Rampersad, Arnold. "Du Bois's Passage to India: *Dark Princess.*" W. E. B. Du Bois, *On Race and Culture: Philosophy, Politics, Poetics.* Ed. Bernard W. Bell, Emily R. Grosholz, and James B. Stewart. New York: Routledge, 1996.

Reed, Adolph L., Jr. *W. E. B. Du Bois and American Political Thought: Fabianism and the Color Line.* New York: Oxford University Press, 1997.

Robinson, Cedric J. *Black Marxism: The Making of the Black Radical Tradition.* London: Zed Press, 1983.

Said, Edward. *Orientalism.* New York: Vintage, 1994.

Stoddard, Lothrop. *The Rising Tide of Color against White World Supremacy.* New York: Scribner, 1922.

Tate, Claudia. Introduction to *Dark Princess,* by W. E. B. Du Bois. Jackson: University Press of Mississippi, 1995. ix–xxviii.

Weinbaum, Alys Eve. "Reproducing Racial Globality: W. E. B. Du Bois and the Sexual Politics of Black Internationalism." *Social Text* 67, 19.2 (Summer 2001): 15–39.

barrios of the world,
where we live and
strive,
where rich and poor
separate
their worlds
into different realitie
barrios of the world,
paradoxes seething
with rage/unsanity

a new world cometh

—Ricardo Sánchez,
"Barrios of the Worl

B. V. Olguín

Barrios of the World Unite!: Regionalism, Transnationalism, and Internationalism in Tejano War Poetry from the Mexican Revolution to World War II

Relocating Mexican American Subjectivity

The relatively recent canonization and commodification of Mexican American literature, along with new archival discoveries in the field, have led to dynamic debates about Mexican American literary history and, more importantly, Mexican American and Chicana/o ontology.[1] Earlier New Critical readings, such as Juan Bruce-Novoa's 1982 *Chicano Poetry: A Response to Chaos*, inevitably have given way to more incisive Marxist and materialist feminist readings, including Ramón Saldívar's 1990 *Chicano Narrative: The Dialectics of Difference*, Angie Chabram-Dernersesian's 1992 "I Throw Punches for My Race, but I Don't Want to Be a Man," Alfred Arteaga's 1997 *Chicano Poetics: Heterotexts and Hybridities*, and Sonia Saldívar-Hull's 2000 *Feminism on the Border: Chicana Gender Politics and Literature*. Scholars of nineteenth-century Mexican American literature like Genaro Padilla, Rosaura Sánchez, Erlinda Gonzales-Berry, and Tey Diana Rebolledo have made even more compelling arguments for a broader and more complex treatment of Mexican American subjectivity.[2] Their ongoing archival discoveries reveal that we must account for contradictory class, gendered, and racialized Mexican American subject positions as well as shifting and radically ambiguous national affiliations that involve relations to power that are variously, and sometimes simultaneously, hegemonic and subaltern.[3] As such, their work can be seen as a forerunner of the current shifts in American, ethnic, and women's studies toward models of transnationalism that attempt to map out the complex relationships between alterity and agency across time and place.[4]

In her 1998 article, "Minefields and Meeting Grounds: Transnational Analyses and American Studies," Priscilla Wald laments that this transnationalist trend is so ideologically inchoate that it leaves us "no longer sure where we are" (216). Despite Wald's apt critique of the dangerous lack of historicism sometimes associated with transnational dislocations, I have shown elsewhere how Mexican American war narratives have exploited this ambiguity to enable materialist and immanently internationalist remappings of Mexican American and modern Chicana/o subjectivities.[5] George Mariscal similarly has observed these possibilities in the introduction to his 1999 edited anthology, *Aztlán and Vietnam: Chicano and Chicana Experiences of the War*, as have other scholars of post–Vietnam Chicana/o literature. Significantly, most criticism on the transnational aspects of Mexican American and Chicana/o literature has focused on the post–Vietnam era. Whereas recent critical attention has been directed toward the historical period preceding the U.S.-Mexican War from 1846 to 1848, there has been a dearth of scholarship on Mexican American literature, especially poetry, from the early 1900s to the 1940s. Despite the significance of this period in American literary history—the heart of American modernism—introductory surveys of Mexican American poetry, such as Juan Bruce-Novoa's aforementioned work, Cordelia Candelaria's 1986 *Chicano Poetry: A Critical Introduction*, and Rafael Pérez-Torres's 1995 *Movements in Chicano Poetry: Against Myths, against Margins*, neglect this corpus altogether. Other prominent scholars situate poets from this period as part of the "Mexican American Generation," thereby embedding them within a generational topography that reduces their works to overdetermined "assimilation narratives."[6]

These lacunae notwithstanding, groundbreaking criticism on African American literature between the two world wars, such as William Maxwell's 1999 *New Negro, Old Left*, James Smethurst's 1999 *The New Red Negro*, and Alan Wald's 1994 *Writing from the Left*, has enabled us to complicate such reductive readings of early twentieth-century minority discourses on identity. Indeed, as these studies have shown, black writers from the 1920s to the 1940s, especially those associated with the Communist Party's Popular Front, posed significant challenges to the hegemonic narrative of nation by invoking a complex claim to American citizenship and black nationalist identity while simultaneously militating for internationalist revolution. They did so precisely as the United States sought to consolidate its status as the premier capitalist empire through commerce and warfare. That is, amid intense economic crisis, global warfare, and radical political action, black writers cultivated a vernacular poetic that imagined an alternative utopian social space that situated African American ontology both within and without the continental United States. In his 1996 reprise, "The 1930s Left in U.S. Literature Reconsidered," Alan Wald calls for an expanded historiography of this era that accounts for the exigencies introduced by women and minority writers. Following Wald, I propose to examine how Texas Mexican—or Tejana and Tejano—poets from the 1900s to the early 1940s simultaneously ground Mexican American ontology within a regional space as well as within the broader historical materialist struggles that led to a proliferation of wars in the first half of the twentieth century. I submit that their explorations of the complex and conflictive relationship between Mexican Americans, capitalism, and American imperialism anticipate contemporary discourses on Mexican American transnationalism even as Tejana and Tejano poets from this era pressured the postmodernist relativism that informs much of the criticism on transnationalism that Priscilla Wald identifies as problematic.[7]

A complete history of the Latina/o literary Left prior to 1960, as well as Mexican American and broader Latina/o participation in the Popular Front, remains to be written. However, I argue that Mexican American war literature, especially Tejana and Tejano war poetry, provides a good entry into these relationships. As I will show, this corpus is particularly well suited to enabling further explorations of the relationship between Mexican American regionalism, transnationalism, and internationalism precisely because of the unique social locations of these authors as combatants for and against the United States.[8] For instance, whereas Mexican-born anarchist poet Sara Estela Ramírez exploited her ambiguous national affiliations to militate for a complex model of Mexican and Mexican American internationalism before and during the Mexican Revolution of 1910, Mexican American war poetry by Margil López and Américo Paredes explores how the Mexican American soldier occupies an equally contradictory transnational and proto-imperialist subject position as a GI, or rather, "Government Issue," materiel. Collectively, these authors show how Mexican American soldiers are both active agents and subjects of a nation that in large part is built upon a war of expansion and conquest against their ancestors, and that subsequently consolidates its status as the premier capitalist imperialist power during this period in part through the legendary (though highly problematic) heroics of Mexican American GIs.[9] The unique social location of Mexican Americans, especially Mexican American soldiers, thus not only overdetermines Mexican American anomie, but also enables—and at times demands—that they interrogate the very notion of a nation-state and the Mexican American space within. These three poets enable such an assessment.

Expanding upon Ramón Saldívar's notion of the Mexican American "dialectics of difference," I will show how these authors use a variety of poetic forms and genres to present complicated recognition scenes in which Mexican American soldiers are actualized as coherent subjects not only as the antitheses to or agents of Anglo-American capital. Rather, these authors articulate poetic personas through racially nuanced yet oftentimes contradictory affiliations and claims to sameness with people of different races, ethnicities, and nationalities throughout the world who also are involved in conflicted relationships with capitalism and U.S. imperialism. The resultant configurations of Mexican American identity pose compelling challenges to long-accepted paradigms. Writing at a time and in an ideological context in which Mexican American citizenship was rendered radically inchoate as a result of the proliferation of borderlands insurgencies by Tejano seditionists, the mass-scale induction of Mexican Americans into the U.S. armed forces, and the persistence of legal segregation that circumscribed their status in civil society, these authors enable us to map the contours as well as the potential—and potential limits—of transnational configurations of Mexican American ontology. Indeed, they offer us the opportunity to explore alternative constructions of Mexican American subjectivity before it becomes reified through romantic cultural nationalist discourses in the 1960s and 1970s (which figured Chicano male warrior heroes fighting to reclaim the ancestral lands of Aztlán) or relativized by problematic postmodernist celebrations of Mexican American liminality.[10] That is, Tejana and Tejano poets writing during the period framed by the Mexican Revolution to World War II not only anticipate the creation of the concept of Aztlán and the borderlands as foundational metaphors for regionalist and cultural nationalist configurations of Mexican American ontology; they also refashion and relocate the southwestern United States and its Mexican

American subjects onto the world at large through transnationalist and immanently internationalist stagings of the Lacanian recognition scene. In their poetry, Mexican Americans are consolidated as subjects through their reflection and recognition in others—both enemies and allies of the United States—which ultimately facilitates more complex assessments of Mexican American spatial ontologies then and now.

The U.S.-Mexico Border as Global Battleground: Sara Estela Ramírez's Materialist Feminist Revision of the Epic Heroic Corrido

Until recently, the most salient attempts to theorize Mexican American poetics were grounded in the epic heroic corrido, the nineteenth-century octosyllabic ballad form that, according to Américo Paredes's foundational 1958 study, *With His Pistol in His Hand*, is consolidated in the clash between two economic orders: semifeudal Mexico and the nascent capitalist United States. Scholars Ramón Saldívar and José Limón have further proposed the corrido as a residual form for contemporary Chicana/o literary sensibilities to conceptualize modern Mexican American, or Chicana/o, identity in historical materialist terms while still exploring its regionalist dimensions.[11] However, Chicana feminist scholars Sonia Saldívar-Hull, Angie Chabram-Dernersesian, and María Herrera-Sobek lucidly have critiqued the hypermasculinist ontologies arising from the reification of the corrido subject.[12] Even before these contemporary revisions of the male warrior hero, however, early-twentieth-century political activist, educator, and writer Sara Estela Ramírez proposed a feminist and revolutionary revision of the ideologically problematic social bandit who populates the nostalgic geopoetic landscape of the epic heroic corrido.[13] A member of the Partido Liberal Mexicano (PLM—Mexican Liberal Party) who also is recognized for her collaborations with brothers Enrique and Ricardo Flores Magón along with other anarchist revolutionists, Ramírez introduces a materialist and gynocritical war poetry that partially decenters the male warrior hero precisely as this masculinist and highly regionalist genre reaches its apex. Moreover, her verse enables us to reimagine the spatial ontologies of Mexican Americans beyond problematic "oppositional" models of Chicana/o identity (which inadvertently reassert U.S. hegemonic claims to the Southwest by asserting Chicanas/os as a minority Other), or even the more recent recuperations of the Mexican American bourgeois subject.[14] Instead, through her activism and writing, Ramírez proposes the Mexican American borderlands subject as invested with a simultaneously local resonance and global importance that arises from the historically significant wars that are waged there. Mexican American ontology is inalienably grounded in conflicts such as the U.S.-Mexican War of 1848, which is oftentimes articulated as a racialized regional struggle between Mexicans and Euramericans.[15] But Ramírez enables us to examine how Mexican Americans also are interpellated as immanently internationalist subjects through wars like the Mexican Revolution, which her party, the PLM, regarded as part of the global struggle against capitalism.

Ramírez has received growing critical attention since Emilio Zamora's and Inés Hernandez-Tovar's early archival work on her writings and has since become a fixture in reconstructed genealogies of Chicana literary figures.[16] Following Hernandez-Tovar, Teresa McKenna most recently has identified Ramírez's work as a "precursor to contemporary Chicana literary production" (113). Given that modern Chicanas have reclaimed figures as far back as Malintzín and Sor Juana Inés de la Cruz, this recuperation of Ramírez certainly is viable, even though Ramírez was born in the state of Coauhuila, Mexico, in 1881 and remained a Mexican citizen until her death in Laredo, Texas, in 1910.[17] Yet I believe that Ramírez was as much Mexican as she was Mexican American and, as Louis Mendoza similarly has argued, her shifting national affiliations were the result of a strategic nationalism that effectively rendered her citizenship moot. Mendoza aptly observes that Ramírez "viewed nationalism as a strategem for living with the contradictions produced by class struggle in the racialized context of the United States" (119). I will add that her shifting national allegiances not only were a stratagem, but also served as a point of departure in her seditionist activities on both sides of the border. As such, she enables us to resist popular postmodernist constructions of the border as an amorphous free-floating "transnational" space and, instead, situate it as a global battleground in the fight against the commodity fetish. Indeed, Ramírez was a member of the PLM, an internationalist anarcho-communist cadre organization whose president, Ricardo Flores Magón, urged its partisans to "convert all the countries into one large single country, beautiful and good, a country of human beings, a country of man and woman with one single flag: that of universal fraternity" (Gómez-Quiñones 60). Moreover, Ramírez and other PLM members also were associated with famous internationalists like John Reed and Emma Goldman, who used the United States as a base of operations to militate for anarchist revolution both in the United States and abroad. Accordingly, PLM militants were branded and imprisoned as seditionists—or rather, *anti*-nationalists—by the Mexican and U.S. governments alike. In other words, Ramírez was a materialist transnationalist fighting for Magón's "one single large country" even as she was and continues to be integral to the Chicana feminist cultural nationalist genealogy. I argue that her enduring legacy is due in large part to her gynocritical martial verse, which militates for a radical revision of the overdetermined regionalist and masculinist conceits of the epic heroic corrido, under whose shadow she lived, wrote, taught, and fought.

Ramírez performs a critique of the masculinist conceits of the corrido while still preserving the global resonance of the historical materialist struggle that undergirds the genre. Her poem, "March 21: To Juarez," which was published in 1908, foregrounds these complex geopoetics and politics.[18] Significantly, Zamora as well as Mendoza provocatively link the poem to a planned anarchist insurrection in Mexico that was to have coincided with the publication of this poem in the anarchist newspaper *El Demócrata Fronterizo* (The Borderlands Democrat). According to other scholars of the PLM, an attack on Ciudad Juarez, Mexico, was to be mounted by anarchists from El Paso, Texas, that would be the signal to other PLM partisans to join the insurrection against Mexican dictator Porfirio Díaz. Mendoza suggests that the scheduled publication of the poem a month before the attack was intended as "a call to action" (118).[19] Though no conclusive evidence has been found, I submit that the poem's gloss of the engagé format of the corrido nonetheless alludes to this authorial intent. This martial tone and extratextual resonance is evident from the first stanza:

> It is true that the deeds of my homeland, which I adore,
> As well as her heroes
> Number in the thousands.
> How many pages of gold
> In that history of epic songs!
> How many sublime strophes on those pages
> Where liberty traced her name
> With clear, indelible, red letters! (lines 1–9)

Indeed, the entire poem is rife with heroic references to "titans" and "gladiators / With arms of steel destroying / The thrones of rude oppressors!" (lines 21–23); it concludes by invoking the indigenous hero of the title —Zapotec Indian Benito Juarez—who was elected president of Mexico several times in the 1860s and 1870s. Famous for his fight against and eventual victory over the occupying French forces of the self-proclaimed emperor of Mexico, Napoleon III, Ramírez characterizes Juarez as the "tutelary god . . . / who guides our steps" (lines 52–53). On the surface, this poem appears to be simply a nationalist paean that celebrates the heroics of the leader of the Cinco de Mayo battle in which the French occupation forces were defeated in Puebla, Mexico, in 1868. But just as this battle continues to serve as a touchstone for European imperialism —French Foreign Legion recruits still pay homage to their "martyred" comrades by facing toward Puebla during their training graduation ceremonies—it also illustrates how modern Mexican national identity, like Sara Estela Ramírez's own identity, is intertwined with nationalist struggles against imperialist powers that internationalists insist was always already part of the global struggle against imperialism and, ultimately, capitalism. Rather than degenerating into the problematically nostalgic Mexican literary genre of *indigenismo* (indigenism) that was to follow the Mexican Revolution, Ramírez's poem tropes the color red (e.g., "clear, indelible, red letters") not merely in terms of an indigenous nationalist hero, but as an immanently internationalist metaphor that eventually becomes a metonym for communism after the Bolshevik Revolution.

The internationalist allusions in the above poem are made more manifest in other compositions such as "The Struggle for Good" (178–80), which reads as an allegorical, and at times quite literal, lesson in dialectical thought. This poem, which is ignored by all scholars of Ramírez's verse, begins by tackling one of the fundamental premises of communism—human nature:

> Innate in humanity is the desire for good.
> Everything tends to improve, to perfect itself.
> Nature shows us how life arrives
> at perfection, from the rudimentary
> phases; and that same nature does not
> only make itself responsible for the
> development of matter, but also takes
> upon itself the moral development of
> the masses that constitute communities,
> of the communities that constitute
> societies and of societies whose
> heterogeneous and harmonious combina-
> tion constitutes humanity. (lines 1–15)

This narrative poem, which dispenses with the poet's earlier uses of hyperbolic and figural language while still attempting to make effective use of poetic devices such as meter, repetition, enjambment, and crescendo, is fundamentally didactic. The lesson continues with the author lamenting the usurpation of nature and power and the mystification of the masses ("It is sad, nevertheless, to see / that ascendant march of humanity to- / ward darkness," lines 16–18). However, as in other poems such as "Reef" (183), this poem offers a resolution by privileging experience, especially privations, as the dialectical vehicle for empowerment (e.g., "the stumblings hurt much, but / they teach much," lines 62–63). In fact, when read in relation to her speeches to workers and PLM partisans, the didactic engagé tone of this poem resonates more like a motivational speech than a piece of art, thereby imbuing the composition with the same extratextual imperative evidenced in "March 21: To Juarez," albeit with a far more overtly anticapitalist trajectory.[20]

More importantly, concurrent with her internationalist dialectical materialism, Ramírez's borderlands subject is regendered as female through a complex blend of cultural nationalist and gynocritical poetics that further transform the masculinist and regionalist conceits of the corrido genre. Anticipating Gloria Anzaldúa's 1987 groundbreaking testimonio, *Borderlands/La Frontera*, by almost a century, Ramírez invokes Mesoamerican motifs to ground her subject in a specific place—squarely atop and simultaneously on both sides of the U.S.-Mexican border—while still enabling broader ruminations on Mexican (American) identity and power across time. A member of Las Hijas de Cuahtemoc (Daughters of Cuahtemoc), a women's auxiliary of the PLM named after the last Aztec emperor, who was executed for refusing to submit to Spanish rule, Ramírez regenders the warrior heritage through poems such as "Rise Up!," which is dedicated "To Woman" (194). In this poem, like others such as "Aurora" (162–63), Ramírez broadens her feminist nationalist politics by invoking the gynocritical mother-daughter paradigm. She begins by noting that "one who is truly a woman is more than goddess or queen" (lines 12–13). After all, "Gods are thrown out of temples; kings are / driven from their thrones, woman is always woman" (lines 17–18). In the last two stanzas, Ramírez uses the imperative that forms the title of the poem to pair her still somewhat ambiguous celebration of womanhood with the warrior ethos that, ironically, defines the epic heroic corrido:

> Only action is life; to feel that one
> lives is the most beautiful sensation.
> Rise up, then, to the beauties of life;
> but rise up so, beautiful with qualities,
> splendid with virtues, strong with energies. (lines 23–27)

When read in relation to poems like "March 21: To Juarez" and "The Struggle for Good," this poem enables Ramírez to both invoke and partially transform the warrior hero paradigm of the border ballad: she regenders it as a female archetype who is at once grounded in Mexican history and the U.S.-Mexican borderlands region while still retaining a global, even metaphysical resonance that is also always materialist. For Ramírez, this new warrior is a heroine, a woman, whose resilience and longevity supercede the ephemeral rule of male patriarchs because, the poem suggests, of the female power of regeneration.

Ramírez further situates her warrior heroine within—as well as beyond—the genealogy of Mexican women warriors that Elizabeth Salas has traced to Mesoamerican times in her 1990 study *Soldaderas in the Mexican Military*. Ramírez's subject also anticipates contemporary revisions of the soldadera by Mexican American authors such as Elena Rodriguez, whose 1997 autobiographical novel, *Peacetime: Spirit of the Eagle*, presents a Chicana feminist and cultural nationalist rendition of the Mexican American GI. Moreover, similar to Chicana poets Gloria Anzaldúa, Judy Lucero, and Alma Villanueva, Ramírez successfully merges a gynocritical poetics with a materialist politics to propose an extratextual activist discourse.[21] Ramírez is a feminist and, moreover, a revolutionary. Mendoza has aptly noted that

> Ramírez's writings belong to a literature of political and social movement that anticipated the need to counter narrow notions of identity. For her, geographical movement across national borders was strategic, as part of a larger purpose of political education and propagandizing. The Mexican diaspora into the United States has been spurred by the economic, political and physical violence that accompanies capitalism and colonialism, and it should be seen as part of the continuing legacy of transnationalism. (119)

I will add that Ramírez's verse further problematizes conventional discourses on nationalism and even transnationalism by paralleling some Marxist and postcolonialist recognitions of the historically unique and immanently revolutionary potential of national minorities and nationalist insurgencies.[22] That is, Ramírez enables us to relocate the Mexican American subject as simultaneously local and global, with particular attention to the status of Mexican Americans in world history and, more precisely, the internationalist struggle against capitalism. The U.S.-Mexican border, she illustrates, has always been a global battleground, and Mexican Americans not only have been part of it from the very beginning but they are also constituted in it.

When Juan Came Marching Home Again: Place, Space, and Mexican Americans in World War I

My remapping of Mexican American ontology as transnational and potentially internationalist is enabled by one of the least likely writers, Margil López. His ultrapatriotic poem, "To the Memory of the Mexican American Heroes (Who Died in the Great War, Defending the Democratic Principles of the American Union)," serves as a symbolically significant epilogue to J. Luz Saenz's 1932 memoir about his service as a U.S. Army enlisted man during World War I, *Mexican Americans in the Great War: And Their Contingent in Support of Democracy, Humanity, and Justice.*[23] Following Jacques Derrida's provocative notion that the supplement frames as well as performs the nucleus of a text, I submit that López's closing poem not only undergirds Saenz's lethal model of patriotism. Rather, through peculiar performative contradictions, the poem ultimately enables a decentering and critical remapping of Mexican American ontology beyond the geopolitical boundaries of the United States that Saenz purported to preserve through his service in the U.S. Army. While the PLM was using South Texas as a staging ground for its revolutionary activities in Mexico, and while a series of anti-American insurgencies by the infamous *sediciosos* (seditionists) were erupting throughout the U.S.-Mexican borderlands (including many concentrated around the South Texas region of Saenz's hometown), Saenz celebrates his military service in France under the command of General John J. Pershing. Ironically, Pershing is infamous to many Mexicans and Mexican Americans for his invasion of Mexico in an unsuccessful attempt to capture Mexican revolutionary leader Pancho Villa, who had invaded and briefly occupied Columbus, New Mexico, in 1916. Rather than being anomalous footnotes to U.S. imperialism, however, Saenz's patriotic memoirs and López's framing poem are both part of a large tradition of patriotic Mexican American war narratives extending from the American Civil War to contemporary Tejano music about the Persian Gulf War as well as the recent war in Afghanistan that variously celebrate the Mexican American male warrior hero in U.S. military history.

Although this corpus of Mexican American war narratives is ideologically inchoate, most texts inevitably are in dialogue with one another through their racialized troping of citizenship and, above all, death. Whereas writers such as Vietnam veterans Charlie Trujillo and Danel Cano have focused on the obvious contradictions of Mexican Americans fighting and dying for a country that denies them the full rights of citizenship, López attempts to celebrate Mexican American soldiering and self-sacrifice as a legitimating claim to citizenship. Yet his contradictory signifying practices inadvertently deterritorialize Mexican Americans in troubling though ultimately productive and potentially empowering ways.[24] That is, even though López foregrounds a problematic topos that alternately will be rehearsed and rejected by Mexican American soldier-authors in subsequent generations, his poem's unique spatial poetics decenter conventional racial and geographic configurations of American identity: "To the Memory of the Mexican American Heroes" boldly proclaims *Mexican* Americans as the prototypical *American* subjects who, significantly, actualize their American identity in Europe, far outside the geopolitical boundaries of the United States. This spatial relocation enables a profound reconstruction for Mexican American ontology and, ultimately, destabilizes Anglocentric models of U.S.-American identity in general.

As suggested by the poem's subtitle, López's displacement of Anglocentric notions of American identity revolves around the reification of Mexican American mortality rates. In a study of Mexican American veterans in his 1996 *Border Visions: Mexican Cultures of the Southwest United States*, Carlos Vélez-Ibáñez notes that the disproportionately high mortality rates for minority soldiers arise from salient racism in the military establishment whereby minorities are placed in more dangerous combat situations than white soldiers (201). I contend that morbid celebrations of these mortality rates by authors like López also may arise from their attempts to reject the complicated political legacy bequeathed by earlier Mexican American soldiers. These include Juan Seguín, who fought against Mexico in the Texas-Mexican War from 1935 to 1936 and then against the United States in the U.S-Mexican War a decade later, as well as Rafael Chacón and Santiago Tafolla, two of many Mexican American soldiers who fought on opposite sides of the American Civil War before deserting to escape racist persecution by their own troops.[25] Even though no evidence exists to confirm that López was cognizant of these particular figures, his poem nonetheless is preoccupied with dispelling the notion that minority soldiers are inferior and cannot be trusted. Following the assimilationist cultural politics of the League of United Latin American Citizens (LULAC), of which Saenz was a founding member, the poem addresses this issue by alternately celebrating and collapsing Mexican American difference.[26] "To the Memory of the Mexican American Heroes" first invokes the problematic notion of a Mexican American warrior culture through references to Mexican American GIs as "intrepid warriors" who posses a "Spartan magnificence" (line 7). In this way, the poet inadvertently parallels the eugenicist discourse about a minority warrior cast. In "The Role of Working-Class Latinos/as as Cannon Fodder for the Next Century," Mariscal illuminates the exploitative nature of this trope when he notes how it commonly is deployed by imperial powers with large minority populations who are used as canon fodder in the armed forces. Following this problematic invocation of a Mexican American warrior caste, López then safely collapses the celebration of Mexican American difference with a poetic erasure of it through martyrdom. In so doing, he echoes the controversial legacy of rejection and postmortem appropriation surrounding his predecessor Juan Seguín. In a morbid spectacle of rejection and appropriation, Seguín was disinterred from his original burial place in Nuevo Laredo, Mexico (where he had fled to avoid assassination by his former enemies *and* allies, both of whom labeled him a "Mexican Benedict Arnold"). Seguín was later reburied in Seguin, Texas, as part of the Sesquicentennial Celebration, during which he was recognized as a Texan and American "hero."[27] Similarly, López's Mexican American heroes are included in the American polis only after they are safely dead. (Even those who survived would return to a society that still practiced legal segregation against its nonwhite residents, thereby placing their citizenship under erasure.) Like other narratives by Mexican American soldier-authors such as Raul Morin's 1963 anthology, *Among the Valiant*, and Roy Benavidez's autobiographies *Medal of Honor* and *The Three Wars of Roy Benavidez*, López's Mexican American heroes are figuratively and literally erased precisely at the moment that their agency and identity as American citizens are actualized.

Although this paradoxical and problematic claim to citizenship is obvious, it nonetheless becomes significant for the way it enables the poet to extend U.S.—and especially Mexican American—ontology into Europe and vice versa. More precisely, López's poem permits the recentering of the Mexican American figure not only as a national subject but also as a transnational (if not antinational) one by staging the self-actualization drama as a reverse migration. Here, the poem both invokes and decenters the language of colonialism by presenting the mestizo subject in a return trip to the "old world." Written in a bombastic formal Spanish common of Mexican American occasional verse of the era, the poem begins:

Sing heroic children of the new continent,
the civic virtues, with laurels sing,
of intrepid warriors who with head high
died in defense of our freedom. (lines 1–4)

The poem continues with the invocation of an important symbol of national identity:

> The Eagles of America crossed the ocean,
> planted in Europe their military genius . . . (lines 13–14)[28]

Though it is safe to assume that the "Eagles of America" refer to the U.S. national symbol, the bald eagle, rather than the Mexican national icon, the golden eagle, the poem nonetheless involves a racialist poetics that inevitably renders the notion of America and Americanness as ambiguous categories. Significantly, the reverse migration does not involve a search for one's European roots. This travel narrative is occasioned by a war against the "cowardly Germans." Although the referent is associated with Keiser Wilhelm's German army, the epithet is imbued with ambiguity due to the large population of German Americans who settled around López's hometown of Sarita in South Texas. The poem, which already traffics in eugenicist discourses through its invocation of a "warrior cast" of Mexican American "Spartans," also ironically places white supremacist discourses of American identity under erasure through its free use of epithets against Europeans, which indirectly places Euramerican patriotism under suspicion.

Although it is important to not overstate the significance of this slippage in the poem's racialized symbolic system, it is equally important to signal the recurrent performative contradictions and ambiguities in the descriptions of the geopolitics of Mexican American citizenship, especially because they both demand and enable a productive historicist remapping of Mexican American spatial ontologies. Another instance of such slippage occurs in López's discussion of Mexican American heroism, which he frames as "civic valor," thereby reconfiguring an otherwise universal trait as also a civic, or rather, local phenomenon. Significantly, the poet further presents Mexican American heroism as a recognition scene between the Mexican American soldier and Europeans when he writes: "What an example of heroism you left for those / nations that reside over there in the old world!" (lines 35–36). Here, López's vantage point in the "new world" is oriented toward the "old world," which becomes the performative space for the actualization and recognition of Mexican American heroism and citizenship, or rather "civic valor." Moreover, within this precarious balance of local resonance and global performance of Mexican American citizenship, López ultimately proposes Mexican American soldiers as prototypical Americans rather than simply a subordinate minority Other. Though the poem does not conclusively resituate Mexican American citizenship in Europe or the world at large—after all, it frames a very patriotic and celebratory claim to inclusion in the American polis—this verse nonetheless inadvertently permits such a relocation. That is, it reifies Mexican American soldiering and sacrifice in Europe amid yet another Western imperialist contest not unlike the one that undergirded the transformation of Mexican Americans into a U.S. minority. But this new ontological space is located far outside the Rio Grande region.

Even though López celebrates those who survived to return home with "glory and splendor" (line 24), the fact remains that many Mexican American GIs did not come marching home to a welcoming population. Many were killed, and those who did survive were forced to confront the conflictive and constraining status of race in their claims to American citizenship, which ultimately placed their nationalist and even transnationalist performances of identity under erasure. In other words, López's claim that the battlefield self-sacrifice of Mexican Americans legitimates their claim to U.S. citizenship—which corresponds to other representations by Mexican American authors—ultimately is radically insufficient and even self-defeating. The persistent effacement of Mexican American identity through warfare and during war also provides a productive space in which to reimagine Mexican American ontology beyond a reductive claim to difference or a lethal claim to sameness. Although López deliberately does not explore this possibility, his complex and contradictory troping of Mexican American citizens as exemplary Americans whose attributes are illustrated in Europe nonetheless enables this very synthesis by subsequent generations of soldiers and authors.[29]

Toward an Internationalist *Soldado Razo*?: The Local and the Global in Américo Paredes's World War II Poetry

Américo Paredes, who served as an enlisted reporter assigned to cover the U.S. occupation of Japan after World War II for the U.S. Army newspaper *Stars and Stripes*, further synthesizes Ramírez's internationalist concerns and López's contradictory nationalist conceits through his portrayal of a semi-autobiographical Mexican American GI subject—the *soldado razo* or buck private—as a palimpsest.[30] In his poetry about his military experiences and observations shortly after World War II, Paredes presents this figure simultaneously as an agent, subject, and potential enemy of capitalism and U.S. imperialism. Inexplicably, this dimension of his poetics has been overlooked or undertheorized in current criticism. For instance, scholars have entirely ignored *Cantos de Adolescencia*,

Paredes's first collection of poems written from 1934 to 1939. On the other hand, Ramón Saldívar, José Limón, José David Saldívar, Rafael Pérez-Torres, and others have celebrated *Between Two Worlds*, Paredes's second collection of poetry that covers the period from 1930 to 1970, as paradigmatic of Mexican American poetics for its counterhegemonic tone, its incorporation of indigenous rhythms and forms, and its purportedly postmodernist explorations of Mexican American hybridity.[31] However, even as these recent examinations of Paredes's work challenge simplistic constructions of the "Mexican American Generation" as "assimilationists," they nonetheless fail to provide a full assessment of his complex negotiation of identity and ideology in his verse. I argue that Paredes's poetic corpus as a whole illustrates Mexican American interpellation even as it gestures toward complex subaltern reconfigurations of Mexican American subjectivity that also are immanently Marxist and internationalist. Through complexly racialized and problematically gendered signifying practices, Paredes intersperses nostalgic regionalist and pantheistic paeans to South Texas and the Rio Grande region alongside poems that extend the performance of Mexican American spatial ontology beyond the U.S.-Mexican borderlands by relocating it onto a new geopoetic terrain that spans the area from Aztlán to South America and even from Arkansas to Asia and beyond. In this way, he offers an alternative reconstruction of Mexican American subjectivity that not only extends Ramírez's provocative relocations and López's inadvertent dislocations, but also anticipates and even pressures current American studies criticism on transnationalism.

From the opening pages of *Cantos de Adolescencia* and *Between Two Worlds*, Paredes resists the reification of the Mexican American subject as the hypermasculinist regional figure who looms significant in his later scholarship on the epic heroic corrido. Instead, he invokes the problematic trope of the tragic mestizo to illustrate how the ambiguous ontological space occupied by Mexican Americans is embedded with layers of material history. In poems such as "A México" (To Mexico, *CDA* 9), "Himno" (Hymn, *CDA* 10), and "México, la ilusión del continente" (Mexico, the Illusion of the Continent, *CDA* 11), as well as "The Mexico-Texan" (*BTW* 26–27), "Alma Pocha" (*BTW* 35–36), and the mixed-genre piece, "Tres Faces del Pocho" (Three Faces of the Pocho, *BTW* 38–45), Paredes employs Mexican American bilingual vernacular speech not so much as a celebratory performance of hybridity, as Pérez-Torres has suggested in *Movements in Chicano Poetry* (271). Rather, Paredes foregrounds his alternative reconstruction of Mexican American ontology by first rendering Mexican American subjectivity as tragically hybrid. In "The Mexico-Texan," for instance, he writes:

For the Mexico-Texan he no gotta lan',
He stomped on the neck on both sides of the Gran',
The dam gringo lingo he no cannot spik,
It twisters the tong and it make you fill sick.
A cit'zen of Texas they say that he ees,
But then, why they call him the Mexican Grease?
Soft talk and hard action, he can't understan',
The Mexico-Texan he no gotta lan'. (lines 5–12)

Scholars such as Homi Bhabha and Henry Louis Gates have invoked the Hegelian master-slave dialectic to convincingly argue that such linguistic transmutations enable "mimic men" or "vernacular intellectuals" to undermine the authority of the imperial power over its colonized subjects by disrupting the integrity of the colonialist narrative.[32] But I contend that Paredes mimics the Mexico-Texan's hybrid pidgin English to underscore his status as a tragic antihero whose bicultural and biracial heritage is as much a liability as it is an asset. In a sarcastic tone also known as *cábula* or *choteo*, which are Chicano and Afro-Cuban discursive practices akin to the double-voiced signifying that Gates and others have observed at work in African American literature and popular culture, Paredes repeatedly emphasizes that even though the Mexico-Texan has the "privilege" of celebrating two independence days—the American Fourth of July and the Mexican Sixteenth of September—"'He no gotta country, he no gotta flag.' / He no gotta voice, all he got is the han' / To work like the burro; he no gotta lan'" (lines 30–2).[33] Indeed, the Mexico-Texan is in a drunken stupor precisely because of the proliferation of "independence day" celebrations:

And only one way can his sorrows all drown,
He'll get drank as hell when next payday come aroun',
For he has one advantage of all other man,
Though the Mexico-Texan he no gotta lan'
He can get him so drank that he think he will fly
Both September the Sixteen and Fourth of July. (33–38)

In "The Borders of Modernity," Ramón Saldívar aptly notes that such passages reveal how Paredes "sought to create poetic figures to account for what some are today denoting as the postnational Latino subject in the midst of the subject's formation. This subject in process, the displaced and dispossessed object of official narratives of American history, the Mexican American that Paredes describes, existed in an empty discursive realm" (75). Following Saldívar as well as the observations that Lisa Lowe makes about the antithetical nature of Asian American citizenship that arises from racialist legislation throughout American history, I maintain that Paredes's Mexico-Texan also can be seen as a Mexican American permutation of the antithetical citizen: in the cruel circular logic of the lower Rio Grande region at the turn of the twentieth century that links land ownership to civic legitimacy, the dispossessed Pocho is consigned to the margins as a negative reference point who serves to buttress the limits of the English-language Anglo-capitalist norm. He is the embodiment of underdevelopment that enables the new capitalist empire to thrive.[34]

Paredes, however, invokes the problematic trope of the tragic mestizo to offer more than simply pathos-laden laments about hybrid subjectivity, as María Herrera-Sobek proposes in "Nation, Nationality, and Nationalism: Américo Paredes' Paradigms of Self and Country." I argue that "The Mexico-Texan," like the companion poems "México, la ilusión del continente" (*CDA* 11), in which the poet laments "I spend my twenty terrible years / confused about things Anglo and things Latino" (lines 5–6), and "Alma Pocha" (*BTW* 35), which represents the "Pocho," or acculturated subject, as "bloodied" and "sprinkled with tragedy" (lines 2, 7–8), collectively presents a historicist allegory on the peonage that follows the Treaty of Guadalupe-Hidalgo through which Mexico was forced to cede to the United States over one-half of its national territory—along with the inhabitants—at the end of the U.S.-Mexican War in 1848.[35] Indeed, in "México, la ilusión del continente," Paredes describes the Pocho in terms of national separation and ontological schism ("Life has thrown me onto foreign land / outside of my wounded country," lines 1, 4), as well as a longing for reunion ("you will be my light, the light that guides me, / the eagle, the cactus and the serpent," lines 29–30).[36] In this poem, as in others such as the sonnet "Flute Song" (*BTW* 24), in which the poetic persona laments, "Why was I ever born / Proud of my southern race, / If I must seek my sun / In an Anglo-Saxon face" (lines 5–8), the Mexican American subject is not actualized as the semifeudal social bandit supplicating for his own right with his pistol in his hand. Rather, Paredes's Mexican American subject is situated in the historical conflict between a semifeudal rural economy and the global rise of capitalism.

In the second stanza of "Alma Pocha," which is written entirely in

Spanish, Paredes explicates the contours of this interstitial space in materialist terms:

> En tu propio terruño serás extranjero
> por la ley del fusil y la ley del acero;
> y verás a tu padre morir balaceado
> por haber defendido el sudor derramado;
> verás a tu hermano colgado de un leño
> por el crimen mortal de haber sido trigueño.
> Y si vives, acaso, será sin orgullo,
> con recuerdos amargos de todo lo tuyo;
> tus campos, tus cielos, tus aves, tus flores
> serán el deleite de los invasores;
> para ellos su fruto dará la simiente,
> donde fueras el amo serás el sirviente.
>
> In your own land a foreigner you will be
> by the law of the rifle and the law of steel;
> and you'll see your father shot to death
> for having defended the fruits of his labor;
> you'll see your brother hung from a limb
> for the mortal crime of having been a farmer.
> And if perhaps you live, without pride it will be,
> with bitter memories of all that was yours;
> your lands, your skies, your birds, your flowers
> will be the delight of the invaders;
> for them your fruit will sprout
> where once you were master a servant you will be. (lines 10–23)[37]

Although the linguistic geography of Paredes's "Pocho" poems—which vacillate from monolingual English and Spanish to a code-switching vernacular hybridization of both—certainly renders Mexican American ontology as ambiguous, these poems clearly and deliberately propose a didactic meditation on the historical materialist subtext of Mexican American subjectivity through their invocation of the violent dispossession of Mexican Americans following the U.S.-Mexican War. More importantly, these poems perform a significant displacement of the warrior hero paradigm: by presenting him as hanging dead from a tree, without pride, and also working as a servant, Paredes provides a far more complex treatment of the performances of Mexican American subjectivity than the cultural nationalist discourses he adumbrates. Indeed, the balance of his poems about his experiences as a Mexican American soldier/subject read as a poetic meditation on utopian desire that ultimately challenges cultural nationalist and postmodernist readings of his verse.

In *Mexican Ballads/Chicano Poems*, and "Américo Paredes and the Transnational Imaginary," respectively, José Limón and Ramón Saldívar propose Paredes's 1935 poem "Guitarreros" (Guitarists, *BTW* 29) as an antiromance. They aptly note that it chronicles the passing of a feudal patriarchal order and the mass-scale introduction of capital that follows. I maintain that Paredes's poetic treatments of land and identity in this and other poems throughout *Cantos de Adolescencia* and *Between Two Worlds* also undergird a mapping of the contours of this new order and the new Mexican American ontological space within—and without—it. These poems show that within the new epistemical order of modern capitalism that this war inaugurates in the Americas, Mexican Americans are not only tragically ambiguous cultural agents and antithetical citizens, but also complexly situated transnational subjects whose identities are always already situated in a global struggle over the commodity fetish that has rendered them peons. Expanding upon Saldívar, who argues in "The Borders of Modernity" that "Paredes cites the local communal aspects of national culture, language, and race as the mainstays to freedom in contrast to Roosevelt's universalizing liberal ethico-political discourse of national unity that seeks to extend the local unity globally" (79), I believe that Paredes's verse also attempts to collapse the binary gap between the global and the local.

Indeed, in the very first poem in *Between Two Worlds*, "The Rio Grande" (*BTW* 15), which originally was published in Spanish in a slightly different form as "El Rio Bravo" in *Cantos de Adolescencia* (26) and subsequently served as Paredes's epitaph, the poet traffics in the rather clichéd but nonetheless significant pantheistic image of water.[38] His troping of water presents an allegorical discourse on the conflicted nature of Mexican American history that ultimately demands a more global relocation of Mexican American subjectivity. Paredes's English version of this 1934 poem begins:

Muddy river, muddy river,
Moving slowly down your track
With your swirls and counter-currents,
As though wanting to turn back. (lines 1–4)

This image of the Rio Grande fighting against itself corresponds to earlier characterizations of the tragic mestizo. However, when the conflicted Rio Grande is paired in the eighth stanza with an allusion to the ancient Euphrates River that runs near the biblical city of Baghdad (line 32), the symbol begins to resist the troubling essentialist notion of race that informs the tragic hybrid subject of other poems. Ironically, despite the poem's title, the composition deliberately gestures away from the continental United States, and even the U.S.-Mexican border region, as the quintessential performative space for Mexican American subjectivity. It is here that Paredes extends López's productive dislocations. Specifically, in this stanza Paredes's poetic persona is situated sleeping "by the margin of the sea" (line 36), where the Rio Grande empties into the ocean in "swirls and countercurrents," thereby linking the entire world—the ancient and the new—through the pantheistic trope of water. In *Border Matters*, José David Saldívar observes that Paredes's Rio Grande poems "replace[] conventional poetic topoi from the Western canon with South Texas–Mexico border ones" (56). I will add that the Rio Grande, which functions as a palimpsest embedded with the cultural capital of the Mississippi, and perhaps even the Thames, Rhine, Euphrates, Nile, and Amazon Rivers, thus enables Paredes to gesture outward from this South Texas–Mexican border by lyrically proposing that Mexican American subjectivity is performed at the turbulent intersection of the regional and the global. However clichéd this allusion may be, it ultimately permits a far more profound (though still problematic) synthesis of Mexican American ontology in yet other poems.

Paredes continues this transnationalist allusion in "Himno" (*CDA* 10) and "Night on the Flats" (1934—*BTW* 17). Both poems recall the pantheist nationalist poetics of Walt Whitman's 1892 *Leaves of Grass* as well as Whitman's anticolonialist analogues such as José Martí's nineteenth-century collection, *Versos Sencillos* (Simple Verses) and Pablo Neruda's 1950 anticolonialist long poem, *Canto General*, all of which were known to the poet. Moreover, his 1934 "El sueño de Bolivar" (Bolivar's Dream, *CDA* 12–13) and the 1939 ode "A César Augusto Sandino" (*BTW* 53) together extend the pastoral allusions toward a lyrical meditation on the political status of Mexican Americans in the world at large. In "El sueño de Bolivar," for instance, Paredes invokes one of the most revered nineteenth-century Latin American independence leaders by describing him as the "the son of Mexitli the Yaquís" (line 3).[39] That is, he links Bolivar to the war god of the native tribe that resides in the U.S.-Mexican borderlands from Arizona to California. As an anthropologist, Paredes was aware that many Mexican Americans claimed Yaqui ancestry. More importantly, he affirms that Bolivar's unrealized dream of uniting the Americas under one Latin American flag will one day be achieved:

No ha caído en tierra infértil
la semilla que sembraste
y que regada está con sangre;
lo que echaste tú a los mares
sobre las inquietas aguas
llegará a la playa un día.

It has not fallen on infertile land
the seed you sowed
and that is watered with blood;
that which you threw into the seas
over the turbulent waters
one day will arrive on the shore. (lines 35–40)

Significantly, these prophetic martial verses were written by a Mexican American poet who claimed to be not only a descendant of the original population of South Texas but also of a seditionist father who, Paredes notes in the epigraph to his 1958 *With A Pistol in His Hand: A Border Ballad and Its Hero*, "rode a raid or two" (np). That is, the poem suggests a confluence of the Latin American past with the Mexican American present through the figure of the male warrior hero. Even though this rhetorical move is undergirded by patriarchal conceits, these transhistorical and transnational associations enable Paredes to elevate the Pocho from his earlier status as a tragic figure of the U.S.-Mexican border to a potential hero of the Americas.

In "A César Augusto Sandino," another martial poem, written in 1939, fourteen years after "El sueño de Bolivar" and five years after Sandino's assassination by the U.S.-backed Somoza family dictatorship, the poet further synthesizes his Pan-Americanist gestures in terms of the Pan-American solidarity that José Martí proposes in his foundational 1891 treatise *Nuestra América* (Our America).[40] In this poem, Paredes pays homage to a figure renowned for his fight against the invasion and occupation of Nicaragua by the U.S. Marines in the 1920s. A generation later Sandino was adopted as a nationalist icon for the anticapitalist Sandinista National Liberation Front, which triumphed in 1979 and subsequently rewrote the country's national anthem to include a line that proclaims the United States as the "enemy of humanity." A similar anti-imperialist polemic is inscribed throughout Paredes's poem. In fact, his Spanish-language ode also includes a transnational recognition scene that provides yet another synthesis of Mexican American spatial ontology. Toward the middle of the poem, the author writes:

Tú desdeñaste el yugo. Yo te canto,
yo que he llorado y he sufrido tanto
el yugo colectivo de mi raza.
    You dismantled the yoke. I sing to you,
    I who have cried and have suffered so much
    the collective yoke of my people. (lines 9–11)

This linkage between a sovereign nation fighting against U.S. imperialism with Mexican Americans, who were civically constituted in a U.S. imperialist war the previous century, is a topos in Mexican American literature, especially war literature. In fact, Paredes's internationalist allusion is reminiscent of Alejandro Murguía's 1990 collection of testimonial fiction, *Southern Front*, which recounts his service as a Chicano internationalist volunteer in the Sandinista Revolution in the 1970s.[41] In both these texts, Mexican Americans are actualized as (Pan-)Americans through their identifications with Sandinistas. As such, the tragic mestizo trope of earlier poems is transformed as the past lament is now replaced by song. Significantly, whereas Paredes's contemporaries such as Saenz and López articulated ultrapatriotic poetic personas, Paredes characterizes the Mexican American subject as a potential transnational agrarian warrior hero who is decidedly anti–United States and immanently anticapitalist.[42]

Despite the recurrence of a masculinist gaze in poems such as "Gringa" (Whitegirl, *BTW* 107), "A una Sajona" (To an Anglo Woman, *CDA* 37), "Mercenaria" (Mercenary, *BTW* 78), and "Japonesa" (Japanese Girl, *BTW* 85), Paredes's verse can thus be read as a complex discourse on desire that relocates the Lacanian reflection onto a different racial and geopolitical topography—from the Americas to Asia—where Paredes spent almost a decade of his life after leaving the U.S. Army. That is, even as his poetry is infused with clichéd antagonistic depictions of Anglo women as beautiful yet treacherous ("A una Sajona") and exoticist descriptions about Asian women ("Japonesa") as having been "made for love" alongside empathetic love poems addressed to noble Mexican and Latina women, he also proposes an alternative to this fetish in other poems such as "Pro Patria" (*BTW* 84).[43] In this poem, Paredes invokes a cross-racial subaltern cadre of "my people" that pressures conventional cultural nationalist configurations of Mexican American identity while also proposing, at least provisionally, a resolution to his own commodification of women. The poem begins:

In the mud huts of China,
The tile-roofed paper houses of Japan,

In the straw-thatched jacales of old Mexico,
The rain-blackened shacks of Arkansas,

Here is my fatherland, these are my people,
My beloved,
Black, yellow, brown—
And even if their eyes are blue—

These are my people,
The bleeding wounds upon the feet and hard hands
Of humankind. (lines 1–11)

This poem, which seems to resist the ultranationalist inclinations alluded to in the title, privileges the subaltern of all countries: from the Third World battlefields of Asia to the hills of Arkansas in the American heartland. Significantly, the poet overcomes the racial binaries of his fetish poems by invoking the working and subaltern classes, the ones with "the bleeding wounds upon the feet and hard hands" (line 10). As if to emphasize this collapsing of racialist configurations of the poet's "people," he calls attention to his inclusion of whites by noting, in a pronounced enjambed line further accentuated by dashes at both ends, that "even if their eyes are blue," they are "my people" (line 8). Moreover, Paredes avoids the simplistic racialized and gendered binaries of other poems and instead juxtaposes the downtrodden masses with the "sleek bastards in the swallowtails, / They who can say which course the earth shall take, / How it should swing on its axis, / The sons-of-bitches in the striped pants" (lines 12–15). Although the epithet "sons-of-bitches" corresponds to the sexist metaphors in his other World War II poems, "Pro Patria" nonetheless ends with the author's poetic persona figuratively transcending his role as a male GI through new alliances with other subordinates of a hierarchical episteme like capitalism. The poem ends: "It is for this we breed / More numerous / Than a triumphant soldier's dreams" (lines 21–23). Here, breeding is disarticulated from the masculinist racialist signifying practices of his "love" poems and reconfigured as a transgressive act of cross-racial class solidarity free of the eugenicist notion of miscegenation. Instead, Paredes invokes the idea of a multiracial and transnational subaltern alliance through a Marxist methodology, which he develops in other poems as well as in his narratives. Similarly, both Ramón Saldívar and John Michael Rivera have made provocative linkages of Américo Paredes and Mexican American communist Emma Tenayuca, who served as a template for some of Paredes's short fiction.[44] "Pro Patria," when read in the context of the various recognition scenes that undergird much of his poetic corpus, indicates that Paredes—oftentimes figured as the quintessential precursor to Chicano cultural nationalism—was not only a transnationalist, but perhaps even an immanent Marxist internationalist.

Conclusion: Toward a Genealogy of the Mexican American Literary Left

Immediately after World War II—the conflict that enabled the United States to consolidate its status as the premier empire in the world—Américo Paredes proposes a radical model of Mexican American ontology that anticipates the work of yet other Mexican American soldier-authors in the 1950s and early 1960s, such as Rolando Hinojosa and Ricardo Sánchez. For instance, in *Korean Love Songs*, Hinojosa's collection of poetry based on his own combat experiences during the Korean War, Mexican American and other ethnic minority troops attempt to resolve their ambiguous status as minority GIs in a variety of troubling ways after their commanding officer—General Walker—links Mexican Americans with the North Korean enemy. Hinojosa's poem cites the actual army memo that ostensibly was designed to allay fears that the Chinese had entered the war, which reads in part: "We should not assume that / Chinese Communists are committed in force. / After all, a lot of Mexicans live in Texas" (lines 18–22).

In Hinojosa's subsequent narrative poems, minority troops like Jehú Malacara fanatically dedicate themselves to killing the enemy in the hope of proving their heroism. On the other hand, Lieutenant Brodsky, an American Jew, commits suicide because he simply refuses to engage in the unrestrained killing of a racialized enemy so soon after similar atrocities against his ancestors in World War II. Yet another character in Hinojosa's narrative verse, Sonny Ruiz, takes General Walker's linkage to the ultimate extreme by fleeing the battlefield and going into self-imposed exile in Japan, where he marries a Japanese woman and assimilates into Japanese society. He thereby becomes the paradigmatic Mexican American–cum–Asian enemy/ally who will find his analogues in the Chicano literature of the Vietnam War.[45] Rather than merely illustrating how a cultural nationalist model of Mexican American identity is radically inchoate and ideologically unstable, Hinojosa's war poetry, like the other war poetry by Ramírez, López, and Paredes, in fact demands a more complex assessment of Mexican American ontology that reconciles the local, highly regional contours of Mexican American identity with the global, transnational, and immanently internationalist performances of it.

Ricardo Sánchez, an army veteran from the 1950s who came to be renowned as a Chicano convict or Pinto poet in the 1960s and 1970s, proposes the syncresis that enables this tense balance. Often derisively described as an ultranationalist "Movement poet," Sánchez actually proposes a radical revision of the central metaphor in Chicana/o cultural nationalist discourse—the barrio. In "Barrios of the World," cited as the epigraph to this essay, Sánchez didactically explains why the dislocations proposed by the authors above are in fact necessary and productive. His depiction of the "barrios of the world" as subaltern archipelagoes of poverty and subordination deliberately signals an inalienable link between racial abjection and underclass status in the United States. He thus foregrounds other linkages across time and place. Renowned for his militant poetics and attendant activist participation in groups such as the Brown Berets and La Resistencia, the immigrant rights arm of the Revolutionary Communist Party, USA, Sánchez follows and extends the poetic discourses on Mexican American spatial ontology by the aforementioned poets. Despite being a Tejano himself, Sánchez proclaims that Chicano ontology is located in the "barrios of the world / where rich and poor separate." He adds that the attendant paradoxes and contradictions—the hallmark of the Mexican American milieu—presage "a new world" in which identity is constructed not merely in terms of race, ethnicity, or even regionalism, nationalism, and transnationalism, but rather through new priorities that are fundamentally materialist and internationalist.

Notes

1. Although "Mexican American" and "Chicana/o" are sometimes used interchangeably, I make a distinction between the two. In this study, "Mexican American" is a descriptive term that refers to the Mexican descent population living in the United States from the end of the U.S.-Mexican War in 1848. "Chicana/o," which gained a counterhegemonic resonance in the 1960s and 1970s during the Chicana/o civil rights movement, generally refers to the post-1960s generations of Mexican Americans. My reference to Mexican and American Chicana/o literary history corresponds to these distinctions.

2. See Padilla; Rosaura Sánchez; Gonzales-Berry; and Rebolledo; as well as Rebolledo and Márquez.

3. See especially Sánchez and Pita's discussion of the complex negotiations of power and subordination by nineteenth-century Mexican and Mexican American women in the introduction to Amparo Ruiz de Burton's novel, *The Squatter and the Don*.

4. For general overviews of the debates about globalization and transnationalism in American studies, see the 2000 special issue of *American Studies* edited by Yetman and Katzman, as well as the 1998 special issue of *Cultural Critique* edited by Wiegman. For explorations of the complex intersections between transnationalism, feminism, and ethnic studies, see Kaplan, Alarcón, and Moallem.

5. See Olguín, "Sangre Mexicana/Corazón Americano."

6. For examples of this reductive generational paradigm, see Leal and Raymond Paredes.

7. For a related critique of transnationalism, see Marcial Gonzalez's critique on the ideological contradictions and postmodernist conceits in borderlands theory.

8. Though scholars such as Ernest Chavez and journalist Elizabeth Martinez provide lucid examples of Chicano Leftist activism across time and place, no one has yet to produce a thorough history of the Chicana/o and Latina/o literary Left. Alan Wald's preliminary mappings in *Writing from the Left*, as well as in "The 1930s Left in U.S. Literature Reconsidered," provide a compelling blueprint for such a study even as he fails to distinguish *Latinesca* literature (i.e., the literature produced by non-Latina/os) with Latina/o-authored texts.

9. Mexican American soldiers are renowned for having earned the highest number of Medals of Honor per capita than any other racial or ethnic group in the United States. Many of these medals were awarded posthumously.

10. For a critique of the ideological conceits inherent to the male warrior hero paradigm, see Chabram-Dernersesian, "I Throw Punches." Pérez-Torres presents such a celebratory treatment of Chicana/o hybridity in *Chicano Poetry*, whereas Arteaga provides a historicist alternative in *Chicano Poetics*.

11. See Ramón Saldívar, *Chicano Narrative*, and Limón, *Mexican Ballads*.

12. See Saldívar-Hull; Chabram-Dernersesian; and Herrera-Sobek, *Mexican Corrido*.

13. For a critique of the reactionary tendencies and limited revolutionary potential of social bandits vis-à-vis rebels and revolutionaries, see Hobsbawm, *Bandits*, *Primitive Rebels*, and *Revolutionaries*.

14. For an example of recent attempts to recenter the nineteenth-century bourgeois Mexican American subject, see Aranda.

15. For arguments that the U.S.-Mexican War was the result of racism such as the white supremacist idea of Manifest Destiny, see Mirandé and Acuña. For a Marxist interpretation of the economic causes of the war and its legacy, see Barrera.

16. See Zamora, Hernandez, and Hernandez-Tovar.

17. Malintzín, also known by the epithet "La Malinche," was Hernan Cortez's translator and mother to his children. For a critical overview of the status of this historical figure in Mexican and Chicana thought, see Alarcón. For a review of Malintzín in Mexican and Chicana literature, see Messinger Cypess. Sor Juana Inés de la Cruz was a sixteenth-century nun in colonial Mexico renowned for her bilingual and feminist poetry and plays. For a Chicana feminist recuperation of this historical figure, see Gaspar de Alba.

18. Cited in Hernandez-Tovara 159–61. Unless otherwise noted, all page numbers for and translations of Ramírez's poems are from Hernandez-Tovar.

19. For PLM insurgent activities, see also Gómez-Quiñones.

20. For excerpts of Ramírez's speeches, see Hernandez-Tovar 189.

21. For the gynocritical poetics and materialist politics in Chicana poetry, see Olguín, "Mothers, Daughters, and Deities."

22. See Lenin's thesis on national minorities in his *State and Revolution.*

23. There is no pagination of López's poem, which appears as one of several appendices to Sanez's text.

24. See Trujillo, *Soldados* and *Dogs from Illusion.* See also Cano.

25. For a broader discussion of Seguín, see De La Teja; for Chacón, see Dorgan Meketa; for Tafolla, see Padilla.

26. For a general history of LULAC, see Márquez.

27. For this episode, see De La Teja.

28. Unless otherwise noted, all translations of López's poem are mine.

29. For a similar troping of Mexican American self-sacrifice and citizenship, see Mike Stroot's 1985 documentary film, *Hero Street, U.S.A.*

30. Paredes served in the U.S. Army from 1940 to 1946 and subsequently worked for the army and the Red Cross as a uniformed civilian. For more biographical information on Paredes, see Limón, "Américo Paredes" and *Mexican Ballads*; Ramón Saldívar, "Américo Paredes"; and Calderón and López-Morin.

31. See Ramón Saldívar, "Borders of Modernity"; Limón, *Mexican Ballads*; José David Saldívar, *Border Matters* and "Looking Awry at 1898"; and Pérez-Torres. All subsequent references to *Between Two Worlds* in the text will be indicated as *BTW* and *Cantos de Adolescencia* as *CDA.* Unless otherwise noted, all translations are mine.

32. See Gates and José David Saldívar, "Looking Awry at 1898." For an overview of various models of hybridity and liminality, see Ashcroft, Griffiths, and Tiffin.

33. *Cábula*, which refers to the Chicano creative and oftentimes sexualized word play and punning, is common among Chicano convict poets such as Ricardo Sánchez. For a discussion of *choteo*, see José David Saldívar, "Looking Awry at 1898."

34. See Lowe.

35. For a general discussion of the U.S.-Mexican War and the Treaty of Guadalupe-Hidalgo, see Griswold del Castillo.

36. The original Spanish verses are: "En tierra ajena me arrojó la vida / fuera de mi patria herida," and "será mi luz, la estrella que me guía, / el águila, el nopal y la serpiente."

37. This translation borrows from Ramón Saldívar's in "Borders of Modernity."

38. Medrano tells us that this poem was read as Paredes's ashes were released into the mouth of the Rio Grande.

39. The original Spanish-language verse is "hijo del Mexitli el Yaqui."

40. For comparative analyses of U.S. minority literatures and Martí's Pan-Americanist discourses, see José David Saldívar, *Dialectics of Our America*, and Pytell, "Comparative American Studies."

41. For Murguía's testimonial fiction, see Olguín, "Sangre Mexicana."

42. For an overview and critique of the generational paradigm that Paredes disrupts, see Mendoza.

43. Several love poems in *Cantos de Adolescencia* and *Between Two Worlds* are addressed to Mexican and Latina women. *Between Two Worlds* also includes poems to his Uruguayan Japanese wife. For a critique of Paredes's masculinist homosocial poetics, see Olguín, "Reassessing Pocho Poetics."

44. According to Saldívar, Tenayuca served as the template for the central character in Paredes's short story, "The Hammon and the Beans."

45. For these Asian and Mexican American encounters, see Mariscal, *Aztlán*, and Olguín, "Sangre Mexicana."

Works Cited

Acuña, Rodolfo. *Occupied America: A History of Chicanos*. 3d ed. New York: Harper and Row, 2000.

Alarcón, Norma. "Traddutora, traditora: A Paradigmatic Figure of Chicana Feminism." *Cultural Critique* 13 (Fall 1989): 57–87.

Anzaldúa, Gloria. *Borderlands/La Frontera: The New Mestiza*. San Francisco: Aunt Lute Press, 1987.

Aranda, José F. "Contradictory Impulses: María Amparo Ruiz de Burton, Resistance Theory, and the Politics of Chicano/a Studies." *American Literature* 70.3 (Fall 1998): 551–79.

Arteaga, Alfred. *Chicano Poetics: Heterotexts and Hybridities*. Cambridge: Cambridge University Press, 1997.

Ashcroft, Bill, Gareth Griffiths, and Helen Tiffin. *The Empire Writes Back: Theory and Practice in Post-Colonial Literatures*. New York: Routledge, 1989.

Barrera, Mario. *Race and Class in the Southwest: A Theory of Radical Inequality*. Notre Dame, Ind.: University of Notre Dame Press, 1979.

Benavidez, Roy P., and John R. Craig. *Medal of Honor: A Vietnam Warrior's Story*. Washington, D.C.: Brassey's, 1995.

Benavidez, Roy P., and Oscar Griffin. *The Three Wars of Roy Benavidez*. San Antonio: Corona Publishing Co., 1986.

Bhabha, Homi. "Of Mimicry and Man: The Ambivalence of Colonial Discourse." *October* 28 (Spring 1984): 125–33.

Bruce-Novoa, Juan. *Chicano Poetry: A Response to Chaos*. Austin: University of Texas Press, 1982.

Calderón, Héctor, and José Rósbel López-Morin. "Interview with Américo Paredes." *Nepantla* 1.1 (2000): 197–228.

Candelaria, Cordelia. *Chicano Poetry: A Critical Introduction*. Westport, Conn.: Greenwood Press, 1986.

Cano, Daniel. *Shifting Loyalties*. Houston, Tex.: Arte Público Press, 1995.

Chabram-Dernersesian, Angie. "I Throw Punches for My Race, but I Don't Want to Be a Man: Writing Us—Chica-nos (Girl, Us)/Chicanas—into the Movement Script." *Cultural Studies*. Ed. Lawrence Grossberg, Cary Nelson, and Paula A. Treichler. New York: Routledge, 1992. 81–95.

Chavez, Ernest. "Imagining the Mexican Immigrant Worker: (Inter)Nationalism, Identity, and Insurgency in the Chicano Movement in Los Angeles." *Aztlán* 25.2 (Fall 2000): 109–35.

De La Teja, Jesús F., trans. and ed. *A Revolution Remembered: The Memoirs and Selected Correspondence of Juan N. Seguín*. Austin: State House Press, 1991.

Dorgan Meketa, Jacqueline. *Legacy of Honor: The Life of Rafael Chacón, a Nineteenth-Century New Mexican*. Albuquerque: University of New Mexico Press, 1986.

Gaspar de Alba, Alicia. "The Politics of Location of the Tenth Muse of America: An Interview with Sor Juana Inés de la Cruz." *Living Chicana Theory*. Ed. Carla Trujillo. Berkeley, Calif.: Third Woman Press, 1998. 136–65.

Gates, Henry Louis. *The Signifying Monkey: A Theory of Afro-American Literary Criticism*. New York: Oxford University Press, 1988.

Gómez-Quiñones, Juan. *Sembradores, Ricardo Flores Magón y El Partido Liberal Mexicano: A Eulogy and Critique*. Los Angeles: Aztlán Publications, 1973.

Gonzalez, Marcial. "The 'Borderlands' as Cultural Identity in Chicana/o Literary Studies: A Dialectical Critique." *Twentieth-Century Americanisms: The Left and Modern Literatures of the United States*. Ed. James Smethurst and Bill V. Mullen. Chapel Hill: University of North Carolina Press, 2002.

Gonzales-Berry, Erlinda. *Pasó por aquí: Critical Essays on the New Mexican Literary Tradition, 1542–1988*. Albuquerque: University of New Mexico Press, 1989.

Griswold del Castillo, Richard. *The Treaty of Guadalupe-Hidalgo: A Legacy of Conflict*. Norman: University of Oklahoma Press, 1990.

Hernandez, Inés. "Sara Estela Ramírez: Sembradora." *Legacy: A Journal of Nineteenth-Century American Women Writers* 6.1 (1989): 13–26.

Hernandez-Tovar, Inés. "Sara Estela Ramírez: The Early-Twentieth-Century Texas-Mexican Poet." Doctoral diss. University of Houston, 1984.

Herrera-Sobek, María. *The Mexican Corrido: A Feminist Perspective*. Bloomington: University of Indiana Press, 1990.

———. "Nation, Nationality, and Nationalism: Américo Paredes' Paradigms of Self and Country." Keynote address, Pasó por aquí: Américo Paredes Symposium, Austin, May 3, 2001.

Hinojosa (Smith), Rolando. *Korean Love Songs*. Berkeley, Calif.: Editorial Justa, 1978.

Hobsbawm, Eric J. *Bandits*. London: Delacort, 1969.

———. *Primitive Rebels*. Manchester, U.K.: Manchester University Press, 1959.

———. *Revolutionaries*. New York: Pantheon, 1973.

Kaplan, Caren, Norma Alarcón, and Minoo Moallem, eds. *Between Woman and Nation: Nationalisms, Transnational Feminisms, and the State*. Durham, N.C.: Duke University Press, 1999.

Lacan, Jacques. *Ecrits*. Paris: Seuil, 1968.

Leal, Luis. "Mexican American Literature: A Historical Perspective." *Modern Chicano Writers: A Collection of Critical Essays*. Ed. Joseph Sommers and Tomás Ybarra-Frausto. Englewood Cliffs, N.J.: Prentice-Hall, 1979. 18–30.

Lenin, Vladimir I. *The State and Revolution*. New York: International Publishers, 1935.

Limón, José E. "Américo Paredes: A Man from the Border." *Revista Chicano-Riqueña* 8.3 (Summer 1980): 1–5.

———. *Dancing with the Devil: Society and Cultural Poetics in Mexican American South Texas*. Madison: University of Wisconsin Press, 1994.

———. *Mexican Ballads/Chicano Poems: History and Influence in Mexican American Social Poetry*. Madison: University of Wisconsin Press, 1992.

López, Margil. "To the Memory of the Mexican American Heroes (Who Died in the Great War, Defending the Democratic Principles of the American Union." J. Luz Saenz, *Los Mexico-Americanos en la Gran Guerra: Y su contingente en pro de la democracia, la humanidad, y la justicia*. San Antonio, Tex.: Artes Gráficas, 1933. np.

Lowe, Lisa. "The International within the National: American Studies and Asian American Critique." *Cultural Critique* 40 (Fall 1998): 29–47.

Lucero, Judy A. "Humilidad" [*sic*]. *La Palabra* 2.2 (Primavera) (1980): 90.

———. "Ocho poemas de amor y desesperación." *De Colores* 3.1 (1976): 57–58.

———. "Memoriam: Poems of Judy A. Lucero." *De Colores* 1.1 (Winter 1973): 71–79.

Mariscal, George. *Aztlán and Viet Nam: Chicano and Chicana Experiences of the War*. Berkeley: University of California Press, 1999.

———. "The Role of Working-Class Latinos/as as Cannon Fodder for the Next Century." Conference presentation, Twenty-eighth Annual Conference of the National Association for Chicana and Chicano Studies, Tucson, Ariz., April 7, 2001.

Marquez, Benjamin. *LULAC: The Evolution of a Mexican American Political Organization*. Austin: University of Texas Press, 1993

Martí, José. "Our America." *Heath Anthology of American Literature*, 2d ed. Ed. Paul Lauter. Lexington, Mass.: Heath, 1994. 821–29.

Martinez, Elizabeth. *De Colores Means All of Us: Latina Views for a Multi-Colored Century*. Cambridge: South End Press, 1998.

Maxwell, William J. *New Negro, Old Left: African-American Writing and Communism between the Wars*. New York: Columbia University Press, 1999.

McKenna, Teresa. *Migrant Song: Politics and Process in Contemporary Chicano Literature*. Austin: University of Texas Press, 1997.

Mendoza, Louis G. "Confronting *la Frontera*, Identity, and Gender: Poetry and Politics in *La Crónica* and *El Demócrata Fronterizo*." *Recovering the U.S. Hispanic Literary Heritage*. Vol. 3. Ed. María Herrera-Sobek and Virginia Sánchez Korrol. Houston, Tex.: Arte Público Pres, 2000. 103–23.

Messinger Cypess, Sandra. *La Malinche in Mexican Literature: From History to Myth*. Austin: University of Texas Press, 1991.

Mirandé, Alfredo. *Gringo Justice*. Notre Dame, Ind.: Notre Dame University Press, 1987.

Morin, Raul. *Among the Valiant: Mexican Americans in WW II and Korea*. Los Angeles: Borden Publishing, 1963.

Neruda, Pablo. *Canto General*. Trans. Jack Schmitt. Berkeley: University of California Press, 1991.

Olguín, B. V. "Mothers, Daughters, and Deities: Judy Lucero's Gynocritical Poetics and Materialist Politics." *Frontiers* 22.2 (2001): 63–86.

———. "Reassessing Pocho Poetics: Américo Paredes' Poetry and the (Trans)National Question." Under consideration, *PMLA*.

———. "Sangre Mexicana/Corazón Americano: Identity, Ambiguity, and Critique in Mexican American War Narratives." *American Literary History* 14.1 (Spring 2002): 83–114.

Padilla, Genaro. *My History, Not Yours: The Formation of Mexican American Autobiography*. Madison: University of Wisconsin Press, 1993.

Paredes, Américo. *Between Two Worlds*. Houston, Tex.: Arte Público Press, 1991.

———. *Cantos de adolescencia*. San Antonio, Tex.: N.p., 1936. Copies located in the Nettie Lee Benson Latin American Collection, University of Texas at Austin.

———. *With His Pistol in His Hand: A Border Ballad and Its Hero*. Austin: University of Texas Press, 1958.

Paredes, Raymond. "Mexican-American Literature: An Overview." *Recovering the U.S. Hispanic Literary Heritage*. Ed. Ramón Gutierrez and Genaro Padilla. Houston, Tex.: Arte Público Press, 1993. 31–51.

Pérez-Torres, Rafael. *Movements in Chicano Poetry: Against Myths, Against Margins*. Cambridge: Cambridge University Press, 1995.

Pytell, Cyrus R. K. "Comparative American Studies: Hybridity and Beyond." *American Literary History* 11 (1999): 166–86.

Rebolledo, Tey Diana. *Women Singing in the Snow: A Cultural Analysis of Chicana Literature.* Tucson: University of Arizona Press, 1995.

Rebolledo, Tey Diana, and María Teresa Márquez, *Women's Tales from the New Mexico WPA: La Diabla a Pie.* Houston, Tex.: Arte Público Press, 2000.

Rodriguez, Elena. *Peacetime: Spirit of the Eagle.* San Jose, Calif.: Chusma House, 1997.

Salas, Elizabeth. *Soldaderas in the Mexican Military: Myth and History.* Austin: University of Texas Press, 1990.

Saldívar, José David. *Border Matters: Remapping American Cultural Studies.* Berkeley: University of California Press, 1997.

———. *The Dialectics of Our America: Genealogy, Cultural Critique, and Literary History.* Durham, N.C.: Duke University Press, 1991.

———. "Looking Awry at 1898: Roosevelt, Montejo, Paredes, and Mariscal." *American Literary History* 12.3 (2000): 387–406.

Saldívar, Ramón. "Américo Paredes." *Updating the Literary West.* Ed. Thomas J. Lyon. Fort Worth: Texas Christian University Press, 1997. 633–37.

———. "Américo Paredes and the Transnational Imaginary." Brackenridge Distinguished Lecture, University of Texas at San Antonio, February 22, 2001.

———. "Bordering on Modernity: Américo Paredes's *Between Two Worlds* and the Imagining of Utopian Social Space." *Stanford Humanities Review* 3.1 (1993): 54–66.

———. "The Borders of Modernity: Américo Paredes's *Between Two Worlds* and the Chicano National Subject." *The Ethnic Canon: Histories, Institutions, and Interventions.* Minneapolis: University of Minnesota Press, 1995. 71–87.

———. *Chicano Narrative: The Dialectics of Difference.* Madison: University of Wisconsin Press, 1990.

Saldívar-Hull, Sonia. *Feminism on the Border: Chicana Gender Politics and Literature.* Berkeley: University of California Press, 2000.

Sánchez, Ricardo. "Barrios of the World." *Selected Poems.* Houston, Tex.: Arte Público Press, 1985. 51–2.

Sánchez, Rosaura. *Telling Identities: The Californio Testimonios.* Minneapolis: University of Minnesota Press, 1995.

Sánchez, Rosaura, and Beatrice Pita. Introduction. *The Squatter and the Don.* Ed. Rosaura Sánchez and Beatrice Pita. Houston, Tex.: Arte Público Press, 1997.

Smethurst, James. *The New Red Negro: The Literary Left and African American Poetry, 1930–1946.* New York: Oxford University Press, 1999.

Stroot, Mike, Director and Producer. *Hero Street, U.S.A.* St. Louis: Busch Creative Services Corp., 1984.

Trujillo, Charlie. *Dogs from Illusion.* San Jose, Calif.: Chusma House, 1994.

———. *Soldados: Chicanos in Vietnam.* San Jose, Calif.: Chusma House, 1990.

Vélez-Ibáñez, Carlos. *Border Visions: Mexican Cultures of the Southwest United States.* Tucson: University of Arizona Press, 1996.

Villanueva, Alma. *Blood Root.* Austin: Place of Herons Press, 1977.

Wald, Alan M. "The 1930s Left in U.S. Literature Reconsidered." *Radical Revisions: Rereading 1930s Culture.* Ed. Bill V. Mullen and Sherry Lee Linkon. Urbana: University of Illinois Press, 1996. 13–28.

———. *Writing from the Left: New Essays on Radical Culture and Politics*. London: Verso, 1994.

Wald, Priscilla. "Minefields and Meeting Grounds: Transnational Analyses and American Studies." *American Literary History* 10.1 (Spring 1998): 216.

Whitman, Walt. *Leaves of Grass*. New York: Bantam Books, 1983.

Wiegman, Robyn. "Introduction: The Futures of American Studies." *Cultural Critique* (1998): 5–9.

Yetman, Norman R., and David M. Katzman. "Globalization, Transnationalism, and the End of the American Century." *American Studies* 41.2–3 (Summer–Fall 2000): 5–12.

Zamora, Emilio. "Sara Estela Ramírez: Una Rosa Roja en el movimiento." *Mexican Women in the United States: Struggles Past and Present*. Ed. Magdalena Mora and Adelaida R. Del Castillo. Los Angeles: Chicano Studies Research Center Publications, University of California at Los Angeles, 1980.

The radical Left of the 1940's and 1950's was not a movement of Anglo-Saxons or their ideology. It was an ethnic movement dominated by Negroes and Jews, and it was the Jews who ideologically influenced the Negroes.
—Harold Cruse, *The Crisis of the Negro Intellectual*

Alan Wald

Narrating Nationalisms: Black Marxism and Jewish Communists through the Eyes of Harold Cruse

From *Crusade* to *Crisis*

In the fall of 1947 left-wing African American novelist Chester Himes (1909–84) endured a "hurt" that profoundly altered the direction of his literary and personal life. Prior to that time, he felt invigorated by the modest success of *If He Hollers Let Him Go* (1945), his proletarian novel about racial and sexual tensions in the wartime Los Angeles workforce. He thus looked forward with excitement to the publication of his new, four-hundred-page, gut-wrenching, sensational psychological thriller—*The Lonely Crusade* (1947)—about the association of blacks and Jews in the Communist movement. The topic anticipates by twenty years a large part of Harold Cruse's *Crisis of the Negro Intellectual* (1967), albeit the methods and conclusions of the two narratives, one marketed as fiction and the other as scholarship, are notably different. Furthermore, early in the new millennium, the magnitude of curiosity among contemporary scholars and activists about this past alliance of black and Jewish radicalism, and the inheritance of Black Marxism, is unrivaled by any preceding generation.[1]

Scholars now agree that *Lonely Crusade* is Himes's masterwork. It is his most daring self-revelation, an attempt to infuse the dramatic strategies of fictional narrative with a social and philosophical vision equal to, if not transcending, Richard Wright's *Native Son* (1940). Psychologically, *Lonely Crusade* is a confessional autobiography; intellectually, a political and social analysis of racial, gender, and ethnic relations; and ideologically, a personal testament of revolutionary faith.[2]

In his two-volume autobiography, *The Quality of Hurt* (1972) and *My Life of Absurdity* (1976), Himes refrains from discussing his four years as a laborer (1940–44) in Los Angeles, as well as his role as a sometime sympathizer and possibly even brief member of the Communist Party probably beginning in Cleveland in the late 1930s and ending in Los Angeles in the early 1940s. He had, after all, already dramatized his experiences in his first two novels. In later interviews, he acknowledged that the black and Jewish Communist characters in *Lonely Crusade* were modeled on identifiable Leftists, and the events in the life of protagonist Lee Gordon were based on his own experiences.[3]

Lonely Crusade brought disaster from every quarter. Himes's wife, Jean, against his wishes, secretly read part of the manuscript while they were staying in a shack on the California-Nevada state line. Believing that she was the basis of the character Ruth, betrayed wife of Lee Gordon, she fled into the mountains. Found there hours later in a dazed condition, she declared that the marriage was over. Himes believed that this was a decisive factor in the deterioration of their relationship, which ended three years later.[4] Moreover, sales were less than his first novel (4,000 copies at best, as opposed to about 7,000 for *If He Hollers Letter Him Go*), publicity events were canceled, and the anticipated hostility from the Communist press was joined by bitter denunciations from black and Jewish publications.[5]

A quarter of a century later, meditating on reactions to the risk he had taken in this novel in frankly confronting "the truth," Himes wrote: "Of all the hurts which I had suffered before—my brother's accident [blindness due to an explosion for which Himes felt responsible], my own accident [falling down an elevator shaft and permanently damaging his back], being kicked out of college, my parents' divorce, my term in prison, and my racial hell on the West Coast—and which I have suffered since, the rejection of *The Lonely Crusade* hurt me the most. Because I had gone out on that limb."[6] As a result, he decided to leave the United States.

He also began suffering from a five-year writers' block before reemerging as a novelist who had distanced himself from the radical, proletarian tradition.

A first reading of *Lonely Crusade* might appear to confirm Cruse's famous argument *Crisis* that the postdepression Communist movement was at its core a tense alliance of Jewish Americans and African Americans, the former serving as chief ideologists. In *Lonely Crusade*, the Communist movement is the only game in town for radicalizing black workers, and the leading left-wing philosopher is Abe Rosenberg (Rosie), an elderly member of the Jewish Communist Party. The most fully developed black Communist, Luther McGregor, is a skilled rank and filer who carries out his assignment to befriend Lee (a neophyte union organizer who attempts to win the pro-union vote of white and black workers at an aircraft plant), loyally implementing whatever line his ideologists have determined.[7]

Moreover, throughout the novel, as is the case in Cruse's *Crisis*, where blacks and Jews are referred to as the "two nationalisms," Jews are nearly always described as the most numerous ethnic group in the Communist Left. Indeed, in the eyes of protagonist Lee, Jews share many personality traits that especially fit them for Party membership. At one point, in a line that could have come from *Crisis*, Lee declares to Rosie: "You know, Rosie, you always have the answer. Is it the Jew in you or the Communist?"[8]

On the other hand, there are symptomatic divergences. For Himes's Lee Gordon, the "Semitic stereotype" has certain unattractive physical features, something that Cruse never remotely suggests. Rosie, for example, is "the picture of the historic Semite"—short, fat, with a bald head and "frog-like" body. Party functionary Maud Himmelstein, "as Jewish in appearance as the Jewish stereotype," is "mannish-appearing," with a rasping voice and the stub of an arm that jerks spasmodically. Further, in arguments with Rosie, Lee gives vent to anti-Semitic charges that extend far beyond even the most unpleasant innuendos of *Crisis*. Lee insists that Jewish greed has confined blacks to ghettos, Jewish mothers spoil their sons, and Jews are generally more antiblack than white Christians.[9]

It is difficult not to be offended by all the anti-Semitic statements that spew from the lips of Himes's main character (and the ugly visual images that form in his mind), and not to be skeptical of the Machiavellian villainy that Himes attributes to the Party.[10] Yet *Lonely Crusade* ultimately strives to explode what I call the "group caricature"—the conflation of diverse individuals to a common behavioral pattern by virtue of ethnicity, race, gender, or class—to which Lee and other characters are held victim.

In fact, as the plot lunges relentlessly through catastrophe after catastrophe, Rosie steps outside the Jewish stereotype to emerge as the moral center of the narrative. A devoted Party member, he challenges Party authority on behalf of Lee, even though it results in Rosie's own expulsion. When Lee, facing a police frame-up for the murder of a racist officer, feels abandoned and sinks into a swamp of despair, Rosie finds him and nurtures him back to life. In the process Rosie imbues him with the revolutionary Marxist (but non–Communist Party) philosophy that Lee ultimately appropriates in his own way to allow his psychological reintegration and his self-determined actions at the climax of the work.

A parallel evolution occurs in the character of the black Communist, Luther. Initially, Luther seems to reaffirm two anti-Communist stereotypes, that of the "dupe" and of the cynical manipulator of others. Even worse, his appearance, in Lee's eyes, reproduces the most disgusting white racist stereotypes that parody the African American as an "ape" and a sex machine. However, as the novel gathers steam toward its climax, Luther is revealed as an individualist (first) and black nationalist (second), with powers of self-control and native intelligence that outdistance all other characters in the book. A strong hint that Lee's antiblack, anti-Communist racist stereotype of Luther is a naive oversimplification comes earlier in the novel. Luther steps forward to sing the full text of "Signifyin' Monkey" before a group of black workers, quelling their disunity and establishing his community links. At the end, he adds the significant final statement, "Thass me!"[11]

The surface narrative of *Lonely Crusade* thus bombards the reader with outrageous images of Jews, blacks, Communists, and white women.[12] But the ideology of the text can be interpreted as a courageous—if highly problematic—effort to transcend narrow group caricature, even while recognizing the powerful emotional reality of the "dirty hell of race."[13] Lee Gordon is a black man who transcends the illusion of finding his masculinity through the sexual conquest of white women. This transcendence comes about through a combination of bitter experiences, observation of the actions of his union comrades (especially the heroic Joe Ptak and the loyal Smittie), and Rosie's philosophizing; it occurs at the precise historical moment of the industrialization of the multinational workforce in Los Angeles. What Lee learns is that authentic dignity and manhood can be acquired by playing a vanguard role in the larger cause of the militant class struggle, which objectively benefits the short- and long-range interests of African Americans as well.[14] In the final scene, the lineup of the union against the police impels every character who identifies with the union, including the racist president of the local, to unite in protecting Lee from arrest. Even his enemies in the Communist Party are driven by necessity to join the struggle.

In contrast, Cruse's *Crisis* moves in the opposite direction. It commences with a welcome attempt to render Marxist analysis more sophisticated by shifting from mechanistic class explanations to historical materialist ideas about the centrality of culture and ethnicity; the latter are adapted from V. F. Calverton's refreshing 1920s writings on "Cultural Compulsives" (cultural tendencies of collectives) and Milton Gordon's 1964 *Assimilation in American Life* (which views Protestants, Catholics, and Jews as the three main power groups). Within a short time, however, Cruse reveals himself to be a far greater prisoner of vulgar group caricature regarding the reification of imagined and exaggerated cultural traits of ethnicities than the Communist Party ever was in its reductive use of class analysis. Moreover, Cruse projects conspiratorial and invidious motives onto his various targets, who are mainly Jews, Caribbean blacks, and African American Marxists. His view is not merely that "Jews . . . ideologically influenced the Negroes" in the Communist Party. He goes much further: "The radical Left in America has developed in such a way that the Jewish ethnic group, one of the smallest in the country, had more political prestige, wielded more theoretical and organizational power, than the Negro who in fact represented the largest ethnic minority. Consequently, all political and cultural standards on the radical Left were in the main established and enforced by Jews for, and on, Negroes."[15] For Cruse's narrative, the roots of this situation can be traced to the late 1920s. At that time, myriad scholars believe, the CPUSA underwent a progressive transformation into an increasingly dependent acolyte of Stalin's Soviet foreign policy, following the expulsion of the majority leadership steered by Jay Lovestone, who was associated with Bukharin's "Right Opposition" political current in the Soviet Union.[16] Cruse, instead, saw the seeds of the Party's destruction planted by its Caribbean-born black members, whose psychological hang-ups as a group prevented them from developing political and cultural leadership. This paved the way for Jewish control.[17]

The "Jewish Crusade"

At the time of its publication, Cruse's book was called anti-Semitic by a few left-wing reviewers such as *Black Scholar* editor Robert Chrisman, but the specifics of his treatment of Jewish Communists in *Crisis* have never been discussed.[18] The charge of anti-Semitism is complicated by Cruse's eschewing any biological explanation for Jewish group behavior.[19] Besides, Cruse appears to be recommending that black intellectuals act more like Jews in realizing their "cultural compulsives." Further, the use of "anti-Semitic," courageous on the part of a radical black reviewer in the late 1960s, when there was a tendency to refrain from sharp public criticism of other militants, may lack precise meaning today; since then, the term has been employed frequently and irresponsibly to smear anyone who dares to criticize the Israeli state. What is more important to establish is that the group caricature aspect of Cruse's narrative is methodologically unsound, leading to factual misrepresentations ultimately deleterious to the assessment of past successes and failures in the movement to eradicate racism from our society.

For example, whereas many scholars have remarked on the devoted work, and the personal risks taken, by Communists in their mobilization to defend the famous "Scottsboro Boys" in Alabama, Cruse depicts the campaign only as a "propaganda windfall." He explains that "the importance of this episode goes far beyond its organizational and propaganda aspects. For, as Quentin Reynolds once pointed out, it coincided with the exact period in which *The Daily Worker* was able to purchase its own printing presses."[20] Yet this inference of misappropriation of contributions to the Scottsboro defense fund, many of which came from poor people in Harlem, is groundless. Reynolds contends only that some unidentified "Harlem leader[s] hinted broadly" that the source of the new Party presses was "black donations." However, this remark is preceded by the assertion that "no one knows just how much money was raised by the Communist Party." In regard to the *Daily Worker* presses, Reynolds notes that "there were many who joked about the source which had supplied the money." So Reynolds, who documents nothing in his book, is making it plain that he places no confidence in the allegations, which might easily be a street witticism or motivated by the envy of a Party rival. Moreover, Reynold's work has all the features of a crude Cold War anti-Communist tract; one wonders why Cruse does not go all the way and cite Reynolds's (undocumented) declaration that it was "certain" that the Communist Party secretly favored the victims receiving the death penalty "because nine young Negroes executed would be far more useful."[21]

Cruse then states that the "true indication" of who really benefited from the Communist Party policy at the time can be seen in the launching in June 1937 of a modest monthly magazine called *Jewish Life*. Thus Cruse "proves," without any reliable facts, that Jews promoted a pseudoantiracism to procure money from blacks to promote their own Jewish nationalism. He thereby establishes the ideological precept to which his narrative becomes captive.[22]

Even when his contentions contradict other, more dispassionate scholarship available to him, Cruse proclaims that Jews as a group are the most devious Communists. For instance, he avows, "the only ones who talked Americanization but did not fall for it 'culturally' were the Communist Jews who never overlooked a single stratagem for the preservation of Jewish cultural identity." Of course, abundant evidence exists for a range of attitudes toward Jewish identity in the Communist Party. Six years before Cruse's study, Nathan Glazer published the acclaimed *Social Basis of American Communism* (1961) that considered Communist Jews and African Americans, a work that is not cited by Cruse. In his book Glazer concedes that Jews were numerically the largest ethnic group in the Communist Party but observes that "once the diversity of the Jews who entered the Communist Party is realized, any simple interpretation of the relationship between Jews and the Communist Party fails." Morris U. Schappes, who functioned for decades as a Jewish Communist Party cultural leader before his expulsion, insisted in 1970 that the dominant view in the Communist Party was never for ethnic group survival of Jewish Americans, but what he calls, perhaps with some exaggeration, "national nihilism."[23]

Unfortunately, the "simple" interpretation that Glazer avoided is precisely what Cruse serves up, spiced with conspiratorial innuendos:

> The Jews . . . with their nationalistic aggressiveness, emerging out of the Eastside ghettoes . . . demonstrate[d] through Marxism their intellectual superiority over the Anglo-Saxon goyim. The Jews failed to make Marxism applicable to anything in America but their *own* national-group social ambitions or individual self-elevation. As a result, the great brainwashing of the Negro radical intellectual was not achieved by capitalism, or the capitalistic bourgeoisie, but by Jewish intellectuals in the American Communist Party.[24]

Here, again, Cruse, the prisoner of group caricature, runs roughshod over elemental facts. Most Jews named by Cruse—ones who allegedly strived, from Jewish nationalist motives, to establish "theoretical dominance over the Negroes in the interpretation of the Negro Question in the United States"—hailed from backgrounds and upbringings remote from "Eastside ghettoes."[25] James Allen (1906–90, born Sol Auerbach), depicted by Cruse as an ur-villain for his books and pamphlets on African American history and politics, was a doctoral candidate at the University of Pennsylvania in Philadelphia, the city where he was raised. Herbert Aptheker (b. 1915) came from a wealthy New York family and earned a doctorate at Columbia. V. J. Jerome (1895–1965, born Jerome Isaac Romaine) attended high school in England and studied philosophy at New York University.

To establish that these Jews identified as "white" and saw Marxism as "a white- (if not Jewish-) created social science [that] had to be 'taught' to Negroes in the manner in which one teaches backward peoples Western Democracy," Cruse offers the following rationale: "In Harlem, during the 1949–51 Negro-white inner-party conflict over white leadership, several white Communists indignantly replied that 'it was white people who brought the ideas of Marxism to Harlem in the first place!'" How do we refute such evidence if we were not present? And even if such a foolish statement were made, what does it mean? How should we weigh this contention against the numerous autobiographical writings by former black Communists that contain no such anecdotes?[26]

The problem of evidence in *Crisis* is crucial. In essence, Cruse's account of the relationship between Black Marxism and Jewish Communists can hardly be treated more seriously than Himes's fiction in *Lonely Crusade*. Both accounts, whatever "truths" they may reveal through the insights of intelligent perception applied to a certain degree of personal experience, must be assessed differently from, say, the scholarly works of John Hope Franklin. Both *Lonely Crusade* and *Crisis* are accounts by exceptionally thoughtful, passionate, and angry intellectuals, intended to challenge prevailing notions and offer superior visions of truth about the nature of racism.

There is no reason to dispute the likelihood that there were arrogant, racist, chauvinist, aggressive, or otherwise insensitive Jews in the Communist movement, and that Cruse may well have encountered some of them. Nor should we deny that common histories and backgrounds can produce similar patterns of thought and behavior. The leap to conspiratorial group caricature, however, is a far different matter. Cruse has scant basis for claiming that "the Jewish sense of inferiority, or pride, or envy mixed with a challenging claim of counter-superiority, spurred Jewish Communists to capture as many second-level posts of command as possible. The great threat to this goal was no longer the Anglo-Saxon in the Party, but the Negro."[27] Moreover, Cruse himself cites material that patently refutes many of his arguments. For example, a passage from a book by Melech Epstein, referred to by Cruse for other polemical purposes, includes this information: "The number of Negro [Communist] party organizers and officers was out of all proportion to the small number of Negro members. It became an unwritten rule [in the 1930s] that every committee must include a certain proportion of Negroes. More Negroes were sent to Party schools in Moscow and here. The South . . . was dotted with Negro organizers." How can these statements be reconciled with Cruse's earlier claim that Jews were driven by their "cultural compulsive" to capture all of the secondary leadership posts, while seeing blacks in the Party as the main threat to this objective? Are not such positions as organizers, officers, and members of leading committees adjudged secondary command posts? Are not Party schools designed to educate members to assume such leadership roles?[28]

Most disheartening is Cruse's elucidation of the Party's "turn" to the Popular Front. Since the 1950s, scholars have debated the extent to which the 1935 reorientation was a knee-jerk reaction to the call of the Seventh World Congress of the Comintern or was the result of the accumulated wisdom of national and local experience with sectarian misadventures. Cruse, however, offers a unique theory: "Under Jewish Communist prodding, the Communist Party took up the anti-Hitler crusade in the late 1930s." As a result of this crusade, a "very large corps of Negro volunteers went to Spain during the Spanish Civil War of 1936–1939 to fight and die for Spanish democracy." Comparable to black financial contributions to the Scottsboro defense that were sacrificed on the altar of Jewish cultural nationalism, the blood of African Americans was spilled in Spain on behalf of the "Jewish crusade against Hitler."[29]

In his passion to find evidence to confirm this thesis, Cruse cites a statement by Langston Hughes to convey the impression that Hughes, too, thought that the Abraham Lincoln Brigade exploited naive blacks: "With so many unsolved problems in America, I wondered why would a Negro come way over to Spain to help solve Spain's problems—perhaps with his very life. I don't know. I wondered then. I wonder still." This passage appears at the beginning of the section entitled "Citation for Bravery" in Hughes's autobiography. Yet the next sentence reads: "But in my heart I salute them." Clearly Hughes admires and honors the internationalism of black American fighters in Spain, and his "wonder" is more an expression of awe at their heroism than skepticism about their choice. It is regrettable that Cruse did not give us a longer excerpt from this section of Hughes's memoir. Hughes explicitly transcends the group caricature of *Crisis*; his interviews with black Americans in Spain show that their motives varied and were self-selected. Some thought that "by fighting Franco they felt they were opposing Mussolini [who had invaded Ethiopia]. Others said that they had come to Spain to fight against the kind of people who oppress Negroes in the American South. Others said they had come to oppose fascism, and help prevent its spread in the world." Hughes should not be enlisted to support Cruse's cynical argument.[30]

The Lost Legacy of Black Marxism

Black Marxism is presently the focus of a small number of books, each offering various interpretations of the phenomenon. Cedric Robinson's sympathetic but skeptical *Black Marxism: The Making of the Black Radical Tradition* (1983) argues that Marxism and black radicalism frequently merge in common cause but ultimately are driven by incompatible social dynamics. Robin Kelley's celebratory *Hammer and Hoe: Alabama Communists during the Great Depression* (1990) and *Race Rebels: Culture, Politics, and the Black Working Class* (1994) see the Communist movement as providing space for a congenial blending of internationalist class struggles and black nationalist aspirations.[31] In political theory and history, African American scholars like Angela Davis, Manning Marable, and Gerald Horne have continued to keep Black Marxist traditions alive,[32] while Earl Ofari Hutchinson's 1995 *Blacks and Reds* treats the relationship as a once-heroic development whose time has manifestly passed.

Chester Himes's narrative of blacks and Jews in *Lonely Crusade* shares more with this contemporary body of scholarship than does Cruse's *Crisis*. Even though Himes's novel is no less belligerent toward the Communist Party, it depicts the agency and autonomy of black Communist Party members in a way that is consonant with the views of Robin Kelley, Mark Naison, and others. Luther and Bart (the African American leader of the Communist Party in California) are not delineated as malleable instruments created top-down by Party bureaucrats, whether they be "Jewish nationalists" or "Stalinists." Although these characters in certain respects appear as "grotesques,"[33] they have a history of experiences influencing how they interact with Communist ideology and institutions.

In *Crisis*, the second group, after Jews, under sustained assault by Cruse, is not Anglo-Saxons (or Protestants or Catholics), but Black Marxists themselves—especially cultural workers. Most of the hostility is directed toward novelist John Oliver Killens (1916–87) and playwright Lorraine Hansberry (1930–65), although actress Ruby Dee (b. 1924), actor Ossie Davis (b. 1917), singer Paul Robeson (1898–1976), novelist Julian Mayfield (1928–84), and several others come in for some hard knocks. Cruse's method here is remarkably similar to his relentless "exposé" of the Jewish nationalists. Whether in their Communist or post-Communist phases,[34] these figures are characterized as middle-class integrationists (sometimes "left-wing integrationists") who have betrayed the African

American "cultural compulsive" rooted in Harlem, for which Cruse stands seemingly alone as the representative.[35]

Hansberry, for example, is repeatedly clobbered with an unsubstantiated newspaper report that quotes her as saying that *A Raisin in the Sun* is "not a Negro play." This quotation has since been discredited by Robert Nemiroff, but it is crucial to Cruse's misrepresentation of the play as "one of the most significant examples of th[e] use of Negro 'workers' in drama to reflect middle-class values." Moreover, Cruse claims that Killens, Hansberry, Davis, and Dee, "because of their apparent social and professional exclusiveness, as well as their associations with Harlem left-wing cultural organizers, were considered to be a clique by people involved in Harlem cultural life."[36] The problem here corresponds to that in Cruse's statements about Jewish arrogance. One cannot disprove his claim that an individual or even people adhered to this view. But what is the weight of the claim? What does it mean? What documentation does he offer that this assessment was a majority view or even a popular one?

As in the case of his assault on Jewish Communists, Cruse combines his attack on Black Marxists with many clear-sighted observations about the hypocrisy of cultural institutions in the United States, the sham of the melting pot myth, the centrality of cultural issues, the need for exacting intellectual work, and the indispensability of African Americans' right of self-determination. Thus there is a temptation to assent to Cruse on other, more challenging issues, especially where contrary evidence is not readily available.[37]

Additionally, *Crisis* retains authority because it has secured a niche. It is one of the few sources that associates black cultural institutions with Communist Party supporters, such as the American Negro Theater (ANT), the Negro Playwrights Company, the Committee for the Negro in the Arts, the Harlem Writers Club, the Harlem Writers Guild, and *Freedomways*. It is also the sole book acknowledging, with details, the existence of a substantial post–World War II black Communist cultural presence in many artistic venues and genres. Cruse's treatment of the Communist Party raises a crucial problem of Leftist history and culture that many subsequent left-wing scholars of black radicalism have hesitated to address: the question of Stalinism—generally meaning the ultimate subordination of the Communist Party to the authority of the Soviet Union, the employment of bureaucratic organizational methods modeled on the Soviet Communist Party, and the reliance on Soviet cultural dictators such as André Zhdanov for literary orientation.

The issue of Stalinism, often used as a club by enemies of the Left as well as by radical rivals of the Communist Party, has usually been ignored, sidestepped, or dismissed by those seeking to reclaim the heritage of the interracial antiracist struggle pioneered by the Communist movement; some, who have no particular sympathy for the Soviet Union, would simply like to regard consideration of Stalinism a dead dog of Cold War anticommunism.[38] Cruse, who seems to feel that a special category is necessary for the Soviet brand of communism, hurts his own case by never offering an explanation for the influence of Stalinism on the Communist Party; worse, he frequently describes the Party's bureaucratic methods as an exercise of Jewish power. Cruse takes enough false steps in his handling of Stalinism to virtually discredit the whole effort. Still, a more critical analysis of the Black Marxist experience than lately has prevailed must accompany the welcome celebrations of the heroic "resistance" of black radicals if their suffering and commitment are to be rendered usable for antiracist cultural workers and activists of the present.

Fortunately, some scholarly publications already contradict many of Cruse's inaccurate allegations about Black Marxism. His accusation that Communists were "integrationists" and his notion that integrationism and nationalism are necessarily the primary categories of analysis have been criticized as misleading.[39] But his misconception on this topic persists due to the dramatic appearance of "Black Power" in the 1960s and the new ultramilitant stance (often accompanied by calls to "pick up the gun") that renders it too easy to collapse previous radicalisms into mid-twentieth-century liberalism. However, the liberal idea of integrating African Americans "equally" into existing socioeconomic structures is significantly different from the Communist Party's aim of joining blacks (while maintaining their cultural identity) and whites together in an effort to overthrow the social order and reconstruct new, egalitarian socioeconomic forms.

The Party's policy of assigning white members to do political work in black areas, such as Harlem, and the openness of black Communists to allowing whites to contribute to black radical news and cultural magazines have somewhat confused the debate about integrationism. Cruse is possibly sound in asserting that all-black Communist Party units, and perhaps even all-black publications, would have been more inviting to potential black recruits and might have encouraged more black leadership and autonomy. The presence of whites, especially if confident, articulate, and bonded together through a common political analysis, can be intimidating and even stultifying to newly radicalizing and perhaps younger, less-experienced members of a subaltern group. But the equation of integrated political units with a political strategy of integration, or as necessarily leading to a certain cultural policy (adaptation to middle-class values), is deceptive and can be refuted by the work of many writers from the Black Marxist tradition.

The Literary Record

In 1989 a remarkable but little-noticed novel for "Young Adults" by Alice Childress appeared under the title *Those Other People*. Graced with a cover featuring four serious-looking teenage faces with luminous eyes, two African American and two white, two female and two male, *Those Other People* offers a political plot reminiscent of the 1954 classic Marxist movie produced by blacklisted Hollywood Communists, *The Salt of the Earth*. The irrepressible theme of that McCarthy-era script was nothing less than the central message of the U.S. cultural Left: "The indivisibility of equality."[40]

Composed by Communist screenwriter Michael Wilson, *Salt of the Earth* dramatized with subtlety and poignancy how people of color (Chicanos engaged in a miners' strike in New Mexico) had to discover the arduous way, through personal experiences erupting in kitchens and bedrooms as well as in the workplace, to unite around the demands of women as well as men. It also dramatized how working people of all ethnicities had to overcome backward prejudice, joining together to support the demands of the most oppressed, in order to win a victory for the benefit of all.

Appearing three-and-a-half decades after *Salt of the Earth*, *Those Other People* depicts a painful movement toward a parallel unity. This time the common struggle is in Minitown, New York, and the unity is forged among an African American brother and sister enduring racial discrimination; a white, very young temporary computer instructor who faces persecution for his gay sexual orientation; and a white, blond, fifteen-year-old schoolgirl who is sexually harassed and nearly raped by a macho gym teacher.

Not only does the theme of *Those Other People* recall earlier left-wing cultural productions like *Salt of the Earth*; the form of this novel, too, resonates with features of the radical "collective novel," much theorized and heavily promoted in the 1930s.[41] Each of the nineteen chapters of *Those Other People* is the voice of a different character. The text not only gives expression, via these dramatic monologues, to the thoughts and perspectives of the four teenagers who become the group protagonist. It also imparts voice to racist and sexist characters who are allowed to rationalize their own behavior and to explain how they formed the opinions they hold about "those other people."

Although belonging to a relatively obscure genre of mass cultural production that has received little attention as counterhegemonic practice, *Those Other People* actually expresses an extraordinary culmination of six decades of radical resistance culture revolving around class, gender, and race. Above all, it springs from the legacy of Black Marxism in the United States. Its author, Alice Childress (1921–94), was part of the left-wing African American theater community drawn to Communism in the late 1930s; she remained a steadfast supporter, and possibly even a member, of the Communist Party throughout the Cold War era. She was also one of the "original members of the Harlem in-group" accused by Cruse of being "pro-integration," and she allegedly "policed" the April 1965 Negro Writers Conference on behalf of Killens's "leftwing literary elite."[42]

Childress's remarkable narrative not only carries on a traditional left-wing view, that unity in struggle does not necessarily mean abrogation of self-determination, but it also bonds that tradition with contemporary issues. Moreover, the semi-obscured legacy of Black Marxist cultural work includes not just the writing since the 1960s by dozens of subtle and thoughtful artists like Childress, but at least one extraordinary text of the Cold War era itself, Killens's 1954 novel *Youngblood*.[43] Thus Cruse's shallow indictment of Black Marxists as tools of Jewish Communists, who cynically promote integrationism for all but themselves, has the potential to do injury not only to our understanding of political practice, but also to literary history.

Cruse's censure of *Youngblood* as a dramatization of Leftist liberal integrationism and as a socialist-realist tract effectively obscures one of the key documents of the complex double vision of postwar Black Marxism. Indeed, one finds in *Youngblood* a view of black-white unity far in advance of the version of nationalism to which Cruse's group caricature led him in 1967—a view somewhat compatible with the "race traitor" and "whiteness" theorizing of the 1990s.[44]

The primary focus of *Youngblood* is a black family in a black community in Georgia, but Killens understands that a minority alone is incapable of transforming society. Class allies must be found, so a parallel narrative to the Youngblood family ordeal develops around a white worker named Oscar Jefferson. Killens subtly depicts the formation of a burgeoning alternative psychology in Jefferson: an outlook based on a negative view of the costs of identifying "white," which will one day break the social construct of the "cracker" consciousness into which Jefferson is being socialized. This rejection of W. E. B. Du Bois's famous "wages of whiteness" does not grow out of Oscar's altruism, or a sense of noble self-sacrifice, or even pity; Killens locates the source of Oscar's potential liberation from the illusions of his white skin privilege in three other zones.

First, Oscar is bitter that cracker behavior has forever ruined his relationship with his mother, who was forced to falsely accuse Oscar's best friend, African American youth Jim Kilgrow (Little Jim), of rape. Oscar has come to see his father's patriarchal relationship to himself and his mother in the fashion that a class-conscious worker sees a boss. Thus, when Oscar leaves home and goes to work, he has the capacity of perceiving white bosses not as his friends, but as people who will use him as his own father used his mother and himself to frustrate and warp desire.

Second, Oscar has a reservoir of experiences in ordinary life that contradict the cracker ideology into which his environment is trying to interpellate him. Many of them stem from his childhood friendship with Little Jim, when he witnessed everyday behavior among the Kilgrows, especially the father-son relationship. These experiences, felt but untheorized, go counter to the racist category of "Nigger" that had been transmitted to him by his father, his father's boss, and church and state authorities. Indeed, the Kilgrow family comportment was far more attractive than the behavior model his own family afforded.

The third and final constituent necessary to shatter the eroding bonds holding Oscar to the illusions of privilege through his "whiteness" is the example of black resistance. First, the knowledge that the Kilgrow family had fought back with arms against racists; second, the sight of Joe Youngblood standing up to his hated boss, alone and against all odds; and third, the community resistance demonstrated by African Americans when they transform the town's annual jubilee from entertainment bordering on a minstrel show to a powerful affirmation of black cultural pride.

Thus in 1954 *Youngblood* dramatized a parallel perspective to the political analysis frequently associated with black Trotskyist C. L. R. James, so influential in recent decades. James's view, articulated in the late 1930s in "The Revolutionary Answer to the Negro Problem" and other essays,[45] was that the African American political struggle served a vanguard function —by taking the initiative and setting an example, as it had done throughout U.S. history. The African American vanguard could best win allies by showing others how to fight, not by subordinating its special interests out of apprehension of being seen as divisive to the interracial unity obligatory for class struggle.

In the latter part of *Youngblood*, Oscar Jefferson sees the Youngblood men affirm their masculinity—in contrast to the abusive methods of the crackers—by standing up for the dignity of the oppressed and by uniting as men with women and entire families on an egalitarian basis in struggle. He instinctively feels that this is more meaningful, more vital, more beautiful, and more desirable than the privileges of his white skin color, which have brought only self-hate, shame, and family discord. This growing awareness leads to Oscar's support of the unionization of the town's black hotel workers and to his enlistment in the armed camp of black workers defending the wounded Joe Youngblood from white vigilantes.

Youngblood can be criticized in many areas, including, perhaps, its idealization of the proletarian family as a revolutionary site. But if the novel is to be charged with advocating integrationism or assimilationism, it is integration with the ordinary culture of African America—not for a moment with an elite, patriarchal Eurocentric culture.[46] Associating Killens with left-wing integrationism misses the profoundly revolutionary implications of his book; it is white Oscar Jefferson who finds "manhood" and family dignity, and who heals the Oedipal contradictions of his own youth, through *his* momentary integration with black resistance culture.

The narrative of the "two nationalisms" in Cruse's *Crisis* agonizingly blends the insightful with the outrageous. For the antiracist political and cultural movements of the present, however, the stakes are high in regard to whether we accept his version as an accurate record of the Black Marxist experience. If Cold War African American Leftists are to be tossed into the dustbin as dupes of Jewish nationalism, much will be expunged from cultural history and political consciousness. Contemporary antiracist political practice will needlessly proceed with an impediment, unaware of the resources to be gained from the profound sense of continuity that might be available to it.

Notes

I am grateful to Robert Chrisman, Patrick Quinn, Mark Solomon, John Woodford, and the 1997–98 Fellows at the University of Michigan Institute for the Humanities for providing critical feedback on a draft of this essay. I also appreciate the suggestions of the anonymous readers for *Science and Society*, where this essay first appeared in vol. 64, no. 4 (Winter 2000–2001): 400–23.

1. Chester Himes, *If He Hollers Let Him Go* (Garden City, N.Y.: Doubleday, 1945) and *The Lonely Crusade* (New York: Knopf, 1947); Harold Cruse, *The Crisis of the Negro Intellectual* (New York: Morrow, 1967).

2. Stephen J. Rosen, "African-American Anti-Semitism and Himes' *Lonely Crusade*," MELUS 20, no. 2 (Summer 1995): 47; Harold Bloom, ed., *Richard Wright's Native Son* (1940; reprint, New York: Chelsea House Publishers, 1996).

3. Chester Himes, *The Quality of Hurt: The Early Years: The Autobiography of*

Chester Himes (Garden City, N.Y.: Doubleday, 1972) and *My Life of Absurdity: The Later Years: The Autobiography of Chester Himes* (Garden City, N.Y.: Doubleday, 1976). "There wasn't a single event in the story that hadn't actually happened. My characters were real people." Quoted in Michel Fabre and Robert Skinner, *Conversations with Chester Himes* (Jackson: University Press of Mississippi, 1995), 126. According to Edward Margolies and Michel Fabre in their *Several Lives of Chester Himes* (Jackson: University Press of Mississippi, 1997), 44, "[Dan] Levin served as the prototype of Abe Rosenberg in *The Lonely Crusade*." Levin was a pro-communist writer who befriended Himes in Cleveland and later helped him settle in Paris. My own research indicates that the character of the Los Angeles Communist Party leader, Bart, is based on Georgia-born African American Pettis Perry and the biography of the pathological black communist, Luther McGregor, is similar to that of Mississippi-born Eluard Luchell McDaniel, a veteran of the Abraham Lincoln Brigade who published dialect stories while working on the Writers Project in San Francisco in the 1930s. African American novelist and former Party member Lloyd Brown, who wrote a scathing review of *Lonely Crusade* in *New Masses* (September 9, 1947), recalled Perry telling him that Himes had been expelled from the Party in Los Angeles for sexually harassing white women and that he took his revenge on Perry and others through his vicious portraits in the novel. Neither Himes nor any Himes scholars have ever acknowledged Party membership, although they agree that he attended cell meetings and other activities, so the question of official status remains inconclusive. Interview with Lloyd Brown, 1990.

4. Himes, *Quality of Hurt*, 93.

5. In retrospect, some of the mainstream reviews seem rather favorable, but overall, they offered little solace to Himes.

6. Himes, *Quality of Hurt*, 102.

7. In this case, in the spring of 1943, the Party made antifascist unity a priority. Many Left critics believed that this orientation downplayed the class struggle in general and the special needs of black workers in particular so as not to disrupt wartime production.

8. *Crisis*, 476 ("The Two Nationalisms"); Himes, *Lonely Crusade*, 52.

9. Himes, *Lonely Crusade*, 151, 272, 244, 152–58.

10. What he writes is little different from the depictions of Communism in Ralph Ellison's *Invisible Man* (1952) and Richard Wright's *The Outsider* (1953), two novels that were surely more influenced by Himes's work than scholars have acknowledged.

11. Himes, *Lonely Crusade*, 28 ("dupe"), 81 ("ape"), 318-30, 204 ("Thass me!").

12. Though space does not permit a discussion of gender in Himes, *Lonely Crusade* was far ahead of *Crisis* in its integration of gender and patriarchy into its analysis.

13. Himes, *Lonely Crusade*, 369.

14. Twenty-three years later, Himes stated: "The situation I described was how things were during the Second World War. All that has changed now. The political statements I made in *Lonely Crusade* are no longer valid." Quoted in Fabre and Skinner, *Conversations*, 94.

15. *Crisis*, 516. Cruse states that this same characterization applies to liberal civil rights organizations.

16. The most influential case for this interpretation appears in Theodore Draper, *American Communism and Soviet Russia* (New York: Viking, 1960). Subse-

quent scholars have convincingly challenged the one-sidedness of Draper's view as it related to rank-and-file practice in the United States but have not refuted evidence of the Party leadership's unbreakable tie to Soviet foreign policy.

17. "The West Indian-American Negro braintrust could not utter a single theoretical idea about themselves. . . . This situation led inexorably to the period of Jewish dominance in the Communist Party. It culminated in the emergence of Herbert Aptheker and other assimilated Jewish Communists, who assumed the mantle of spokesmanship on Negro affairs, thus burying the Negro radical potential deeper and deeper into the slough of white intellectual paternalism" (*Crisis*, 147). Other oversimplified and negative characterizations of black Caribbeans appear elsewhere, such as "West Indian Americans and West Indian Britishers are forever boasting about their origins in front of American whites and American Negroes, but they are always 'from there' or 'leaving there' for greener pastures elsewhere" (ibid., 251).

18. "There is a vicious anti-Semitism throughout the work." Robert Chrisman, "The Crisis of Harold Cruse," *Black Scholar* (November 1967): 78.

19. Admittedly, formal repudiation of biological explanations is also a common ploy of antiblack racists who use "cultural" and "historical" explanations to justify their attribution of negative traits to African Americans.

20. *Crisis*, 148. A recent study acknowledging the Communists' courage is Carroll Van West's "Perpetuating the Myth of America: Scottsboro and Its Interpreters," *South Atlantic Quarterly* 80 (Winter 1981): 36–48.

21. Quentin Reynolds, *Courtroom: The Story of Samuel S. Leibowitz* (New York: Farrar, Straus, 1950), 311, 260. Of course, one cannot rule out the misappropriation, or improper channeling, of defense funds. There are people who could have rationalized that giving money to the *Daily Worker* was objectively in the interests of the case, since the paper was a main defender of the imprisoned youth. Moreover, it is logical that the Party's impressive work for the defense would bring in a slew of donations to the Party itself. However, the plausibility of any of these explanations should not mean a belief in the charges. Most important, the accusation of misappropriation of funds for Party presses is not repeated in the major scholarship on the case itself, even though the Party is heavily criticized for ultraleft and sectarian tactics. See Dan Carter, *Scottsboro* (Baton Rouge: Louisiana State University Press, 1979), and James Goodman, *Stories of Scottsboro* (New York: Pantheon, 1994).

22. *Crisis*, 148.

23. Ibid., 152; Nathan Glazer, *The Social Basis of American Communism* (New York: Harcourt, 1961), 132–33; Morris U. Schappes, "The Jewish Question and the Left," New York, *Jewish Currents Reprint* (1973): 5. Glazer insists that there were a range of attitudes in the Party from those who were committed to Jewish-specific interests such as the survival of Yiddish to those "who had no interest at all in any Jewish concern" (p. 132).

24. *Crisis*, 158.

25. Ibid.

26. Ibid. I am referring to former black Communists such as Harry Haywood, *Black Bolshevik: Autobiography of an Afro-American Communist* (Chicago: Lake View Press, 1978); Nelson Perry, *Black Fire* (New York: New Press, 1994); and James Yates, *From Mississippi to Madrid* (Seattle: Open Hands Publishing, 1989).

27. *Crisis*, 163. In some cases Cruse simply transforms a half truth into a falsehood through overkill. On the same page he states categorically, "Needless to

say, no one in the Communist Party spoke theoretically for Jews but other Jews." Two Party pamphlets, *Anti-Semitism: What It Means and How to Combat It* (New York: Workers Library, 1943) and *Should Negroes and Jews Unite?* (New York: Negro Publication Society of America, 1943), the contributors of which include non-Jewish Communist Party leader Earl Browder and African American L. D. Reddick, should suffice to check Cruse's overzealousness. Cruse could have safely written "[it was rare," instead of "no one," but it would have been inconsistent with the hyperbole of his argument. Another example is his statement that "the privileges and prerogatives of the lowest rank and file white [in the Party] outweighed those of the highest Negro Communist leader" (p. 227). In Earl Ofari Hutchinson's *Blacks and Reds: Race and Class in Conflict, 1919–1990* (East Lansing: Michigan State University Press, 1995), hardly a pro-Communist book, the author cites Eslanda Robeson, married to Paul Robeson, as a source for an incident in which two young black Party members had a longtime Party stalwart, a white woman, censured and ejected from a Party meeting because the white woman told them to stop talking during the meeting (p. 231). Hutchinson relates similar incidents where rank-and-file black members punished white members.

28. *Crisis*, 164. Cruse is undaunted in persisting in this line of argument, in sustained passages as well as in short references, as if the matter had been proved. On p. 169 he writes: "In Negro-Jewish relations in the Communist Left there has been an intense undercurrent of jealousy, enmity and competition over the prizes of group political power and intellectual prestige. In this struggle, the Jewish intellectuals—because of superior organization, drive, intellectual discipline, money and the motive of their cultural compulsives—have been able to win out."

29. Ibid., 168.

30. Ibid.; Langston Hughes, *I Wonder as I Wander* (New York: Rinehart, 1956), 354.

31. Cedric J. Robinson, *Black Marxism: The Making of the Black Radical Tradition* (Totowa, N.J.: Biblio Distribution Center, 1983); Robin D. G. Kelley, *Hammer and Hoe: Alabama Communists during the Great Depression* (Chapel Hill: University of North Carolina Press, 1990) and *Race Rebels: Culture, Politics, and the Black Working Class* (New York: Free Press, 1994). Further, Mark Naison astutely discusses relations between the Communist Party and Harlem cultural figures in *Communists in Harlem during the Depression* (Urbana: University of Illinois Press, 1983). Haywood's *Black Bolshevik* provides considerable inside information. For additional bibliographical references, see footnotes to my essay, "Lloyd Brown and the African American Literary Left," in Alan M. Wald, ed., *Writing from the Left: New Essays on Radical Culture and Politics* (London: Verso, 1994). A more recent addition to the literature is Claudia Rosemary May, "Nuances of Un-American Literatures(s): In Search of Claudia Jones; A Literary Retrospective on the Life, Times, and Works of an Activist-Writer" (Diss., University of California–Berkeley, 1996). Four recent books—by Mark Solomon, Bill Mullen, James Smethurst, and William Maxwell—have added considerably to our understanding of Black Marxism. I have tried to summarize the achievements of these scholars in a two-part review essay, "African Americans, Communism, and Culture," *Against the Current* 84 (January–February 2000): 23–29 and 86 (May–June 2000): 27–34.

32. See Angela Y. Davis, *Women, Race, and Class* (New York: Vintage Books, 1981). Among Marable's many books, the section "Radical Democracy and So-

cialism" in his *Speaking Truth to Power: Essays on Race, Resistance, and Radicalism* (Boulder, Colo.: Westview Press, 1996) addresses the issue most directly. Gerald Horne has produced three informative books, *Black and Red: W. E. B. Du Bois and the Afro-American Response to the Cold War, 1944–1963* (Albany: State University of New York Press, 1986), *Communist Front? The Civil Rights Congress, 1946–1956* (Rutherford, N.J.: Fairleigh Dickinson University Press, 1988), and *Black Liberation/Red Scare: Ben Davis and the Communist Party* (Newark: University of Delaware Press, 1993).

33. This is also true of the characters in Ralph Ellison's acclaimed *Invisible Man* (New York: Random House, 1952).

34. He avows that Killens and company were "shaped by a special kind of literary and political conditioning [with] its literary, artistic, and political origins . . . to be found in the radical left-wing movement in the Harlem of the late 1940s and early 1950s," and that they have "remained prisoners of that tradition, to date" (*Crisis*, 206).

35. The "entire Negro integrationist elite speaks through *Freedomways*" (*Crisis*, 248), Killens and Hansberry's "Robeson idolatry was middle class to begin with" (p. 252), and the aim of Robeson's *Freedom* newspaper was to "foist middle-class social aims upon the so-called working-class movements" (p. 230). Cruse refers to the "left-wing integrationists" in Killens's group (p. 410), and, in contrasting Richard Wright's plebeian background with Cruse's antagonists, he offers what is probably another example of overkill in his categorical, undocumented statement that "not a single Negro writer or dramatist sponsored and promoted by the leftwing has followed the difficult route traveled by Wright" (p. 267).

36. Ibid., 246, 275, 508 ("not a Negro play"), 236, 199. See Robert Nemiroff, "A Cautionary Note on Resources," *Freedomways* 19, no. 4 (1979): 286.

37. One can hardly disagree with his opening claim: "America, which idealizes the rights of the individual above everything else, is in reality, a nation dominated by the social power of groups, classes, in-groups and cliques—both ethnic and religious. The individual in America has few rights that are not backed up by the political, economic and social power of one group or another." *Crisis*, 8.

38. For example, Penny M. Von Eschen, in her excellent study *Race against Empire: Black Americans and Anticolonialism, 1937–1957* (Ithaca, N.Y.: Cornell University Press, 1997), neither addresses the issue of Stalinism nor goes into detail about Party relations with the various projects of her protagonists. Another perspective is suggested by Barbara Foley, who equates all forms of anti-Stalinism with anti-Marxism in *Radical Representations: Politics and Form in U.S. Proletarian Fiction, 1929–1941* (Durham, N.C.: Duke University Press, 1993).

39. One of the most lucid critiques of Cruse appears in the chapter "Escaping the Ghost of Harold Cruse" in Jerry Gafio Watts, *Heroism and the Black Intellectual: Ralph Ellison, Politics, and Afro-American Intellectual Life* (Chapel Hill: University of North Carolina Press, 1994), 3–23. Watts writes: "In many respects, Cruse's 'crisis' was a sectarian ploy. He wanted to frame the issues of black intellectual life and politics along a rather simpleminded axis between black nationalism and integrationism" (p. 8).

40. See Alice Childress, *Those Other People* (New York: Putnam, 1989) and Deborah Silverton Rosenfelt, ed., *The Salt of the Earth* (New York: Feminist Press, 1978), 94.

41. See Granville Hicks, "Complex and Collective Novels," in Jack Alan Rob-

bins, ed., *Granville Hicks in the New Masses* (Port Washington, N.Y.: Kennikat Press, 1974), 26–33. These essays were originally serialized in the *New Masses* in April and May 1934.

42. *Crisis*, 515, 500 (quotations). Childress worked with the left-wing American Negro Theater for eleven years and published her first play, *Florence*, in the October 1950 issue of the Communist journal *Masses & Mainstream*. Her pro-Communist convictions in the Cold War era are clear, even if there is some uncertainty about her precise organizational affiliation. Dr. Annette Rubinstein, a former Communist Party member, believed that Childress was a Party member. Rubenstein to the author, March 23, 1996. African American novelist Lloyd Brown, also a former Party member, recalled only that "Alice Childress [was] a talented woman communist writer [who] hoped that not being in the Party would keep her from being labeled." Brown to the author, March 22, 1996. Extant scholarship on Childress, including La Vinia Delois Jennings's book *Alice Childress* (New York: Tawyne Publishers, 1995), is silent on the entire subject.

43. See John O. Killens, *Youngblood* (New York: Dial Press, 1954).

44. See Noel Ignatiev and John Garvey, eds., *Race Traitor* (New York, Routledge, 1996), and Mike Hill, ed., *Whiteness: A Critical Reader* (New York: New York University Press, 1977).

45. See Scott McLemee and Paul Le Blanc, eds., *Selected Writings of C. L. R. James, 1939–1949* (Atlantic Highlands, N.J.: Humanities Press, 1994).

46. It is worth noting that Cruse is accurate in reminding us that Killens published a hatchet-job review of Ellison's *Invisible Man* due to Ellison's switch to anticommunism; however, Cruse then proceeds to do exactly the same thing—judge Killens's novel by his alleged politics. See *Crisis*, 235.

Barbara Foley

From Communism to Brotherhood: The Drafts of *Invisible Man*

That Ralph Ellison was during the late 1930s and early 1940s a fairly close fellow traveler of the Communist Party of the United States of America (CPUSA) remains one of the best-kept secrets of U.S. literary history. To no small degree, Ellison himself helped to veil his Leftist past. A biographical sketch accompanying a review of *Invisible Man* in the April 1952 *Saturday Review of Literature*—for which it was surely the author who supplied the information—alluded to Ellison's having "lectured at Bennington and NYU, worked in a factory, for a psychologist, and at free-lance photography; tinkered with audio-electronics, and done a wartime stint in the Merchant Marine." When he received the National Book Award (NBA) less than a year later, it was noted in the *Saturday Review* that the suddenly famous young novelist had been a "published writer since 1939, with articles, short stories, and criticism appearing in *Horizon*, *Cross Section*, *The Reporter*, *The New York Times Book Review*, and this magazine." Omitting mention of the approximately two dozen pieces of journalism and fiction that had appeared in the *New Masses* during the late 1930s and early 1940s, Ellison was clearly bent upon dissociating himself from the organized Left. In subsequent interviews and writings, he emphatically distanced himself from communism, insisting that he had always viewed Leftist politics with suspicion and that the Brotherhood of *Invisible Man* was not to be specifically associated with the CPUSA.[1]

Although many critics over the past half century have taken Ellison at his word—about both himself and his novel—the record indicates otherwise. The *New Masses* writings, as well as his contributions to the New York branch of the Federal Writers Project (FWP), give clear indications of Leftist sympathies and, in fact, exhibit the young writer's willingness to follow the often dramatically shifting Party line. The recent publication of several more short stories from this period—discovered after Ellison's death under the dining room table in his apartment by literary executor John Callahan—reveals that the apprentice Ellison repeatedly sought to express a Leftist vision through the medium of fiction of a decidedly proletarian cast. Early letters from Ellison to his mother and to his high school English teacher, Josie Craig Berry, also portray a young man animated by a radical political outlook.[2]

Yet *Invisible Man* is, unequivocally, a text of the Cold War, manifesting a thoroughgoing antipathy to the organized Left and participating fully in the discourse of anticommunism pervading the moments of its reception in 1952 and its garnering of the National Book Award the following year. Until the entire Ellison archive at the Library of Congress—including his journals and correspondence—becomes open to the general public, we can only speculate about the reasons why Ellison relinquished, and finally turned against, his former Leftist sympathies and affiliations. The drafts of *Invisible Man* are, however, now available for viewing; they reveal that the process by which Ellison created his Cold War classic—what we might term its "anticommunistization"—was hesitant and gradual. Indeed, the careful symbolistic patterning for which the novel is so famous—for example, the accreted meanings associated with blindness; the repeated instances in which the hero is given slips of paper determining his destiny; the homologous character structures of his antagonists, from Norton to Brother Jack—was, evidently, absent from the novel begun in a Vermont barn doorway in the summer of 1945. Moreover, although the entire text was reworked extensively, the section dealing with the hero's Brotherhood experiences seems to have gone through particularly dramatic revision. In this essay I shall indicate the key elements in the hero's Harlem organizing experience that were reworked in such a way that the text's initially positive—albeit ironically tinged—portrayal of the Red-black relationship devolved into the portrait of Brotherhood perfidy familiar to readers of the published text.[3]

Before I begin, it is important to note that the drafts of *Invisible Man* at the Library of Congress, numbering in the thousands of pages, contain multiple versions of many passages and chapters. Even though Ellison appears to have categorized the sections of the novel under various rubrics (e.g., "At Mary's," "Brotherhood—Arena Speech," "Brotherhood—Parade"), the page numbers follow different sequences, and it is often very difficult to trace the order in which the various sections, and the many revisions within chapters, were composed. What I present here are thus provisional findings and tentative conclusions about the compositional process involved in the sections of the novel focusing on the Brotherhood. Because the drafts of Ellison's 1952 novel contain such provocative evidence of his changing political standpoint, however, I decided to proceed, hoping that my efforts here will contribute to the revisionary estimate of Ellison's relationship to the Left that is long overdue. If this project contributes to further rethinking about the relationship of other African American writers to the U.S. Left, I shall be rewarded all the more.[4]

Ellison appears only gradually to have reduced his Communist characters, black and white, to the cartoonish exemplars of Stalinist authoritarianism appearing in the 1952 text. Cool and aloof in the published text, Brother Hambro, the invisible man's theoretical mentor, is originally named "Stein," has "three blue stars . . . tatooed on the back of his left hand," and exhibits considerable humility regarding the Brotherhood's attempt to gain a beachhead in Harlem. "We don't know too much about your people," he tells the protagonist. "We thought we did but we don't, even though some of us still think we do. What we have is a theory. . . . So instead of trying to tell you how or what to do I'll tell you to work it out in your own way." Lincolnesque in stature and bearing, the avuncular Stein/Hambro observes that "to be part of a historical period, a people must be organized and able to make themselves felt as a force. To do this a group must find its voice. It must learn to say 'yea' or 'nay' to the crucial decisions of the times." Harlem's Negro population, the Brotherhood theoretician urges, must act rather than react, and prevent lynchings and riots before they happen, "swerv[ing] the developing forces away from the destructive event and transforming it into [a] socially useful one." Where the Brotherhood in the 1952 text is shown abandoning

Harlem in the hope that a riot will occur, in the earlier drafts its chief ideologist wishes Harlem's inhabitants to become conscious historical agents so that they may stave off disaster. That the sympathetically portrayed Stein/Hambro of the early drafts is demonstrably Jewish further suggests Ellison's intent to defend U.S. communism from attacks that would portray it as a Jewish conspiracy.[5]

In the drafts, other Brotherhood leaders lack the robotic traits attributed to them in the published version of the novel. As we work backward, various puns and wordplays disappear. Brother Wrestrum ("restroom"), in one previous version designated as "Brother Thrilkild," is "Brother Elmo" in a still earlier version. That Ellison recognized the political implications of his changing portrayal of Wrestrum/Thrilkild/Elmo is shown in his penciled comment, "a totalitarian type, eager to regiment all aspects of life"—a notation signaling a growing intention to caricature, as well as a Cold War–era awareness that there is indeed such a thing as a "totalitarian type." Brother Jack, demonic in the 1952 text, is considerably more likable in earlier incarnations. At the Cthonian party, there is no scene where Brother Jack asks the hero to become "the new Booker T. Washington" and proposes the mechanistic toast "To History." In the chapter about the arena rally, the statement that "Brother Jack spoke about economics and politics" is crossed out and changed to "Brother Jack spoke coldly." In the early version, too, there occurs no meeting in which the invisible man is chastised by the leadership for political incoherence and opportunism; instead, he and Brother Jack go out for a beer. When the protagonist later realizes that the Brotherhood has been losing its base of support in Harlem, he notes, in an early draft, "When I met Brother Jack he was as bland as ever, but now that I admitted to myself that I no longer liked him I told myself that I was being subjective." This formulation was changed to "When I met Brother Jack he was as bland as ever, but now I admitted to myself that my old uneasiness had returned." As Ellison worked toward his final draft, apparently it was crucial that his hero should never acknowledge having felt positively at any point toward the Brotherhood leader. Furthermore, Ellison seems to have added only late in his writing the climactic scene in which Brother Jack's eye pops out and he starts gabbling in a foreign tongue (presumably Russian), thereby signifying the hero's invisibility to the Russian-ruled Reds. Finally, although in all the drafts the warning note handed to the hero by Brother Tarp is said to be written in a handwriting that the hero "faintly recognize[s]," all do not contain the culminating episode in which the hero, having crawled down a manhole during the riot, finds in his briefcase the note enabling him to identify

Brother Jack as his hidden enemy. Rather than having conceived in advance a narrative structure in which Norton, Bledsoe, Emerson, and Brother Jack possess homologous character structures, Ellison evidently discovered only after extensive rewriting that—as noted to himself in a marginal comment—the novel's "antagonists must all be connected, merged into every other antagonist. White against black."[6]

Indeed, if we move from the portrayal of individual members of the Brotherhood to the more general representation of the organization's relationship to the African American working class, the drafts of *Invisible Man* suggest that, at least when he first conceived the New York sections of the novel, Ellison wished to pay a degree of tribute to the CPUSA's work in bringing a class-conscious politics to Harlem. In an early draft, it is not the recognition that he is in debt to Mary Rambo and needs money, but instead the impact of seeing a Brotherhood-sponsored march through Harlem after the eviction demonstration, that decides the hero to cast in his lot with the Left:

> There were hundreds of them, marching six or eight abreast in a kind of wild discipline beneath a blaze of phosphorescent flares. . . . I now saw the whites, not old and at the head, . . . but young, of all ages and mixed indiscriminately throughout the procession. . . .
>
> Their chanted words were now becoming distinct:
>
> *No more dispossession of the dispossessed*
> *We Say,*
> *No more dispossession of the dispossessed!*

In the wake of the parade, a group of boys do a riff on the marchers' slogan:

> *I dispossessed your mama 'bout half past nine,*
> *She said, "Come back, daddy, any ole time."*
> *I dispossessed your sister at a quarter to two,*
> *Said, "If you stay 'til six, daddy, you will do."*
> *I dispossessed your grandma at a quarter to one,*
> *She said, "Daddy, daddy, daddy, thy will be done."*
>
> "Jesus Christ," I thought, looking at the strutting, nose thumbing boys. I haven't heard anything like that since I left home. They were playing the *dozens* in the same rhythm as the chant.

The message of the march, moreover, resonates with the invisible man's inherited beliefs and present mood. One of the speakers, a white man, "talked in economic terms, . . . describ[ing] scenes of eviction and dispossession and men laid off from jobs, and the work of unions and the activities of strike-breakers and the attempts to set white workers against black workers." The rally concludes with the singing of "John Brown's Body," and the invisible man joins in, remembering that his grandfather "had often sung [the song] in a quavering voice when by himself." Curious and thrilled, the hero ascends the speaker's platform, is congratulated on having sparked the march by his speech earlier that day, and decides to take the job previously offered by Brother Jack.[7]

Ellison's decision to omit the parade scene from the 1952 novel is critical. Whereas in the published text the arid theorizing of the Brotherhood is shown to be out of touch with the pulse of Harlem, here Harlem youth take up the rhythms of the Left, just as the Communists couple new, radical lyrics with the songs of the black church. The parade testifies to the multiracial mix of people brought together under the banner of Brotherhood, with whites of all ages blending through the crowd. Moreover, the speech underlines the politics of class-conscious multiracial unity. By contrast, the closest Ellison gets to voicing the discourse of the depression-era CPUSA in *Invisible Man* is in the arena speech, where the hero speaks against "dispossession" and in praise of the "uncommon people" (334–38). The words "white worker" and "black worker," however, never appear. The hero's resistance to the unfamiliar scene dissolves, finally, when he hears whites and blacks join in singing "John Brown's Body," a favorite song, he muses, of his skeptical, subversive grandfather—who, in the epilogue to the 1952 novel, is quoted not as a proponent of the tradition of Brown, but rather as a believer in the message of the Founding Fathers (560–61).[8]

Another omitted episode depicts the hero overhearing a conversation in a tenement called "The Jungle," where the Brotherhood has been attempting to organize a rent strike. One man comments on his having become friends with a white Brotherhood couple, noting that "these here fays dont act like ofays, they act like people!" Though at first he was skeptical of the white man's offer of friendship, the Harlemite now concludes: "This is something much bigger than I thought. I'm in it for good now. They invite me to they house, I invite them to mine; they serve me saurkraut and winnies [*sic*]. I serve em red rice and beans, and we building the movement together." The Red-inspired multiracial unity that the invisible man glimpsed at the parade to Mount Morris Park is apparently being built on the interpersonal level as well.[9]

Indeed, the invisible man's entire experience as a Brotherhood organizer, viewed retrospectively as sheer hoodwinking and manipulation in the 1952 text, is depicted quite nostalgically in the drafts. In the published text, Ellison restricts his account of the hero's Brotherhood organizing to a description of the "Rainbow of America's Future" poster campaign and a brief account of a parade of "fifteen thousand Harlemites . . . down Broadway to City Hall," in which he features a cohort of dancing teenagers, "the best-looking girls we could find, who pranced and twirled and just plain girled in the enthusiastic interest of Brotherhood" (371). In what appears to be the earliest draft of this material, the protagonist omits the prancing girls and offers a fuller description of the demonstrations he helped to organize:

> At the time we were stepping up the fight against evictions and unemployment and it was my job to work closely with other community leaders. Oh in those days I worked. Speaking, studying, throwing the old ideology around; marching, picketing. It was nothing to pull five thousand men and women into the streets on short notice; or to lead them to mass with groups from other sections for a march straight down Broadway or Fifth, or even Park, to City Hall. We must have worn an inch or two off the surface of the streets. Just give me the hungry and dispossessed and I could make them forget black and white and rush a squad of police, or throw an iron picket line around City Hall or the Mayor's Mansion.

Whereas the Brotherhood in the 1952 text is shown to engage in only one march on City Hall, in the earlier draft it does so routinely. And whereas in the published novel the Brotherhood exploits the nubile bodies of young black women to further its cause, in the draft the Harlem masses respond favorably to the Brotherhood for what seem to be more principled reasons. Even though the retrospective narrator speaks somewhat caustically of "throwing the old ideology around," he looks back on his earlier activism with some fondness.[10]

In this early draft, moreover, the protagonist speaks of the non-Harlem Brotherhood sections with affection and respect:

> They were like no other people I had ever known. I liked . . . their selfless acceptance of human equality, and their willingness to get their heads beaten to bring it a fraction of a step closer. They were willing to go all the way. Even their wages went into the movement. And most of all I liked their willingness to call things by their true names. Oh, I was trully [*sic*] carried away. For a while I was putting most of my salary back into the work. I worked days and nights and

was seldom tired. It was as though we were all engaged in a mass dance in which the faster we went the less our fatigue. For Brotherhood was vital and we were revitalized.

Ellison later penciled in a number of telling revisions. "They were willing to go all the way" became "they seemed willing to go all the way." "Their wages went into the movement" became "a good part of their wages went into the movement." The narrator adds to the statement that he contributed "most of my salary" the comment that "money was not so necessary, when we found so much in our group." Such alterations suggest Ellison's growing desire to ironize the protagonist's naive faith in his comrades, downplay the extent of their shared commitment, and suggest that the Brotherhood has clandestine ties with the wealthy class it purports to wish to overthrow. It would appear that Ellison came to view even these qualifications as implying too positive a portrayal of the Brotherhood, however, for he eventually cut the entire passage from the novel.[11]

Furthermore—and of crucial importance in the representation of Leftist history in *Invisible Man*—the drafts do not accuse the Brotherhood of sacrificing Harlem on the altar of Soviet expediency in the period following the collapse of the 1939 Nonaggression Pact and the Nazi invasion of the Soviet Union. In the published novel, the invisible man learns that the Brotherhood has lost its base in Harlem as "a result of a new program which had called for the shelving of our old techniques of agitation" and "a switch in emphasis from local issues to those more national and international in scope," in which "it was felt that for the moment the interests of Harlem were not of first importance" (418). Ellison would later make the implied charge here explicit: "The Communists recognized no plurality of interests and were really responding to the necessities of Soviet foreign policy, and when the war came, Negroes got caught and were made expedient in the shifting of policy."[12]

In the drafts, the reasons given for the Brotherhood's diminished influence in Harlem are a good deal more complex. In a handwritten version appearing to be the earliest account, the hero observes that he lost some influence with "the committee" early on by mistakenly carrying out a campaign to free a young Negro writer who had been imprisoned for murder—but who, when freed (largely as a result of the hero's efforts), commits another murder. Thus when the hero tries to caution the Brotherhood about the riot brewing in Harlem, the organization rejects his warnings not because its abstract theory cannot admit the possibility of contingency and chaos, but, in large part, because the invisible man's credibility has been damaged. More strategic reasons are cited as well:

> We found that with the slight rise in the nation's economy our issues were being won too quickly. . . . And it was at this point that the opposition went into action [and] picked Harlem for the showdown and we were given a shock. . . . First membership began falling off, but we were unaware because for some reason the Harlem committee falsified their reports, making it appear that things were going smoothly, or were at least stable. But History forced the truth. I learned that a deal had been made with a congressman back during the time of my first speech and now . . . with electiontime drawing near and we would have to throw our support behind him, the people were not responding.

The criticism lodged here focuses primarily on the perils of reformism: the Party pays the price for its involvement in electoral politics. But it appears that what precipitates the crisis in the Brotherhood's relationship to Harlem is the attack from the "opposition," which "picked Harlem for the showdown," rather than any pattern of manipulation and betrayal on the part of "the committee." Although opportunism is evident in the Harlem leaders' handing in "falsified . . . reports," there is no clear suggestion that the organization has abandoned the fight against racism.[13]

Among the most significant revisions of the Brotherhood materials in the early drafts of *Invisible Man* is Ellison's decision to efface a young white woman named Louise. In the 1952 text, the hero's interactions with white women in the movement are confined to his flirtation with Emma, mistress to Brother Jack, an attempted seduction by the red-robed wife of a Brotherhood leader, and his abortive relationship with Sibyl, another leader's wife, who lusts to be taken in violence by a black man. The woman who was once Louise remains only as the nameless young woman who, in the eviction scene, tells the hero that "you certainly moved them to action." She disappears from the novel after he last glimpses "her white face in the dim light of the darkened doorway" (277–78). In the drafts, however, the shadowy young woman plays a meaningful role. Encountering her at the Cthonian on the evening of the eviction and the parade, the invisible man is taken with her beauty and flirts with her openly, testing the limits of her antiracism. Though initially skeptical about her motives for belonging to the Brotherhood, he is attracted by her honesty and openness. Her father is a wealthy businessman, she tells him; she hopes through her Brotherhood activity to undo some of the damage her source of wealth has done. Furthermore, the hero is shown to be fully aware of his own mixed and conflicting motives in wishing to make a romantic conquest of such a markedly "white" woman. The following passage is marked "omit" in the margin:

> And I knew at that moment that it was not her color, but the voice and if there was anything in the organization to which I could give myself completely, it was she. If I could work with her, be always near her, then I could have all that the Trustees had promised and failed to give and more. And if she was not the meaning of the struggle for the others, for me she would be the supremest prize of all. "Oh you fair warrior," my mind raced on, "You dear, sweet, lovely thing, for you I'd rock the nation with a word. You'll be my Liberty and Democracy, Hope and Truth and Beauty, the justification for manhood, the motive for courage and cunning; for you I'll make myself into this new name they've given me and I'll believe that Brother Jack and the others mean what they say about creating a world in which even men like me can be free. . . .["] I took a drink and for an instant I remembered the Vet laughing in the bus as it shot away from the campus. . . . So I would *play* the fool, and if it was my being black that made me desire the white meat of the chicken, then I'd accept my desire along with the chitterlings and sweet potato pie.

Louise's subsequent appearances in the draft text are fragmentary. There is a rather bizarre two-page imitation of the style of *Finnegan's Wake*, in which an unspecified voice riffs on "Sweet Georgia Brown" as the hero meditates on the whiteness of Louise. There is also a handwritten paragraph describing the invisible man's forcing her to sit under a sunlamp so that she will be less visibly white when they go out. But Louise is referred to several times as the invisible man's love interest: when he follows the parade, he searches for Louise in the crowd, and later it is his pursuit of Louise to "The Jungle" that results in his overhearing the conversation about the hip red "ofays." On the day when he has his grand confrontation with "the committee," the protagonist remarks that he had originally wished to spend the day with Louise; when he cuts his ties with the Brotherhood, his greatest regret is losing her. She was evidently a figure of central importance in Ellison's first conception of the novel's Harlem section.[14]

Ellison seems to have removed Louise from the novel only by degrees. In various later drafts she appears—albeit not as "Louise"—as the wife of Tod Clifton. In the 1952 text, Clifton is an exemplar of martyrdom, betrayed by the Brotherhood and then murdered by the Nazi-like New York police; while attractive to all the young women in the

Brotherhood, he is single and uninvolved. In at least two of the drafts, however, Clifton's mourning the collapse of his marriage with a young white woman is among the most important facets of his role. In the earlier draft, it is Clifton who reports having put his wife under a sunlamp to minimize her whiteness; moreover, he voices uneasiness at having felt that they were in a showcase marriage, "symbolic of this and symbolic of that." Penciled-in editorial changes show Clifton later stating to the invisible man his suspicion that Louise may have married him "under orders" from "the committee"; the hero demurs, thinking, "He hates himself. . . . He doesn't believe that she—any white girl—could love him simply because she is white." In the later draft, Clifton openly charges the Brotherhood with having used Louise as "nigger bait." "I didn't know whether we were together for love or for discipline," he says. "We were like that couple in a sign advertising one of those jungle movies; she was the blonde and I was the gorilla." Although Clifton's final bitter comment unambiguously affirms the anti-Communist charge that the CPUSA used white women to attract African American men to the movement, the evolution of Clifton's wife from her earlier incarnation as Louise shows that Ellison originally had in mind a much more psychologically nuanced—and self-critical—depiction of the appeal of white women to black men in the radical movement. Ellison's eventual elimination of the Louise character from the text suggests, however, his desire to avoid anything resembling a three-dimensional portrayal of interracial sexuality. Emma, Sibyl, and the woman in the red robe were easier to handle.[15]

For all the bitter anticommunism Ellison poured into this last conversation between Clifton and the invisible man, apparently he was not yet ready to accuse the Brotherhood of driving Clifton to his death. For none of the early drafts contains a description of Clifton's murder by a policeman in midtown Manhattan. In one version, the hero sees Clifton performing the grotesque dance with his Sambo doll only in a nightmare, not in reality. In another—seemingly still earlier—draft, the man whom the hero encounters handling the dancing Sambo dolls is not Clifton but "one of the younger brothers. One of the most enthusiastic." The young man chants:

What makes him happy?
What makes him wantta dance? heh?
This Sambo, the joy boy?
He's more than a toy, he's Sambo the dancing doll.
He lives in the sun shine of your smile, thats his secret[.]

> Ladies and Gentlemen, only 25 cents, because he likes to eat!
> Shake it Sambo, Shake it and take it. . . . Thank you.

That a young Negro comrade should engage in such grotesque self-caricature obviously raises important questions about his relationship to the Brotherhood. But it remains unresolved here whether we are witnessing an allegory of internalized racism or one of Leftist oppression. Moreover, the young man is not murdered by a policeman, so the cost of his falling out of history is not so high. In the 1952 text, by contrast, Clifton's chant contains unambiguous allusions to the Brotherhood as the source of his humiliation. The doll will "kill your depression / And your dispossession"; it begs for a "brotherly two bits of a dollar." But that the Brotherhood's betrayal of Harlem would propel Clifton into this desperate self-parody, and hence into murder at the hands of New York's finest, was clearly not in Ellison's mind when he first imagined the scene with the dancing Sambo dolls.[16]

As is suggested in the parade and tenement episodes, early drafts of *Invisible Man* represent the Brotherhood as both relevant to and welcome in Harlem. The openness of Negro migrants to Red politics is further explored in the draft portions of the novel set in Mary Rambo's boardinghouse. In the 1952 text, the Harlem characters who stick most in the mind are those who are the least proletarianized. The street peddler Peter Wheatstraw, master of verbal wizardry, recalls such legendary folk trickster characters as Brer Rabbit and Sweet-the-Monkey. Mary Rambo is perhaps most memorable for her owning the grotesquely racist cash-bank that the invisible man cannot get rid of, as well as for her statement, "I'm in New York, but New York ain't in me": both narrative details stress her rural backwardness. Such still-unassimilated migrants as Wheatstraw and Rambo correspond to types whom Ellison interviewed during his stint as an investigator of Harlem living conditions for the FWP in the late 1930s; indeed, Rambo's signature declaration directly replicates the words of one of Ellison's interviewees. But during his FWP research Ellison also encountered a number of Harlemites who displayed acute class consciousness; that he chose to omit from the 1952 text the voices of radical Negro migrants turned proletarian was a choice rather than a necessity.[17]

The early drafts of *Invisible Man* reveal that Ellison originally intended a more politically and sociologically variegated portrayal of Harlem's working-class population than appears in the 1952 text. Mary Rambo is not just a kind voice and face appearing mysteriously when the dazed hero reels out of the hospital after his electroshock therapy (a scene absent in the early drafts), but instead a worker at Harlem Hospital who takes him in after he has been injured in a brawl with a white racist. Hardly the folkish isolate of the published novel, this Rambo runs a boardinghouse where, among other things, the Brotherhood is the topic of everyday dinner conversation. The widowed Mrs. Garfield—whose husband "worked with his hands and believed in unions and strikes and things"—comments that "[our people] are acting really radical," since "every evening or so when its [*sic*] not too cold you can see a group of both colored and white holding meetings." Mr. Portwood, who admires the Brotherhood because "they got some colored big-shots right along with the whites [*sic*] ones," opines that perhaps the invisible man "ought to join up with them. Or maybe be a union leader so our folks can get some of the good jobs."[18]

Above all, it is the hovering shadow of Leroy, the former inhabitant of the invisible man's room, that dramatically shapes Ellison's original representation of the philosophy and politics embraced by Harlem's migrants. A young man—about the hero's age—who left the South at the age of fifteen after "escap[ing] from a mob," Leroy lived at Mary's for three years and then went to sea, where he became best friends with a white sailor (also a native of the South) by the name of Treadwell. Visiting Mary's apartment with the news that Leroy "drowned at sea," Treadwell notes that because Leroy was a union militant he "might have been pushed off the ship." The invisible man's sense of identification with this touchstone character—he even wears some of Leroy's clothes—was to serve as an index to his expanding consciousness: as Ellison commented in a marginal notation, "IVM must sum up LeRoy in his own mind at different stages of his own development."[19]

In several of his meditations on the status of African Americans, Leroy manifests a markedly radical tendency:

> Would it be that we are the true inheritors of the West, the rightful heirs of its humanist tradition—especially since it has flourished through our own dehumanization, debasement, through our being ruled out of bounds; since we have been brutalized and forced to live inhuman lives so that they could become what they consider "more human"? Doesn't the pattern of our experience insist that we seek a way of life more universal, more human and more free than any to be found in the world today? . . .
>
> To be redeemed my life demands something far larger, broader: A change in the rules by which men live. For now for me to be more

human is to be less like those who degrade me. Is to be more appreciative and respectful of those who differ from me in both my thoughts and my actions. I wish to be, in my thinking, neither black nor white, and in my acting, neither exploited [nor] [exploiter]. And yet I'm willing to accept the human responsibility of soiling my hands with the blood of those who spill my blood whether wearing a hood and using a gun or sending out the orders in a telegram.[20]

The thoughtful tone of Leroy's journal anticipates the epilogue to the 1952 text. When Ellison eliminated Leroy from his novel, he transferred to his narrator some of his character's concern with what it meant for African Americans to be the "true inheritors of the West, the rightful bearers of its humanist tradition." But Leroy's remarks are inflected by a number of Marxist assumptions that are wholly alien to his successor. African Americans possess the greatest capacity to understand social reality because they have been most oppressed by and alienated from it: Leroy's thinking closely parallels Frederick Engels's formulation of the dialectical relation of knowledge to class in the *Anti-Duhring*. Moreover, in postulating that his "we" are objectively positioned to bring into being a "pattern of life" that will be "more universal, more human and more free," what Leroy describes in all but words is the classless society of the "Internationale," where the revolutionary proletariat will abolish class and become "the human race." "The change in the rules by which men live" apparently entails the abolition of both race ("I wish to be, in my thinking, neither black nor white") and of class ("and in my acting, neither exploited [nor] [exploiter]"). The process by which this "change in the rules" will be achieved will be, of necessity, violent, leading Leroy to "accept the human responsibility of soiling my hands with the blood of those who spill my blood." That he announces his willingness to act violently against both those who are "wearing a hood and using a gun" and those who are "sending out the orders in a telegram" evinces his awareness of the class purposes served by the likes of the Ku Klux Klan, whose members function as shock troops for elites using racism as a means of social control. Leroy might as well be a card-carrying member not just of the National Maritime Union—to which, incidentally, Ellison himself belonged for several years—but of the CPUSA.[21]

Indeed, Leroy's comments on Frederick Douglass show him to the left of contemporaneous Communist doctrine:

Frederick Douglass, a typical 19th century idealist. Made the mistake of throwing his best energies into speeches. Had he spent his time in organizing a revolt he would have been a far more important man

> today; he would have fathered a tradition of militant action around which men could rally today. What method? Why guerrilla warfare, the tactic and strategy of John Brown, a man more reasonable in his so-called madness than Douglass dared allow himself to admit.

Always a CPUSA hero, Douglass occupied an especially important position in the Red pantheon in the war years. During the Civil War Douglass had urged fugitive slaves and freedmen to join the Union army, even under the prevailing conditions of intense racial discrimination, in order to defeat the greater enemy that was the slave power. Eager to find historical precedent for their call upon African Americans to postpone an all-out antiracist struggle until after the defeat of fascism—including acceptance of a Jim Crow army—the CPUSA explicitly analogized Douglass's stance with its own some eighty years later. Leroy, however, expresses skepticism about Douglass and prefers the legacy of John Brown, contrasting the former's reliance on rhetoric with the latter's "tradition of militant action."[22]

Mary Rambo's departed lodger also serves to draw out the radical potentialities in others, most significantly Treadwell. Noting that Leroy disturbed a number of his deep-seated prejudices, Treadwell describes how their friendship gave him insight into the role that racism had played in externalizing and deflecting his own antipathy to the different sorts of authority by which he—and, by extension, all southern white male workers—were being controlled:

> We're trained to hate you, to suppress and repress you. It is our major dicipline [*sic*], our equivalent of a state church, or a recognized military cult, or the entering the service of the king. And so thorough is the dicipline [*sic*] that everything else that we're trained to suppress becomes mixed up with it—hate for the father, mother, brother; sexual impulses, unclean thoughts,—everything becomes mixed up with the idea of suppressing you. So that its [*sic*] hard to change anything deeply within us without images of you rushing into our minds.

Thanks to Leroy, Treadwell has come to realize the extent to which white supremacy functions ideologically to bind white workers to their own oppression; Freud is recruited into an alliance with Marx.[23]

One conversation with Leroy particularly sticks in Treadwell's mind. Describing a group of U.S. white college students disembarking at Le Havre from Treadwell and Leroy's ship, Leroy remarked that the students were "some of the most fortunate and unfortunate people in the world" because, as "unconscious vessels of our whole way of life," they would assume that they were going to visit "an inferior people" and miss the cultural riches before them. By contrast, Leroy opined, there were "only two really and deeply human groups in the whole country," namely "yours and mine. We fight each other and hate each other and fear [one] another. And yet our hope lies in the fact that we do. We're the only two groups that aren't ashamed to admit that we're the most miserable bastards in the world. And that all the money and power in the world is no cure for it." Here Leroy examines the differential effects of ideology on different sectors of the population. Interpellating the youth of the U.S. elite—"unconscious vessels of our whole way of life"—as superior to the people of all other lands and times, the gospel of American supremacy deprives them—"some of the most fortunate . . . people in the world"—of their full humanity, making them "some of the most . . . unfortunate" as well. Paradoxically, it is the black and white members of the working class—pitted against one another in violence and fear, "the most miserable bastards in the world"—who, by virtue of their having no stake in the survival of the system, have the capacity to "feel love or even real joy." To be "really and deeply human" results from the experience of oppression, which positions its victims to understand that "money and power" are what violate their humanity in the first place. This is a distinctly Marxist formulation of epistemic privilege.[24]

We cannot at this point know why Ellison eliminated the boardinghouse characters in general, and Leroy in particular, from *Invisible Man*. The effect of this decision, however, was to omit his most concrete demonstration of the openness of the black working class to a politics of class-conscious multiracial unity—indeed, in Leroy's case, of the extent to which many key components of those politics were already embraced by Harlem's most advanced denizens. One cannot help wondering what the novel would have looked like if the invisible man of the 1952 text had used the radical Leroy as a benchmark in "the different stages in his own development." Given the drafts of *Invisible Man*, the final version is irretrievably haunted by the ghosts in Mary Rambo's kitchen.

The drafts of *Invisible Man* do not signal that Ellison originally set out to write a proletarian novel. Even in formation his text was more about identity than commitment, internal change than social transformation; in various places, moreover, its treatment of American communism is undeniably satirical. But the political stance implied in Ellison's early depiction of his hero's encounter with the organized Left is hardly that of a Cold Warrior and in fact suggests considerable admiration for various facets of the Communist activity in Harlem with which Ellison himself was quite familiar. Furthermore, revisions in the drafts—on the level of sentence, passage, and episode—reveal that Ellison changed his mind, and his text, only gradually. Anticommunistization was, it appears, a process, not a single act. If an alternative text of the novel were to be culled from the early drafts, the result would lack much of the rhetorical tidiness that no doubt contributed to the novel's receiving the NBA in 1953 and that continues to make the text so seductive to pedagogues teaching their students to read for pattern and irony. The drafts show that Ellison did not originally pattern the novel around the homologous character structures that, in the more thesis-driven 1952 text, render equivalent the invisible man's white antagonists, thereby equating Jim Crow racism with elite dominance with communism. Indeed, the greater political complexity of the drafts requires us to historicize the novel in ways that a New Critical reading does not, thereby enabling us to query the politics accompanying the formalist logic of the well-wrought urn and to remember that the Cold War was fought on the aesthetic as well as the explicitly political front.

Read in the light of its early drafts, *Invisible Man* suggests a new meaning to the trope of invisibility, for Ellison engaged in an act of purposive self-disappearing when he produced his revised text. Just as Mary Rambo's boardinghouse is peopled by the ghosts of Mrs. Garner, Mr. Portwood, Treadwell, and Leroy, throughout the 1952 text there roams the specter of a Ralph Ellison who once "bent closer, excited," eager to spread the news of a multiracial radical working-class movement in the making.

Notes

1. Eloise Perry Hazard, "The Author," *Saturday Review of Literature* 36 (April 12, 1952): 22; Rochelle Girson, "Sidelights on Invisibility," *Saturday Review of Literature* 36 (March 14, 1953): 20, 49. For Ellison's later statements dissociating himself from the Left and disavowing any equation of the Brotherhood with the CPUSA, see Andrew Geller, "An Interview with Ralph Ellison," *Tamarack Review* (Summer 1964): 7, and Ellison, *Going to the Territory* (New York: Random House, 1986), 59, 202, and *Shadow and Act* (New York: Random House, 1964), xxi. Leftist poet and journalist Melvin B. Tolson stated that he and Ellison had been "in the radical movement" together and referred to Ellison—somewhat angrily—as an "Ex-Communist." Quoted in Robert M. Farnsworth, *Melvin B. Tolson, 1898–1966: Plain Talk and Poetic Prophecy* (Columbia: University of Missouri Press, 1984), 299–300. For more on Ellison's radical journalism, see my "Ralph Ellison as Proletarian Journalist," *Science and Society* 62 (Winter 1998–99): 537–56, esp. 539–41.

2. That the old canards about African Americans and communism persist into

these presumably post–Cold War years is evidenced in a relatively recent article appearing in the flagship journal of African American literature; see Jesse Wolfe, "'Ambivalent Man': Ralph Ellison's Rejection of Communism," *African American Review* 34 (Winter 2000): 621–38. Some of Ellison's FWP pieces are contained in Ann Banks, ed., *First-Person America* (New York: Knopf, 1980); some unpublished writings are in the microfilm version of the FWP's "The Negro in New York" writings (reels 2 and 3) at the Schomburg Library, New York City. A number of Ellison's previously unpublished radical short stories are reproduced in John C. Callahan, ed., *Flying Home and Other Stories* (New York: Random House, 1996). For more on Ellison's proletarian short stories, see my "Reading Redness: Politics and Audience in Ralph Ellison's Early Fiction," *Journal of Narrative Technique* 29 (Fall 1999): 323–39. Though access to Ellison's correspondence is still restricted, two letters to his mother have been reproduced in Callahan's "'American Fiction Is of a Whole': From the Letters of Ralph Ellison," *New Republic* (April 1, 1999): 35–37. A 1937 letter from Ellison to Berry, in which he boasts of his association with the Young Communist League–sponsored magazine the *Champion*, is among Berry's papers in the Western History Collections, University of Oklahoma, Norman. Berry subsequently noted Ellison's editorial activity in her regular column in the *Oklahoma City Dispatch*.

3. On the dates on which the NBA was announced and awarded, the *New York Times* was replete with articles about the Smith Act trials and the need for a foreign policy to "defeat red encirclement" (*New York Times*, January 28, 31, 1953). The keynote address at the NBA ceremony, delivered by William O. Douglas of the U.S. Supreme Court, focused on the need to help Asian nations like Malaysia "coordinate their efforts in the counter-revolution against Communism." "Address of Justice William O. Douglas," NBA Award Ceremony, New York City, January 27, 1953, Random House Papers, Special Collections, Butler Library, Columbia University. For the term "homologous character structures" I am indebted to my friend Gregory Meyerson.

4. Ellison's letters to Richard Wright show that both men were angered by the reception of *Native Son* by certain members—especially African Americans—of the CPUSA leadership. They also reveal, however, that Ellison agreed with certain aspects of the Party line until as late as 1948. Of particular interest in the Ellison-Wright correspondence are the letters of April 22, 1940, August 18, 1945, June 24, 1946, and February 1, 1948, box 97, folder 1314, Richard Wright Papers, Beinecke Rare Book and Manuscript Library, Yale University, New Haven, Conn. Ellison began work on *Invisible Man* while staying with Amelie and John Bates, an interracial Leftist couple who lived in Waitsville, Vt. John Bates—whose brother Ad was active in CPUSA-led union work—posed as the invisible man in Gordon Parks's photo essay on Ellison's novel that was published in *Life* magazine on August 25, 1952, pp. 9–11. For the information about John and Amelie Bates, I am indebted to their daughters Beth and Grace, whom I interviewed in Waitsville in August 1996.

5. "Brotherhood," folder 1, box 142, Ellison Papers, Manuscript Division, Library of Congress, Washington, D.C. (hereafter cited as EP). The same draft contains a further description of the invisible man's childhood memory of a "tall, fastidious Jew" who was "more aristocratic than all the Southern aristocrats in the town put together." The locus classicus of the branding of white Communists as Jews bent upon control of African Americans remains Harold Cruse's *Crisis of the Negro Intellectual* (New York: Morrow, 1967).

6. "Brotherhood," folders 3, 5, and 6, box 143, EP; "Brotherhood—Arena Speech," box 143, EP; Ellison, *Invisible Man* (1952; reprint, New York: Random House, Vintage Books, 1982), 300, 303. The page numbers of all subsequent quotations from the novel will be cited parenthetically in the text.

7. "Brotherhood," folder 2, box 143, EP.

8. For more on the CPUSA's practice of matching radical antiracist lyrics with familiar tunes, see Robin D. G. Kelley, *Hammer and Hoe: Alabama Communists during the Depression* (Chapel Hill: University of North Carolina Press, 1990).

9. "Brotherhood—Fired Tenement," box 143, EP.

10. "Brotherhood," folder 3, box 143, EP.

11. Ibid.

12. Ellison, *Going to the Territory*, 296.

13. "Brotherhood," folders 2, 5, box 143, EP;

14. "Brotherhood—Louise," box 143, EP. Here is a sample of the Joycean passage: "Astonding [*sic*], you erred her fair. go to the head of the roof! Suns! The rush of wings, who neighed? Cops with horseshoes anvil the streets. . . . Impossible. Snowdisillusion (continued on page plucked from diseviction) time floating like flake into her drawers, snow fleeting disillusion its best to grab her though with fragment clinging reads: My Nigra Primus Provoed by me out of Minny rummed and throwed into cuba libre, ignorant acreless muleless a side of macon a jog of goergum this first Aprooled dies irae of '71 too soon to be forgot. Color? Brown." "Brotherhood—Louise," box 143, EP. We may be grateful that Ellison decided to omit this material from the 1952 text. Notably, representation of the protagonist's racial insecurity is not limited to the Louise chapters in the early drafts. Ellison describes the protagonist's attempt to find acceptance among the Harlem elite: "I took to going around to well known places and trying to adopt the values of 'society.' I read all the books on attiquette [*sic*] and all the 'how to win friends' books. I dressed fastidiously, spending much of my salary and many tedious hours on my toilet. I tried all of the preparations for straightening the hair. I piled them on until my hair turned dry and red and fell out by the handfuls. But I wasn't discouraged. I was desperate. I smeared strong bleaching ointments on my face until it was for a time a mass of running sores and that forced me to stay within the house for months, but at best I achieved only a muddy, green-tinged complexion." "Bar Scene—Downtown," box 142, EP. Clearly Ellison originally intended a much sharper ironization of his protagonist than appears in the 1952 text.

15. "Brotherhood," folders 1, 4, box 143, EP. For an instance of the charge that the CPUSA dangled white women before black men, see J. Saunders Redding, *On Being Negro in America* (Indianapolis: Bobbs-Merrill, 1951): 51–70. Marvel Cooke, active in the Harlem CPUSA for many years, claimed that this charge was without foundation; interview with author, 7 October 1995.

16. "Brotherhood," folder 4, box 143, EP.

17. The prototypes for Rambo and Wheatstraw are apparent in Ellison's FWP interviews that are reproduced in Banks, *First-Person America*, 244, 250–52. See also Foley, "Ralph Ellison as Proletarian Journalist," *Science and Society* 62 (Winter 1998–99): 537–56, esp. 541–43.

18. "At Mary's," folder 1, box 142, EP. In 1963 Ellison published an early version of the Mary Rambo material, featuring her as a worker in Harlem Hospital, as "Out of the Hospital and under the Bar," in Herbert Hill, ed., *Soon, One Morning* (New York: Knopf, 1963), 242–90.

19. "At Mary's," folders 1 and 2, box 142, EP. In a ruminating note to himself, Ellison characterized Leroy as "a young student who came North to study. An orphan he is self educated and distinctly different from those who like him were born in the South. He has learned to read, and has linked up his humanity with that of Humanity generally. He is interested in problems of leadership. He is Leader, psychologically, who has seen the dichotomy of his position as consisting of a need to act on folk level, or of building up organization whereby he can operate on more sophisticated urban level. In folk he can see only limited possibilities, which are nevertheless vital. On the other hand he feels need to possess the meaning of the entire American culture, if not emotionally, intellectually—although he does not believe that such a division is necessary." "At Mary's," folder 2, box 142, EP. In another draft passage the invisible man describes the books Leroy has left behind, including "Darwin, Marx and Freud, Frazier, Malinowski and Raglan; a study of Luther Burbank, a Bible, a work on navigation, the eneid [*sic*], a Shakespeare, a work on mathematics, something titled 'How to Abandon Ship,' something titled 'Sickness unto Death,' and a large work titled 'Myth and Leadership: A Study of the Leader and His Mission.'" "At Mary's," folder 1, box 142, EP. It is difficult to avoid the conclusion that Ellison envisioned aspects of himself in Leroy (whose name he sometimes spelled "LeRoy").

20. "Brotherhood," folder 2, box 143, EP.

21. Frederick Engels, *Herr Eugen Duhring's Revolution in Science: Anti-Duhring*, trans. Emile Burns (New York: International, 1939), 104.

22. "Leroy's Journal," box 145, EP. Some African Americans criticized the CPUSA for withholding full support from the "Double-V Campaign," an effort to use the crisis of the war to push a full civil rights agenda. Although Leroy may be read as joining in this criticism, it should be noted that his designation of Brown as greater than Douglass hardly fits in with the implicitly or explicitly anti-(white) Communist cast that the charge often assumed. For more on Ellison's views on the Double-V Campaign, see his various commentaries in the *Negro Quarterly*, a short-lived radical black magazine that Ellison coedited with African American radical (and sometime CPUSA member) Angelo Herndon, especially "Editorial Comment," *Negro Quarterly* 1 (Winter 1943): 294–303. The entirety of Douglass's July 6, 1863, speech urging full African American participation in the Civil War was reprinted in the *Communist* (the CPUSA's theoretical organ) in 1942, with a preface by James Ford. "Negroes and the National War Effort," *Communist* 21 (April 1942): 262–64. See also Ben Davis Jr., "The Communists, the Negro People, and the War," *Communist* 21 (August 1942): 633–39, and A. B. Magil, "Lessons of the Civil War for Our Day," *Communist* 21 (August 1942): 644–62. See also the symposium "Have the Communists Quit Fighting for Negro Rights?," *Negro Digest* 3 (December 1944): 57–70.

23. "At Mary's," folder 2, box 142, EP. Ellison further treats the damaging effect of white supremacist consciousness on the white working class in his remarkable story, "A Party Down at the Square," in Callahan, *Flying Home and Other Stories*, 3–11; see my commentary on this story in "Reading Redness." Ellison's interest in yoking Freudian psychology with Marxist analysis is displayed in his 1945 review of Gunnar Myrdal's *American Dilemma*; see Ellison, *Shadow and Act*, 303–17.

24. "Leroy's Journal," box 145, EP.

Mary Helen Washington

Alice Childress, Lorraine Hansberry, and Claudia Jones: Black Women Write the Popular Front

Until very recently Cold War scholarship routinely resegregated the 1950s, giving us versions of the white Hollywood Ten, white Red Diaper babies, white HUAC hearings of the House Un-American Activities Committee (HUAC), white Red feminism, and a white blacklist.[1] In the 1990s a new generation of scholars began to reverse that trend, but most of us still have no sense of the important cultural and political work done by U.S. blacks in the Cold War decades, or the extent of the repression blacks faced during that time, or how Cold War pressures deeply influenced racial issues.[2] But, as books like Thomas Borstelmann's *The Cold War and the Color Line* (2001), Mary Dudziak's *Cold War, Civil Rights* (2000), and Gerald Horne's *Black and Red* (1986) suggest, in the logic of the Cold War, being black equaled being Red.[3] White people who were called before HUAC found themselves under suspicion for having black friends, or being in an interracial marriage, or listening to black music—as if that mighty one drop of black blood could even produce a Communist. Even John Foster Dulles, certainly no friend to

The Committee for the Negro in the Arts. From left: Walter Christmas, Ruth Jett (founder), Charles White, Janet Duncan, Frank Silvera, Viola Scott Thomas, and Ernie Crichlow, New York City, 1950s.

the Left, "lamented [in 1953] the problem of getting colored people cleared by the FBI."[4] Whether on the Left or the Right, African Americans were, by virtue of their blackness, subversives in the Cold War. Prominent black writers frantically debated in the December 1950 issue of *Phylon* whether they should simply eliminate black characters and race material from their fiction in an attempt to be acceptable to mainstream publishers and audiences. Then, as the Red Scare was bearing down on black organizations, Walter White, head of the NAACP, a blue-eyed man light enough to pass for white, suggested a permanent solution to charges of black disloyalty: he advocated in the December 1949 issue of *Negro Digest* a serious exploration of a potion called monobenzyl ether of hydroquinone to turn black skin white and, like an "atomic bomb," conquer the color line.[5]

Paul Robeson and W. E. B. Du Bois are still the only black figures referred to as major players of the Cold War period, but Jack O'Dell contended that "every organization in Negro life which was attacking segregation per se was put on the subversive list by Attorney General Tom Clark." That list of subversives named the Council on African Affairs, which operated out of Robeson's office on 125th Street; Robeson's newspaper *Freedom*; the Committee for the Negro in the Arts, organized to fight for jobs and dignity for black artists, writers, musicians, and actors; and Club Baron, one of the few playhouses producing interracial and black plays in the 1950s. Blacks on the subversive list—to name just a few—included Ruby Dee, Ossie Davis, Sidney Poitier, Coleman Young, Harry Belafonte, Hazel Scott, Lorraine Hansberry, (actor) Canada Lee, Lena Horne, Elizabeth Catlett, Charles White, and Alice Childress. Finally in 1953, when it looked as though the ranks of black leaders would be decimated by this purge, blacks formed the national Committee in Defense of Black Leadership to support those who were being smeared as subversive. Esther Jackson, one of its organizers, noted how little of this history has been preserved: "It's little known that there were several hundred African Americans who were either arrested or under contempt during the McCarthy period."[6] Thus, the 1950s as a period of creative black struggle has disappeared or been omitted from most histories, including most African American literary histories, and the terms "U.S. radicalism," "left-wing," "Old Left," "New Left," and "Communist" have come to signify white history and black absence.

This essay is intended to reclaim those terms by reconnecting writer Alice Childress and her 1956 novel, *Like One of the Family*, to a black Leftist cultural front that continued in Harlem long after the "official" Popular Front was considered dead. In the process, I hope to show that Childress and a network of black women on the Left—most prominently Lorraine Hansberry and Claudia Jones—developed a model of feminism that put working-class women at its center. I also argue that Leftist politics (read: communism) was a vital—even essential—grounding of African American cultural production in the 1950s. Because African American canonization practices have always followed the lead of the Cold Warriors, excising the black Left, we know African American literature of the 1950s through writers like Richard Wright (he tried to be a Communist but publicly renounced the Party in 1944), or, more typically, through Ralph Ellison's conservative, anticommunist, high modernist *Invisible Man;* thus the black cultural radicalism of the 1950s has been almost totally obliterated.[7] As activist and artist during that period, writing fiction and producing plays, as well as campaigning against political repression and racism, Childress counters the notion of the 1950s as a decade without dissent. Unlike Wright and Ellison, she stayed connected to Leftist circles throughout the fifties, concocting for herself, in true Popular Front fashion, a politics that was part Marxist, part black nationalist, part feminist, and part homegrown militancy.[8] She then spent the next forty years erasing or disguising her Leftist past.

Herbert Aptheker (at left), Ewart Guinier, and Alice Childress at a reception on the publication of the collected works of W. E. B. Du Bois, edited by Aptheker, New York City, 1975. (Courtesy of Bettina Aptheker)

Alice Childress, *Like One of the Family*, and the Black Leftist Cultural Front

Although Childress's name is unfamiliar to many, she does not belong in the category of unknown African American writers. Her career as actor, playwright, novelist, short story writer, journalist, and essayist stretches from the late 1930s until her death in 1994. Although best known as a playwright (she is the only African American woman to have written, produced, and published plays for four decades), Childress appeared with the American Negro Theater in the 1940s, receiving a Tony Award nomination for her role as Blanche the prostitute in the 1944 Broadway hit *Anna Lucasta*, which she starred in with her husband Alvin Childress. Her 1955 *Trouble in Mind* won an Obie for the best off-Broadway play of the 1955–56 season. Three of her plays have been televised: *Trouble in Mind*, on BBC in 1955; *Wine in the Wilderness*, on the PBS affiliate WGBH, Boston, in 1969; and *Wedding Band* (first produced in 1966 at the University of Michigan, then in 1972 at Joseph Papp's Public Theater, starring Ruby Dee), a prime-time special on ABC in 1973. Her 1973 novel, *A Hero Ain't Nothin' but a Sandwich*, for which she wrote the screenplay, was made into a 1978 feature film starring Cicely Tyson and Paul Winfield. She published two later novels, *A Short Walk* (1979) and—her last—*Those Other People* (1989), about a young white gay teacher trying to survive the bigotry of a small-town school system.

Obviously sensitive to the liabilities of her Left connections, Childress began revising her personal history, and perhaps salvaging her career, with her autobiographical essays of the 1970s and 1980s. Here she constructs herself as a loner, inspired to write about the masses because of her own experiences and determination.[9] In one piece Childress cites slavery, racial discrimination, and her own family history as the sources for her ideas about the working class, with no acknowledgment of the role of Karl Marx or the Harlem Left in her life. Maintaining the pose of embattled loner, she says she taught herself to "break rules and follow my own thought," declaring that "a feeling of being somewhat alone in my ideas caused me to know I could more freely express myself as a writer." This is reminiscent of Betty Friedan, who reemerged in the 1970s as a middle-class feminist without a trace of her radical Leftist past.[10] But from the Works Progress Administration (WPA) to the left-wing American Negro Theater, Robeson's radical newspaper *Freedom*, the pro-Left Club Baron playhouse and Greenwich Mews Theater, the blacklisted Committee for the Negro in the Arts, and the Communist Party, Childress almost always worked collaboratively with people on the Left, most importantly with writer Lorraine Hansberry on *Freedom* and with Communist activist Claudia Jones. She was close to and almost certainly a member of the Communist Party.

Though almost none of the scholarship on Childress before 2000 mentions her left-wing background, she left a fairly obvious trail. Herbert Aptheker, a leading Communist in the fifties who became her friend when she began publishing in *Masses and Mainstream*, told me that during the worst days of the McCarthy era, Childress allowed him to use her uptown apartment for meetings with underground Communists.[11] She also helped to organize the Committee for the Negro in the Arts, a group that ensured the blacklisting of Sidney Poitier, Harry Belafonte, playwright William Branch, artist Elizabeth Catlett, and undoubtedly Childress herself.[12] Childress worked on the arts committee to free black Communist Ben Davis and on the Harlem Committee to Repeal the Smith Act, both of which helped to earn her an FBI file. Anyone familiar with the history of the Left would know that all of the institutions that Childress was most closely associated with in the fifties—*Masses and Mainstream*, Club Baron, the Jefferson School of Social Science, *Freedom*, the Sojourners for Truth and Justice, the American Negro Theater, and the Committee for the Negro in the Arts—were virtually a compendium of the New York Left. In view of her activities, the FBI organized "a discreet surveillance" and began to compile the hefty file in which she is identified as a member of the Harlem Regional Committee of the Communist Party. Blacklisted, Childress went to Aptheker to try to get her first novel, *Like One of the Family*, published in 1956. Although this

A page from Childress's FBI file.

Office Memorandum • UNITED STATES GOVERNMENT

TO : Director, FBI (100-379156) DATE: JAN 26 1953

FROM : SAC, New York (100-104258)

SUBJECT: ALICE CHILDRESS
SM-C

The above captioned individual is the subject of a security investigation in the NYO. Information to date reflects ALICE CHILDRESS has been a member of the CP since 1951 and during that year was an instructor at the Jefferson School of Social Science. The subject has also been affiliated with the following groups since 1950:

The Frederich Douglass School, The American Peace Crusade, Civil Rights Congress, Teachers Union, Congress of American Women, Sojourners for Truth and Justice, New Playwrights, May Day Parade, National Council of the Arts, Sciences and Professions and the Committee for the Negro in the Arts.

Investigation in NY further revealed that the subject's husband is [redacted] who is [redacted]

b7C

These facts are being submitted to the Los Angeles Division for information purposes.

1-Los Angeles

ALL INFORMATION CONTAINED HEREIN IS UNCLASSIFIED DATE 4/10/80 BY SP-5 RJS/RB

RECORDED - 18

100-379156-3

JNG:SW

FEB 11 1953

full-length "proletarian" book appeared that year and she wrote consistently until her death, most of her writing, like Childress herself, has been almost completely excised from the record by both black and Marxist literary historians.[13]

Childress's experimental novel, *Like One of the Family*, can only be understood in the context of the Cold War. Its protagonist, a black domestic named Mildred Johnson, is a Harlemite, an internationalist, a race woman, and a left-wing activist, in some ways a spiritual cousin to Langston Hughes's Jesse B. Simple, with strong ties to the black community, an ease with vernacular speech, and a militant racial perspective. Speaking in the first person often to her friend Marge, Mildred is both insider and outsider, a working-class woman with a low-paying job and a knowledgeable political operative who is intended to be a model of resistance. Like Simple, Mildred scrapes by on little money, yet she has a rich social and political life, partying at her friends' newly acquired homes, or going dancing by moonlight but also organizing to support civil rights, or attending meetings about Africa. Her lifestyle is far more bourgeois and intellectual than that of Simple, who hangs out at the local bar and often speaks when he is lit up by alcohol. Mildred is in many ways Childress's politically idealized self, always presenting a black Leftist viewpoint with such self-assurance that I always found this novel problematic and was reluctant to teach it in my classes. Even though Mildred's voice is powerfully employed against the exploitation of black workers and racial stereotypes, her monologues seemed to me static and one-sided, without the complexity required of a novel. What I now realize is that it is important to read the Mildred monologues as they first appeared—not in the autonomous and static text of the novel, but in a left-wing newspaper in the midst of Cold War tensions, dramatically transformed by their position on the page and by their dialogic relationship to their audience and to the other stories in the paper.

The Mildred monologues originally were produced as columns called "Conversations from Life" in Paul Robeson's *Freedom*. From August 1951 until the paper's closing issue in August 1955, Childress wrote more than thirty columns in which Mildred spoke out against the McCarthy-HUAC hearings, against the arrest of people under the Smith Act, against colonialism in Africa, against assassinations of black militant leaders, and against the growing anticommunism among black leaders.[14] In the novel, or what I call the "book version," Childress eliminated or changed references that may have seemed dated or no longer relevant, but in the process she also excised the sharp political critique of the columns. In some cases references to communism or to specific political events were eliminated, so that the intensity of the original moment is lost. For example, in the column about the 1952 Democratic National Convention, Mildred denounces Adlai Stevenson for choosing a southerner, Senator Sparkman of Alabama, for his running mate, but in the book version, she simply refers to "some politicians."

As a collaborative text, Mildred's "Conversations" were effective because of their relationship to the other articles in *Freedom*, each article and column anticipating the next one, encouraging and supporting political risk and pursuing the paper's goal of developing a politically informed black community. In the June 1953 Africa issue, for example, Childress's column is preceded by eleven pages devoted to the art, politics, and cultures of Africa. Included are columns by Du Bois and Robeson, pictorial maps illustrating colonial domination, a summary of U.S.

2 FREEDOM January, 1

McCarthy Bans Books That Honor Negroes

WHEN the State Department at the prodding of McCarthy "banned" several hundred works of some 40 authors from the shelves of U.S. libraries overseas, the N.Y. Times noted that "the nearest to a common factor" for removing the books "appeared to be the refusal (by the authors) to tell Federal investigators about communist affiliations."

But an examination of the list of banned books will reveal that conspicuous among the titles that fell victim to McCarthy were the outstanding contributions concerning racial discrimination, particularly anti-Negro oppression, in the United States.

Anti-Communist Banned

For example, the banning of books by two well-known anti-communists, Walter White and the Swedish Rockefeller-financed scholar, Gunnar Myrdal ("A Rising Wind" and "An American Dilemma") dramatically attests to the pure and simple anti-Negroism of McCarthyism.

During World War II, Mr. ... troops then stationed (1944) in England, all of them, with the exception of a single anti-aircraft group, did only manual labor.

A Southern View

Mr. White also quoted from "an official order of an American colonel of Southern birth": "Colored soldiers are akin to well meaning but irresponsible children. . . . They cannot be trusted to tell the whole truth. Among the peculiar characteristics of the whole race (are) excitement, fear, religion, dope, liquor. . . . They individually or collectively can change form with amazing rapidity from a timid or bashful individual to brazen boldness or madness. The colored individual likes to 'doll up,' strut, brag and show off. He likes to be distinctive and stand out from others. Everything possible should be used to encourage this."

Such reporting, by McCarthyite standards, is "subversive" and should be removed from overseas libraries. The fact that protest resulted in restoring this book to the ... cial Problems of Negro Education," a work commissioned by the federal government when he served as research associate for President Roosevelt's Advisory Committee on Education in the late thirties. At the hearing the author described his work as "analysis of the horrible discrimination against Negroes in education."

Is Education Subversive?

Professor Wilkerson, formerly a member of the Howard University faculty, pointed out that the book contained "nothing about communism" but rather concerned itself with a "weakness of American democracy." He said, "if the proposals had been followed" that were laid down in his book, "it would have strengthened democracy." His question: "Is there something about a book on Negro education that is subversive?" provoked a typical McCarthy outburst when the Wisconsin senator gavelled, "We'll ask the questions!"

And most of the questions had to do with everything else but the book. Particularly did Senators Mundt and McCarthy stress the witness' alleged advocacy of "force and violence." But Mr. Wilkerson doggedly tried to keep the hearings on their ostensible subject, a book on discrimination against Negroes in American education. His refusal to knuckle under to intimidation finally prompted Senator Mundt wearily to call for the book's removal from the overseas libraries. For McCarthy the opportunity proved too tempting. He openly proclaimed himself a book-burner when he snapped defiantly: **"I don't care what they do with that book . . . whether**

From the N. Y. Amsterdam

15th Amendment

Another Negro called before the McCarthy committee was Mrs. Eslanda Goode Robeson. McCarthy was particularly taken aback when Mrs. Robeson, in declining to discuss her private beliefs and opinions, underscored the rights of the Negro people by invoking the 15th Amendment to the U.S. Constitution. This bulwark of the Constitution guarantees equal rights regardless of race or color. When she elected the 15th Amendment in addition to the 5th—McCarthy snapped, "You have no special rights because of your race!" He overruled Mrs. Robeson's position, but not without a final word from the famous anthropolo-

violence. The only force violence I have seen has that against the Negro peo

Jim Crow Elections

McCarthy tried with a perate politeness to assure Robeson that the only re no Negroes were on the mittee was that there we Negro senators. The only crimination he saw was crimination by the vot This apology by McCarthy Jimcrow elections is not He knows the score—and clear where he stands on issue—with the Dixiecrats. Robeson took a few minute to provide the "naive" Mc thy with a few elementary in American life: "Most groes are in the South."

Mrs. Robeson Proves Too Much For Sen. McCarthy

Ike, 'Book Burning' McCarthy At Odds

Senator Would Burn Wilkerson's Study Exposing Discrimination

White Asks Dulles About Ban On Book

Coverage of the State Department's banning of books from U.S. libraries. (Freedom, January 1954, 2)

companies reaping profits all over the continent, and a series of pictures juxtaposing apartheid signs in South Africa with Jim Crow signs in the United States. The purpose of Mildred's "Conversation" on page twelve—at the end of the issue—is to make readers feel a personal investment in this empirical "evidence." Mildred has just returned from a meeting on African art and history and is telling her friend Marge about the "pack of lies" about Africa they get from the movies: "All our education about Africa comes from bad moving pictures . . . you know how they show us bunches of 'wild folk' goin' crazy and bein' et up by lions, tigers, and snakes. We see pictures about Africans dancin' all day and drummin' all night . . . and ain't it funny how the animals always eats the African and not the white man?" Mildred says that most of the extant African cultural artifacts can only be seen in the British Museum, that Africans belong to many groups, and that the South Africans are waging a war against colonialism that is exactly like the battles of African Americans against Jim Crow. Thousands of South Africans are breaking the apartheid laws—"Just like if you was to walk in a Mississippi waitin' room,

The 'Big Truth' is the Answer To the 'Big Lie' of McCarthy

Freedom

"Where one is enslaved, all are in chains!"

Vol. IV, No. 1 — JANUARY, 1954 — 10c

By PAUL ROBESON

JUST JOIN ME for a moment in taking a look at what kind of country this could be if peace reigned in the world. What could we do with the 40-to-50 million dollars of your money and mine which an arrogant government now spends to build up a war machine here at home and all over the world.

How many counties are there in the South with large Negro populations but not a hospital which Negroes can enter? How many thousands of our people have had their life's blood drip away, like Julia Dericotte (whom I knew, and Bessie Smith, one of our great artists, because the county hospital would not take them in? Could not some of these billions be used to build hundreds of hospitals and clinics in rural and city areas, South and North, for Negro and white Americans who now lack adequate medical facilities?

Peace Means Security

Let's talk about schools for a moment. How many millions—no billions—are really needed to eliminate segregation in education, or to push the level of Southern education up to the inadequate achievement of the North? The money that's now spent for a single H-bomb plant could do this if we really had peace.

Or take housing. Have we eliminated the unpainted rural shacks with the rain pouring inside; the urban tenements and shanties with inadequate plumbing or no plumbing at all, the rat-infested slums in the major cities of the country? Nobody who has traveled through the South or taken a look at the fire-traps here on Chicago's Southside would say that we have. But can we replace these horrible excuses for human habitation with comfortable sturdy homes for all white, are going to have decent homes to live in then we must have peace.

Yes, peace and vast programs of peace-time construction—hospitals, schools, homes, roads, community centers, bridges and dams—would mean jobs—jobs in the tens of thousands and millions for workers who are now beginning to feel the brunt of layoffs in the electrical trades, in the auto industry, in textile, steel and packing—and you can just keep filling in the others.

Path to Freedom

Every consideration of the interests of the Negro people, every concern for their security, their fight for equality, their dignity, demands that every gathering of Negro Americans declare that we must have peace, not war! Let Mr. George Schuyler marry Joe McCarthy if he wants to—we beg to be excused from the ceremony. Let the decrepid Max Yergan lounge around in illusions of 19th century imperialist omnipotence, if he will—we have other ideas. We are convinced by everything that has happened in this nation and abroad that the path to Negro freedom lies in firm conjunction with the giant strides which humanity is taking in all other countries of the world, barring none, toward enforcing the peace and silencing the warmakers.

Now, if you preach this doctrine of peace, friendship and brotherhood among the world's peoples—you may still run into a little trouble in the United States. That old devil McCarthy may set out to get you!

Reject 'Big Lie'

But a lot of Americans are waking up to the fact that to be the victim of an attack by McCarthyites may not be fatal.

NAACP Says: "Stand Firm" on "The Precious Charter of Our Liberty"

THE CONSTITUTION of these United States unequivocally guarantees to all Americans freedom of speech, thought and assembly. If these liberties should be lost, weakened or destroyed either by legislation or by direct or indirect intimidation, our crusade for civil rights will be seriously hampered.

Already there is discernible a pattern which tends to link the advocacy of full equality for Negroes and other minorities to subversion or "un-Americanism."

In some communities, textbooks, courses of study and teaching techniques dealing with human relations and minority group situations have been condemned or eliminated on the ground that these are not "American."

In examinations designed to test the loyalty of applicants for or holders of positions in government, a question frequently asked persons is whether they believe in the equality of the black and whites races or entertain Negroes socially in their homes.

In many areas the advocates of low-cost public housing are already branded as socialists, while those advocating non-segregated housing are called communists.

Professors and teachers who declare that segregation and discrimination based upon color are undemocratic are suspect, as are those who assert that scientific inquiry supports the thesis of the basic equality of peoples, regardless of race or color.

Books which displease Senator McCarthy or others are to be banned, if not burned. We recall that it was a controversial book, **Uncle Tom's Cabin**, which helped mightily to strike the shackles of slavery from the ankles of America's slaves.

In the atmosphere of inquisition which is whirling unchecked in our nation's capital until it now borders upon the proportions and destructiveness of a tornado, it is conceivable that any organization working for interracial democracy may be challenged for its campaign against race prejudice, discrimination and inequality.

In this day of pilloring, of browbeating, of branding, of cunning indictments, we call upon our people to stand firm upon the platform of the Americanism of the founding fathers as set forth in the Declaration of Independence,

Leading Racists Back McCarthy

By CHARLES ALLEN

When [Senator] McCarthy joined in the attempt to block the appointment of Mrs. Anna M. Rosenberg to the post of assistant secretary of defense in the Truman administration, the Wisconsin senator worked closely with one of the foremost racist of America today, Gerald L. K. Smith. Smith and his organization, the Christian Nationalist Crusade, are blatantly anti-Negro.

Since the 1948 national convention of Smith's Christian Nationalist Crusade, anti-Negroism has been an official plank in its platform. This writer possesses a tape recording of part of this convention. In one speech by a Smith lieutenant, Smith's followers roared in raucous approval when he ranted: "Now we're not demagogic about the Negro problem. . . . We're going to speak what we believe, we're going to seek what is the only solution of the problem of black and white mixture in the United States. We advocate a constitutional amend-

(Continued on page 3)

Coverage of McCarthy's attacks on civil rights. (*Freedom*, January 1954, 1)

tear down the 'white' sign and sit yourself down!" Such conversations thus framed the issues in the language of "ordinary" people, making them important to their everyday lives and encouraging them to think and act in more radical ways.

In the March 1952 column, Mildred intends to expose the anticommunism that is beginning to dominate black newspapers, noting that some folks have been "wearin' their finger out pointin' at each other, callin' names, tellin' who they thinks is an agitator and who they thinks is Communist, who they thinks is a white folks' you know what." Since the word "Communist" is not used in the book version, the entire context for the arguments and tensions in the social club is lost. Moreover, in the novel there is a softening of racial critique: When one club member objects to white support of a memorial for two slain civil rights leaders, Mildred maintains that blacks should encourage white support because otherwise whites may decide to stay at home or even join the opposition. But in the original column, Mildred says that whites need to support the memorial because of their complicity in these terrorist acts: "Any white folks who are ashamed, disgraced and fightin' mad because of the behavior of their own people [should] also put their money in it."

Drawing of Paul Robeson by Charles White. (*Freedom*, February 1953, 1)

Childress joined Paul Robeson and the other *Freedom* contributors in January 1954 to produce a relentless broadside against Joseph McCarthy and HUAC. Mildred attacks McCarthyism as a form of legalized terror in which everyone—from the army to the post office to ordinary housewives—is being investigated. The justification for all of this repression, she tells Marge, is that "under Communism, you'll lose your freedom, the freedoms we prize so much like reading what you want, saying what you want, choosing your friends like you want, publishing any book or paper you want to publish, reading what you like, have equal rights that citizens are supposed to have." She predicts that "we are all going to suffer much more until we wake up and defend the rights of Communists." In the February 1955 issue, when cautioned by a white employer that her involvement with Robeson will only cause her trouble, Mildred responds: "Somebody has made trouble for me, but it ain't Paul Robeson. And the more he speaks the less trouble I'll have."

One of the significant features of *Freedom* was its aim of producing an informed readership, not a group of demoralized people; it did so by adopting a tone of militant resistance and by focusing on organized efforts to fight discrimination and political repression. Mildred's "Conversations" were an essential ally in that strategy, complementing the political energy of the paper, but speaking from a working-class and female viewpoint.

Lorraine Hansberry and *Freedom*: A Founding Text of Black Left Feminism

In 1950 twenty-year-old Lorraine Hansberry left the University of Wisconsin in Madison for New York and within a few months began working at *Freedom*, first as a secretary-receptionist and later as a writer. Some critics suggest that Hansberry, who had been involved in the CPUSA as an undergraduate, found the greatest support and theoretical basis for her commitment to women's emancipation through the Harlem Left, most importantly through the women writers at *Freedom*. Thelma Dale, the paper's general manager, was a labor organizer and a founding member of the Congress of American Women (CAW), the first independent women's organization endorsed by the CPUSA; Yvonne Gregory contributed articles on women's activism and black women artists. The opening issue of the paper (November 1950), which featured an article by labor leader Vicki Garvin on the fight of the office workers' union for jobs for black women, included the line that was part of the paper's ethos: "A people can rise no higher than its women." Eslanda Robeson and Shirley Graham Du Bois were staff and editorial writers, determining policy and pushing the paper in feminist and socialist directions. By the March 1953 issue, Lorraine Hansberry, now almost twenty-three, had her own byline on page one—right next to Robeson's.

In due course Hansberry was assigned the job of roving reporter and staff writer and sent to cover national and international stories of women's liberation struggles. In this capacity she wrote about women's movements in Egypt, Argentina, China, Korea, Brazil, Kenya, and Jamaica, always focusing on women fighting both for peace and women's equality. In October 1951, in Washington, D.C., she covered a gathering of over one hundred black women, "the wives, mothers, and victims" of race hatred who called themselves "Sojourners for Truth and Justice," an organization led by pro-Communist women, including Childress, marching in the spirit of Tubman and Truth to demand the death of Jim Crow. That month, an entire page of *Freedom* was devoted to articles on the Sojourners, all written by Hansberry in what became her signature style at the newspaper. Calling attention to the radical leadership of women, Hansberry makes special note of the fact that, when the Sojourners gathered at a Washington church, two spaces were left empty, one for

Communist leader Claudia Jones, who had been imprisoned under the Smith Act, and one for Rosa Ingram, confined in a Georgian jail for killing a white man who tried to rape her. In an appeal to young readers, Hansberry observes that "in New York, young women gave paychecks and new-clothes money to send and be sent as Sojourners."

At every opportunity Hansberry foregrounds black women's labor issues, advocates women's equality, and focuses on international women's movements. But the most creative and ingenious way the paper strengthened its coverage of women—a practice undoubtedly initiated by female staffers—was by inserting photographs of women in articles even when they were mostly about men. For example, in Hansberry's story on the Kikuyu people's anticolonialist struggle against the British, the accompanying photo is not of the men in prison but of the Kikuyu women marching on the prison compound.

Yet to a contemporary audience the feminist politics in *Freedom* might seem inadequate, for the paper makes no critique of male dominance and power. Indeed, the paper is silent on domestic abuse, sexual harassment, womanizing, and the absence of women in powerful leadership positions or their relegation to domestic work in the home. Nor does it refer to Hansberry's own struggles over her sexuality or Childress's divorce from Alvin Childress for his role as Amos in *Amos 'n' Andy*. But it is unfair to impose contemporary standards of feminism on the women at *Freedom*. Despite the limitations of their time—they wrote when there was no national feminist discourse coming from any quarter—they climbed the ladder of responsibility at the paper and searched out angles that would spotlight women. Moreover, they worked to create a sense of international solidarity among women of color, and they placed black working-class women at the center of their concerns, laying the groundwork for a powerful, progressive American feminism in this so-called containment decade. Contrary to the mainstream image of the award-winning Broadway author of *Raisin in the Sun*, Lorraine Hansberry of *Freedom* was a militantly left-wing, antiracist, anticolonialist, socialist feminist, whose activities in the 1950s earned her a three-binder FBI file.

Claudia Jones, the CPUSA, and *Like One of the Family*: The Circle Complete

It is likely that, for Alice Childress, another important connection with the Left was Claudia Jones, who in 1950, at age thirty-five, was the highest-ranking black woman in the American Communist Party. In 1949 Jones had published in the Left journal *Political Affairs* an essay about black working-class women entitled "An End to the Neglect of the Problems of the Negro Woman." I believe that when Childress invented Mildred Johnson for her *Freedom* columns and for her novel *Like One of the Family*, she was attempting to answer Jones's concerns about the way Popular Front literature ignored black women.[15] Although I have pieced together the relationship between Childress and Jones with only meager scraps of information, I know that at some point in the 1940s or early 1950s they crossed paths. Both traveled in the same Left-progressive circles in Harlem and knew many of the same people. Born in Trinidad and raised in Harlem, Jones was the secretary of the CPUSA's National Women's Commission and well known on the Left. She was also a part of Harlem's "Sugar Hill" set of artists and intellectuals that included Langston Hughes and Childress.[16] In 1951, the same year that Jones was jailed for violating the Smith Act, Childress became active on the Harlem Committee to Repeal the Smith Act, and so certainly she knew Claudia Jones.[17] In view of these connections, it seems more than a coincidence that Childress's fictionalized domestic worker Mildred voiced ideas that were very similar to those put forth by Jones.

Jones's essay in *Political Affairs* denouncing the Left's "gross neglect of the special problems of Negro women,"[18] set off a firestorm among Party members as it charged that this neglect was apparent in all ranks of the Left—in the labor movement, among Left-progressives, and in the Communist Party. With facts gathered from the U.S. Department of Labor, Jones assembled a catalog of evidence to show that, as the most oppressed group in America, black women *ought* to be central to Leftist strategies and concerns.

In what must have provoked at least mild white Leftist soul searching, Jones cites the subtle ways that white progressives act out "chauvinism" toward black women, including criticizing their domestic help as not being "friendly" enough, or talking to them about how exploited they are—as if they were unaware of their own condition, or calling them "girl" or "the maid." Progressives, Jones says, have been known to express surprise that Negroes are professional or to make remarks like, "'Isn't your family proud of you?'" Or they might ask a professional woman to recommend someone in her family who does domestic work. Sometimes white union women told black women that they would keep the money so that "nothing will happen to it."[19] In one community, white progressive mothers tried to have their children removed from a school when it became 60 percent black. Jones claimed that domestic workers were told that they were backward and not yet ready to join the Party.

Jones opened up another can of worms when she surfaced what was often tucked into the margins of left-wing analyses of race: the degree to which black women felt or actually were ostracized socially.[20] Contrary to Mike Gold's memory of a black woman Communist who could dance like a dream, Jones says that black women walked around with empty dance cards at progressive and Party social affairs. All too often white men and women and Negro men participate in dancing, "but Negro women are neglected." She also notes that black women are rejected for not meeting "white ruling-class standards of 'desirability'" like light skin. Her criticism that Party members and progressives failed "to extend courtesy to Negro women" was ominous in its implications: even on the Left, black women were considered inferior to whites.[21]

One white Communist woman called Jones's article "reverse chauvinism." Almost in anticipation of this criticism, Jones cautions with the example of white women suffragists, who failed to link their struggles with those of blacks. Echoing Frederick Douglass, she argues that "the Negro question in the United States is *prior* to, and not equal to, the woman question."[22] But, unlike Douglass, Jones does not subordinate women; she insists that the black working-class woman must be at the center of Left theorizing, because she embodies the three most important elements of the Left: the woman, the Negro, and the worker.

When Alice Childress revised and expanded her "Conversation from Life" columns in *Freedom* for *Like one of the Family*, Mildred's monologues became a virtual dramatization of the issues in Jones's essays. Mildred becomes an enlightened, politically conscious domestic worker, the center of the novel, as if to show, in collaboration with Jones and Hansberry, the possibilities of leadership in the very women whom progressives were excluding. Throughout the book, Mildred is shaping a gospel of social justice with messages about the dignity and importance of labor. In the chapter called "Hands," she pays tribute to working people by tracing the line of labor required to create the objects we use every day—from the tablecloth that began in "some cotton field tended in the burning sun" to her friend Marge's nail polish. In an encounter with a woman who is angry at "them step-ladder speakers," obviously a reference to the CPUSA's tradition of speaking on street corners, Mildred launches into a sermon on the value of "discontent:" "Discontented brothers and sisters made little children go to school instead of working in the factory, and "a gang of dissatisfied folk brought us the eight-hour workday, women's right to vote, the minimum wage, unemployment insurance, unions, Social Security, public schools, and washing machines." Contrary to the view of Childress's protagonist as a "sassy" black domestic, Mildred is laying out a platform of labor rights for domestic workers that includes

The 'Many Others' In History

A Conversation from Life

By ALICE CHILDRESS

[illegible]

(Continued on Page [illegible])

Above: Alice Childress, "A Conversation from Life: The 'Many Others' in History." (Freedom, n.d.)

A Conversation from Life

By ALICE CHILDRESS

Want to be a 'Freedom Associate'?

Come on in, Marge, and take a load off your feet. Fix yourself some coffee and while you're at it—you can fix me some too. . . . Girl, I had me one fine weekend. . . . I told you I was going to spend a couple of days with Jim and Mable, and believe me when I tell you, I had one fine time. They know everybody under the sun and they all came in Saturday night . . . And did we ball! Mable's back yard is about as big as a postage stamp but we all got out there and made barbecue on the grill. . . . What old lanterns? We was workin' strictly by moonlight . . . big fat full moon, too, girl!

We had cans of beer buried in a tub of ice, home made potato salad, good old spareribs smothered in Jim's special barbecue sauce, and frankfurter weenies. . . . And don't ask about the hot yeast rolls and cornbread!

Marge, the weather was tantalizin' . . . real warm and every once in a while a cool breeze would brush its hand across your face and throw it's arm around your shoulder, and then you'd hear the trees whisperin' to each other . . . and between the smell of the rose bushes and the barbecue, you'd get a whiff of hot coffee comin' from her kitchen door. . . . HONEY, THEY LIVE!

And Jim can just keep you laughin' with those tall tales of his, and Mabel sings sweet enough to break your heart. . . . Well, we stayed out there and sang and laughed until the night air got a little crisp, then we gathered everything up and went downstairs to the basement. Jim has built a little bar to one side and Mabel has made red and white checked curtains for the windows and tablecovers for the four card tables. . . . And, Marge, you should have seen how she had candles stuck in bottles. Yes, indeed, from moonlight to candlelight! Then we danced awhile . . . and who wasn't no wallflower was me. But then, on the other hand, nobody was. . . .

After a time we all sat back sippin' tall cool drinks while Mable and Jim talked to us about joinin' "Freedom Associates." That's a little group that gives teas and parties and picnics and cocktail sips and bus rides and dinners and beach parties and birthday celebrations and forums on Africa and the West Indies and . . . and . . . well, I couldn't tell you how much more. . . .

Of course it's fun, but on top of that we're sellin' subscriptions to a clean, truthful newspaper, FREEDOM. . . . Yes, I said "we" because I joined "Freedom Associates." Of course, you can join it, Marge. Here's a copy of FREEDOM. . . . Now you read every bit of it from front to back and if you like it and want to play "Fairy Godmother" to a newspaper and at the same time have a lot of fun . . . you let me know and I'll write the paper and get you in. . . . Oh, they got branches in practically every city, and where there isn't any, they'll help you set up one.

I particularly want you to join, Marge, because I plan to make some changes in the organization and I'll need you to help me. . . . Well, I think we should have buttons or badges, so folks know who you are . . . and I think we should have committees . . . Birthday . . . Church . . . Friends of Africa . . . Goodwill . . . and committees all such as that. . . . No! I ain't gonna tell you another word until you join!

. . . Don't be silly, of course your boy friend can belong. I just told you Jim's a member! No, Marge, it won't cost you nothin'—except a free evenin' once in a while. . . . Don't you want to be a "Freedom Associate?"

Left: Alice Childress, "A Conversation from Life: Want to Be a 'Freedom Associate'?" (Freedom, July 1953, 8)

just wages and fair treatment by white employers.[23] The Mildred character put flesh and blood on the issues articulated in Claudia Jones's essay. Whereas Jones was writing for the intellectual elite, Childress was addressing the women who suffered the same slights and indignities as Mildred, giving them a theory of labor rights, an authorization for dissent, and a language to speak against injustice, constructing them and herself as bona fide figures of the Left.

Childress in the 1960s and Beyond

Alice Childress's work as playwright and novelist continued long after the Popular Front period—until her death in 1994—and so the inevitable question arises: Did her revolutionary consciousness survive when the period of radical social activism was over? There is ample evidence to show that Childress's work was always informed by progressive thinking and radical activism. She wrote her first play, *Florence*, in 1950 to counter the sexism of the men of the Harlem Left, demonstrating that women's stories were at the heart of, not peripheral to, racial issues.[24] In her 1955 play *Trouble in Mind*, she fought against racial stereotyping in the theater, and in her most-produced play, *Wedding Band* (1966), about the relationship between a black woman and a white man living in the South, where they cannot legally marry, she countered both the Left's fictions of interracial solidarity and the imperatives of a 1960s-style black nationalism.[25]

But it is her final literary production, the novel for young adults entitled *Those Other People* (1989), that may best reflect, in contemporary terms, Childress's continuity with Popular Front politics. The main character, Jonathan Barnett, is a young, white, gay computer instructor at a small-town high school, where he witnesses a sexual assault on one of the female students by another male teacher. As school officials attempt to protect the accused teacher and blackmail Jonathan, anonymous callers threaten to reveal the young instructor's sexual identity if he testifies. Jonathan finds an ally in Tyrone Tate, a black student who is trying to fight the elitism of his upper-class parents as well as the small-town bigotry of the white school and town. Each of the major characters tries to avoid being summoned to testify under oath, knowing that the controversy can ruin reputations, cost jobs (get name and face on television), or even incur physical danger.[26] Obviously, memories of the McCarthy-HUAC witch hunts were never far from Childress's consciousness, and in her final literary act she seems to be offering this legacy to the next generation: a narrative of interracial solidarity and political re-

New York Shakespeare Festival
PUBLIC THEATER
Produced by **Joseph Papp**

presents

Wedding Band

by
Alice Childress

Directed by
Alice Childress and Joseph Papp

Setting by
Ming Cho Lee

Costumes by
Theoni V. Aldredge

Lighting by
Martin Aronstein

with
(in alphabetical order)
James Broderick **Juanita Clark** **Jean David**
Ruby Dee **Calisse Dinwiddie** **Vicky Geyer**
Albert Hall **Hilda Haynes** **Polly Holliday**
Brandon Maggart **Clarice Taylor**

Associate Producer
Bernard Gersten

Productions at the Public Theater are made possible in part by support of the New York State Council on the Arts and the National Endowment for the Arts.

Publicity poster for the New York Public Theater's production of Wedding Band.

sistance influenced in large measure by the ideologies and practices of the black Popular Front.

Childress "actively contested" as well as energetically espoused the politics of the Left, but so little has been done to historicize the role and contributions of black women on the Left that I can only cautiously claim that she was able to "shape its contours." In her 1998 essay on Claudia Jones, Rebecca Hill says, and I agree, that in exposing the triple oppression of black women, black women in the Left-leaning National Negro Congress (of which Childress was a member) were far ahead of the CPUSA in their gender analysis. But the names of these women—Claudia Jones, Thelma Dale, Ada B. Jackson, Charlotte Hawkins Brown, Halois Moorehead, Lorraine Hansberry, Alice Childress—are rarely included in feminist, black, or Leftist histories.[27] Only recently have we begun to see names like Thelma Dale, who pushed for the unionization of domestic workers, or the one hundred black women who formed the Sojourners for Truth and Justice, or the women activists at *Freedom* written into Leftist history. In 1998 Esther Cooper Jackson, one of the founders of the Southern Negro Youth Congress, told me that in the 1940s SNYC activists in Birmingham, Alabama, had already begun to deal with "The Woman Question" in their personal and professional lives. Robin D. G. Kelley documents that the young SNYC radicals working in the South for racial justice also campaigned against sexism, pushing for women to move "away from mimeograph machines" and into leadership positions and calling men into account for male chauvinism.[28] Some women like Esther Cooper Jackson and Augusta Jackson Strong kept their original names after they married. Even Gwendolyn Brooks, whose association with the Left is not well known, was clearly influenced by and producing left-wing feminist ideas.[29] These women do, in fact, constitute a radical tradition. If it is largely an unrecorded history, it is mainly because the Cold Warriors tried to wipe the country clean of left-wing ideas. But, in some measure, we can also fault the practice of scholarly segregation in which writing about the Left has been the province of white (mostly male) analysts who have produced discursive chronicles not at all commensurate with the powerful histories that these women actually made.

Notes

1. This applies to any number of books on the Cold War published before 1990, including Alan Nadel, *Containment Culture: American Narratives, Postmodernism, and the Atomic Age* (Durham, N.C.: Duke University Press, 1995); Stephen J. Whitfield, *The Culture of the Cold War* (Baltimore: Johns Hopkins University Press, 1991); Judy Kaplan and Linn Shapiro, eds., *Red Diaper Babies: Children of the Left: Edited Transcripts of Conferences Held at World Fellowship Center, Conway, New Hampshire, July 31-August 1, 1982, July 9–10, 1983* (Somerville, Mass.: Red Diaper Productions, 1985); and Kate Weigand, *Red Feminism: American Communism and the Making of Women's Liberation* (Baltimore: Johns Hopkins University Press, 2001). I am referring to any discussions of the Cold War, anticommunism, or the Old and New Left that marginalize, minimize, or ignore the important roles of blacks in that era.

2. These scholars, to whom I am most indebted for my research on Childress

and black women on the Left, have begun to challenge the absence of black voices in Cold War scholarship: Michael Denning, *The Cultural Front: The Laboring of American Culture in the Twentieth Century* (New York: Verso, 1997); Barbara Foley, *Radical Representations: Politics and Form in U.S. Proletarian Fiction, 1929–1941* (Durham, N.C.: Duke University Press, 1993); Gerald Horne, *Black and Red: W. E. B. Du Bois and the Afro-American Response to the Cold War, 1944–1963* (New York: State University of New York Press, 1986); Robin K. G. Kelley, *Hammer and Hoe: Alabama Communists during the Great Depression* (Chapel Hill: University of North Carolina Press, 1990); William J. Maxwell, *New Negro, Old Left: African-American Writing and Communism between the Wars* (New York: Columbia University Press, 1999); Bill V. Mullen, *Popular Fronts: Chicago and African-American Cultural Politics, 1935–1946* (Urbana: University of Illinois Press, 1999); Mark Naison, *Communists in Harlem during the Depression* (Urbana: University of Illinois Press, 1983); and James Edward Smethurst, *The New Red Negro: The Literary Left and African American Poetry, 1930–1946* (New York: Oxford University Press, 1999). I have been helped at every stage in this essay by Alan Wald's many articles and by his encyclopedic knowledge of Cold War and black literature. His book, *Exiles from a Future Time: The Forging of the Mid-Twentieth-Century Literary Left* (Chapel Hill: University of North Carolina Press, 2002), is a major contribution to the study of black writers on the Left.

3. See Thomas Borstelmann, *The Cold War and the Color Line: American Race Relations in the Global Arena* (Cambridge: Harvard University Press, 2001); Mary L. Dudziak, *Cold War Civil Rights: Race and the Image of American Democracy* (Princeton, N.J.: Princeton University Press, 2000); and Horne, *Black and Red.* All three of these books make the point that blacks involved in civil rights activities were subjected to particular scrutiny by Joseph McCarthy and HUAC.

FIND

4. Borstelmann, *Cold War and the Color Line*, 109.

5. *Negro Digest*, December 1949, 39.

6. O'Dell and Jackson are quoted in Charles Cheng, "The Cold War: Its Impact on the Black Liberation Struggle within the United States," *Freedomways* 13 (Fourth Quarter 1973): 198.

7. See Childress, *Like One of the Family: Conversations from a Domestic's Life* (Boston: Beacon Press, 1956), and Ellison, *Invisible Man* (1952; reprint, New York: Random House, Vintage Books, 1982). One of the most provocative and useful books about literature and the Cold War is Thomas Hill Schaub's *American Fiction in the Cold War* (Madison: University of Wisconsin Press, 1991). But Schaub still uses *Invisible Man* as the representative text of the 1950s, ignoring the more radical black writing of the Cold War era. For an analysis of the conservative politics of Ellison's novel, see Barbara Foley, "The Rhetoric of Anticommunism in *Invisible Man*," *College English* 59, no. 5 (September 1997): 530–47.

8. See Childress, *A Hero Ain't Nothin' but a Sandwich* (1973; reprint, New York: Puffin Books, 2000), *A Short Walk* (New York: Coward, McCann, and Geoghegan, 1979), and *Those Other People* (New York: Putnam, 1989). Like most left-wing writers of the 1950s, including Frank London Brown and Lloyd L. Brown, Childress is rarely even listed in the index of most African American literary anthologies.

9. Her most important essay is "A Candle in a Gale Wind," in Mari Evans, ed., *Black Women Writers, 1950–1980: A Critical Evaluation* (New York: Anchor Press, 1984), 114–15. Critics have blindly followed Childress's lead and ignored the evidence of her Leftist past. She has been labeled a liberal, a materialist feminist,

FIND

a race militant, a didactic black activist, but never a left-wing writer and activist. One commentator attributes her devotion to working-class characters to her modest beginnings as a high school dropout working to support herself. Some analysts have decided that Childress can be understood only in the context of feminist literary criticism; indeed, in my own critiques, I have always, until now, considered her in the contexts of race and gender. In the one full-length biography of Childress, La Vinia Jennings's *Alice Childress* (New York: Twayne, 1995), there is no mention of her left-wing politics and activities. Of course, Childress was notoriously secretive about her life. Jennings found that she changed her birth date from 1916 to 1920, maintaining that women should always keep their age a secret. In a telephone conversation of January 26, 2001, Jennings told me that the birth records of Childress's daughter Jean had been "sealed" and that she was unable to locate a marriage certificate for Alice and Alvin Childress in any New York borough, despite Alice's lifelong residence in New York City.

FINO

10. In his study *Betty Friedan and the Making of the Feminine Mystique: The American Left, the Cold War, and Modern Feminism* (Amherst: University of Massachusetts Press, 1998), Daniel Horowitz documents the origins of Friedan's feminist politics in the left-wing labor movement of the 1940s and 1950s, a connection that Friedan eliminates in her famous text, *The Feminine Mystique* (New York: Norton, 1974). In this book, according to Horowitz, Friedan sought to distance herself from these Leftists, claiming that her feminism developed in response to the problems of middle-class white suburban women.

11. Herbert Aptheker, interview, San Jose, Calif., November 2000.

12. In an interview on March 2000, William Branch insisted that the committee "appealed to all politically aware black artists of the 1950s," not just those on the Far Left. "Its area of concern was the degrading images of blacks that were standard fare in the media. It aimed to fight against a culturally segregated world that relegated blacks to menial and stereotypical roles and that denied mainstream jobs to black artists." Nevertheless, the *Daily Worker* provided extensive coverage of the founding of the committee and its activities.

First blk ♀ proletarian novel

13. According to Barbara Foley (*Radical Representations*), Margaret Walker's novel *Jubilee* (Boston: Houghton Mifflin), published in 1966 though written much earlier, is the first proletarian novel by a black woman. But that achievement belongs to Childress's *Like One of the Family*, which predates *Jubilee* by ten years. Were Childress's left-wing activism and writings given more attention by radical scholars, that distinction would be obvious.

14. In her 1998 book, *Many Are the Crimes: McCarthyism in America* (New York: Little, Brown), Ellen Schrecker says that because of the reports on Africa by the African American press and the work of influential leaders like Paul Robeson and W. E. B. Du Bois, "the civil rights movement [in the 1940s] had a global perspective," covering freedom struggles and strikes in Africa, denouncing imperialism, and linking American racism to South African apartheid. With the destruction of the Left, however, "the black community simply let Africa drop off the map," with the result that "Americans, both black and white, know less about Africa today than they did in the 1940s" (pp. 375–76).

15. Claudia Jones, "An End to the Neglect of the Problems of the Negro Woman," *Political Affairs* 28, no. 6 (June 1949): 51–67.

16. Carl Dorfman (Claudia Jones's lover in the 1930s), interview, New York City, May 21, 2001.

17. In "Narrating Nationalisms: Black Marxism and Jewish Communists

through the Eyes of Harold Cruse," *Science and Society* 64, no. 4 (Winter 2000–2001): 418, n. 26, Alan Wald notes another source for Childress's Communist connections.

18. Jones, "End to the Neglect of . . . the Negro Woman," 51.

19. Ibid., 60–61.

20. Despite the importance of "The Woman Question" in the CPUSA, black women activists were highly disgruntled about their treatment by the Left. They complained about being kept out of high positions in the trade union movement and about the "lopsided interracialism" of the Party that meant black men were often romantically involved with white women when they, black women, often were involved with neither black nor white men. In a 1981 interview, Louise Thompson Patterson noted that when she married William Patterson, "there was a real celebration on the part of many black women to see that one of the leaders of the Communist Party had married a black woman" (Horne, *Black and Red*, 385, n. 2). Mark Naison (*Communists in Harlem*) also reports that there was a "strong undercurrent of sexual tension and jealousy" over the fact that black men and white women seemed "to gravitate toward one another in Party circles," a situation that occasioned the joke among blacks that "the 'ass struggle [was] replacing the class struggle'" (pp. 280–81) (Naison heard this joke from Howard "Stretch" Johnson in an interview with Johnson, July 23, 1971.) Paul Robeson was secretive about his affairs with white women; he was particularly concerned about how marriage to a white woman would affect his standing among blacks. In these early years, a group of black women went so far as to ask the Party for a ban on interracial marriages, which Communist Party leader Abner Berry said would be counterrevolutionary although he recognized the emotional legitimacy of their grievances. Esther and James Jackson told me (interview, Brooklyn, N.Y., January 1998) that black men in SNYC, recognizing the frequency of interracial relationships between black men and white women, took a pledge in the late 1930s to marry only black women because they intended to work in the South, where an interracial marriage could interfere with their work. The one white woman, Anne Florant, who married a SNYC worker and went south to work, passed for black.

21. Jones, "End to the Neglect of . . . the Negro Woman," 60.

22. Harriet Magil, from an interview with Katherine Campbell, New York City, February 17, 1981, quoted in Kate Weigand, *Red Feminism: American Communism and the Making of Women's Liberation* (Baltimore: Johns Hopkins University Press, 2001), 107 ("reverse chauvinism"); Jones, "End to the Neglect of . . . the Negro Woman," 63.

23. Childress, *Like One of the Family*.

24. In the early 1940s Childress was a founding member of the left-wing American Negro Theater, where she first began to write plays herself. She says that she wrote *Florence* in response to the men at the ANT (including Sidney Poitier) who said that racial issues could only be represented by black men. Friend and fellow activist Poitier (*This Life* [New York: Knopf, 1980]) describes Childress's influence during what he calls "that period of my life": "She opened me up to positive new ways of looking at myself and others, and she encouraged me to explore the history of black people (as opposed to 'colored people'). She was also instrumental in my meeting and getting to know the remarkable Paul Robeson, and for that alone I shall always be grateful" (p. 122).

25. Childress had to fight on all fronts to get *Wedding Band* produced. For sev-

eral years this play was considered so controversial that no commercial producer would touch it. When it was finally produced by Joseph Papp at the New York Public Theater, a heckler in a dashiki made loud, hostile remarks during the love scenes, almost spoiling opening night. Even Childress's good friend and fellow Leftist, novelist John Killens, said that the heroine's struggles for a relationship with a white man were the wrong politics for an era of intense militancy. When the play was televised as a two-hour special on ABC in 1973, eight affiliates refused to broadcast it, and some aired it only after midnight. Papp told Childress that she would have to make the white male, not the black woman, the lead character if she wanted to take the play to Broadway. She refused. Undaunted by these obstacles, Childress produced a play that critiqued the position of every character in the play—from black nationalism, to white liberalism, to white racism, to bourgeois black elitism. I see this play reflecting a politically mature Childress, grounded by her experiences on the Left in the 1940s and 1950s and moving to a complex, nuanced, and remarkably prescient view of the interrelations of race, class, and gender.

26. Childress, *Those Other People.* Childress is deliberately using Cold War language and imagery to suggest the practices of the HUAC.

27. Rebecca Hill, "Fosterites and Feminists, or 1950s Ultra-Leftists and the Invention of Amerikka," *New Left Review* 228 (March–April 1998): 67–90.

28. Esther Cooper Jackson, interview, Brooklyn, N.Y., January 1998; Kelley, *Hammer and Hoe*, 112.

29. In "Why Negro Women Leave Home," a March 1951 essay for *Negro Digest*, Brooks celebrates women who went to work during the war and acquired, along with the "good taste of financial freedom" (p. 28), an ability to critique sexism, develop new interests in the world, and, if necessary, contemplate divorce.

Rise up, you Cracker boy.
Sing your ballads,
Dream your future.
—Don West, "Cracker Boy"

Rachel Rubin

Voice of the Cracker: Don West Reinvents the Appalachian

In 1970, in the pages of the *West Virginia Hillbilly*, poet Don West looked back over more than a century's history of "discovery" of Appalachia by various observers from the North. West wrote, "The southern mountains have been missionarized, researched, studied, surveyed, romanticized, dramatized, hillbillyized, Dogpatched and povertyized again" ("Romantic Appalachia"). As this incancatory list indicates, West was keenly aware not only of how outsiders have pictured poor white southerners, but also of the political consequences of that representation. This awareness, perhaps more than anything, shaped his career, which was varied. In addition to writing poetry, West was also a radical preacher, a union organizer, a farmer, a teacher, a radio commentator, a deck hand on a Mississippi steamboat, cofounder with Myles Horton of the Highlander School (1935), and the founder of the Appalachian South Folklife Center (1965), where West rebuilt the library that had been burned down in Georgia by the Ku Klux Klan in 1958, along with the house West lived in with his wife.

West's biography offers plenty in the way of explanation for his savvy about the representation of Appalachia and Appalachians. He was born in 1907 into a farming family in Devil's Hollow of Gilmer County, Georgia. By the age of fifteen, West had attended school for a total of five terms and had begun traveling seven miles by mule to Oakland Junior High School. But around this time, neighbors accused his father of being a moonshine "reporter"—that is, an informer who reveals to revenue officers the locations of illegal moonshine stills. This was a serious accusation that could lead to social ostracization or worse; as a result, the family decided to leave Devil's Hollow. An uncle of Don's got him a place in the Berry School in Rome, Georgia, where he worked his way through school until he was expelled for objecting to the showing of *Birth of a Nation* because of the way it glorified the Ku Klux Klan.

After completing three years of high school in this way, West was accepted to Lincoln Memorial University in Harrogate, Tennessee. He supported himself and his sister through college by gathering laundry, sweeping floors, and washing dishes—still finding time to be a campus leader and to carry baskets of food to the poor (purportedly, however, he often had to borrow the money to buy it). "Most of the faculty was Yankees who had come down . . . as missionaries to save our hillbilly souls," West said much later of the college. "We didn't like that" (James 1D).

From Lincoln Memorial, West went to Vanderbilt University, where his classmates included prize-winning writer Jesse Stuart (who wrote the introduction to West's first book of poetry, *Crab-Grass*, and served as best man at his wedding) and poet James Still, both of whom had also graduated from Lincoln Memorial. At genteel Vanderbilt the three Appalachian writers, who were friends, came to be known as "the barefoot boys"; although they followed different career paths, each found subject and inspiration in his rural background. At Vanderbilt, West completed a degree at the School of Religion and began preaching in slums and in little mountain churches; according to Stuart (who refers to West in autobiography as "Ron East"), West was kicked out of three churches for calling for justice on earth instead of a reward in heaven (Stuart 141). Until his death in 1992, West continued to write poetry, to farm, and to organize in Appalachia, especially at his Appalachian South Folklife Center (known as "Pipestem" for the town in West Virginia in which it was located), which has been the site of an annual folk music festival, a children's summer camp, a community meeting place, and a center for regional history. When West, in his eighties, began to winter in Florida, he involved himself in tenants' organizing in St. Petersberg and worked there with Mexican immigrant farmworkers.

As these few details show, a biography of West, who was tagged a "mountain socialist" by his colleague Myles Horton for his straightforward and energetic activism, would be a great contribution to the history of the South and of the American Left. Such a volume has yet to be written and cannot be undertaken here. This essay will focus largely on West's considerable but remarkably neglected body of poetry. By "neglected," I mean from the academic/critical point of view; West's fourth book of poetry, *Clods of Southern Earth*, which was published in 1946, sold over 15,000 copies by subscription before coming from the press. (This was reported in the *Atlanta Constitution* as a record for a first book of poetry—which is remarkable even though it was not, in fact, West's first book of poetry.) West's poetry was sold largely through union meetings and other gatherings of sharecroppers, miners, and farmers in what Jeff Biggers calls a "populist poetry crusade" (Biggers 160). To date, however, there is only one published academic article about West's poetry—by journalist and writer Biggers, who knew West toward the end of his life—and a few brief mentions in other articles or books.[1] I want to show that a look at West's poetry can provide a useful way to explore how the cultural Left—from its valorization of the folk in the 1930s through the era of the civil rights movement—sought to craft an image of the poor white southern highlander who was politically aware and culturally empowered. West himself more succinctly imagined such enlightenment in his 1933 poem "Clodhopper": "Clodhoppers of the world, unite! You have nothing to lose but your clods!" (*Clods* 45).

As in "Clodhopper," a major preoccupation of West's poetry is the political awakening of poor whites in the South. This is not to say that West pictures southern workers as naive to begin with: since toil is the defining experience of these people's lives, the men and women who populate his poems have a class consciousness and a sense of right and wrong that represents, in West's vision, the best of what is really "American." Indeed, a revisionist history of the United States, from the point of view of workers, is an important project of West's; throughout his writing (both poetry and prose) he insistently traces the freedom-loving values of working Americans, black and white, back to the first settlers of Georgia. Therein, according to West, lies the true history of the United States, a tale that has yet adequately to be told: "Someday I intend to do it, to tell about these people with rough hands, big feet, and hard bodies; about the real men and women of the South" (*O Mountaineers!* 19). West did attempt to write this history, albeit in brief, in a 1970 pamphlet titled "People's Cultural Heritage in Appalachia."

West's invocation of a "people's history" of the South waiting to be written is connected to his sense of a "people's art" of the South that he sees himself as producing. His vision of the poet's role is to direct a native class consciousness, to call it to action as would a union organizer organizing a collective job action or a preacher calling for professions of faith through acts of charity (both jobs that West held):

Listen. . . ! I'm an agitator—
  They call me "Red,"
The color of Blood,
  And—"Bolshevik!"
. . . .
I sing to a submerged South,
  And she responds
With deep sobs of misery,
  She stirs
And anger sets on her lips.
. . . .
I am speaking!—Listen!
  I, the poet
In overalls, working man,
  Mountaineer
  Agitator! (*Clods* 24)

As "poet in overalls," West both embodies and enacts the identity formation of the politicized poor white through formal choices that consciously elevate traditional mountain artists—quilt makers, balladeers, fiddle players, revival workers—as his most important "literary" ancestors.

In his insistence on the vernacular and the regional as an alternative to the commercial and the mass-produced, West's stance is entirely in keeping with discussions that occupied the organized Left (in particular, the Communist Party of the United States) about the role of the "folk" or "traditional" cultural practices in challenging the "mainstream" cultural productions that are designed to promote and maintain the interests of industrial capitalism. West was associated with the CPUSA—his work is included in the important collection, *Proletarian Literature of the United States* (1935), and he contributed fairly frequently to Communist-led or Communist-sympathetic journals such as *New Masses*, the *Daily Worker*, and the *Liberator*. This attention from Left political organizations to the political potential of "folk" art yielded not only West's poetry, but also a large (and still understudied) body of material that constitutes a bottom-up portrait of the rural South, including ballads and protest songs by Aunt Molly Jackson and Emma Dusenberry, the volume of southern folklore collected by Benjamin Botkin, and Lee Hays's labor-organizer plays performed at the Commonwealth College in Polk County, Arkansas.

In a number of ways, West invokes and pays tribute to folk artists in his books of poetry. His anthology, *O Mountaineers!*, is illustrated with drawings of his neighbors in Pipestem, West Virginia, including a quilter, a fiddler, and a banjo player. All of his books contain poems about these creative figures. A good example is "Ballad Singer," which he wrote in 1940:

He sang his songs of living
Of corn in rocky soil
And men and women giving
Their lives to honest toil. (*Clods* 136)

Or "The Fiddler" of the same year:

Sam bent to his fiddle and hugged it close
And tore off a soulful tune
Till the silent hills seemed to rise right up
To clutch at a low-slung moon. (*Clods* 64)

But West goes beyond just populating his poems with folk artists; he shapes his aesthetic by approximating the technique of nonwritten (and sometimes nonverbal) forms. For example, in "Ballad for Hattie Carroll," who was an African American maid who was beaten to death by a wealthy guest in the posh Baltimore hotel where she worked while others looked on, West begins with the traditional singer's call to his or her listeners:

Come all you poor and honest people
You who would like to understand
And listen to a sad, sad story
Of happenings in this troubled land. (*O Mountaineers!* 35)

In "Ballad for Bill Moore," West likewise uses the ballad form—presenting the ballad itself as a carrier of "real" Americanness. Moore was a white southerner who walked southern roads carrying a sign that read, "End segregation in America—Eat at Joe's both Black and White." He was shot and killed on a stretch of highway near Attala, Alabama, on April 23, 1963. West's poem about Moore borrows both language and structure from the folk hymn, "Jesus Walked This Lonesome Valley." The hymn's lyrics are as follows: "Jesus walked this lonesome valley, he had to walk it for himself, O nobody else could walk it for him, he had to walk that lonesome valley for himself." West's version is a deliberate echo of the hymn:

O Bill Moore walked that lonesome highway
He dared to walk there by himself;
None of us here were walking with him,
He walked that highway by himself.

He walked for peace, he walked for freedom,
He walked for truth, he walked for right
End segregation in this country
Eat at Joe's, both black and white. (*O Mountaineers!* 55)

West, of course, was well acquainted with the tradition of writing topical words to fit familiar tunes—a mainstay practice of the labor movement since the nineteenth century; in fact, in 1937 West put together a songbook, *Songs for Southern Workers*, in which a number of hymns or other familiar tunes are given new, political lyrics intended to "express[ ] the thoughts of people towards unionism, bosses, exploitation, etc." (*Songs* n.p.) Furthermore, as Cary Nelson has pointed out (Nelson 140), in the 1930s miners' songs were starting to be published in books, creating a congenial context for West's (and other poets') politicized work with the ballad form on the printed page.

In addition to West's many poems that draw on the ballad form, other poems, such as "Highlander Youth," draw on the oratorical style of the southern Protestant preacher for their incancatory, biblical sense of intensity and furor:

I hear the deep groan
Of abiding pain
Scourging the hills
With a crimson stain
Of mountain blood. . . . (*Clods* 125)

West combines folk-inflected forms with a use of mountain dialect that sometimes emphasizes an orality of the poems and connects them to the art of the fiddler, the preacher, and the ballad singer. But more often, I think, the dialect is painstakingly represented on the page in a way that ultimately emphasizes the written-ness of the poems, creating a tension between oral and written, rural and city, "folk" and literate—a tension that gives West's elevation of the "folk" historical context and makes his formal choices more pointed. In other words, West is not springing (or claiming to spring) full-formed from the bosom of the folk, using words and phrases that come "naturally" to him. (Nor is he simply unsophisticated, as he is often dismissed.) He is rather making an argument about the value and political potential of folk cultures—at a moment when those cultures appear to be pressingly endangered by the need of the industrial economy to bring formerly self-sufficient Appalachia under its reign. For example, "Last Wish" is written entirely in dialect, some of which is "sight" dialect only ("mountins" would not be pronounced any differently than "mountains"). In this poem, factory work has meant literal death; the mountain speech, presumably being used by Jim's wife or lover, comes to represent the mountaineer's vulnerability, here operating on a cultural or linguistic plane:

Climbin' mountins from sun to sun
A-toilin' all day long,
A-weavin' flowers in calico,
Singin' a lonesome song . . .

Singin' a soulful song all day,
Climbin' a rugged hill
Since Jim was kilt by factory wheels,
Workin' in Atco Mill . . .

Thur's one more hill afore I go—
Hit's fudder up the sky,
A windy know whur fierce and low
The storms pass Jim's grave by . . .

And one more wish afore I pass
Out of this factory town—
I want to see my people jine
To tear thur misery down . . . (*Clods* 53)

But in the "last wish" of the poem's title, also related in dialect, is the potential for the factory workers to "jine / To tear thur misery down."

West's valorization here of the folk voice, specifically in terms of its ability to intervene in the exploitation of the capitalist economy, is emblematic of the stance that characterized the Left's approach to culture in the 1930s, when folk culture, as opposed to the elitism of "high" culture and the commercialism of "mass" culture, seemed to provide a foundation on which a truly revolutionary worker's culture could be based.

In the packaging of his books, West shows considerable desire to be seen as a "folk" poet. By "packaging" I mean his own introductions, introductions by other people, blurbs on the back of the book, and headnotes that he writes to some of the poems. In the foreword to his fourth book, West writes:

> You may be one of those Americans who say you don't like poetry anyhow. No one can blame you for that. I've often felt that way, too. Maybe it's because too many poets write in the old tradition. Using an obscure and "subtle" private language, they write only for the little clique of the "highly literate" elite. . . . You say you want a poem with its roots in the earth; a poem, that finds beauty in the lives of the common people, and perhaps a poem that may sometimes show reasons for the heartache and sorrow of the plain folks and sometimes point the way ahead. I don't blame you. I sort of feel that way, too. (*Crab-Grass* 16)

But West's deceptively simple "folk" poems are thrown into sharp relief in his collections because they are frequently interspersed with very "modern" poems in free form, using "high" diction, "standard" English, and dense syntax. In this ranging between "folk" and "modern," "high" and "low," "standard" and "vernacular," he strikingly resembles Langston Hughes, who was a hugely important influence on West.[2] Two poems that West wrote about workers at about the same time demonstrate this contrast. "Harlan Coal Digger, 1934" is almost imagist in composition; with its lack of verbs and intrusive punctuation (such as the preponderance of ellipses), it is oriented to the written page, rather than to recitation:

> Home . . . a box . . .
> on four pegs . . .
> oozy, drippy shoes . . .
> Acrid odors
> From under the cat-scorcher . . .
> (*O Mountaineers!* 88)

"On Piney Spur" (1933), in contrast, utilizes the rhyming quatrain of the traditional ballad and is written in heavy dialect:

> When the factory got my Love
> It slowed her dancin' feet
> Till she could skeercely climb the hill
> To whur we used to meet.
> (*O Mountaineers!* 163)

A dialectic emerges, wherein categories such as "high," "written," and "standard" on one side and "oral," "folk," and "vernacular" on the other are seen to be mutually dependent rather than mutually exclusive.

Such juxtapositions show that, like Hughes and other poets of the American vernacular, West is using dialect and "folk" forms in a self-conscious fashion that calls attention to language as a thing-in-itself, as a cultural artifact, not a container of culture. But as such, mountain language is exposed to the same forces that have plundered Appalachia for natural resources and cheap labor. For this reason, West is careful to point out that when it comes to "folk art," it really matters who is looking (or reading, or listening) and with what motivations. In the comment with which this essay opens, West catalogs centuries of "discovery" of Appalachia. "Romanticization" is one on the list of things "done to" mountain people—and this could easily happen if Appalachian art is approached with a condescending sentimentality. In "Appalachian Blues," West takes to task three groups of intruders: first, those "who come to study us / to see what is wrong with us, that we are poor"; second, those "do-gooders, missionaries of numerous persuasions"; but he is perhaps harshest toward those who belong to third category:

"Folksy ballad hunters
Discoverers of mountain music
and mountain musicians—
Columbuses discovering Appalachia . . .
Circuit riding freaks. (*O Mountaineers!* 242)

"Columbuses discovering Appalachia": here West limns for his readers a cultural imperialism that necessarily results from the status of the southern Appalachian region as, in the words of West in an essay about the area, "a colonial possession of Eastern based industry" ("Romantic Appalachia" 212). The Columbus metaphor draws the same comparison between the fate of Appalachians (and Appalachian culture) and the fate of American Indians (and American Indian culture) that prompted Harry Caudill to call the region "America's paleface reservation" (Munn 30). In "On Piney Spur," mountain culture (and the labor of the people who produce it) is, along with coal, the raw goods to be looted from the area by the colonizers for the sake of profit.

The lines from "Appalachian Blues" quoted above are the final lines in West's collection *O Mountaineers!*, the ones with which he closes the book in which he has gathered what he thinks is most important from his earlier books of poetry. Plainly, then, these words are meant to leave the reader—or, at least, certain readers—with a caution about how to approach West's own "folk" art. West shares this potentially confrontational stance toward the reader with other writers of Appalachia who possess West's awareness of the cultural vulnerability that mountain people face as money interests transform their towns and hollows—and commodify their traditions and customs. This list would include Mildred Haun, who draws a viciously satirical picture of a museum representative come to Tennessee to acquire folk art, and novelist Harriette Arnow, who depicts a more sympathetically drawn art teacher who nonetheless sees the protagonist's carving as so exotic that he asks her what country she is from. In addition to other chroniclers of the colonization of Appalachia, West shares this stance with other identity-centered, "ethnic" writers, such as Jewish novelist Mike Gold (who pictures a gang of small boys throwing garbage at wealthy people on a tour bus) and Chinese American writer Frank Chin (who invents an opportunistic character who literally gives tours through Chinatown).[3]

Thus, West's reinvention of the cracker serves as a cultural assertion set in belligerent opposition to the romantic notion of Appalachians as what Berea College president William Goodell Frost famously called in 1899 "our contemporary ancestors," untouched by time and untainted by "progress" (Frost 93). In his important book *All That Is Native and Fine*, David Whisnant demonstrates compellingly the ways in which outsiders invested in a limited and sentimental notion of Appalachian culture have actually fabricated, or at least altered, a "native" culture to serve the marketplace. For instance, the "well-born" founders of the Hindman Settlement School in Knott County, Kentucky, possessed a "veneration . . . for local culture [that] was *selective*, and the mechanism of selectivity was the colored lens of their own culture, which was for all practical purposes the genteel popular culture of the turn of the century" (Whisnant 51). In concrete terms, this had a visible impact on which forms of native culture were to be revered and preserved, and which forms were to be discouraged: "Child ballads and dulcimers were good; banjos and the newer music to be heard at the railheads and county seats were not" (Whisnant 56).

As the denigration of the banjo, with its West African roots, and of "newer music," with its implication of cross-racial cultural contact, indicate, romanticizing the Appalachian folk served particular and concrete political agendas, such as white supremacy and anti-immigrationism. In Mary French Caldwell's 1930 essay, "Change Comes to the Appalachian Mountaineer," white Appalachians are held up as a possible bulwark against horders of European immigrants and African Americans flooding American cities: "These people have in their veins the blood of the builders of the nation, in their minds the native intelligence of the Anglo-Saxon, and in their hearts a deep loyalty to their country and an abiding faith in God. If they are sometimes illiterate, narrow-minded, provincial and a trifle 'hide-bound,' at least they are not Communists or atheists, and the ease with which their minds may be developed is amazing" (Caldwell 219). A romantic vision of Appalachia, then, performed ideological work that was not necessarily in service of Appalachians themselves. It could also, according to Whisnant, "become a diversion, a substitute for engaging with the political and economic forces, processes, and institutions that were altering the entire basis of individual identity and social organization in the mountains" (Whisnant 13). West, meanwhile, was determined to use the "folk" tradition as a way to agitate about the very processes that the romanticized vision of the "folk" tended to elide.

In addition to the figure of the romantic mountaineer, West is also responding to the image of a comic or dangerous "hillbilly" that by the first decades of the twentieth century was already dominant in popular culture (appearing in movies, comic strips, newspaper reporting, and music). Like the romantic mountaineer, this version of the invented Appalachia could also act as a deliberate and consequential diversion from "the hurly-burly of politics and commerce and industry" that was shaping the region. Allen Batteau shows in *The Invention of Appalachia* how the notion of "feuding hillbillies" was invoked and bolstered in order to disregard the political content of violence during the Battle of Matewan in 1920 between West Virginia coal miners and tyrannical coal camp operators. When newspapers ran stories with headlines like "Strike Feudists Pour Hail of Lead into Mingo Town" or "Highlander Ethics Perpetuated," the class content of what was essentially guerrilla warfare was rendered invisible (Batteau 111).[4]

When West says that Appalachia has been "Dogpatchized," he is referring to this popular image of the comic/dangerous mountaineer. Dogpatch is the setting for the comic strip *Li'l Abner*, which was drawn by Connecticut native Al Capp and which debuted in 1934. Dogpatch is a mythical "hillbilly" community, where lazy and dirty residents revel in their own filth and ignorance (the main character winning at one point the label of "stupidest man in the universe"). During this period—the decade or so leading up to the publication of West's poetry—the most popular comic strips, including Capp's, reached an audience of 50 million readers or more practically every day of the year (Mazón 33). *Li'l Abner* vied for this mass audience with Billy DeBeck's strip *Snuffy Smith*, which debuted the same year as *Li'l Abner*, and with the drawings of cartoonist Paul Webb, who drew hillbillies for *Esquire* magazine from 1934 to 1948. Along with Capp's and DeBeck's, Webb's hugely popular cartoons quickly became a locus classicus for comic representations of hillbillies. Aversion to work is arguably the most common theme of Webb's cartoons, which generally pictured men lying on the ground with a jug of moonshine nearby. Capp, DeBeck, and Webb shared this thematic concern; other frequently recurring themes were dirtiness, backwardness, and sexual depravity (in Webb's case, with relatives, with animals, and with children).

Thus, the fact that West has so many poems about work becomes a polemic in the face of popular figurations of the poor white as inherently lazy. His poem "Stereotypes," for instance, works by cataloging epithets thrown at poor whites, allowing them to accumulate until finally they ring hollow in the face of the nobility of work:

Redneck, Cracker,
Goober picker
Eat poke sallet
Drink pot licker.

Wool hat, hooger
You're my brothers
All of us had
Poor white mothers.

Linthead, white trash
Red dirt eaters
Lonesome water
Makes repeaters.

And hillbilly,
Do you think we should
Class ourselves with
The Peckerwood?

We are the ones
The big folks claim,
Who lynch the blacks
And bring them shame. (*O Mountaineers!* 50)

In this poem and many others, West confronts the conventional wisdom that dictates that poor southern whites are the most racist Americans. (In materialist fashion, he insists that the real racists are the ones who make profits off the stolen or exploited labor of African Americans.) This is one way, according to West, in which the fate of the hillbilly in popular discourse is linked to the racism faced by African Americans. West was moved to write a kind of anxious fan's letter to Langston Hughes, in which he chides Hughes about his use of the word "cracker," citing one of his columns in the *Chicago Defender*, although Hughes had also used the epithet in poems like "Ballad of Sam Solomon" (1943):

Sam Solomon called on
Every colored man
To qualify and register
And take a stand
And be up and out and ready
On election day
To vote at the polls,
Come what may.
The crackers said, Sam,
If you carry this through
Ain't no telling what
We'll do to you. (Hughes 295)

In 1943, the year "Sam Solomon" was published, West wrote to Hughes: "I admire you and your writing as much as I do anyone I know of. But I think I shall always say that its [*sic*] wrong for any educated Negro to single out the 'cracker,' 'poor white trash' and any other group of working white folks, as the chief enemy of the working people."

In his letter to Hughes and in much of his writing, West insists that the same forces that benefit from racism against African Americans have encouraged this kind of classism as a strategy to drive a wedge between groups of working people who should be allies. In other words, white supremacy and hillbilly bashing serve to bolster each other, rather than standing in opposition—or even in reaction—to each other. Indeed, James Klotter has written that the stereotypes used to denigrate white Appalachians are frequently reapplied versions of the stereotypes used to denigrate African Americans. He points out that accounts by the earliest literary writers, historians, folklorists, and sociologists found Appalachians to be wily, superstitious, and lazy, open to visitors but at the same time likely to engage in violence. "Instead of 'Sambo' and 'Nat' came 'Abner' and 'Joab,'" writes Klotter (Klotter 52). (Klotter even quotes one writer's account of Kentucky mountaineers that dwelled on how much the group loved to eat watermelons!)

By underscoring the financial benefit to those living in "the big houses / on the hills" who taught the poor white to say "nigger" (as West puts it in "Voice of the Cracker," the poem from which the title of this essay is taken), West's poetry demystifies what David Roediger (borrowing from W. E. B. Du Bois) has referred to as *The Wages of Whiteness*. Indeed, West's body of work could usefully be considered within the purview of what are known as "whiteness studies," because his poetics depend on the ways in which labor and economics have created the two mutually defining categories of "white" and "black." Ultimately, West appears optimistic about the everyday workability of black/white alliance in class struggle: he has a poem called "Unity Is an Ax," a title that is, for those from the country, at once declamatory and homey.

This growing acknowledgment of the mutuality of race-, region-, and class-based oppression helps to explain the decades-long evolution of the Highlander Folk School, which Don West and Myles Horton, fellow products of a Christian socialist tradition in the South, cofounded in 1932. Located in Grundy County, Tennessee—one of the country's ten poorest counties at that time—Highlander began as a labor school but quickly became the principal training center of the CIO in the South. West quickly became involved in the organizing struggles of coal miners, textile workers, and others, moving around when he felt there was a need. He began to use his poetry in organizing struggles during this time: West found that he could make connections between sympathetic intellectuals and struggling workers by reading his poetry at universities.

But in the postwar years, the CIO, responding to the pressures of the Cold War by hastily caving into the demands of the Taft-Hartley Act, insisted that Highlander end its long-standing association with left-wing trade unions. Highlander's leaders refused, and the school's primary function as a labor school ended as a result. (West himself was called before the House Committee on Un-American Activities in the mid-late 1950s.) Highlander began to devote itself more to the problems and needs of farmers in the region, and by the 1950s and 1960s it had further evolved into a central training and meeting place for black and white civil rights activists; it was largely responsible for the establishment of "Citizenship Schools" across the South where adult African Americans learned to read so that they could register to vote.[5]

West's early work at the Highlander school provided a crucial model for his central aesthetic: imagining a politicized folk. Furthermore, by proclaiming and naming this folk to be the truest Americans, he situates his own work within the Popular Front mandate for American unity against fascism and its allies.[6] In this way, West seeks to wrest back control of hillbilly culture from derision and condescension. At the same time, as proletarian writers were more famously doing in urban settings, he seeks to redefine poetry itself as a tool or weapon of class struggle, rather than a commodity to generate profit. For this reason, there is no copyright to *In a Land of Plenty: A Don West Reader*. Instead, West writes a note to the reader on what would have been the copyright page: "To challenge the power of oppression is the poet's responsibility. . . . Thus no copyright, no effort to restrict us. Groups or individuals are welcome to reproduce or use any or all parts of this book" (West, *Land of Plenty* n.p.). He is offering his poetry as a partial corrective to the problem of representation succinctly described by David Whisnant: "To this day there are a thousand people who 'know' that mountaineers weave coverlets and sing ballads for every one who knows that millions of them have been industrial workers for a hundred years, have organized unions and picketed state and nation capitols in pursuit of their constitutional rights, and have laid their bodies in front of strip-mine bulldozers and overloaded coal trucks" (Whisnant 13).

West's deliberate reinvention of the hillbilly rests on a keen awareness of how the mountaineer has been drawn from without, whether through contemptuous stereotyping or condescending romanticization. The awakening he calls for among poor whites—a conversion story in the style of both Mike Gold and the Bible—depends on a realization of whose interests, and what ideology, these images have served. Finally, in his movement to carve out an ethnic identity for Appalachians that combines class consciousness, radical politics, and "folk" tradition, West finds in the mountaineer a figure who—precisely because he is one of "America's mongrels"—can take the national stage:

O this is the story
Of you and the rest
And if I am lying
My name's not Don West.

Notes

1. Outside of the academy, West still has his moments. For instance, Warren Doyle (known as the person to walk the entire Appalachian Trail the most times) has made a tradition of reading West's poetry to an annual meeting of a group of long-distance hikers; before he died, West had read to the group each year. The Appalachian Studies Association, whose mission includes both scholarship and advocacy, chose West as one of its "Appalachian heroes" in 2001 and produced a T-shirt with his picture. Future academic inquiry on West will be indebted for some time to come to the work of journalist/writer Jeff Biggers, whose thorough and visionary research in archives and through interviews will go far in allowing the historical record on West to be set straight. In addition to Biggers, several scholars are finally beginning to give West his due; these include oral historian Victoria Byerly, author of an as-yet unpublished biography of West; labor historian Jim Lorence, who is currently working on West's organizing efforts; and Ph.D. student Chris Green, who has given a conference paper on the poetry of West and Muriel Rukeyser.

2. West praised Hughes's poetry in a number of different places. For instance, he thanks Hughes in the acknowledgments to his fourth book for "teaching me through the beauty of his own work"; Hughes, in turn, called West's work "the poems of our heartbeats." West also wrote a poem for Hughes, called "To My Brown Brother (For Langston Hughes)," which he published in his chapbook *Deep, Deep Down in Living.* This chapbook is extremely rare and hard to find, and, at this point, there is no certainty as to where and when it was published. Jeff Biggers, who located a copy and kindly shared this poem with me, suggests that it might have been published by the Highlander Folk School in 1932.

3. The novels in which these authors create characters who respond with hostility to being gaped at are Mildred Haun's *The Hawk's Done Gone* (1940), Harriette Arnow's *The Dollmaker* (1954), Mike Gold's *Jews without Money* (1930), and Frank Chin's *Donald Duk* (1991).

4. Annabel Thomas's *Blood Feud* (1998), a novel set in the Appalachians of southern Ohio, seeks to reinsert class politics into the feud jeremiad.

5. In 1959 the state of Tennessee confiscated the Highlander Folk School's land and revoked its charter, forcing the school to move to Knoxville, where it still operates under the name Highlander Research and Education Center.

6. The stationery that West used during a stint in the mid-1940s as superintendent of the Lula, Ga., public schools proclaims below the address, "Education for Victory over Fascism Both Foreign and Domestic." West's days at Lula make fascinating study: he was apparently so successful during his stewardship of this African American school system that *Seventeen* magazine published an article about it. West himself wrote of the job with appreciation in a letter to Langston Hughes: "It has been an experience for me to have a Negro school under my supervision."

Works Cited

Arnow, Harriette. *The Dollmaker.* 1954. New York: Avon Books, 1972.

Batteau, Allen W. *The Invention of Appalachia.* Tuscon: University of Arizona Press, 1990.

Berger, Arthur Asa. *Li'l Abner: A Study in American Satire.* 1969. Jackson: University Press of Mississippi, 1994.

Biggers, Jeff. "The Fugitive of Southern Appalachian Literature: Reconsidering the Poetry of Don West." *Journal of Appalachian Studies* 5.2 (Fall 1999): 159–80.

Caldwell, Mary French. "Change Comes to the Appalachian Mountaineer." 1930. Reprinted in McNeil, *Appalachian Images in Folk and Popular Culture.* 217–25.

Chin, Frank. *Donald Duk.* Minneapolis: Coffeehouse Press, 1991.

Doyle, Warren. Telephone interview with author. April 2002.

Frost, William Goodell. "Our Contemporary Ancestors in the Southern Mountains." 1899. Reprinted in McNeil, *Appalachian Images in Folk and Popular Culture.* 91–106.

Gold, Michael. *Jews without Money.* 1930. New York: International Publishers, 1942.

Haun, Mildred. *The Hawk's Done Gone and Other Stories.* 1940. Nashville: Vanderbilt University Press, 1987.

Hughes, Langston. "Ballad of Sam Solomon." *Collected Poems of Langston Hughes*. Ed. Arnold Rampersad and David Roessel. New York: Knopf, 1994. 295.

James, Sheryl. "A Radical of Long Standing." *St. Petersberg Times*, March 22, 1989.

Klotter, James C. "The Black South and White Appalachia." *Blacks in Appalachia*. Ed. William H. Turner and Edward J. Cabbell. Lexington: University Press of Kentucky, 1985.

Mazón, Mauricio. *The Zoot-Suit Riots: The Psychology of Symbolic Annihilation*. Austin: University of Texas Press, 1984.

McNeil, W. K., ed. *Appalachian Images in Folk and Popular Culture*. Ann Arbor, Mich.: UMI Research Press, 1989.

Munn, Robert F. "The Latest Rediscovery of Appalachia." *Appalachia in the Sixties*. Ed. Walls and Stephenson. 25–30.

Nelson, Cary. *Repression and Recovery: Modern American Poetry and the Politics of Cultural Memory, 1910–1945*. Madison: University of Wisconsin Press, 1989.

Roediger, David. *The Wages of Whiteness: Race and the Making of the American Working Class*. New York: Verso, 1999.

Still, James. Interview with J. W. Williamson. *Interviewing Appalachia: The Appalachian Journal Interviews, 1978–1992*. Ed. J. W. Williamson and Edwin T. Arnold. Knoxville: University of Tennessee Press, 1994.

Stuart, Jesse. *To Teach, To Love: What Teaching Means to a Famous American Teacher-Writer*. New York: World Publishing Co., 1970.

Thomas, Annabel. *Blood Feud*. Knoxville: University of Tennessee Press, 1998.

Walls, David S., and John B. Stephenson. *Appalachia in the Sixties: Decade of Reawakening*. Lexington: University Press of Kentucky, 1972.

West, Don. *Clods of Southern Earth*. New York: Boni and Gaer, 1946.

———. *Crab-Grass*. Nashville: Art Print Shop, 1931.

———. *In a Land of Plenty: A Don West Reader*. Minneapolis: West End Press, 1982.

———. Letter to Langston Hughes. 1943. James Weldon Johnson Collection, Beinecke Rare Book and Manuscript Library, Yale University.

———. *O Mountaineers! A Collection of Poems*. Huntington, W.Va.: Appalachian Movement Press, 1974.

———. *People's Cultural Heritage in Appalachia*. Huntington, W.Va: Appalachian Movement Press, 1970.

———. *The Road Is Rocky*. New York: New Christian Books, n.d.

———. "Romantic Appalachia." 1972. Reprinted in Walls and Stephenson, *Appalachia in the Sixties: Decade of Reawakening*. 210–16.

———. *Songs for Southern Workers: 1937 Songbook of the Kentucky Workers Alliance*. Huntington, W.Va: Appalachian Movement Press, 1971.

Whisnant, David. *All That Is Native and Fine: The Politics of Culture in an American Region*. Chapel Hill: University of North Carolina Press, 1983.

Michelle Stephens

The First Negro Matinee Idol: Harry Belafonte and American Culture in the 1950s

In a 1996 interview with Harry Belafonte for the *New Yorker*, Henry Louis Gates Jr. made an observation that is reflected in the title of this essay. Gates pointed out, "For a couple of years in the late fifties, Belafonte was arguably the most desirable man in the Western world."[1] In that piece Gates constructed his own narrative to explain the Belafonte phenomenon, but his account was not published in isolation. Between June and September 1996, Belafonte actually did a series of interviews, including one at the Schomburg Center in New York with Cornell West and two more that ran as stories in the August and September issues of *People* and *Ebony*, respectively.[2] That collection of articles served as the real occasion for this piece, because they replicated key contradictions in the image of Belafonte that first emerged during the height of his popularity in the 1950s.

These contradictions are stark in the two very different histories of Belafonte that the 1996 articles reconstruct. The interviews he did with journalists from *People* and *Ebony*, for example, focus on his activities in the years after his initial success—his work for the State Department as cultural ambassador to the Peace Corps and goodwill ambassador to the United Nations International Children's Emergency Fund (UNICEF) and his present-day significance as a member of the black cultural elite, one who owns his own production company, Belafonte Enterprises. Essentially, for the readership of *People* and *Ebony*, Harry Belafonte is a humanitarian cultural entrepreneur.

The interviews with West and Gates tend to go in the opposite direction—they spotlight Belafonte's history before the 1950s and during the turbulent 1960s. It is a very particular *political* history, one of Belafonte's formation as part of a generation of depression-era black radicals, a generation best symbolized by Paul Robeson.[3] These are serious pieces, excavating the political genealogy of a radical race hero. Gates, for example, resolves his own question of the meaning of Belafonte's larger cultural and political legacy in two eloquent phrases: "Harry Belafonte: Was he not Negro manhood at its finest? Was he not the perfect hybrid of popular culture and political conscience?"[4]

Humanitarian cultural entrepreneur, radical race hero—who is and was Harry Belafonte? What happens when we also place Belafonte in the context of ethnic performers of the 1950s such as Desi Arnaz? What should be interesting here to scholars of twentieth-century Americanism is not just the history of Belafonte's radicalism or his entrepreneurship, but rather the process by which he could so smoothly come to represent the "perfect hybrid" of both. If Belafonte's initial political formation came from his associations with a generation of Popular Front black radicals—the "black cultural front," so to speak—his ultimate transformation into "Negro manhood at its finest" also reflects a process Hazel Carby has encapsulated in her use of the term, the American "race man."[5] Belafonte's career perfectly describes the process by which black radical cultural forms are "imaginatively incorporat[ed] . . . into the national cultural community through the figure of the black male."[6]

Furthermore, Belafonte's personal, cultural, and political history illuminates some key dynamics in the relationship between the United States and the Caribbean at the very moment of the construction of a discourse of the American Century. Ultimately, this essay argues that, in the 1950s, Harry Belafonte became a key cultural figure for a racialized vision of American ethnicity, one that was compatible with the needs of an internationally expanding American state. The development of the tourist industry and the military expansion of the United States into the Caribbean during this period provide important contexts for understanding the racialized sexual politics of ethnic performances such as

Belafonte's. Essentially, the 1950s saw Belafonte's black, ethnic, working-class consciousness, forged in both Caribbean and American radicalism, transformed to fit a quintessentially liberal story of American, interracial integration.

In the 1996 interview with Cornell West, Belafonte continually placed his own career alongside that of his mentor, Paul Robeson. In the early 1950s, faced with the opportunity to become a jazz and pop singer like Billy Eckstine, Belafonte made the conscious decision to buck the trend and become a folk singer. It was the Robeson mantle, a black folk singer whose power lay precisely in his ability to represent *both* black and white folk from across the world, that Belafonte hoped to inherit. As Michael Denning has pointed out, in Robeson's performances of the song "Ballad for Americans" he articulated a vision of a "laboring," multi-ethnic America that stood in opposition to racialized narratives of nationhood such as the film *Birth of a Nation.*[7] This was also the political context in which Belafonte understood the significance of his own West Indian background for American popular culture.

In expressing his ethnicity, Belafonte aimed to communicate the actual laboring conditions of West Indian life. In the interview with West, Belafonte described his own feelings about the Caribbean work song that has made him so popular in the United States: "When I sing 'The Banana Boat Song,' most people see it as some whimsical, fanciful little tale. . . . But to me, it's about a human condition. . . . Most of my family [in Jamaica] were plantation workers. . . . They chopped sugarcane, and chopped bananas, and loaded ships, and did all these things under tremendous difficulty and pain and anguish. . . . Song was sometimes our only relief from the burden of life."[8]

Belafonte's song of the ethnic self was not just an act of communication performed with the intent of transcending racial difference. He aimed to focus on the particular life-world of West Indian laborers. In this regard, Belafonte described himself as following the dictates of Robeson: "If art was not political, to me it wasn't even art. It was Paul Robeson who once said to me, 'The purpose of art is not just to show life as it is but to show life as it should be.' That became my motto. And very early on when I turned to singing and he came to hear concerts of mine, he said, 'Harry, get them to sing your song. And then they'll have to come to know who you are.'" For Belafonte, the song of the ethnic self was not just a song of identity, but a song with the express political intent of mobilizing class consciousness. As he further described: "I al-

ways thought that if people came to embrace my art and began to sing my song, they would want to know who I am. And if I could get them to the next level of that curiosity, I would politicize them to death."[9]

It is fascinating to rethink Belafonte's career in light of his self-placement in the context of the black Popular Front. Describing his formative years as a teenager growing up in Harlem, Belafonte recalled both the everyday presence of "the icons and the heroes of the time"—"If I walked up and down Seventh Avenue long enough, I would bump into Du Bois, I would bump into Duke Ellington, I would bump into Paul Robeson"—and the influence of what they had to say about the American world in which he lived.[10] Yet Harry Belafonte is not now, nor has he ever been, a Paul Robeson. Despite his best efforts, his cultural legacy is predominantly that of the "charming" and "whimsical, fanciful little tale" of "The Banana Boat Song," revived for a postmodern audience in Tim Burton's 1988 film *Beetlejuice*. Despite even Gates's attempts to revise that song's history, when belting out "Day-O" few Americans are thinking about the proletarianization of the West Indian working classes.[11]

If we place Belafonte's and Robeson's careers side by side, we see the profound effects of history on the options available to a black male artist in shaping his cultural image. Belafonte's success as a humanitarian cultural entrepreneur, as a "race man" even in the nineties, can be related to his failure as a "laboring" ethnic performer. What we see in Belafonte's performances of his ethnicity throughout the 1950s is the transformation of his ethnic working-class story into the interracial romance of American integrationism.

As Hazel Carby points out, in the 1930s Robeson also wrestled with competing narratives of the meaning of his black masculinity in the context of white American modernism.[12] The degree to which he was able to resist those narratives rested precisely on his unwavering and highly visible commitment to the Popular Front social movement that gave the "cultural front" its initial impetus and driving force. In Belafonte's case, however, though he may have gained the values of the Popular Front from the coincidence of his being born at the tail end of that generation in 1927, he was actually not a part of the group of second-generation American immigrants who formed the ranks of the CIO after 1934. Rather, for most of the years immediately following the crash of 1929, from between the ages of five and twelve, Belafonte was living in Jamaica, the island of his mother's birth.

If anything, it was his West Indian mother who more properly represented that Popular Front, ethnic, class consciousness. As Belafonte pointed out in one oblique reference to politics during his *People* interview: "She was feisty against rich people who would look upon her as an artifact rather than a human being."[13] Belafonte's mother, Melvine Love, is an important character in an unauthorized biography of Belafonte written by music critic Arnold Shaw and published in 1960. In Shaw's portrayal of Love, we see the traces of the laboring ethnic body from the 1930s: "Melvine Belafonte was at times a domestic servant and, when opportunities appeared, a dressmaker. People who know her describe her as a sharp, rather touchy woman with a pronounced West Indian accent. . . . Without being hostile, she was wary of white people. . . . She was, and is today, an extremely proud woman."[14] Melvine Love Belafonte marks the only place in Shaw's narrative where this particular depiction of West Indian ethnicity—as belligerent, proletarian, and unassimilated—emerges. Instead, despite the mention of his early years in Jamaica and the influence of his West Indian mother on his identity, Shaw's account of Belafonte is most decidedly a story of American race relations and a cultural document of white American integrationism.

In Shaw's biography, then, we find an invaluable record of Belafonte's full-fledged construction as a "Negro matinee idol" in the 1950s. From the outset Shaw describes the young Harry as an "angry black man," an anger generated from his experience of racial segregation growing up in Harlem. Quickly it becomes apparent that one of the ways in which Belafonte transcended his anger was by transcending his West Indian mother. Melvine Love was the ghost that must be exorcised for Belafonte's true story to emerge—the romance of his relationship with white female America.

In retelling the story of Belafonte's controversial divorce from black NAACP activist Marguerite Byrd, and subsequent second marriage to white, Jewish dancer Julie Robinson, Shaw speculates: "There is some question as to whether Harry was ever really in love with Marguerite. . . . It may well be that Harry fell in love, not so much with a person but with an image of what he himself wanted to be—perhaps, the image of what his mother wanted him to be. This resulted in an attachment that was not easy to sever. The loyalty of a son to a mother."[15] Shaw sums up Harry and Marguerite's divorce in 1957 with the succinct comment, "Harry had succeeded in destroying the mother image."[16] Two things become evident as Shaw's pseudo-Freudian (psycho)analysis of Belafonte's life and career continues. Belafonte's ethnic class anger against America was mediated first by his transcendence of his West Indian mother, who was "wary of white people," and second by his acceptance of, and love for, a white woman. In other words, what is centrally at stake in Shaw's account is the ethnic and racialized Other's forgiveness of white America.[17]

If the American story of the assimilation of the ethnic Other usually rests on the ethnic Other's moment of conversion—that is, the willingness to renounce his or her Otherness to become American—in the case of Harry Belafonte assimilation required the black ethnic to perform a different kind of cultural work. Through him white Americans felt able to forgive themselves, because they were forgiven by the ethnic Other. As Belafonte observed after a backstage visit from some of his adoring fans, "I was like the badge of honor. . . . I had a responsibility to understand that they had been confused and did not know any better about some of the things they used to do and say, and it was up to me to forgive them."[18]

Submerged within Shaw's descriptions of Belafonte's relationship with his white female audience, we see the real "cultural labor" that went into producing the "first Negro matinee idol." If the black male's racial anger is usually figured through his desire to rape the white female, Belafonte's capacity to "forgive" took the form of his willingness to seduce her. Nothing could demonstrate this more effectively than the lengthy and painfully contrived language of Shaw's opening "Curtain Raiser." This loose preface begins with one of those moments when a thousand words may actually convey the best picture and therefore bears quoting at some length:

> In the darkness, all eyes sweep toward one spot with anticipation. Suddenly, a single beam cuts a long cone of pink light. At the end of it, a face appears.
>
> It is a handsome face, clean-cut, boyish, the black hair, close-cropped, the dark eyes, large and intense, the lips, full and sensuously expressive.
>
> A husky resonant voice rises out of the breathless quiet like a fountain of silk and velvet.
>
> In the soft shadows, avid female eyes search out the white of his shirt, open at the neck in a seductive *V* that seems to plunge almost to his navel. Dreamily, they contemplate the attractive figure, sheathed in black, form-fitting slacks, cinch-belted. . . . Magnetically, they are held by his tight, catlike movements, and the feeling he communicates of coiled tension and erotic power.
>
> Harry Belafonte, the first Negro matinee idol, is on.[19]

In centering on Belafonte's relationship with his white female audience, Shaw sexualizes the black folk singer. The drama of his singing performances is about his erotic relationship to that audience, rather than about the social message he hoped to transmit. Here we see not the laboring of an ethnic performer to represent artistically his marginalized culture, but the sensual laboring of a black male body to succeed in the sexual economy of white American culture. This is precisely one dimension of "Americanization" that Belafonte admired his own mother for fighting against—the perceiving of the ethnic black body as an "artifact" or fetish, rather than as a human being.

Shaw's biography really does stand as an urtext in understanding how Belafonte, the "King of Calypso," the "first Negro Matinee Idol," was perceived, was constructed, and performed in the 1950s. Yet one might ask, why Belafonte and why the 1950s? Here, I would argue, is where history and geopolitics enter the stage, for the cultural work that went into creating Harry Belafonte as a sexual icon did not occur in a historical vacuum.

The second half of the 1950s saw the convergence of three seemingly unrelated events, of both international and domestic significance, that would necessitate the incorporation of this particular kind of black, male, ethnic performer in the second half of the twentieth century—the U.S. military presence in Trinidad, the resistance of the Caribbean through the figure of the Trinidadian calypso singer, and the containment of an alienated black American consciousness, as anticipated by Richard Wright (in *Native Son*), within U.S. borders.[20] The convergence of these three events can serve as an occasion to reflect on different insurgent cultural forms, as well as ways of imagining black political rebellion in the African diaspora and their relative "compatibility" with the cultural and political discourses of the United States.

In 1941 publishing magnate Henry Luce used the occasion of the United States's participation in a second European war to publish his manifesto of American expansionism, "The American Century."[21] Luce's manifesto would soon have direct consequences in the Caribbean, specifically in Trinidad. In 1940 the U.S. government acquired a number of military bases in Trinidad, including one on Chaguaramas Bay. The "American Occupation," as this period was called on the island, was a controversial affair. For though in 1920, after the U.S. invasion of Haiti in 1915, Eugene O'Neill's play *Emperor Jones* had been able to imagine the American presence on Caribbean soil without much native cultural resistance, the same was not true of Trinidad in the 1940s. As Ivar Oxaal points out, American activities in the Caribbean were now being closely observed and commented on by the singers of the Trinidadian folk, calypso performers who were radicalized by the American Occupation.[22]

Calypsonians such as the Mighty Sparrow commented on the U.S. presence in Trinidad throughout the 1940s and 1950s. In his 1958 hit

"Yankees Back Again," Sparrow noted that in the postwar period American soldiers were being replaced by American capitalists, and he used the image of slavery to represent America's buying and selling of West Indian laborers abroad:

Well, the days of slavery back again . . .
Since the Yankees come back over here
They buy out the whole of Point-à-Pierre
Money start to pass, people start to bawl
Point-à-Pierre sell the workmen and all.

Fifty cents a head for Grenadian
A dollar for born Trinidadian
Tobagians free, whether big or small
But they don't want no Bajans at all.[23]

In Sparrow's lyrics, the alienation of the black worker and the fetishization of the black ethnic body come together; as he portrays the buying and selling of workers—the turning of ethnic labor into currency on the world market—he also suggests the construction of various ethnic identities themselves as competing commodities in a global cultural market.

The existence of real native resistance in the Caribbean to U.S. claims for world hegemony would produce cultural transformations within American society. For if the 1940s and 1950s saw the expansion of American capital's confidence in its right to travel and exert its influence globally and hemispherically, these years also saw an intolerance on the part of the U.S. government to accept freedom of movement as a fundamental right of its own radical black citizens. In 1940 another significant event occurred in American culture—Richard Wright published, and later produced as a film, *Native Son*, his account of black American working-class alienation.

Both *Native Son* and the U.S. presence in Trinidad can be read against the backdrop of an earlier cultural document of U.S.-Caribbean relations and black "rebellious masculinity," the 1920 Eugene O'Neill play, *Emperor Jones*, adapted for the screen in 1933 with Paul Robeson in the leading role.[24] In 1940, when Wright published *Native Son*, he was less focused on the story of individual psychological trauma and the violent effects of racial oppression on the black male psyche. Wright's lament on the novel's favorable reception reflected his sense of failure at using Bigger Thomas to represent the alienation of the black American collective as a whole. Bigger Thomas, the brutal and brutish black character, was a further historical elaboration of Paul Robeson's native, black savage,

Brutus Jones, who in the film version of O'Neill's play escapes to a Caribbean island after murdering both a fellow Pullman porter and a prison guard.

In *Emperor Jones*, Brutus Jones ultimately becomes the Garveyesque black emperor of "an island in the West Indies as yet not self-determined by White Marines."[25] In this opening stage direction, O'Neill referenced the 1915 invasion of Haiti by U.S. Marines. But with the United States's increased presence in the Caribbean, the power of Brutus Jones was precisely that he too, as an African American, gained the potential to step beyond the imaginative borders of the United States. This "Emperor of a small West Indian island" was very much a West Indian character, probably modeled historically on Jamaican immigrant Marcus Garvey, whose UNIA parades were passing through Harlem in 1920, the year that *Emperor Jones* was first performed in New York. But Emperor Jones was also a symbolic cultural form, one that represented a type of spectacular male black leadership and rebelliousness that defied the terms of black racial identity as they were understood in 1920s America. Marcus Garvey, for example, was no "race man," and his extremely visible presence would expand the limits of how the New Negro could be imagined and "portrayed" during the Harlem Renaissance.[26]

Equally dangerous, Garvey's politics spoke most powerfully to a specific segment of the black American population, the group least likely to find social acceptance in America and therefore the group least interested in its own cultural Americanization, the black working poor.[27] For Paul Robeson, the counter to black working-class alienation was hope, but this was a hope primarily based on black Americans' ability to travel freely in and out of the United States, both physically and conceptually.[28] This was also the hope mobilized by Garvey's failed dream of a black-owned fleet of ships, the "Black Star Line," that could allow black citizens to assert their "right to travel" the Atlantic pathways of the modern world system. By the 1940s this, ultimately, was the hope that Wright's "native son" lacked: "Trapped on the roof," Bigger Thomas counts his bullets and leaves the last one for himself" as the agents of the state, the police, moved in ever-tightening, concentric circles, surrounding him.[29] Indeed, by the late 1950s the U.S. government had revoked both Robeson's and W. E. B. Du Bois's passports, and C. L. R. James's deportation in 1953 mirrored Garvey's deportation thirty years earlier.

In the 1920s O'Neill's *Emperor Jones* worked culturally to displace the threat that the radicalized, rebellious, and traveling black male body posed to the American nation-state. This was the threat that a figure like Marcus Garvey represented, as he traveled throughout both the American South and the diasporic, colonial world. In the figure of Brutus Jones, a role Paul Robeson made famous, O'Neill's first modern American drama sent the black troublemaker to the islands—native to black America or the Caribbean, the black radical was ejected from the American republic and returned to the colonies. Attempts to contain the radicalism of America's own traveling native sons in the 1950s could only be threatened by the presence of a radical, ethnic Caribbean voice in the United States. In the political culture of 1950s America, the "King of Calypso"—the inheritor of Garvey's dream of a West Indian empire, the second-generation Caribbean American native son—had to be integrated within the nation as the "Negro matinee idol" if only to prevent him from becoming America's Mighty Sparrow.

In 1927, the year of Harry Belafonte's birth, Marcus Garvey was deported; by 1957, the moment of Belafonte's cultural emergence, Paul Robeson had been contained. In the intervening years, since his return to Harlem from Jamaica as a teenager in 1939, it had taken Belafonte over a decade to establish himself as an ethnic performer in his own right. The forces that had conspired to punish Robeson were working to facilitate Belafonte's success.

What American cultural world was Harry Belafonte laboring in by 1954, when he made his first major screen appearance in the film *Carmen Jones*? No 1950s audience could have viewed the final scene without an immediate cultural reference back to Bigger Thomas, suffocating and strangling both his white and black female counterparts in *Native Son*. If that image was not vivid enough, Arnold Shaw underscored the similarity with an anecdote from behind the scenes of the film. According to Shaw, Belafonte threw himself into the role with such zest and passion that, "in the final scene where he murders Carmen for her faithlessness, Otto Preminger became worried lest he hurt Dorothy Dandridge. . . . 'When you strangle the lady,' Preminger warned, 'don't put wrinkles in her neck.'"[30] It was precisely this "violence," sexualized even further in Shaw's accounts of Belafonte's stage performances, that was ejected from the body of the black performer through his love for white women.

This historical lens also contextualizes Belafonte's 1957 performance in *Island in the Sun*, the production that, almost single-handedly, helped to create him as the "first Negro matinee idol." Based on the novel by Alec Waugh, the film was described explicitly by its producer, Darryl Zanuck, as an analogy for American race relations. It remains a classic in U.S. cultural history because it portrayed, for the first time, an interracial romance using a black actor, Belafonte, and a white actress, Joan Fontaine.

The fragmented nature of *Island in the Sun* perfectly captures the strange, finished product that was Harry Belafonte by the end of the 1950s. All the traces of American nationalist and internationalist discourse, post-1945, are present in the film and in his character, David Boyeur. Boyeur is a trade union organizer—the return of the repressed from the 1930s socialist, Popular Front past—reemerging to thwart American internationalism in the Caribbean in the figure of the West Indian nationalist. This imagined island, representing a Caribbean in the throes of decolonization that would result in Jamaican and Trinidadian independence in 1962, suffers mainly from the problem of "color." Belafonte the star, with the political and cultural legacies of his black fathers—the radical race men of Popular Front Harlem—and his ethnic, proletarian, West Indian mother, are sent off to the islands, this time explicitly to work out the "color" problems of American race relations as they spill over to the rest of the world.

The narrative trajectory of *Island in the Sun* holds no surprises. The Caribbean American "native son" is transformed into a "race man" as he wrestles with his love for Joan Fontaine's character. By the time the movie ends, it is no longer relevant that the characters do not ultimately consummate their love. The very innocence of their romance, composed of a forgiveness on Belafonte's part that does not, however, cross the sexual border, confirms that the work of the film has been done: the cleansing of the American soul.

In the context of the contested relationship between the United States and the Caribbean in the 1950s, we can better understand the cultural work that a Caribbean ethnic, a Calypso King, would perform—one who could forgive America's increased presence in the Caribbean in exchange for the promise of an equal place in American national popular culture. In 1950s America, the mobility of black cultural forms and performers, both domestically and internationally, depended on the imprimatur of the U.S. state. To leave the black Atlantic for the Asian Pacific for a brief moment, Burmese writer Wendy Law-Lone opens her novel, *The Coffin Tree*, with the following scene:

> Someone was singing . . . Shan coming home with another of his annoying calypsos.
>
> When I was a lad jes three foot three
> Sartin questions occurred to me
>
> Calypsos were a recent import: Harry Belafonte had passed through [Burma] on a U.S. government cultural tour, and had sung at

Town Hall. Shan had perfected the husky Belafonte tenor. . . . He was walking up the long driveway to the house, singing into the wind:

> So I asked me father quite seriously
> To tell me de story bout de birds and de bees.[31]

In Law-Lone's narrative Belafonte travels with the approval of the U.S. State Department, becoming the premier representative of a now fully incorporated, racialized ethnic, whose light love songs in dialect—stories of "de birds and de bees"—could embody the symbolic coupling of the (third) world's "darker peoples" with America. This was precisely what made Belafonte "the most desirable man in the Western world."

Belafonte's emergence and subsequent popularity in the mid-1950s was shaped to address the needs of the audiences of the American Century. Whereas Paul Robeson spoke to black and white audiences who used folk culture to protest their social and economic alienation, by 1957 what black and white America were seeking in the figure of the black folk performer was forgiveness for, and reconciliation with, a now inescapable American world destiny. But remaining vigilant to the principle that men shape their freedom out of what is given to them, Belafonte paid the price of "forgiveness" for very large future gains. In the late 1950s and early 1960s he was the only black performer with the cultural capital and financial power needed to support and subsidize Martin Luther King Jr.'s civil rights movement.

Rather than hold Harry Belafonte up as either a symbol of race success or ethnic failure, I would place him beside contemporaneous conceptions of Caribbean American ethnicity. One of these has been the shadow figure of this essay, Belafonte's West Indian mother Melvine Love. In 1959, as the Caribbean American male performer was at the peak of his success, Bajan writer Paule Marshall was publishing her classic narrative of the West Indian *female* immigrant, *Brown Girl, Brownstones*.[32] When Marshall walked the streets of Brooklyn she saw, not Du Bois, Ellington, and Robeson, but her own mother and the other invisible, laboring West Indian women of Caribbean American ethnic culture.

The later emergence and prominence of the Caribbean woman writer throughout the 1980s—Marshall and her contemporaries such as Michelle Cliff, Jamaica Kincaid, and Audre Lorde—expanded the representation of Caribbean ethnic identity to include a black, female consciousness, often with an oppositional sexuality, one very different from the fetish of black masculinity represented by the calypso crooner.[33] Marshall, like Belafonte, survived both the civil rights and the black power eras to stake her claim on U.S. culture as part of this later black cultural movement of the 1980s. In *Brown Girl, Brownstones*, her 1959 song of the ethnic self, Marshall heralded not America's continued romance with the ethnic race man, but a new praise song for his widows and daughters.[34]

In the brief essay, "Three Black Women Writers: Toni Morrison, Alice Walker, Ntozake Shange" (1981), cultural critic C. L. R. James, himself a blend of Trinidadian and American radical impulses, identified black women working in the United States as the founders of a new "social movement" for the American twentieth century. He wrote: "Black women in America for hundreds of years have been scrubbing, sweeping, cleaning, picking up behind people: they have been held in the background; kept for sex. And now [women writers] have taken these Black women and put them right in the front of American literature."[35] Much more needs to be said about the work of these writers than can be covered here. Suffice it to say that Melvine Love lived on in the writings of her literary daughters who understood personally the significance of working immigrant women in the history of twentieth-century Americanism.

Notes

1. Gates, "Belafonte's Balancing Act," 134.

2. West, "Harry Belafonte, 3 June 1996, Schomburg Center, New York," *Restoring Hope*; Silverman and Arias, "*Day-O* Reckoning"; Norment, "Legend Roars Back."

3. Here Paul Robeson functions very much as symbol rather than history, for as James Smethurst pointed out to me, there was an active black Left subculture in the 1950s that included artists and intellectuals such as Richard B. Moore, Lorraine Hansberry, and John Henrik Clarke. These were the very intellectuals Harold Cruse would critique in his 1967 polemic, *The Crisis of the Negro Intellectual* (New York: Morrow). This was also the generation from which Paule Marshall emerged, with a distinctly female vision of Caribbean ethnicity in her novel *Brown Girl, Brownstones*.

4. Gates, "Belafonte's Balancing Act," 133.

5. See Hazel V. Carby, *Race Men*, and Michael Denning, *Cultural Front*.

6. Carby, *Race Men*, 45.

7. Denning, *Cultural Front*, 9.

8. West, "Harry Belafonte," *Restoring Hope*, 4–5.

9. Ibid., 5.

10. Ibid., 26.

11. Recalling its appearance in *Beetlejuice*, Gates ("Belafonte's Balancing Act," 143) has this to say about "The Banana Boat Song"—"the impression you're left with isn't how silly the song was but how bewitchingly catchy it still is . . . you find yourself wanting to join in the chorus."

12. Carby, *Race Men*, see esp. chapters 2 and 3, 45–101.

13. Silverman and Arias, "*Day-O* Reckoning," 64.

14. Shaw, *Belafonte*, 20.

15. Ibid., 199.

16. Ibid., 205.

17. See also Gustavo Pérez Firmat (*Life on the Hyphen*) for a parallel analysis of Desi Arnaz's role as Ricky Ricardo on the *I Love Lucy* television show.

18. Shaw, *Belafonte*, 192.

19. Ibid., 1.

20. The film version of Wright's *Native Son* is specifically mentioned in Shaw's biography. Actress Janice Kingslow, who originally auditioned for Otto Preminger to play opposite Belafonte in *Carmen Jones*, was also called for *Native Son* by Wright but subsequently turned down by the film's French director for looking "too white." Wright, Kingslow, and Belafonte were all performing in the same racialized cultural world. Shaw, *Belafonte*, 155.

21. Luce, "American Century," 23.

22. See Oxaal, *Black Intellectuals*.

23. Lyrics quoted in Gordon Rohlehr, "Sparrow as Poet," in Anthony and Carr, *David Frost Introduces*, 88.

24. The term "rebellious masculinity" comes from Montesinos Sale, *Slumbering Volcano*.

25. O'Neill, *Emperor Jones*, 3.

26. I am referencing here the 1926 questionnaire published in the NAACP magazine *Crisis* entitled, "The Negro in Art: How Shall He Be Portrayed?" Writers from across the black world responded to this critical debate, including Langston Hughes, Countee Cullen, and W. E. B. Du Bois. See also Bernard, *Remember Me to Harlem*.

27. At the time Walter White described these intraracial class distinctions in terms of color, observing "jealousy and suspicion on the part of darker Negroes, chafing at their bonds and resentful of the patronizing attitude of those of lighter color. . . . In New York City this feeling between black and mulatto has been accentuated by the presence of some 40,000 Negroes from the West Indies, and particularly by the propaganda of Marcus Garvey and his Universal Negro Improvement Association." Locke, *New Negro*, 367.

28. See Robeson, "The Right to Travel," *Here I Stand*.

29. This image was compellingly invoked by Wright's friend and contemporary, Trinidadian C. L. R. James, in his review "On *Native Son* by Richard Wright (1940)," in James, *C. L. R. James*, 58.

30. Shaw, *Belafonte*, 141.

31. Law-Lone, *Coffin Tree*, 9–10.

32. Marshall, *Brown Girl*.

33. For female visions of Caribbean American politics and sexuality, see Audre Lorde's *Zami: A New Spelling of My Name* (Watertown, Mass.: Persephone Press, 1982), Paule Marshall's *Reena and Other Stories* (Old Westbury, N.Y.: Feminist Press, 1983), Jamaica Kincaid's *Lucy* (New York: Plume, 1991), and Michelle Cliff's *No Telephone to Heaven* (New York: Plume, 1996).

34. With the publication of *Fisher King*, one could argue that Marshall retells the race man's story itself. Stepping beyond the borders of both an American and a West Indian immigrant narrative, this novel follows the travels of a black jazz musician who leaves New York for Paris in 1949, on the eve of 1950s America.

35. C. L. R. James, "Three Black Women Writers: Toni Morrison, Alice Walker, Ntozake Shange," in Grimshaw, *C. L. R. James Reader*, 411–17 (quotation, p. 411).

Works Cited

Anthony, Michael, and Andrew Carr, eds. *David Frost Introduces Trinidad and Tobago*. London: Deutsch, 1975.

Bernard, Emily, ed. *Remember Me to Harlem: The Letters of Langston Hughes and Carl Van Vechten, 1925–1964*. New York: Knopf, 2001.

Carby, Hazel V. *Race Men*. Cambridge: Harvard University Press, 1998.

Denning, Michael. *The Cultural Front: The Laboring of American Culture in the Twentieth Century*. New York: Verso, 1997.

Gates, Jr., Henry Louis. "Belafonte's Balancing Act." *New Yorker*, August 26, September 2, 1996, 132–43.

Grimshaw, Anna, ed. *The C. L. R. James Reader* (Oxford: Blackwell Publishers, 1992).

James, C. L. R. *C. L. R. James on the "Negro Question."* Ed. Scott McLemee. Jackson: University Press of Mississippi, 1996.

Law-Lone, Wendy. *The Coffin Tree*. Boston: Beacon Press, 1983.

Locke, Alain, ed. *The New Negro*. 1925. New York: Atheneum, 1992.

Luce, Henry R. "The American Century." *Life*, February 1941, 3–40.

Marshall, Paule. *Brown Girl, Brownstones*. 1959. Reprint, New York: Feminist Press, 1981.

———. *The Fisher King*. New York: Scribner, 2000.

Montesinos Sale, Maggie. *The Slumbering Volcano: American Slave Ship Revolts and the Production of Rebellious Masculinity*. Durham, N.C.: Duke University Press, 1997.

Norment, Lynn. "The Legend Roars Back with New Movie and Old Fire." *Ebony*, September 1996, 30.

O'Neill, Eugene. *The Emperor Jones, "Anna Christie," The Hairy Ape*. New York: Vintage International, 1995.

Oxaal, Ivar. *Black Intellectuals and the Dilemmas of Race and Class in Trinidad*. Cambridge, Mass.: Schenkman, 1982.

Pérez Firmat, Gustavo. *Life on the Hyphen: The Cuban-American Way*. Austin: University of Texas Press, 1994.

Robeson, Paul. *Here I Stand*. Boston: Beacon Press, 1958.

Shaw, Arnold. *Belafonte: An Unauthorized Biography*. New York: Chilton Co., 1960.

Silverman, Stephen M., and Ron Arias. "*Day-O* Reckoning." *People Weekly*, August 26, 1996, 61–64.

West, Cornel. *Restoring Hope: Conversations on the Future of Black America*. Ed. Kelvin Shawn Sealey. Boston: Beacon Press, 1997. 3–34.

Fred Ho

Bamboo That Snaps Back!: Resistance and Revolution in Asian Pacific American Working-Class and Left-Wing Expressive Culture

As a stereotype for a U.S. minority group that pliantly bends to adversity, Asian Pacific Americans (APAS) have been metaphorically compared to bamboo. The bamboo metaphor is meant to praise APAS (a so-called positive stereotype) for being quiet, hardworking, and putting up with hardship and oppression with stoicism and patience. APAS are deemed apolitical, accepting of their oppression, with the effect of promoting accommodationism: of collective passivity, nonresistance, and reliance on hard work as the chief means of social mobility. Such stereotypes function to dehumanize and depoliticize a people. An alternative understanding of the bamboo metaphor might be: If bamboo is bent back too far, it will either break or snap back and hit an opponent in the face. Contrary to the "positive" stereotypes—hardworking, silent, passive, model minority—APAS have "snapped back" in a continuous history of resistance to oppression and struggle for full equality, dignity, and liberation.

Historically, the U.S. Left has failed to understand the strategic importance of the "national question" (i.e., how to liberate oppressed nations and nationalities as part of the overall socialist revolution) in devising theory and programmatic applications to unite the hugely diverse multinational U.S. working class. Some socialists, particularly the Trotskyists, do not even recognize the existence of nations and nationalities within our borders much less that they have been oppressed. Rather, they categorize such peoples as "racial minorities" and consider their struggles to be against "racism," which presumes a political goal of integration and assimilation, and which has invariably resulted in condescending, white chauvinist, and racist relations. The brief and exceptional occasions when the U.S. Marxist-Leninist forces acknowledged the national question were in the 1920s and 1930s, when the CPUSA, led by the Comintern, adopted the "Negro Nation" resolutions and committed resources and focus to organize oppressed nationalities, and in the 1970s, when organizations with substantial roots in the national movements of Chicanos, African Americans, Puerto Ricans, APAS, and First Nations/Native Americans (many originating as revolutionary nationalists) developed into Marxist-Leninist groups that became the New Communist movement. Of course, revolutionary nationalists such as the Republic of New Africa and certain Chicano, Hawaiian, and First Nation forces continue to characterize their struggles as national liberation movements. Understanding the APA struggle is part and parcel of understanding the specifics of the national question and the particular challenges of uniting American-born and immigrant sectors; of upholding equality of language (and opposing the dominance of English); of promoting the importance of cultural identity, national consciousness, and pride; and of developing propaganda and effective organizing forms based on the cultural, historical, and social characteristics of the particular nation/nationality.

Indeed, APAS have a long tradition of resisting oppression by any and all means, from social rebellion and protest to building a revolutionary movement. The scope of this essay presumes a familiarity with APA history, which is well documented in many sources given the growth of Asian American studies. Less familiar are the various forms of APA cultural expression. Though APA literature has in recent years received increased attention, this interest by Asian American literary critics and scholars has overwhelmingly emphasized texts written in the English language rather than the ancestral languages of the immigrant groups.

The performing arts (music, theater, dance, etc.) remain an area of relatively little scrutiny even within Asian American studies, albeit now slowly developing with more critical and scholarly writing, including by artists themselves. Asian American media studies have generally stressed the litany of stereotyped images of APAS from mainstream works. APA visual arts, while still not widely examined in academia, has received more exposure in exhibitions and catalog essays.

The focus of this essay is the immigrant working-class forms of APA expressive culture (literature, film, and the visual and performing arts) and the left-wing radical and revolutionary expressions by APA writers, filmmakers, and visual performing artists. It is hoped that this preliminary analysis will spur further historical research and discussion.

Early Chinese American Working-Class Expressive Culture

The first Asian laborers to be recruited and shipped in large numbers to the United States were Chinese—especially in the 1860s to complete the western leg of the transcontinental railroad. When the railroad was finished, the Chinese laborers dispersed to the new western cities such as San Francisco. There they formed small "Chinatown" communities, often in the worst sections, forcibly segregated by both legal restrictions and the constant threat of racist violence. Although it is conjectured that while working on the railroad in the rural areas of the West the Chinese practiced storytelling and sang folk songs, there is no documentation of this cultural activity.[1] The Chinese presence was regarded as temporary: the workers would leave once the railroad was completed. Given the harsh conditions on the frontier and the racist attitudes of whites, as well as the perceived status of the Chinese as temporary workers who were unassimilable and undesirable, their lives and experiences were deemed unworthy of documentation. We have only a few photographs of these Chinese laborers taken in the mid-nineteenth century, and the writings by whites about them exude racist hostility and opposition.

The Chinese immigrants who were unable to return home (most workers could not afford the passage) established their own communities and a thriving cultural life. The most popular form of entertainment, besides gambling, opium smoking, and prostitution, was the opera, specifically Cantonese opera, as most of the laborers originated from the southern province of Kwantung (Canton). Jack Chen, the late Chinese American historian and cultural impresario, observed that in a typical Chinatown, such as San Francisco's, performances of Chinese opera would go on every night. He noted that as many as six theaters existed within the half-dozen square blocks of San Francisco's Chinatown—a theater on every block. Chen documented the "Pear Garden in the West" (the English transliteration for Chinese opera in America) through posters and old photographs revealing a circuit of Chinese opera tours that extended from Vancouver to Central and South America, to Cuba's Chinatown, to New York City.[2]

The spread of Chinese opera to the many Chinese communities that had begun to take root throughout the Americas was spurred in large part by the Taiping Rebellion that erupted in the 1840s, producing two decades of social upheaval in China. Because many leaders of the rebellion were well-known opera performers, the Manchu Ching government (China's last dynasty, composed of foreign invaders) banned the opera. Chinese opera was thus forced to move overseas and establish a sophisticated touring circuit. Various troupes would regularly visit the growing number of small Chinatowns in the Americas. A prominent opera performer, Mei Lan Fang, who traveled to the United States several times during the first half of the twentieth century, was greeted by Chinese American audiences as a superstar.

For the most part, these operas were traditional works. Yet small changes in the form had begun by the early twentieth century, reflecting the emergence of a Chinese American culture. Western musical instruments such as the saxophone, twelve-string guitar, and violin joined the conventional Chinese instruments. In 1904 a Cantonese opera was written about experiences on Angel Island, the Ellis Island of the West Coast, where for three decades (1910–40) Chinese, in their attempt to gain entry to the United States, were detained from weeks to years in prison-like barracks, interrogated and persecuted by U.S. government authorities. Since the initial passage of the Chinese Exclusion Act of 1882, persecution and harassment of the Chinese and other Asians were part of the mounting anti-Asian immigration restrictions and quotas and racist "Yellow Peril" and xenophobic hysteria nationwide. When cheap labor is needed, Asians (along with other immigrants, now primarily from the Third World) have been recruited and brought to the United States in large numbers, but when the U.S. economy declines, these immigrants are excluded and persecuted. This experience contributed to the feeling of dislocation and alienation so commonly expressed in early Chinese immigrant "sojourner" cultural expressions.

The exclusion laws created a bachelor society—a community of overwhelmingly single, male workers in the city ghettos where Chinese resided. Chinese women were not allowed entry to the United States, except the few who were smuggled in as prostitutes or were part of the exempt classes, such as wives of merchants and officials. The impact of these racist exclusion laws was tantamount to genocide, preventing wives and lovers from joining the male workers and thus from procreate. The Angel Island opera expresses the suffering and anger at the mistreatment of the Chinese.

According to Jack Chen, the Chinese opera, which remained popular until the 1940s, served three vital functions in the Chinese American community:

1. It preserved the Chinese cultural heritage in the face of severe racist persecution and hostility by the dominant Euramerican society;
2. It gave the Chinese a sense of history through the various myths, legends, and historical dramas portrayed;
3. It gave the Chinese self-esteem through their heroes, warriors, and great leaders—figures who fought hardship and triumphed over oppression, providing the oppressed Chinese a sense of pride and succor when their existence seemed hopeless.

Chen maintained that Chinese opera "was an educational experience retelling the ancient legends and history; a school for social ethics inculcating the ancient lessons of right living and honorable behavior. It was a living course in literature and aesthetics with its grace and colorful costumes, a school for music, singing, martial and acrobatic skills. Chinese opera is still all of these."

Probably the immigrants' favorite character in Chinese opera was Kwan Kung, the god of war and literature. Kwan Kung, who originally appeared in the classic epic novel, *The Three Kingdoms*, personified loyalty and heroism as a warrior-scholar. The Western Chinese male readily identified with him. Kwan Kung rode a horse (like the American cowboy), was the protector of those who traveled for a living (immigrants, merchants, and touring performers), fought injustice, was loyal to his comrades (important for community identity and solidarity), and was a bachelor who upheld principle and honor—important values on the lawless frontier.

The popularity of Chinese opera reached its height in the early twentieth century, as restrictions enforced by both segregation laws and the threat of racist violence prevented the Chinese from enjoying other forms of American entertainment (e.g., the theater and movies). (The Chinese were deemed pariahs and venal by mainstream America.) By the 1940s Chinese opera declined as motion pictures and television replaced most live performing arts in the United States, as suburbanization and assimilation increased, and as U.S. foreign policy severed relations with the new, communist Peoples Republic of China. Only recently has Chinese opera started to make a comeback in America; the final removal in 1964 of the century-long racist immigration restrictions and quotas has led to a dramatic increase in Chinese immigration to U.S. cities.[3]

Unlike bourgeois European opera in America, Chinese opera in U.S. Chinatowns is a mass popular cultural form consumed by workers now mostly employed in the restaurant and garment industries. These musical offerings are typically performed in a makeshift theater where patrons go to eat and sip tea, chatter loudly until their favorite scenes appear on stage, then shout their praise or criticize the performance. All of the age-old stories are known to the entire audience, so the details are never important. Audiences come to the opera to be thrilled by new, virtuosic singing and martial arts–like acrobatics. Most non–Chinese Americans would be horrified at the behavior of Chinatown opera goers who eat, smoke, drink, and are rancorous in their approval or disapproval of the shows.

Other significant early Chinese American immigrant working-class cultural forms included the *muk-yu go* (Cantonese woodfish head chants or songs), a thirty-six-syllabic-verse poetic chant accompanied by the metrical beating of a fish head–carved woodblock. Thousands of these chants were compiled in a two-volume collection entitled *Songs of Gold Mountain*, of which 246 were translated into English by Professor Marlon Hom in 1992. Many of them expressed indignation, anger, outrage, protest, frustration, depression, and sorrow for the isolation, persecution, suffering, hardship, and oppression that marked the lives of the Chinese immigrants.[4]

On the Angel Island barracks in San Francisco Bay, thousands of Chinese poems were carved by the detained immigrants. The loneliness, anxiety, confusion, despondency, and anger at their persecution and detention by the U.S. government are all evident in these poems. After the Angel Island Detention Center was closed in the 1940s, many of the poems were forgotten until a later generation of Asian American cultural activists and scholars rediscovered them when the holding center was reopened as a historical museum in the early 1970s. Some of these poems with English translations and excellent historiographical annotations are contained in the book, *Island: Poetry and History of Chinese Immigrants on Angel Island, 1910–1940*, edited by Him Mark Lai, Genny Lim, and Judy Yung. An example follows:

I have ten-thousand hopes that the
revolutionary armies will complete their
victory,
And help make the mining enterprises
successful in the ancestral land.
They will build many battleships and come to
the U.S. territory,
Vowing never to stop till the whitemen are
completely annihilated.[5]

Simultaneous with these immigrant working-class Chinese language forms were more assimilated expressions of Chinese American novels, short stories, and musical theater/nightclub cabaret performers—all basically imitative of white American cultural forms. For example, the night club performers, many of them very talented and hardworking, shown in the Arthur Dong documentary film, *Forbidden City* (named after the nightclub of that name), performed to white-only audiences, pandering to their interest in the exotic. Although it may be argued that the Duke Ellington Orchestra did the same thing in its jungle musical revues at the white-patronized Cotton Club during the Harlem Renaissance, the fact is that the Forbidden City performers did not innovate any new forms or anything uniquely Chinese American, whereas Ellington, of course, extended and elaborated radically upon "jazz" and produced a deeper, more significant African American expressive musical culture. The Chinese American performers in such venues as the Forbidden City nightclub in San Francisco imitated mainstream white entertainers and the most commercial styles of their day, such as white big-band swing jazz, vaudeville comedy, and trendy popular dances.[6]

Early Japanese American Working-Class Expressive Culture

The Japanese first arrived in large numbers to the islands of Hawaii in the late nineteenth century to work on sugar plantations. They brought with them many of their peasant folk traditions, including their work songs called *bushi.* The Japanese men worked in the sugarcane fields cutting the long, tough stalks of cane while the women worked in groups outside of the fields stripping cane leaves off the cut stalks (in Hawaiian, called *hole hole*). Unlike the Chinese women, Japanese women were permitted to enter the United States under the Gentleman's Agreement of 1904 between the Japanese and U.S. governments.

The women workers, many of them teenagers, went to the islands through an arranged marriage system as "picture brides." As the term denotes, they agreed to marry men whom they had never met simply through the exchange of photographs. These men, in return, paid for their transportation from Japan to Hawaii, often costing over a thousand dollars, a huge sum considering that these men earned about sixty-nine cents a day for back-breaking labor from sunup to sundown. As one can imagine, when the women arrived on the docks of Hawaii and met their husbands for the first time, they were sorely disappointed. The men often looked nothing like their pictures. They were much older than depicted, sunburned, and haggard from years of stoop labor. These women were in miserable marriages. As they worked, they sang of their sorrows, suffering, hopes, and dreams through a cappella songs based on their familiar peasant melodies, but with words that expressed these new, often bitter, experiences in the United States. Hence, a unique Japanese (Asian) American working-class folk song form developed called the *hole hole bushi*, a hybrid term combining the Japanese bushi song form with the new experiences of hole hole work in Hawaii, no longer as rice farmers or fishing people, but as plantation workers in a burgeoning capitalist agribusiness.

Some hole hole bushi utilized the double entendre as a form of coded message-making by the immigrant women to arrange trysts with men with whom they were having extramarital affairs:

> Tomorrow is Sunday, right?
> Come over and visit.
> My husband will be out
> Watering cane
> And I'll be alone.[7]

Such usage of the hole hole bushi could be construed as a form of protest against patriarchal monogamy.

Hole hole bushi tunes were sung by the Issei, or first-generation Japanese women workers on the sugar plantations of Hawaii. The tradition did not continue, as many of these women left the fields and went to the cities. Today, however, with a resurgence of Japanese American pride and identity, younger people are learning the hole hole bushi, albeit not as field-workers.

On the U.S. mainland, Japanese labored both as industrial workers and as small farmers, who, despite anti-Asian oppression, managed to excel in agriculture, often turning deserts into arable acreage. This success through hard struggle earned the jealousy of greedy white racist agribusiness, bent on dispossessing the Japanese Americans of their land. One of the most traumatic and singular episodes in U.S. history was the World War II internment of Japanese Americans, involving—among other injustices—the seizure of Japanese farmlands and the confiscation of Japanese-owned property. Over 120,000 Japanese Americans on the mainland, two-thirds of them U.S. citizens, were rounded up and herded into twelve desert detention camps, surrounded by armed gun towers and barbed wire, and housed in makeshift barracks from 1942 until the end of the war. This intense oppression produced many forms of resistance, including protests, riots, and legal challenges. After years of organizing by the Japanese American community, the survivors of the camps and their families received a presidential apology and token reparations signed into law by President Ronald Reagan. However, the $20,000 awarded each individual was a paltry amount compared to the money that has been made from the farmlands taken away from the Japanese, not to mention the loss of lives, mental illness, suicide, and general psychological devastation.

During the internment, to affirm their humanity in the midst of inhumane conditions, Japanese Americans created paintings, wrote poems and stories, made sculptures and gardens, and engaged in a myriad of other cultural projects to fend off boredom, to maintain their spirits, and to express their feelings about the internment experience. Japanese Americans have come to call this collective body of expressive culture "Camp Art"—art that was produced in the internment camps (or "concentration camps," as some have referred to them). Some visual artists came to national prominence, including Yasuo Kuniyoshi and Mine Okubo. A stunning collection of transliterations (in Romanji, or Anglicized Japanese) is *Poets behind Barbed Wire*, which contains the poignant poetry composed by four writers during the camp experience.[8]

The Japanese American community has a vibrant tradition of *tanka* syllabic verse poetry circles, with over one thousand such clubs at their height before World War II. Tomoe Tana was the first Japanese American to receive the highest award for poetry from the emperor of Japan. These tanka poems were written both in Japanese and later in English, conforming to the 5-7-5-7-7 five-line syllable verse, and, as explained by Ms. Tomoe Tana, they had to include an image from nature.[9] Japanese festival dances, songs, and other performances continued after the internment, and in the contemporary Asian movement, the tradition of *taiko* drumming was taken up by younger Japanese Americans as they formed numerous *taiko dojos* (Japanese drum corps) in many cities across the country.

Early Filipino American Working-Class Expressive Cultural Forms

Large numbers of Filipinos followed the Japanese both to sugar plantations in Hawaii and to industries and agricultural fields on the West Coast. Many were seasonal workers, laboring part of the year in the salmon canneries of the Northwest and Alaska and part of the year in "factories of the fields."

The Filipinos who immigrated to the United States were primarily from the northern regions of the Illocano- and Visayan-speaking peoples. The Philippines had been colonized by Spain for three centuries, then by the United States as part of the transfer of spoils from the Spanish-American War of 1898. Consequently, Filipino culture had been heavily Hispanicized, and since 1898 Filipino immigrants to the United States shared the contradictory status of being at once Americans and foreign aliens. During its three decades of colonial rule, the United States waged an intensive Anglo-American cultural indoctrination campaign.

Many Filipinos who emigrated to the United States were thus multilingual in their native Filipino dialect, Spanish, and English. One region of the Philippines never colonized by Spain or America—the southernmost Maranao and Magindinao areas—has retained its Muslim and Polynesian cultural heritage, including unique musical and dance forms based on the *kulintang* traditions. Because of Hispanicization throughout the majority of the Philippines, these Muslim peoples and their culture have been regarded as "inferior" and "primitive." Not until the advent of the modern Asian movement did the kulintang traditions become of interest to younger Filipino Americans. Several kulingtang groups are active in Filipino American communities on both coasts.

One of the giants of Asian Pacific American literature is Carlos Bulosan, a Filipino writer who possessed a talent to write in English, a deep familiarity with the folk tales of peasant Filipinos, a profound sensitivity to the stories of the Filipino American *manongs* (first-generation immigrant bachelor laborers in the United States), and a passionate Marxist-influenced humanism. Bulosan, who arrived in the United States in 1931, worked and lived with the manongs and came to know many of their life stories, which he depicted in his epic *America Is in the Heart.* Though subtitled *A Personal History*, the book is actually a composite of the lives of different Filipino immigrant men told as Bulosan's own story. Caught up in the struggles of the Great Depression, Bulosan was heavily influenced by the left-wing socialist-realist writing of the time (discussed in the next section). Bulosan's works consciously depict the lives of Filipino bachelor workers with dignity and poignancy—their constant rejection by white racism, their superexploitation as migrant laborers, and their yearning for love and female affection in a bachelorhood enforced by anti-Asian immigration and antimiscegenation laws, all the while holding on to naive, romantic dreams of acceptance by American society. Bulosan was also one of the preeminent proletarian writers of the era, a period of socialist-realist literature influenced by the Soviet revolution; the anti-colonial struggles particularly in Asia, Africa, the Pacific Islands, and Latin America; and the rise of Leftist movements in the United States during the depression.[10]

Left-Wing Literature of the Late 1920s and the 1930s

Asian Pacific immigrant workers in the United States faced severe oppression during a period of virulent anti–Asian Pacific racist exclusion and persecution, which in part attracted them to the growing left-wing organizing and ideas, especially as promoted by the CPUSA in leading major campaigns for economic and social justice during the late 1920s and throughout the 1930s. During the depression the CPUSA and Communists gained considerable strength among oppressed nationality workers. Much literature is available on the organizing campaigns (against lynching and for racial justice) initiated and led by the Communists among sharecroppers and tenant farmers in the South, unemployed workers councils, and immigrant workers. A few Asian American historians have documented and analyzed the left-wing organizations in the APA communities, most of it concerning the Chinese American Marxists and Leftists by Him Mark Lai.[11]

Another factor contributing to the growth of Marxism and left-wing radicalism in APA communities was the broadening struggle against colonialism and for national liberation in Asia, especially China. But probably the most significant factor was the importance placed on immigrant and oppressed nationality organizing by the CPUSA, particularly after the Third Communist International, where the Party adopted the Negro Nation thesis mandating a special focus on organizing among oppressed nationalities. The Negro Nation thesis considered African Americans to be an oppressed nation with the right to self-determination in the Black Belt South, where blacks were concentrated and were often a numerical majority. Unlike other American Leftists (who were white and white chauvinists), the Communists, through the Comintern resolutions on the Negro Nation, recognized the revolutionary character of the black struggle in the United States, which had the effect of extending to other oppressed nationalities such as APAS and Mexicans in the Southwest. Thus for a period, the CPUSA devoted resources and organizers to these communities. In its heyday of the 1930s, the CPUSA had over a dozen different daily language newspapers, including Chinese, aimed at spreading Leftist influence among the many immigrant groups it attempted to organize. APA Communist organizers were developed on both coasts. They included immigrant workers who were also writers and poets—among them, Happy Gim Fu Lim, secretary of the Chinese Workers Mutual Aid Association (CWMAA) in San Francisco; Ben Fee, president of the CWMAA and later the first Chinese field organizer for the International Ladies Garment Workers Union in New York City, who wrote poetry and short novels in Chinese with Leftist content; and Carlos Bulosan.

One maverick writer was H. T. Tsiang, who self-published three books, including poetry (*Poems of the Chinese Revolution*, 1929), a novel (*China Red*, 1931), and an experimental novel (*The Hanging on Union Square*, 1933). His lively and humorous novel about the tribulations of a Chinese laundryman in New York's Chinatown, *And China Has Hands*, was published by Robert Speller Books of New York in 1937. Scant biographical information has been compiled about Tsiang, but the little gleaned from Chinese newspaper clippings in the files of Chinese American historian Him Mark Lai suggests that he immigrated to the United States as a student-intellectual and based himself initially at Columbia University. He gravitated to the many Left intellectuals and writers of New York City and had his first publication of a poem in the *New Masses*. Not an organizer, he attended many rallies and meetings and hovered around the Left intellectual and activist circles. According to newspaper accounts, by the 1940s he had given up writing and Leftist politics and relocated to Los Angeles, where he found bit roles in Hollywood movies. After the Chinese revolution in 1949, he may have returned home.

What is important to note is that in the first century of APA literature, little was written in English, much less brought out by white publishers. After World War II, authors John Okada (his novel, *No-No Boy*, is considered a "first" among Japanese American fiction) and Louis Chu (his witty novel, *Eat a Bowl of Tea*, set in New York's Chinatown bachelor society, is the story of a young newly married man who finds himself sexually impotent) were published by sympathetic small presses (Chu's personal friend, Lyle Stuart, owned the Lyle Stuart Press). Both authors and their novels have come to be considered pioneers and classics in APA literature. Okada's book captures the anguish and trauma of Japanese Americans in the internment camps. Chu's language is innovative for conveying Chinatown speech. *Eat a Bowl of Tea* is also praised for its realistic and sympathetic portrayal of Chinatown bachelor society.

English-writing APA authors have been the predominant focus of most discourses on APA literature, including the comprehensive *Asian American Literature* (1982) by Elaine Kim.[12] The major flaw in this conceptualization generally and in this otherwise impressive book specifically is that Asian American literature is defined as a literature written in the English language; this definition excludes the vast body of immigrant and working-class expressions. Another conceptual defect of Kim's book is her generational-based model used to categorize APA literature: the "first" generation is "accommodationist" (i.e., seeking acceptance by the dominant American society); the "second" generation is captive to the "sacrifices for success" syndrome (striving to be an example to its race as a "model minority"); and the "third" generation asserts APA pride and sociopolitical identity. The major error in this method is to ascribe social outlook by generation, as APAs evince all forms of sociopolitical characteristics in every generation. Rather, a class analysis would better explain why privileged, English-writing APAs chose to write in English for white publishers and white audiences from whom they sought acceptance and understanding.

Concurrent with the few publications of APA writers by white American publishers prior to the 1970s and 1980s was a much more substantial output of community literary expressions, often written in the immigrants' ancestral language and published by community presses for immigrant readers. These expressions came from the thousands of Japanese tanka poetry clubs throughout Japanese America and from the Chinese-language poetry, chants, and musical songs of U.S. Chinatowns, all of which appeared in community journals, newspapers, and self-published forms.

The Asian Movement and Its Art

The Asian movement (also known as the Asian American movement or the APA movement) emerged simultaneously on both coasts of mainland United States and in Hawaii during the volatile late 1960s and early 1970s.[13] Inspired by the Black Liberation movement, the mass opposition to the U.S. war in Southeast Asia, national liberation struggles in the Third World (especially Asia), and socialist China (especially the Cultural Revolution), the Asian movement grew both on college campuses and in APA communities. The identifier "Asian American" was first adopted by the Asian American Political Alliance, a group of militant student and radical community activists at the University of California-Berkeley in 1968–69. Subsequently, many student groups were formed nationwide (Asian Student Union, Asian American Students Association, etc.), and several networks were organized in the late 1970s, including the Asian Pacific Students Union (APSU) on the West Coast and the East Coast Asian Students Union (ECASU), which now extends from Florida to Maine. These student activists led the fight to create APA studies courses, programs, and departments, which generated further interest in APA literature. Many student journals continue to feature poetry, artwork, comics, and creative writing with varying political perspectives. APA literary and cultural criticism has been primarily the domain of APA academic publications, while creative expressions are featured primarily in student-led publications.

The Asian movement produced a significant alternative, radical cultural drive within the APA communities across the United States, which led to the formation of new organizations devoted to the arts and to cultural organizing. These included the Kearny Street Workshop and Press and Japantown Art and Media in San Francisco (both were multi-arts), Visual Communications in Los Angeles and Asian Cinevision in New York (media groups), taiko dojos in many cities, and groups that focused on literature such as the Basement Workshop in New York (though it also was multi-arts, especially in its early years).

In Hawaii, the only place in the United States where APAs are a majority of the population (and not a small minority), both an APA and a native Hawaiian literary and cultural movement have emerged, sometimes in collaboration and sometimes separately. Bamboo Ridge Press, Seaweeds and Constructions, and other literary projects embraced both local (mostly emphasizing the APA unique sensibility in Hawaii, which was the focus of Bamboo Ridge) and pan-Pacific (including indigenous Hawaiian) literatures. Writers like Darrell Lum, Wing Tek Lum, Juliet Kono, and Gary Paik are part of a local literary movement that addressed the experiences and sensibilities of being APA in Hawaii. This experience tends to be less preoccupied with identity alienation and reactions to white racism than mainland APA writing and more concerned with the uniqueness of APA life in the islands. Other writers and cultural activists such as Japanese American Richard Hamasaki joined with writers of native Hawaiian and other Pacific Islander ancestry to self-publish, record, and organize community forums advocating and disseminating Hawaiian and Pacific literatures. Their works were often ignored, excluded, or marginalized (not even regarded as literature but simply as "writings") both by white-dominated mainstream presses in academia and, sadly, by APA studies and small press publications. Hamasaki and his cultural activist circle have continued to produce recordings and publications that feature traditional as well as contemporary, experimental expressions that draw from Hawaiian legends, chants, and other forms. The distinction must be made between local writers who write about the APA experience in Hawaii and Hawaiian literature, which is the expression of ancestral Hawaiian writers, and writers who identify with the indigenous culture and strife.

Japanese American writer Milton Murayama, who grew up in Hawaii, is significant for initially self-publishing an underground best-seller in the 1950s. Murayama's novel, *All I Asking for Is My Body*, about the struggles and tensions of a Japanese American plantation worker family, was groundbreaking for its use of pidgin dialect, as evidenced in the title of the book.[14]

The Asian movement catalyzed cultural and literary projects too numerous to cite in this essay. Many militant and radical voices emerged. Filipino American poets and writers included the late Serafin Syquia (1943–73), his younger brother Lou Syquia, Al Robles, Virginia Cerrenio, Cyn Zarco, Jessica Hagedorn, and many others featured in the out-of-print anthology, *Liwanag* (1976). Among Japanese American and Chinese American poets and writers were Lawson Fusao Inada, Frank Chin, Shawn Wong, Janice Mirikitani, Wing Tek Lum, Fay Chiang, Thom Lee, Genny Lim, Richard Hamasaki, and others. A short-lived literary/cultural journal *Aion* featured many West Coast progressive and radical APA writers and artists. A developing Leftist APA literary criticism could be found in landmark anthologies such as *Roots: An Asian American Reader* (considered a "classic" that featured essays on politics, community, and identity as well as photography, artwork, and creative writing) and its sequel, *Counterpoint*,[15] as well as in progressive and Leftist newspapers like the *San Francisco Journal*, *Getting Together* (the organ of I Wor Kuen and its predecessor, *Unity*), and *East Wind* (the APA cultural and political journal of the League of Revolutionary Struggle—Marxist-Leninist, another predecessor of I Wor Kuen).

Much of this movement's cultural criticism and views were influenced by Mao Tse-tung's Yenan talks on art and literature, which directed art and artists to "serve the people," to integrate and learn from the working-class masses, and to heighten the national and class struggle. Part of Mao's impact was to motivate these young APA radicals to search for immigrant, working-class forms, traditions, and influences in both documenting APA cultural history and locating sources for inspiration to create a new progressive and revolutionary APA culture. The Asian movement produced the greatest outpouring of expressive culture in all mediums, generated arts-specific organizations with a pan-Asian and political orientation, organized its own presses and publications, and united cultural production with community struggle. Asian American political and cultural activism was greatly influenced by and looked to leadership from the Black Liberation movement and its cultural wing, the Black Arts Movement, which provided examples of independent, self-reliant institution building and cultural production, asserting its own aesthetic and a commitment to fight oppression and build a revolutionary movement.[16] Combining a commitment to activism and to artistic expression, APA poets and performers joined and did their cultural work as part of rallies, demonstrations, fund-raisers, and all types of community programs. Many freely gave of their service, never expecting to make money, much less careers, from their cultural work. Few thought of themselves as professional writers or artists, but rather as professional revolutionaries, some even joining the many new Communist organizations that had emerged during this period of political and cultural upsurge.[17]

Participating in this tremendous upsurge were visual artists Tomie Arai, Jim Dong, Zand Gee, Nancy Hom, and many others on both coasts; musicians such as Dan and June Kuramoto, Mark Izu, Russell Baba, Fred Houn, Benny Yee, A Grain of Sand (the trio of Nobuko/Joanne Miyamoto, Chris Iijima, and "Charlie" Chin); and artists of all disciplines. Many of these individuals gave their talents to support, educate, organize, and raise needed funds for local community and nationwide campaigns, including the campaign to free Korean immigrant prisoner Chol Soo Lee, to build support for the redress of Japanese Americans interned during World War II, to defend the International Hotel in San Francisco's Manilatown-Chinatown, and to help organize Filipino and Mexican/Chicano farmworkers.

Third World literary journals, the precursors to multicultural literature, also featured APA writers such as the *Yardbird* readers, spearheaded by Ishmael Reed and Al Young, and *Time to Greez*, edited by Janice Mirikitani.[18]

Since the 1970s, increasing numbers of APA writers have been published by mainstream presses, with notable successes by Maxine Hong Kingston, Amy Tan, playwright David Henry Hwang, David Mura, Jessica Hagedorn, Lois Ann Hamanaka, among others. Some have won major literary prizes, such as poet Cathy Song Davenport and Garrett Hongo. Asian American academic criticism has given much attention to these writers.

For every oppressed nationality group in the United States, the striving for self-definition continues as a necessary part of the struggle for liberation, for the power to know and embrace one's true history and culture. This is reflected in each generation's quest for identity (e.g., determining the relationship between ancestral, traditional culture, and American/Western cultural forms and experiences; resisting racism and stereotyping; balancing group experience and individual self-expression; defining responsibilities to community; identifying questions of audience, of language). The fundamental question of what is APA literature is rooted in this pursuit of self-definition. Is APA literature any expressive writing by a U.S. resident of Asian/Pacific Islander descent, or does/must it reflect forms, traditions, sensibilities, and experiences of a people? Are APAS an oppressed group, and should APAS and APA artists contribute to the struggle against oppression and for liberation? How this question is addressed remains political, and this political stance informs the APA's artistic and literary sensibilities. The political view of the artist toward assimilation and oppression in terms of actual experience, both group-shared and individual, will shape the ideological and aesthetic direction of his or her creativity.

The emergence of the Asian movement promulgated a wide militant, progressive, and even revolutionary consciousness among the APA communities. The cultural expression of this period rejected assimilation and took up the cause of creating its own aesthetic and organized alternative community-oriented publications and vehicles. In the last decade and a half, however, the Asian movement has ebbed as both the Black Liberation struggle and the U.S. Left in general have undergone repression and co-optation, and as U.S. society has moved rightward. Asian American studies, originally undertaken to support the exertions of APA communities, has increasingly become self-perpetuating academic islands that are divorced from the community. In the mainstreaming of APA studies, APA success stories are more promoted, including some of the aforementioned writers now published and lauded by the mainstream. This ascendant assimilationist tendency sycophantically endorses artists and writers who are anointed by mainstream media and academic circles. For any oppressed nationality in the United States, including APAS, two paths —assimilation versus resistance/liberation—coexist, often in dynamic tension and contradiction. The path of assimilation has sought acceptance, legitimation, validation, and dependency on the white mainstream. The path of resistance and liberation has sought to assert its own aesthetics, find a base of support within its communities, and build its own institutions and vehicles for dissemination. The writers and their writings to differing and varying degrees reflect this contradiction. This essay has focused on the writers and writings, as well as general cultural production and expression, that have consciously resisted white assimilation, opposed APA oppression, and called for social justice and broader, fundamental social transformation, as expressed by David Monkawa:

live poems will graze
on virgin moss growing on
capitalists' graves.[19]

Notes

In this essay, "oppressed nationalities" refer to "minorities" or "people of color" who have faced a history of racism, exclusion, and oppression in U.S. society, who are now generally people of African, Asian/Pacific, Latin American, Caribbean, and indigenous (First Nation, or Native American, or American Indian) descent. "Whites" include all those among the oppressor nationality who enjoy white-skin privileges and have become the dominant cultural and social group in the United States, which today is primarily people of European descent who have accepted becoming "white."

1. Current fiction and dramatic works, such as Maxine Hong Kingston's novel, *China Men* (New York: Vintage Books, 1989), and David Henry Hwang's play, *The Dance and the Railroad* (in *FOB and Other Plays* [New York: New American Library, 1990], portray vibrant storytelling ("talk story") and Chinese folk and opera singing practices among the bachelor laborers. I know of no nineteenth-century scholarly or journalistic accounts of Chinese American cultural activities.

2. This and the next four paragraphs are drawn from Jack Chen, "American Chinese Opera: Chinese American Reality," *East Wind: Politics and Culture of Asians in the United States* 5, no. 1 (Spring–Summer 1986): 14–17.

3. Fuller discussions of early Chinese American music making can be found in Ron Riddle, *Flowing Streams and Flying Dragons: Music in the Life of San Francisco's Chinese* (Westport, Conn.: Greenwood Press, 1983), and Fred Houn, "Asian American Music and Empowerment: Is There Such a Thing as 'Asian American Jazz?,'" *Views on Black American Music*, Black Musicians Conference, University of Massachusetts-Amherst, 1989, 27–31. For woodfish head chants, see Marlon Hom, *Songs of Gold Mountain: Cantonese Rhymes from San Francisco Chinatown* (Berkeley: University of California Press, 1992).

4. See Hom, *Songs of Gold Mountain*, and Fred Houn, "Revolutionary Asian American Art: Tradition and Change, Inheritance and Innovation, Not Imitation!," *East Wind* 5, no. 1 (Spring–Summer 1986): 5–8.

5. Him Mark Lai, Genny Lim, and Judy Yung, eds., *Island: Poetry and History of Chinese Immigrants on Angel Island, 1910–1940* (Seattle: University of Washington Press, 1991), 90–91.

6. Houn, "Asian American Music and Empowerment.

7. Fred Ho and Susan Asai, paper on the *hole hole bushi* presented at the National Asian American Studies Association Conference, Honolulu, 1997.

8. Jiro and Kay Nakano, *Poets behind Barbed Wire: Tanka Poems, Keiho Soga . . .* (Honolulu: Bamboo Ridge Press, 1983).

9. Fred Ho, "Interview with Tomoe Tana," *Asian Week* newspaper (date unknown as my files are in storage; however Mrs. Tana, then in her seventies, au-

dited my Asian American literature course at Stanford University in 1988, during which time I interviewed her).

10. For Bulosan's work, see Carlos Bulosan, *America Is in the Heart: A Personal Story* (1946; reprint, Seattle: University of Washington Press, 1973, and Epilfano San Juan, *On Being Filipino: Selected Writings of Carlos Bulosan* (Philadelphia: Temple University Press, 1995).

11. Him Mark Lai, "A Survey of the Chinese American Left," *Bulletin of Concerned Asian Scholars* 4, no. 3 (1972): 10–21.

12. Elaine H. Kim, *Asian American Literature: An Introduction to the Writings and Their Social Context* (Philadelphia: Temple University Press, 1982).

13. For a comprehensive collection of historical and personal narratives of this period, see Fred Ho, with Carolyn Antonio, Diane Fujino, and Steve Yip, *Legacy to Liberation: Politics and Culture of Revolutionary Asian Pacific America* (San Francisco: AK Press, 2000).

14. Milton Murayama, *All I Asking for Is My Body* (Honolulu: University of Hawaii Press, 1988).

15. See Amy Tachiki, Eddie Wong, and Franklin Odo, with Buck Wong, eds., *Roots: An Asian American Reader* (Los Angeles: Asian American Studies Center, University of California at Los Angeles [UCLA], 1971), and Emma Gee, *Counterpoint: Perspectives on Asian America* (Los Angeles: Asian American Studies Center, UCLA, 1976).

16. Kalamu ya Salaam, "The Magic of Ju-Ju: An Appreciation of the Black Arts Movement," unpublished manuscript given to author.

17. Fred Ho, "Beyond 'Asian American Jazz': My Musical and Political Changes in the Asian American Movement," *Leonardo Music Journal* (San Francisco) 9 (1999): 45–51.

18. *Time to Greez!: Incantations from the Third World/Third World Communications*, ed. Janice Mirikitani (San Francisco: Glide Publications, 1975).

19. David Monkawa, excerpts from "Counter Haikus (An American Calendar)," *East Wind* 5, no. 1 (Spring–Summer 1986): 9.

James Smethurst

Poetry and Sympathy: New York, the Left, and the Rise of Black Arts

New York City is frequently cited as the birthplace of the Black Arts Movement. This is due in no small part to the national reputations of Amiri Baraka, Larry Neal, and the relatively short-lived Black Arts Repertory Theater and School (BARTS) in Harlem. It also has to do with the long-held notion of Harlem as the center of African American intellectual, artistic, and political life. And, of course, a great many important artists and critics associated with the Black Arts Movement—Baraka, Neal, Woodie King, Ron Milner, David Rambeau, Ed Bullins, Sonia Sanchez, Addison Gayle Jr., Jayne Cortez, Nikki Giovanni, David Henderson, Calvin Hernton, Ishmael Reed, Lorenzo Thomas, Askia Touré, Tom Dent, Marvin X, Henry Dumas, the Last Poets, Ed Spriggs—lived in New York for a significant period in the 1960s and 1970s.

As Kalamu ya Salaam and others have pointed out, however, relatively few stable Black Arts institutions were established in the city. BARTS lasted only a year. The major Black Arts journals, publishers, and organizations were based primarily in the Midwest and on the West Coast—though many had New York representatives and some, such as *Black Dialogue*, relocated to New York.[1] During the height of Black Power and Black Arts, Newark was in many respects as important a center as New York—again, owing largely to the work of Amiri Baraka and Baraka's Committee for a Unified Newark (CFUN—later Newark CAP) on the Congress of African Peoples (CAP).[2] Even in the case of Newark and the Newark CAP, the influence on the Black Arts Movement nationally was essentially through political institutions rather than cultural ones. In other words, though the Newark-based Spirit House, journal *Cricket*, and Jihad Press had an impact on Black Arts, this impact was nowhere near as great as the *Journal of Black Poetry*, *Soulbook*, and *Black Dialogue* on the West Coast, Broadside Press in Detroit, or *Negro Digest* (later *Black World*), the Organization of Black American Culture (OBAC), and the Third World Press in Chicago.

The importance of New York for Black Arts lies largely in the role the city's black intellectuals, artists, and institutions played in preparing the groundwork for the movement. As Lorenzo Thomas argues, there was a kind of African American artistic underground in which "scholars of Marxism, left-over Garveyites, and Pan-Africanists" provided "alternative" role models to younger black artists and intellectuals.[3] Larry Neal also claimed in the late 1970s that the influence of the Communist Left on the creation and circulation of African American literature lingered, though "transmuted or synthesized," in the 1960s.[4] Nowhere in the United States was there a greater concentration of older Marxist and nationalist artists and intellectuals than in New York City. It was this density of "alternative" Left, nationalist, and, often, Left-nationalist mentors and role models that intersected with the avant-garde African American artistic community of the late 1950s and early 1960s, centered initially on the Lower East Side, making New York an incubator for Black Power and Black Arts ideologies, poetics, and activists.

Harlem as Exceptional and Representative Cultural Landscape

New York, of course, was the focal point for the political and cultural movement later known as the Harlem Renaissance. Although this movement is still most commonly associated with a wave of literature, music, visual art, dance, and theater by African American artists, much of the impetus for the renaissance came from the emergence and growth of a new black political activism and new political institutions in the period immediately before, during, and after World War I. Harlem became the headquarters of a host of political organizations, including the NAACP, the Urban League, Marcus Garvey's Universal Negro Improvement Association, and the first significant black socialist (and pro-Bolshevik as well as significantly nationalist) organization, the African Blood Brotherhood.[5]

There were other important loci of African American political and literary activities in the 1920s, particularly Washington, D.C., Philadelphia, Boston, and, to a lesser extent, Cleveland and Baltimore. But the literary and political circles there were generally held to be more conservative and more provincial than those in Harlem. Harlem thus came to be seen not only as the "race capital," but also as the cutting edge of African American art and politics.

This sense of Harlem as the focal point of black political and cultural progressivism continued in the depression era. To a certain extent, especially as far as literature was concerned, this sense of Harlem as a "race capital" was an ideological inheritance from the New Negro Renaissance rather than simply a reflection of actual cultural production. In many respects, Chicago was the most vital center of black literary production in the 1930s and 1940s. Washington, D.C., was arguably as important a locus of African American intellectual activity as New York, with dynamic groups of radicals and progressives at Howard University—among them, E. Franklin Frazier, Ralph Bunche, Eugene Clay Holmes, Doxey Wilkerson, and Sterling Brown.

Yet Harlem did retain a claim to political vanguard status. Progressives, like Adam Clayton Powell Jr., and radicals, such as African American Communist city councilman Benjamin Davis and the Italian American congressman from East Harlem, Vito Marcantonio, were prominent figures of the Harlem political landscape. Among black cultural workers in New York, especially writers, visual artists, and theater workers, a huge proportion had some tie to the Popular Front in the late 1930s and early 1940s.[6]

Even as late as the early 1950s, a vibrant Left political and cultural African American subculture still existed in Harlem. The most visible institution of this subculture was perhaps Paul Robeson's journal, *Freedom*. *Freedom* featured work by such artists and intellectuals as Lorraine Hansberry, Alice Childress, John Henrik Clarke, John Killens, Lloyd Brown, W. E. B. Du Bois, Julian Mayfield, Frank Marshall Davis, and, of course, Robeson himself. Clarke, Killens, and Mayfield would mentor a number of Black Arts and Black Power activists, especially in Harlem.

Harlem was also the scene of various large influential activist nationalist groups, generally descended from the Garvey movement, which claimed fewer well-known artists, intellectuals, and politicians than the Left in the 1930s and 1940s but maintained a visible public presence and grassroots popularity. Such nationalism had a long and prominent history in Harlem, reaching back to Garvey and the UNIA (and *Negro World*) and the African Blood Brotherhood (and *Crusader*) during the Harlem Renaissance. In the 1930s and 1940s neo-Garveyites and other nationalists led street demonstrations, orations, and picket lines to protest, for instance, the Italian invasion of Ethiopia, police brutality, and Jim Crow hiring practices by public and private employers in Harlem.[7] In fact, one could characterize the 1930s and 1940s New York forerunners of the later activist civil rights movement (as opposed to the generally more strictly legalistic strategy of the national NAACP) as alternating competition and cooperation between the Left and nationalists of various stripes.

Though the New Negro Renaissance notion of Harlem as an artistic and political center remained (in a more distinctly Left register, perhaps, than in the 1920s), in some ways the community's claim to distinction in the 1930s came, paradoxically, through a new sense of its hyper-"typical" status. In other words, rather than a unique "city of refuge" or a neo-Emersonian figuration of African American future and possibility, invoked both straightforwardly and ironically during the New Negro Renaissance, Harlem became a kind of "everyghetto." In this later, overlapping vision, Harlem embodied the conditions of oppression and poverty that were seen as attending urban black life throughout the United States. Harlem was still distinctive in that its ghettoness, so to speak, was perceived as more intense than that of other communities, due to its size and the concentration of its population. This intensity, further accented by the earlier promise of the Harlem Renaissance, stood as a sour reminder of the deferral of the African American dream. Increasingly, Harlem took on an iconic and, again, somewhat ironic status of "home," as Amiri Baraka would later write, "a place one escapes from" and, importantly, one to which an estranged black artist or intellectual could return, even if, like Baraka, he or she had never lived there.[8]

The Cold War Era

By the late 1950s the political and intellectual landscape of Harlem, and the Northeast generally, had changed greatly—though notions of both Harlem exceptionalism as the "capital of the Negro world" and representativeness as "everyghetto" persisted. The World War II and postwar eras saw the growth of a number of Left-initiated African American organizations and institutions, such as the Civil Rights Congress, the National Negro Labor Council, the journal *Freedom*, and the Left-influenced Harlem-based newspaper, *People's Voice*. By the mid-1950s, however, these institutions and organizations collapsed under the weight of Cold War persecution.[9] Important African American political and cultural activists formerly associated with the Communist Left, such as Max Yergan (a YMCA leader and a founder of the Left-influenced Council on African Affairs), Adam Clayton Powell, musician Joshua White, actor Canada Lee, and Langston Hughes, distanced themselves from the Communists and their allies. Some, like Yergan, White, and Lee became actively anti-Communist—although that did not always save their careers. Others, notably Hughes, retained ties to the Left but were cautious about any public demonstration of those ties. Those political and cultural leaders who maintained open affiliations with the Communist Left, such as Benjamin Davis, Ewart Guinier, Paul Robeson, and W. E. B. Du Bois, found themselves hounded by federal and local governments, blacklisted in their professions, isolated from mainstream political and cultural institutions, and in some cases, as that of Davis, imprisoned.

Beyond these external pressures, the Harlem Left (and the Communist Left generally) was torn by internal problems—often exacerbated by government repression and covert government activity. Mirroring campaigns against "white chauvinism" and "Negro nationalism" within the CPUSA in the late 1940s and early 1950s led to disciplinary proceedings against rank-and-file and leading members, often for a small and sometimes ambiguous remark or act. These campaigns caused considerable turmoil and the loss of important activists, both black and white. Factional battles stimulated by Nikita Khrushchev's 1956 "secret speech" about Joseph Stalin and the Soviet invasion of Hungary that same year further decimated CPUSA membership and largely paralyzed its leadership. The middle and late 1950s saw the expulsion or resignation of such prominent African American Communists as Abner Berry, Harry Haywood, Howard "Stretch" Johnson, and Doxey Wilkerson. Beyond those who were imprisoned, exiled, driven away through the threat of public-sector and private-sector persecution, expelled, or alienated by 1950s factional strife and the revelations about Stalin, many Communists in Harlem (and elsewhere) fell out of regular contact with the organized Left as the infrastructure of the CPUSA and the institutions it influenced disintegrated under the combination of government repression, factionalism, international ideological crisis, and the prevalence of an "underground" mentality in much of the remaining CPUSA leadership.[10]

By the late 1950s activist nationalism in Harlem was also at a low ebb. Nationalist street protests had greatly diminished, possibly because of relative optimism engendered by the promises of early desegregation efforts as well as a general Cold War atmosphere of antiradicalism. Lorenzo Thomas argues that there was a sort of African American McCarthyite attitude in which nationalists were marginalized as "crazy."[11] Another factor may have been, ironically, the increasing influence of the Nation of Islam (NOI). On one hand, the NOI, its new Harlem leader, Malcolm X, and, later, its journal, *Muhammad Speaks*, were powerful, often radical voices for black separatism in Harlem and beyond, reaching a broad section of the black community to a degree not seen since the Garvey movement in the 1920s. In fact, the Chicago and New York staffs of *Muhammad Speaks* were led by such Left veterans as Richard Durham and Joe Walker. On the other hand, the NOI in New York rarely participated in the kinds of grassroots political activities in which early nationalists had engaged.

Of course, there were still nationalist street corner speakers in Harlem, notably Eddie "Pork Chop" Davis, and such visible nationalist presences as the NOI and National Memorial African Bookstore at 125th Street and Seventh Avenue (which would continue to be an important nationalist/Black Arts landmark until its condemnation as part of the Harlem State Office Building site in 1970). And, much like veterans of the Old Left, thousands of Harlemites had engaged in organized nationalist political activities whether or not they were still members of an existing nationalist group. There was also some nationalist (and Leftist) participation in Cold War institutions, particularly the American Society for African Culture (AMSAC). AMSAC was secretly funded by the Central Intelligence Agency. The CIA aimed to channel African American anticolonialism and Pan-Africanism away from the Communist Left (and radical nationalists). However, Leftists and nationalists were able to use AMSAC as a vehicle for a more radical politics with some success. For example, an AMSAC-sponsored Conference of Negro Writers in 1959 included such unrepentantly Leftist (and nationalist) writers as John O. Killens and Lorraine Hansberry.

At the height of the McCarthy period, then, both the Left and activist nationalism were at a relatively low ebb in New York City and other urban centers of the Northeast. Nonetheless, numerous black artists and intellectuals who had been associated with the Left or organized nationalist movements remained. Some, like Du Bois, Robeson, Killens, Hansberry, Ossie Davis, Ruby Dee, Esther Cooper Jackson, John Henrik Clarke, Lloyd Brown, Ernest Kaiser, Alice Childress, and Richard Moore, were more or less unchanged ideologically (or at least retained a sympathy for their old politics)—though their precise organizational affiliations, if any, are often murky.

Many of these writers and intellectuals formed the core of the Left-influenced Harlem Writers Guild (HWG). Although some later commentators, notably Harold Cruse, would posit an unbridgeable gulf between the HWG and the young nationalist writers, in practice there was considerable interaction of the 1960s. For example, the HWG largely initiated the organization of the 1961 demonstration against Patrice Lumumba's assassination that took place outside and inside the United Nations building. Because members of the HWG had formed a sort of extended family for the Congolese United Nations delegation, Lumumba's murder with the complicity of the United States struck them particularly hard. Their response was to contact a wide range of Leftist and nationalist groups within the black community of New York and form a coalition that had not been seen for years, if ever. Among the demonstrators were important future Black Arts activists such as Amiri Baraka, Askia Touré, Aishah Rahman, and Calvin Hicks. HWG members Hicks and Sarah Wright originated the Leftist-nationalist group On Guard for Freedom in an effort to continue the coalition engendered by the United Nations demonstration. Largely through the work of Hicks, Baraka's Organization of Young Men merged with On Guard; thus On Guard came to include many artists and activists who comprised the core of BARTS. On Guard's membership for the most part lived on the Lower East Side but was active in Harlem organizations like the Monroe Defense Committee (created in support of Monroe, North Carolina, NAACP leader Robert Williams, who was famous for lining up armed resistance to Ku Klux Klan terrorism).[12] The HWG also sponsored an important forum at the New School for Social Research in April 1965 that featured such younger writers as Amiri Baraka and Calvin Hernton, as well as older (and not-so-old) artists and intellectuals more normally associated with the HWG and *Freedomways* (and the Old Left), including Alice Childress, Sarah Wright, James Baldwin, John O. Killens, Sterling Brown, Paule Marshall, and John Henrik Clarke.[13]

Some intellectuals who had left or been expelled from the CPUSA, like Richard Moore (expelled in the 1940s for "nationalism"), remained on friendly terms with the Party and those institutions it continued to influence. Moore was a frequent contributor to *Freedomways* between 1962 and 1965—at the same time that his involvement with the more nationalist *Liberator* was greatest. Still others who, like Harold Cruse, were veterans of the cultural wing of the Communist Left had become more or less hostile to the Old Left—though in many cases, such as Cruse's, this hostility was not entirely public until the Black Power movement had clearly begun to emerge.

The work of the Trotskyist Socialist Workers Party (SWP) in the Monroe Defense Committee and Fair Play for Cuba alienated a number of young black militants for what was perceived as a proclivity for sectarian attempts to control those organizations—a proclivity that was also ascribed to the CPUSA and other older "white" Leftist groups. However, the educational institutions of the SWP facilitated the growth of the network of new radical black artists, intellectuals, and activists. Though only a few of the activists who formed BARTS, such as Cornelius Suares and Clarence Franklin, apparently joined the SWP, the early recognition of the importance of Malcolm X by SWP members, particularly George Breitman, led to the circulation of the more radical (in a Leftist sense) ideas of Malcolm X through the SWP's Pathfinder Press. Similarly, the SWP forums that featured Malcolm X played a major role in bringing young black militants from the Lower East Side, Harlem, and elsewhere in the city in contact with each other.[14] After 1962 Maoism, especially through the newly formed Progressive Labor Party, began to have a significant impact on black artists and intellectuals uptown and downtown—in large part through the efforts of Harlem PLP organizer, Bill Epton. Again, relatively few Black Arts activists directly affiliated with the PLP, even when some, such as Baraka, embraced a form of Maoist Third World Marxism. Nonetheless, Epton and the PLP contributed to the circulation of radical ideas and variants of Marxism other than those promoted by the CPUSA and the SWP.

Even black artists and intellectuals who publicly distanced themselves from their previous Leftist politics often maintained contact with those who remained on the Left to one degree or another. For example, the correspondence of Langston Hughes reveals that at the height of the Cold War he kept in close touch with a wide range of Left activists—among them, Alice Childress, Lorraine Hansberry, Theodore Ward, John O. Killens, Louise Thompson Patterson, William Patterson, Ishmael Flory, John Henrik Clarke, and Margaret Burroughs.[15]

Although the institutions of the Old Left had largely been destroyed or isolated, those that remained, such as the national centers of the CPUSA and the SWP, the CPUSA publishing house International Publishers and its SWP counterpart Pathfinder Press, CPUSA and SWP bookstores, the CPUSA-influenced cultural journals *Masses and Mainstream* (later *Mainstream*) and *American Dialog*, the CPUSA newspaper the *Worker*, and the SWP newspaper the *Militant* were more concentrated in New York than anywhere else. And nowhere else, even Chicago, was there such a density of past and present Communists, Trotskyists, and Socialists, black and white. As Gerald Horne has shown, CPUSA leader Benjamin Davis remained a familiar presence in Harlem. Davis, a street speaker who regularly held forth across from the National Memorial African Bookstore, could still draw audiences of hundreds, and sometimes thousands, in Harlem after his release from prison in 1955 until his death in 1964.[16]

When the Cold War began to recede a bit in the late 1950s and early 1960s—in no small part due to the revival of an activist civil rights movement—new, relatively stable intellectual and artistic institutions were created by sometimes uneasy alliances of Leftists, former Leftists, nationalists, and Left nationalists. Some of the artists and intellectuals who organized these new institutions were nationalist intellectuals and radicalized civil rights workers who had become impatient with the limits of Cold War liberalism, seeing it as patronizing, too willing to accommodate itself to a racist power structure, and out of step with the new post-Bandung spirit of radical decolonization as embodied in such leaders as Ghana's Kwame Nkrumah and, particularly, the Congo's Patrice Lumumba. Others were Leftists who were attempting to push the civil rights movement in various directions (e.g., to reject anticommunism, toward a more clearly anti-imperialist, anticolonialist internationalist stance, toward black self-determination, North and South) without rejecting or sharply criticizing it. In many respects, the figure who best embodied the distinctions between these two groups was Martin Luther King Jr. The nationalist group was often sharply critical of King, his philosophy of nonviolence, and what it regarded as an overwillingness to accommodate to northern liberalism and to restrain more radical elements of the movement; the latter Left group was more favorable toward King, seeing him as an ideological work in progress.

One of the first of these new institutions was the journal *Freedomways*, which made its debut in 1961. It was conceived by W. E. B. Du Bois, Edward Strong, Louis Burnham, Esther Cooper Jackson, and other Leftist black intellectuals largely as a continuation of the Left, anti-imperialist, anti–Jim Crow project of Paul Robeson's *Freedom* within the context of the revived civil rights movement and the successes (and failures) of the African, Asian, and Latin American independence movements.[17] Though often critical of African American nationalism, *Freedomways* was more open to nationalist-influenced thought and certainly the notion of African American self-determination (under the rubric of black liberation), than has sometimes been allowed. In fact, especially as the 1960s wore on, the dominant ideology of poets, fiction writers, and other artists associated with the magazine was, as Killens approvingly characterized the ideology of the late Lorraine Hansberry, "Black nationalist with a socialist perspective."[18] Much like the work of Dudley Randall in the 1960s and 1970s and of Langston Hughes in the 1960s, *Freedomways* reminded readers of earlier moments of radical black writing, publishing older writers (and often older poems of these writers) such as Margaret Walker, Claude McKay, Naomi Long Madgett, and Sterling Brown, as well as younger writers like Mari Evans, Nikki Giovanni, David Henderson, Calvin Hernton, Audre Lorde, Haki Madhubuti, Askia Touré, and Alice Walker. A number of these younger writers had participated in the activities and organizations of the Communist Left; others were protégés of older Leftist writers and intellectuals—as in the cases of Nikki Giovanni in her relationship to Killens and of Haki Madhubuti who was mentored by Charles and Margaret Burroughs. Despite Cruse's assessment that the journal was dominated by an old and discredited CPUSA integrationism, young writers prominently identified with the new nationalism, such as Madhubuti and Touré, published in *Freedomways* well into the 1970s.[19] And, as Kalamu ya Salaam notes, Ernest Kaiser's books column in *Freedomways* was a vital annotated compendium of new African American writing in the 1960s (and 1970s and 1980s).[20]

The *Liberator* also combined the new (and old) nationalism with the Old Left in a shifting and sometimes unstable fashion. Initially started in support of African freedom movements by the small Liberation Committee for Africa in 1961 and headquartered in midtown Manhattan, the journal soon morphed into a vehicle for radical African American thought focusing on black struggles in the United States as well as Africa. The early politics of the journal and its publisher Daniel Watts are a little hard to define precisely—in part because what has been written by the participants was, for the most part, retrospectively from the Black Power era and is marked by an anti-Communist nationalism and in part because Watts does not appear to have had a clear ideological center. At times, Watts seemed to take pains to distinguish himself and the *Liberator* from the CPUSA.[21] However, as Harold Cruse and others have pointed out, it is equally clear that Watts had long associated with Communists and other Leftists in the Harlem Writers Guild and other Left-influenced organizations, an association that was reflected in the early *Liberator* masthead and table of contents. In many respects, his political evasiveness about the journal's relationship to the Communist Left, and later such underground or semi-underground Left-nationalist groups as the Revolutionary Action Movement (RAM), was a typical strategy of McCarthy-era radicals who sought work effectively in a very circumscribed political climate. The early writers and advisory board members were largely a mixture of past and present Communists (or Communist supporters) and radical nationalists, including such Left-identified figures as Hugh Mulzac, *Baltimore Afro-American* publisher George Murphy, and Ossie Davis. Some of the nationalists, like Richard Moore, had been Communists and retained cordial public relations with the Communist Left, whatever private reservations they might have had. Others, notably Cruse, were former Communists who had become antagonistic to the Communist Left—though Cruse's public criticism was muted in the early days of the *Liberator*. The journal gradually moved away from the Old Left and vice versa; the final break occurred in 1966, when Ossie Davis and James Baldwin left the advisory board over the issue of anti-Semitism.[22]

It was in no small part frustration with liberalism and enthusiasm about the decolonization movements of Africa, Asia, and Latin America that pushed the *Liberator* to a more militant nationalism (or range of nationalisms since, as Cruse argued, the journal never was completely unified or consistent in its ideology). This frustration was fed by U.S. support of the colonial powers as well as by a lack of federal support for the civil rights movement, particularly the Mississippi Freedom Democratic Party challenge in 1964, at a time when liberal Democrats dominated the White House. This nationalism alienated or forced out the more traditionally Left board members and writers. Though the Leftists were also supportive of the new anticolonial, anti-imperialist movements, the younger militants often associated them with either an ineffectual isolation or a tailing after the more social democratic side of American liberalism or sometimes both. It was, after all, a liberal U.S. administration that was complicit in (and perhaps instigated) the murder of Patrice Lumumba in 1961. A galvanizing event for the new radical nationalists, Lumumba's death inspired a militant demonstration at the United Nations, where Adlai Stevenson's speech to the General Assembly was disrupted by angry shouts and thrown shoes. This protest marked a personal crossroads and was seen as a larger cultural turning point by a number of young militants who would be pivotal in the Black Arts Movement. In some accounts, not only were white sympathizers banned from the demonstration, but also Benjamin Davis and Paul Robeson Jr., son of the famous artist and activist, suggesting a break with the Communist Left and the older mode of radicalism embodied by the CPUSA along the lines of Cruse's *Crisis of the Negro Intellectual*.[23] But since the Left-influenced HWG had such a large part in organizing the demonstration, it does seem questionable that Davis and Robeson would have been excluded simply because of their association with the CPUSA.[24] Nonetheless, regardless of whether Davis and Robeson were actually banned, the story of their ejection from the picket itself marked a certain public rupture with past politics.

There is no doubt that by the mid-1960s the distance between many of the most important young militants and the ideology and remaining institutions of the Old Left had increased. The evolution of the *Liberator* is a good barometer of this change—as well as of how the imprint of older radicals lingered in the work of the Black Arts Movement. Some mark the beginning of the *Liberator*'s importance to Black Arts in 1965, when Larry Neal and Amiri Baraka joined its editorial board at least in part at the urging of Askia Touré—Neal became the arts editor in 1966.[25] Nevertheless, the journal had begun presenting the work of younger black poets like Ishmael Reed, Baraka, and Touré well before Neal and Baraka were added to the board. In addition to poetry, the *Liberator* published a number of essays that were crucial in defining the ideological field of the Black Arts Movement. These included early essays by Harold Cruse (who later became a severe critic of the journal and publisher Daniel Watts), Muhammad Ahmad (Max Stanford), and Touré that broke with Old Left ideology and institutions, though often (especially in the case of Cruse's work) much shaped by Marxist thought. While these writers generally agreed with Leftist conceptions of capitalism and imperialism and were more sensitive to issues of class within the African American community than had often been the case with nationalist writers before and after, they rejected what they saw as the paternalism and arrogance of the Left as well as the notion that white workers would be willing to give up the benefits of racism (and imperialism) to join the struggle of African Americans and other peoples of color around the world.

What Larry Neal brought to the *Liberator* beyond his close ties to many young nationalist black writers (e.g., Baraka, Charles Fuller, and Sonia Sanchez) was his emphasis on an antimaterialist, anti-Western spiritualism. Of course, Neal, like many associated with the journal, rejected the Old Left because they believed that Leftist organizations were essentially run by white people for their own purposes, leaving African Americans without agency. In addition to his adherence to the concepts of black self-interest and black self-determination (a term after all popularized by the Communist Left), Neal rejected "Western" rationalism as embodied in Marxism. Marxism ignored what he called the spiritual component, however accurate its critique of economic exploitation might be. Although this spiritualism was not clearly defined, a commitment to generally non-Christian spirituality became a hallmark of the Black Arts Movement.[26]

Black Bohemia

New York differed from many of the early Black Arts and Black Power centers in that academia played only a minor role in the birth of these movements. A number of those active in the early New York Black Arts scene would eventually hold jobs in academia—though generally outside of New York City and environs. However, no school in New York had the same impact that San Francisco State, Merritt College (Oakland, California), Wayne State (Detroit), Fisk University (Nashville, Tennessee), or the group of historically black schools of Atlanta's University Center did in their respective regions. Instead, as scholars Eugene Redmond, Valerie Wilmer, Aldon Nielsen, Michael Oren, Tom Dent, Lorenzo Thomas, and others have noted, New York was a sort of anti-academic bohemian delta where many streams of black avant garde poetry, fiction, drama, criticism, music, dance, and visual art flowed in the 1950s and 1960s.[27] Poets from the South (Bobb Hamilton, Julia Fields, Tom Dent, Calvin Hernton, A. B. Spellman), Midwest (Askia Touré, Nikki Giovanni, Ted Joans, James Thompson), West (Jay Wright, Sonia Sanchez, Jayne Cortez, and the regionally ambiguous Bob Kaufman), and elsewhere in the East (Amiri Baraka, Larry Neal, Ishmael Reed) joined such New Yorkers as David Henderson, Raymond Patterson, Tom Postell, and Lorenzo Thomas.

Like similar lists of the Harlem Renaissance, such a roll of poets fails to delineate the full dimensions of the black avant garde in New York during this period because it leaves out such musicians as Ornette Coleman, Archie Shepp, Marion Brown, Sam Rivers, Cecil Taylor, and Sun Ra and his Arkestra and such visual artists as Tom Feelings, Bob Thompson, and Joe Overstreet. This list misses the burgeoning black theater movement that took on a new prominence with success of Lorraine Hansberry's 1958 *A Raisin in the Sun*. Many of the poets enumerated above would write for, act in, direct, and even (in the case of Dent) administer black theaters. It also fails to show the extent to which different artistic fields cross-fertilized each other—not only in terms of, say, the well-known impact of "New Thing" or "Free" jazz on the new black (and white) writing, as well as the fact that the interests and projects of the artists themselves were so wide-ranging. Artists known primarily as musicians were also serious writers (Shepp, Taylor, Brown, Sun Ra). Some who became associated with the new music or the new literature were also visual artists (Askia Touré, Ted Joans). Some writers had been high-level musicians (e.g., Jay Wright had played bass for avant garde tenor saxophonist Pharaoh Sanders).

The focal point of this cross-generic activity was not Harlem, but downtown and, increasingly, the new bohemian center of the Lower East Side. In part, the Lower East Side emerged as the locus of the literary and artistic avant garde in New York because rising rents were driving artists out of the older bohemian neighborhood of Greenwich Village. Certainly low rents and the concentration of avant garde artists and institutions in the Lower East Side attracted black artists, who were increasingly drawn there to live or, if they lived elsewhere in the city, to participate in artistic activities and institutions of the neighborhood from readings at the Café Metro to hanging out at Stanley's Bar on Avenue B.[28]

Another attraction was that the community, long a haven for immigrants, was becoming increasingly multiracial, drawing many Asian Americans, a large number of Puerto Ricans, and, to a lesser extent, African Americans, especially east of Tompkins Square Park and south of Houston Street. The symbolic (and often literal) move of black artistic activity from the Lower East Side to Harlem at the beginning of the Black Arts era (actually signaling the beginning of the Black Arts era in New York) had involved the coding of Harlem (aka "uptown") as "black" and the Lower East Side (aka "downtown") as essentially "white." However, part of the original attraction of the Lower East Side was that it was, in fact, far less white than Greenwich Village (despite the village's history as a center of the black community in New York during the nineteenth and early twentieth centuries).[29] Though racial and ethnic relations in the Lower East Side were hardly idyllic, they were somewhat more relaxed than in Greenwich Village, where black bohemians faced the constant threat of violence, especially in the predominantly Italian American south village.

One aspect of the new counterculture on the Lower East Side that has received little scholarly attention is the existence of a politically radical interracial bohemia at the beginning of the 1960s. No doubt this is due in part to the fact that this bohemia grew up while the McCarthy era—Red squads, blacklisting, the House Un-American Activities Committee, the McCarran Act, the Smith Act—was very much alive. Nonetheless, the Lower East Side and the adjoining Union Square area contained an unusual concentration of remaining Old Left institutions, including national organizational headquarters, bookstores, newspapers, journals, and Left-influenced ethnic institutions, such as the Ukrainian Labor Hall, and a Left-wing artistic subculture that included some of the younger artists of the Lower East Side.[30]

This aspect of the growth of what became know as the "New Black Poetry" lurks behind many accounts of the activities of the period. It can been seen in the fact that the first major introduction of the work of the Umbra poets outside of their own journal took place in the pages of *Mainstream*, a CPUSA cultural journal. *Mainstream* was succeeded by *American Dialog*, founded in 1964. Clearly Amiri Baraka has *American Dialog* in mind when he mentions in his autobiography that the Communist Party asked him to be the editor of a new cultural journal in the early 1960s. In fact, Baraka goes on to say that "later, they started a 'black magazine' called *Dialog* and made the photographer the editor."[31] Although *American Dialog* was not really a "black magazine," it was from the beginning far more consistently engaged with the new black cultural radicals, especially writers, visual artists, and "free jazz" musicians, than *Mainstream* had been. This was in no small part due to the efforts of Alvin Simon, an African American photographer who had been a member of Umbra, the Organization of Young Men, and On Guard for Freedom. Simon was a cofounder and "editorial assistant" of the journal—and almost certainly the photographer that Baraka mentions. John O'Neal, leader of the Free Southern Theater, was also listed on the masthead as a "sponsor" of *American Dialog* throughout its eight-year existence. It published such younger writers as Baraka, Julian Bond, Jayne Cortez, Mari Evans, Calvin Hernton, David Henderson, Julius Lester, Clarence Major, Lennox Raphael, Eugene Redmond, Ishmael Reed, and A. B. Spellman. Umbra's first major benefits to raise money for its journal took place in the space of a Communist-led youth group, Advance, on Clinton Street in the Lower East Side.[32]

Both black and white cultural activists associated with the Communist Left played important catalyzing roles in these early activities—among them, Alvin Simon, Walter Lowenfels, Art Berger, and Henry Percikow (in whose workshop such poets as Lorenzo Thomas and David Henderson participated and from whose workshop came, somewhat under duress, much of the early financing for Umbra). Jazz saxophonist and composer Archie Shepp, who would figure prominently in Black Arts activities and who would remain on the Marxist end of the Black Arts political spectrum, was a prominent participant in this Left subculture. Some of the SWP Militant Labor Forums at which Malcolm X spoke and which were important meeting places for uptown and downtown black intellectuals took place nearby in Greenwich Village.

Conclusion

Again, the most crucial contribution of the Black Arts Movement in New York, and the Northeast generally, was not institutional. This is not to dismiss the inspirational effect of the short life of BARTS or the importance (and in a few cases the longevity) of The East in Brooklyn; the New Lafayette Theater, the Studio Museum, *Black Theater*, the National Black Theater, and Liberation Books in Harlem; Spirit House and Jihad Press in Newark; Alma Lewis's School in Boston; and a host of similar institutions in Baltimore, Hartford, Buffalo, Philadelphia, Washington, Pittsburgh, and other small, middle-sized, and large cities in the region. But it seems fair to say that the significance of New York was as an incubator of the movement. Again, this is not to claim that the movement started in New York (as sometimes asserted) and spread elsewhere. There were too many initiatives appearing across the country to trace the birth of the movement to any one place.

Nonetheless, if there was, as Aldon Nielsen and others have claimed, a migration of innovative black writers to New York in the late 1950s and early 1960s, there was also a later emigration that greatly influenced the shape of the movement in other areas. The temporary or permanent relocation of writers active in the radical black literary and political movements in New York in the early 1960s, including Amiri Baraka, Sonia Sanchez, Askia Touré, Edward Spriggs, Tom Dent, A. B. Spellman, Herb Boyd, Lorenzo Thomas, and Ishmael Reed, to the West Coast, the Midwest, the South, and elsewhere in the Northeast had a huge impact on the way the Black Arts and Black Power movements developed in those regions. The emigration of the writers from New York helped give local movements elsewhere the sense of a coherent national movement while at the same time providing activists remaining in the Northeast a clearer picture of what was taking place in other regions. (Of course, New York's continuing character as an artistic delta attracting such major Black Arts figures as Woodie King, Jayne Cortez, Nikki Giovanni, Ron Milner, David Rambeau, and Ed Bullins also facilitated this sense of national coherence.) In turn, the direct encounter with local Black Power and Black Arts organizations in the South and West by East Coast artists and intellectuals provided a point of transmission for ideas and practices that had a major impact on the movement in the Northeast. For example, Amiri Baraka had little to do with the cultural nationalist ideology of Maulana Karenga until his sojourn at San Francisco State. In California Baraka got to see Karenga's Us organization on the ground level. Baraka was impressed by Us's energy, unity, and discipline (which contrasted with the chaos and conflict that had often attended BARTS), influencing his work when he returned to Newark.[33]

The poles of attraction and repulsion between the Old Left (and Old Nationalists) and the young nationalist artists in some ways resemble the push and pull that New York and the myths of Harlem and artistic bohemia exercised on black artists of the 1960s and 1970s. The story of the artistic attractions and disillusionments of Gotham are familiar, as far back as Herman Melville's *Pierre*—and have an African American variant that dates at least to Paul Laurence Dunbar's *Sport of the Gods* and James Weldon Johnson's *Autobiography of an Ex-Coloured Man*. But what is less told in any detail, except in the work of Harold Cruse, who is generally dismissive of the work of the younger black artists of the 1960s before the founding of BARTS, is the importance of the Left, and individuals who emerged from the political and cultural milieu of the Harlem Left (including Cruse) in preparing the field for the Black Arts Movement. The confluence of this Leftist legacy, the long history of activist African American nationalism, the various and often overlapping cultural meanings of Harlem, and the existence of a politically radical artistic tendency within the larger Lower East Side bohemian community had a marked impact on the development of what might be thought of as a Black Arts cadre that helped draw other African American artists and intellectuals to the movement.

Notes

1. Kalamu ya Salaam, *The Magic of Juju* (Chicago: Third World Press, forthcoming), 20.

2. For a study of CFUN-CAP and its impact on the Black Power movement, see Komozi Woodard, *A Nation within a Nation: Amiri Baraka and Black Power Politics* (Chapel Hill: University of North Carolina Press, 1999).

3. Lorenzo Thomas, *Extraordinary Measures: Afrocentric Modernism and Twentieth-Century American Poetry* (Tuscaloosa: University of Alabama Press, 2000), 140.

4. Typescript Interview (12), Larry Neal Papers, box 26, folder 2, Schomburg Center for Research in Black Culture.

5. For New Negro Renaissance radicalism and its relationship to expressive culture, see Ernest Allen Jr., "The New Negro: Explorations in Identity and Social Consciousness, 1910–1922," in Adele Heller and Lois Rudnick, eds., *1915, the Cultural Moment: The New Politics, the New Woman, the New Psychology, the New Art, and the New Theatre in America* (New Brunswick, N.J.: Rutgers University Press, 1991), 48–68, and William J. Maxwell, *New Negro, Old Left: African-American Writing and Communism between the Wars* (New York: Columbia University Press, 1999), 13–62. For the ABB, see Mark Solomon, *The Cry Was Unity: Communists and African Americans, 1917–1936* (Jackson: University Press of Mississippi, 1998), 3–21.

6. For the Left and the Harlem intelligentsia during the Popular Front, see Mark Naison, *Communists in Harlem during the Depression* (Urbana: University of Illinois Press, 1983), 193–226.

7. For nationalist activities in Harlem during the 1930s—particularly those of the UNIA, African Patriotic League led by Ira Kemp, Pan-African Reconstruc-

tion Association, Garvey Club, Harlem Labor Union led by Kemp and Arthur Reid, and Negro Industrial and Clerical Alliance led by Sufi Abdul Hamid—and competition and cooperation between nationalist groups and the Communist Left, see Naison, *Communists in Harlem*, 115–25, 138–40, 261–63, and Cheryl Greenberg, *Or Does It Explode: Black Harlem in the Great Depression* (New York: Oxford University Press, 1991), 114–39.

8. Amiri Baraka, *Home: Social Essays [by] LeRoi Jones* (New York: William Morrow, 1966), 92. For the transformations of the symbolic landscape of Harlem, see James De Jongh, *Vicious Modernism: Black Harlem and the Literary Imagination* (Cambridge: Cambridge University Press, 1990), 151–52.

9. For the impact of the Cold War on African American political activism, see Gerald Horne, *Black and Red: W. E. B. Du Bois and the Afro-American Response to the Cold War, 1944–1963* (Albany: State University of New York Press, 1986), *Communist Front? The Civil Rights Congress, 1946–1956* (Teaneck, N.J.: Fairleigh Press, 1988), and *Black Liberation/Red Scare: Ben Davis and the Communist Party* (Newark: University of Delaware Press, 1994); and Mary Dudziak, *Cold War Civil Rights: Race and the Image of American Democracy* (Princeton, N.J.: Princeton University Press, 2000). For the infrastructure of McCarthyism, see Ellen Schrecker, *Many Are the Crimes: McCarthyism in America* (Boston: Little, Brown, 1998).

10. For example, two longtime residents of Harlem and former members of cultural workers "sections" of the CPUSA, told me that in the mid-1950s the Party structure in Harlem seemed to vanish almost overnight—at least for many rank-and-file members. Both agreed that there were "hundreds" of people in Harlem who still considered themselves Communists but could not find the CPUSA. Most of these former members did not reconnect with the Party later, but some, especially artists and intellectuals, maintained some willingness to participate in activities initiated or supported by a reemergent (if greatly diminished) Communist Left in the early 1960s.

11. Thomas, *Extraordinary Measures*, 138.

12. Sarah Wright, "The Lower East Side: A Rebirth of Vision," *African American Review* 27 (Winter 1993): 594; Interview with Calvin Hicks, Boston, February 13, 2002.

13. See Hoyt Fuller, "Harlem Writers Guild at the New School," *Negro Digest* 14.8 (June 1965): 56–59.

14. Interviews with Amiri Baraka, Newark, N.J., July 15, 2000, A. B. Spellman, Washington, D.C., December 28, 2000, and Calvin Hicks, Boston, February 13, 2002; Amiri Baraka, *The Autobiography of LeRoi Jones* (Chicago: Lawrence Hill Books, 1997), 249–50.

15. In 1962 Hughes wrote Arna Bontemps that Leftist John O. Killens spent a day with him and they "had a long session over literary matters." Bontemps and Hughes, *Arna Bontemps-Langston Hughes Letters* (New York: Dodd, Mead, 1980), 446. One is tempted to view Hughes's statement as a sort of code for any third party reading his mail. In any event, it is one of many examples of how Hughes maintained contact with those artists and intellectuals who had not separated themselves from the Left. For a fuller consideration of Hughes, the Left, and the Black Arts Movement, see James Smethurst, "'Don't Say Goodbye to the Porkpie Hat': Langston Hughes, the Left, and the Black Arts Movement," *Callaloo* 25.4 (Fall 2002): 1225–36.

16. Horne, *Black Liberation/Red Scare*, 293–32.

17. Esther Cooper Jackson, ed., *Freedomways Reader: Prophets in Their Own Coun-*

try (Boulder, Colo.: Westview Press, 2000), xxi–xxii; Interview with Jackson, Brooklyn, N.Y., July 8, 1999.

18. John O. Killens, "Lorraine Hansberry: On Time," 337, in Jackson, *Freedomways Reader*, 335–39.

19. Harold Cruse, *The Crisis of the Negro Intellectual* (1967; reprint, New York: Morrow, 1984), 242–49.

20. Kalamu ya Salaam, *Magic of Juju*, 62.

21. Woodard, *A Nation within a Nation*, 58. But Harold Cruse (*Crisis*, 404–19) associates what he sees as the *Liberator*'s failure to become a truly revolutionary vehicle of black liberation with a persistent Communist influence on the journal's editorial policies until 1966.

22. An article, "Semitism in the Black Ghetto" by Eddie Ellis in the February 1966 issue prompted the departure of Davis and Baldwin. But it is worth noting that in a letter explaining this action, which appeared in *Freedomways* in 1967, Davis reiterated his respect for Daniel Watts and proclaimed himself a "black nationalist," calling into question some characterizations of the split—not to mention *Freedomways*, with which Davis had been long associated.

23. Woodard, *A Nation within a Nation*, 58. The precise events are not entirely clear. Participants in the demonstrations outside and inside the United Nations building to whom I have spoken did not recall Davis's banning—though they read or heard reports of it afterward. In any event, they were unable to affirm or deny whether the banning occurred. A report of the demonstration in the *New York Times* suggests that Davis was prevented by nationalists from taking part in an all–African American picket line at First Avenue and Forty-third Street, but he eventually joined a largely white picket at First Avenue and Forty-second Street. The *Times* article also suggests that Robeson participated in the black picket line unmolested. According to the *Times*, Davis was the first speaker at an outdoor unity rally in Harlem attended by several hundred people. "Riot in Gallery Halts U.N. Debate," *New York Times*, February 16, 1961. The retrospective written accounts of demonstrators that I have seen, including that of Baraka in his autobiography, make no mention of the rejection of Davis and Robeson. Certainly black writers and intellectuals associated with the Left-influenced Harlem Writers Guild helped organize the demonstration. Baraka, *Autobiography of LeRoi Jones*, 267; Wright, "Lower East Side"; Interviews with Calvin Hicks and Esther Cooper Jackson; Maya Angelou, *The Heart of Woman* (New York: Bantam, 1982), 154–66.

24. Wright, "Lower East Side"; Interview with Calvin Hicks.

25. Interview with Askia Touré, Cambridge, Mass., December 2, 2000.

26. For an example of Neal's position, see his exchange with Frank Kofsky in the February 1966 *Liberator*. For an early instance of a rejection of Marxism and the positing of a new African American spirituality by a leading Black Arts activist, see Askia Touré's 1964 letter to James Boggs. James and Grace Lee Boggs Papers, ser. 1, box 2, folder 1, Walter P. Reuther Library, Wayne State University, Detroit.

27. For the African American literary scene in New York in the late 1950s and early 1960s, see Eugene B. Redmond, *Drumvoices: The Mission of Afro-American Poetry: A Critical History* (Garden City, N.Y.: Anchor, 1976), 320–24; Calvin Hernton, "Umbra: A Personal Recounting," *African American Review* 27.4 (Winter 1993): 579–83; Tom Dent, "Umbra Days," *Black American Literature Forum* 14 (1980): 243–94; Amiri Baraka, *Autobiography of LeRoi Jones*, 124–201; Michel

Oren, "A 'Sixties Saga': The Life and Death of Umbra (Part I)," *Freedomways* 24.3 (Third Quarter 1984): 167–81, and "A 'Sixties Saga': The Life and Death of Umbra (Part II)," *Freedomways* 24.4 (Fourth Quarter 1984): 237–54; and Thomas, *Extraordinary Measures*, 118–44.

28. For a brief recollection of Stanley's Bar as a linchpin of black bohemia on the Lower East Side and as an informal venue for wide-ranging intellectual discussion and debate, see Calvin L. Hicks, "African-American Literary and Political Movements, 1960s, on New York's Lowereast Side," Cultural Dimensions, New York, 1994, np. (mimeographed pamphlet).

29. For a recollection of the Lower East Side as a multiracial environment in the 1960s, see Dent, "Enriching the Paper Trail: An Interview with Tom Dent," *African American Review* 27.2 (Summer 1993): 327–44. It is worth noting that the writers themselves did not universally share this vision of a multiracial neighborhood. A number of them recall the Lower East Side in the early 1960s as overwhelmingly white. For this sense of the neighborhood, see Hernton, "Umbra," 579–80.

30. Alvin Simon's account in "Alvin Simon on Umbra" makes this Leftist influence explicit. In a letter to the editor (*Freedomways* 25.1 [First Quarter 1985]: 48–50), Simon writes:

> Among the ideologists who had a major influence, during the "pre-Umbra" period, on the outlook and actions of some key black artists living on the Lower East Side were the Marxists and Marxist-Leninists. During that period, many left-oriented periodicals and literary journals emerged on the Lower East Side and were among the first to publish works of the neighborhood's struggling artists, both black and white. One was the bi-weekly newspaper, *The Worker*, to which I regularly contributed news-stories, photographs, articles, and reviews. Another was the literary and political periodical, *New Horizons for Youth*, of which I was an editorial staff member and which published in 1962 an important piece on the arts by the musician and composer Archie Shepp. (p. 48)

By "Marxist-Leninist" Simon seems to mean "associated with the CPUSA"—the *Worker* was the CPUSA newspaper at the time. One fascinating aspect of Simon's letter is how it demonstrates the lasting impact of Cold War anticommunism. Simon speaks of "Marxists" and "Marxist-Leninists," but nowhere do the words "Communist" or "Communist Party" appear, even when discussing such clearly Communist or Communist-influenced institutions as the *Worker* and *American Dialog*.

31. Baraka, *Autobiography of LeRoi Jones*, 270.

32. Dent, "Umbra Days," 108.

33. Baraka, *Autobiography of LeRoi Jones*, 355–59; Interview with Baraka.

Marcial González

A Marxist Critique of Borderlands Postmodernism: Adorno's *Negative Dialectics* and Chicano Cultural Criticism

Traditionally, Marxists and other Leftists have opposed the existence of national borders (with slogans such as "Smash All Borders!") because borders reinforce nationalism, imperialism, and capitalism while standing as obstacles to the building of proletarian internationalism. In recent years, however, cultural critics have given new meaning to the border by popularizing the terms "borderlands" and "border crossings." For Chicana/o cultural criticism, the borderlands now characterize the contradictory social experiences of Chicanas/os who often speak two languages, identify with two or more cultural backgrounds, and live within numerous other complexities that blur the demarcations of social class, ethnicity, gender, sexual orientation, nationality, and religion. More significantly, the concept of the borderlands has become the central trope for explaining the formation of Chicana/o cultural identity by emphasizing a condition of perpetual liminality and the constant crossing of boundaries. The interstitial quality of the borderlands has also come to be understood as a form of resistance to the status quo, similar to the way that postmodernists think of "hybridity" as counterhegemonic. From a Left perspective, however, the following questions must be raised: Is borderlands theory compatible with a Marxist critique of borders? Does the trope of the borderlands provide a viable conception of cultural identity? And, more importantly, how would Chicana/o criticism look if a dialectical Marxist critique of identity stood in for the postmodernist-inspired concept of the borderlands?

It goes without saying that the powerful metaphor of the borderlands has become a valuable interpretive tool for the study of Chicana/o literature and culture. Anyone who has grown up in a Chicana/o border community will no doubt find it difficult to deny having felt the conflicted experiences of living between two national cultures: related to both, yet belonging to neither fully. The experience of living between two nationalities has been captured brilliantly in the well-known words of La India María, who describes her ambivalent condition in saying, "ni de aquí, ni de allá."[1] Most cultural critics will agree, as I do, with the characterization of Chicana/o literature as culturally conflicted, but the concept of the borderlands, I argue, creates potential theoretical and political problems for Chicana/o cultural criticism with regard to identity formation. These problems do not stem from efforts to describe the material conditions of living on the border or from claims that Chicana/o literature has been significantly impacted, both thematically and formally, by the contradictory social conditions of the border; rather, the problems emerge when critics interpret social ambivalence as the foundation for a counterhegemonic cultural identity.

In this essay, I examine the general advantages of borderlands theory. But I also contend that, despite these advantages, borderlands theory creates potential problems for cultural criticism and political practice. I point out three problems in particular: the tendency to romanticize the border; the political limits of multiculturalism and pluralism, projects promoted by borderlands theory; and the ideological contradictions of theorizing cultural identity nondialectically as a condition of perpetual liminality. In the second half of the essay, I analyze Theodor Adorno's "negative dialectics" and his "critique of identity." In formulating his critique, Adorno draws on the Marxist theory of the commodity exchange abstraction—a theory that, I suggest, stands as a viable alternative to the concept of identity implicit in the trope of the borderlands.

In contemporary Chicana/o literary studies, the border signifies more than simply the geographic line that separates Mexico from the United States; it also represents a politically determined and arbitrarily constructed separation between two national cultures and serves more as an ideological metaphor of power than as a real division. The politically motivated construction of the border does not mean that when immigrants cross it illegally they remain free from physical hardship, the border patrol, unscrupulous *coyotes*,[2] or the harsh and oftentimes deadly conditions confronted when walking across the desert. Rather, it means that the border functions as an unstable, fluctuating, porous demarcation that cannot prevent millions of immigrants from crossing it both legally and illegally year after year. Literary critic Rafael Pérez-Torres distinguishes "the border" from "the borderlands," explaining, "The 'border' divides, separates, categorizes, dispossesses. The 'borderlands' by contrast form a metaphorical and literal space where worlds blend and cross" (35). As Pérez-Torres correctly points out, for many scholars and critics the borderlands have come to represent a condition of cultural, national, and linguistic hybridity. Thus although the border "is a strip of land two thousand miles long and no more than twenty miles wide," according to José David Saldívar, "some believe the U.S.-Mexico border extends all the way to Seattle" (*Border Matters* 8).

Significantly, the border not only fails to prevent immigration, it has likewise been unable to stop working-class immigrant cultures from proliferating in the United States. This unstoppable expansion of immigrant cultures (not only of Latinos but of immigrants from all over the world) in North American society invalidates the concept of a border designed to keep immigrants out. It is worth emphasizing here that the purpose of the border has never been to prevent the crossing of people, goods, money, or culture. It has functioned instead as an instrument of political manipulation to control the supply of labor for certain industries in the United States; in this way the border helps to keep wages down and to undermine unionization drives. The border also has an ideological function: to whip up racist hysteria among U.S. citizens by creating scapegoats of undocumented immigrants, effectively blaming them for high unemployment rates and other depressed economic conditions.[3] Instead of keeping immigrants out, the porous border has produced a wide and overlapping cultural reality constituted by the coexistence of multiple national identities, languages, social classes, and cultural practices. But, as cultural anthropologist Roger Rouse observes, the proliferation of immigrant cultures in the United States has taken place with strong opposition from anti-immigrant individuals and groups that have consistently taken measures to close the border, if not at the actual geographic divide between the United States and Mexico, then at places of employment and public institutions.[4] Rouse points to Proposition 187—California's infamous 1994 anti-immigrant initiative—to explain how "in the United

States, the provisions regarding employer sanctions in the new immigration law have exploded the border for labor and relocated it in a multitude of fragments at the entrance of every workplace" (258). According to Rouse, the "exploded" border has also blurred the once clearly defined divisions between social classes. As he explains, "we live in a confusing world, a world of crisscrossed economies, intersecting systems of meaning, and fragmented identities. Suddenly, the comforting modern imagery . . . of coherent communities and consistent subjectivities, of dominant centers and distant margins no longer seems adequate" (248). Rouse's description of the border as "exploded" echoes Saldívar's claim that the border extends far beyond the "twenty-mile wide strip of land" that separates Mexico and the United States.

Saldívar further describes what he means by the borderlands with the analogous term, "*Transfrontera* contact zone," a phrase intended "to invoke the heterotopic forms of everyday life" (*Border Matters* 14). He draws on Mary Louise Pratt's much-cited concept of the "contact zone," a term she coins to explain, among other things, the ambivalence of texts written by colonized subjects and how these texts unavoidably involve "partial collaboration with and appropriation of the idioms of the conqueror" (Pratt 7). The word "transfrontera" translates literally to "transborder" but also alludes to "transculturation." In other words, the "*Transfrontera* contact zone" is a two-way street, capable of producing an ideological inversion: colonized people collaborate with the colonizer's "idioms," but the colonizer also internalizes the culture of the colonized. From this view, the borderlands can be conceptualized as existing *anywhere* in the world—wherever a subordinated cultural group shares social space with a dominant culture. Thus Saldívar expands his concept of the borderlands beyond the U.S.-Mexican border region to encompass what he refers to as the "global borderlands."

The concept of the borderlands, however, has also come to signify much more than merely a *geographic* space; it also refers to cultural, personal, linguistic, sexual, psychological, and perhaps even spiritual spaces. The goal of the borderlands theorist is to imagine a subject capable of subverting its own subordination by inhabiting these spaces and by constantly migrating across their fixed boundaries without remaining on either side of the divide too long. For Pérez-Torres the "borderlands represent the multiplicity and dynamism of Chicano experiences and cultures. . . . Viewing the borderlands as an interstitial site suggests a type of liminality. The betweenness leads to a becoming, a sense of cultural and personal identity that highlights flux and fluidity" (12). Similarly, Rubén Martínez argues that Chicanos, "a bit like Buddhists, know that stability is a state of movement. To put it simply, these days people who don't move die [and] to stay alive is to move. Economically, culturally, linguistically, sexually" (23). For borderlands theorists, the ideal border subject is able to resist the status quo by staying on the run and by trespassing into normally forbidden areas.

Conceptualized in this way, borderlands culture possesses the potential for transforming society by subverting the hegemony from within. The dominant culture cannot prevent subordinated groups, such as Latina/o immigrants (or even Latina/o professionals), from constantly crossing over into dominant spaces; the subordinated groups therefore challenge the dominant culture's control over these spaces. This process of inhabiting and controlling social spaces could be considered a cultural revolution, similar in scope to what Renato Rosaldo means by "the implosion of the Third World into the first" (85). This kind of "revolution" would not require direct political action; it would occur through the proliferation of various forms of cultural production: art, music, literature, language, folklore, jokes, dance, and lifestyle. With borderlands theory, almost anything can be considered an act of resistance.

For some critics, the concept of the borderlands represents not only the crossing of cultural boundaries, but the crossing of disciplinary divides in academia as well. As Saldívar explains, "in the past ten years the terms *border* and *borderlands* in Chicano/a studies have come to name a new dynamic in American studies—a synthesis of articulated development from dissident folklore and ethnography; feminism; literary, critical-legal, and cultural studies; and more recently gender and sexuality studies" (*Border Matters* xii). Borderlands theory unquestionably offers several advantages for Chicana/o literary criticism. Not least of all, it allows for an interdisciplinary approach to the study of literature and culture, consciously attempting to resist theoretical reductionism by employing various critical approaches, from personal narratives and poetry to poststructuralist and postcolonial theory. Saldívar explains that his work in part "consciously crosses the methodological borders between Marxist and postmodernist criticism" (*Dialectics* xiv). Moreover, he not only uses various methods but also trespasses the divisions that separate national literatures. Rather than study "American literature," which traditionally has been restricted to the literature of the United States, Saldívar proposes to "remap" American literary studies to include the "literatures of the Americas." This "remapping" undermines U.S. nationalism in American studies by encompassing the literatures of the entire Western Hemisphere.

Saldívar and others have done much to expand the critical potential of cultural and literary studies by rethinking traditional paradigms through the prism of the borderlands trope. Yet despite its analytic advantages, borderlands theory nonetheless poses problems that affect both academic study and political practice. By discussing these problems, I hope to initiate a dialogue among critics interested in the interpretation of Chicana/o literature and culture from a Left perspective. Given my limited space, however, I will be able to outline in broad terms only the most important aspects of such a dialogue. To this end, I will refer to the work of Pérez-Torres to illustrate some of the problems with borderlands theory. But I want to emphasize that these problems are by no means limited to Pérez-Torres's work; they are the problems of cultural studies generally and of Chicana/o cultural criticism in particular, three of which I shall now address.

First, some descriptions of the borderlands come close to romanticizing the border by constructing a metaphor for professional academics and students who, many times during their careers, might find themselves "migrating" from one university to another, or crossing personal and psychological boundaries in their everyday struggles, to survive within the academy. The metaphor of the borderlands helps to describe the alienation and contradictoriness of their existence, but when used flippantly it tends to desensitize the horror of the real conditions of the border and of the immigrants who have no choice but to risk their lives crossing it illegally. Pérez-Torres describes how the "Chicano cannibalizes the various worlds from which cultural production emerges. The poet becomes a border crosser, but of a particular type: a coyote, a smuggler, a *pollero* moving people and goods back and forth across aesthetic and cultural as well as geopolitical borders" (246). As much as we might desire for it to be possible, the lives of professional academics and students cannot be compared equitably to those of workers who suffer the inhuman conditions of the real border, where crossing is not a luxury or an act of resistance, but often a matter of life and death. To compare the lives of literary critics to immigrants minimizes the harsh reality of the undocumented worker. In light of this problem, we might recall a poem by Francisco X. Alarcón titled "Mestizo," where the poet describes a subject whose feet

recognize
no border
no rule
no code
no lord. (15)

The poem expresses a romantic desire to disrespect the realities of all borders. In response to Alarcón's poem, Pérez-Torres warns: "The vision of absolute freedom implied by the poem should certainly be viewed with suspicion. The speaker's feet may recognize no border, but just let them actually try to cross one without proper documentation" (211). Pérez-Torres understandably criticizes Alarcón for romanticizing the border, but ironically his criticism contradicts his own romanticized representations of the borderlands as noted above.

In the expanded edition of *Loving in the War Years*, published in 2000, Cherríe Moraga voices concerns similar to my own, first recognizing the advantages of borderlands theory and then criticizing efforts to romanticize the border. She explains that in *Borderlands/la frontera*, first published fifteen years earlier, Gloria Anzaldúa aptly describes the "direct" social experience of living on the border. Moraga also speaks positively of Norma Cantú's autobiographical novel, *Canícula*, highlighting the fact that Cantú materialistically "describes her border home-town of Laredo as a police state, where five kinds of law enforcement agencies patrol the streets" (177). But Moraga also complains that since the publication of Anzaldúa's seminal book, the concept of the borderlands has been appropriated by postmodernism and its power as a conceptual tool for explaining social contradictions has been debilitated. "The border," she argues, "is not the idealized metaphorical site of a new hybridity" (177). She asserts that Anzaldúa's *Borderlands* opened up new and exciting possibilities for border studies until "the academic appropriation of Anzaldúa's 'border' metamorphosed the concept of 'border' and 'borderlands' into a kind of 1990s postmodern homeland for all displaced peoples" (177). Moraga understandably expresses resentment for the ideological debasement of a concept that initially had (and still has) tremendous political potential.

Second, borderlands theory makes claims of subversion and resistance, but it generally perpetuates liberal pluralism in the form of multiculturalism, even if it sometimes sounds like militant ethnocentrism. For instance, Pérez-Torres unabashedly makes use of an ethnocentric discourse to claim that "Chicano culture is not in the business of adding to the trash heap of Euramerican culture" (270). Despite his anti-Euramerican rhetoric, he argues for a method of literary interpretation that resembles Euramerican postmodernism: "The borderlands, the perilous no-man's-land between First World and Third World, the area of flux in which Chicanas and Chicanos negotiate between numerous subject-positions, represents the metaphor and emblem and reality of multiculturalism" (156). How different is this statement really from what Euramerican postmodernists might say about multiculturalism and the crossing of borders? Indeed, how different is Pérez-Torres's multiculturalism from the "trash heap of Euramerican culture" that he attacks?

Paradoxically, Pérez-Torres relies on Euramerican postmodernism to support his argument for multiculturalism and to account for the liberal objectives often associated with multiculturalism. In the same way that nationalists have historically rationalized their potentially reactionary political beliefs by identifying two kinds of nationalism—the fascist and progressive types—Pérez-Torres draws from the work of Hal Foster to identify two strains of postmodernism and multiculturalism: "one of reaction and one of resistance" (14). "Reactionary" postmodernism, for Pérez-Torres, represents the interests of the status quo by reinforcing various means of social control, whereas "resistant" postmodernism seeks to expose rather than exploit social and cultural relations.[5] Similarly, he argues, "reactionary" multiculturalism attempts to reinforce beliefs in the "melting pot," whereas "resistant" multiculturalism emphasizes difference and heterogeneity. Pérez-Torres supports "theories of postmodernity and the multicultural [that] provide powerful tools by which to explore the expanding limits of each other" (150). He adds, the "result is a multiplicity of identities, a perpetual movement among numerous subject positions. None forms a fully privileged realm" (152). Pérez-Torres takes from postmodernism what he needs to construct a subject that seeks recognition of its difference and rejects the racist implications of assimilation. The problem with postmodernist multiculturalism, however, does not lie in its denunciation of racism or in its demands for recognition. On the contrary, these demands are laudable. The problem lies elsewhere and to a large degree remains hidden or mystified and therefore must be extracted from beneath its appearance and unveiled, much in the manner that Marx uncovered the secret that lay hidden in the structure of the commodity—a secret that was to be found not in the reified object itself, but in the social relations of production. Like resistant multiculturalism, borderlands theory attaches itself to the postmodernist critique of metanarratives, universalism, and objectivity—aspects usually associated with modernism. But by promoting multiculturalism, borderlands theory reproduces the very modernist impulse it claims to negate. Multiculturalism, pluralism, and democratic liberalism are not postmodernist doctrines, but *modernist* to the core.

Borderlands theory and resistant multiculturalism thus reinforce the metanarrative of democratic liberalism through the kinds of demands that emerge from these projects: citizenship, recognition, racial and sexual equality, access to social institutions, fair representation in state politics, equal air time on the public media, and above all the opportunity to participate in the life of the nation. Carl Gutiérrez-Jones addresses the problem of liberalism and the reform demands it inspires, explaining that Chicana/o narratives can sometimes become complicit with "an academic framework that is ideologically structured around notions of pluralism, notions that give priority to humanistic universalism and liberal-legal consensus rather than to historically situated cultural conflict" (31). From this perspective, borderlands theory and Chicana/o cultural criticism unwittingly partake of efforts to force the nation to complete the "unfinished project" of modernity, despite being cloaked in postmodernist rhetoric.

To be clear, in pointing out that multiculturalism reinforces the politics of liberalism, I am not saying that cultural critics from marginalized groups should refrain from supporting or participating in these kinds of projects. On the contrary, social conditions demand that antiracists, feminists, gay and lesbian activists, and politically conscious workers, students, and scholars engage in reform struggles. What I want to emphasize, though, is that reformist politics by and large end up reinforcing systemic inequalities unless the political contradictions of reformism are comprehended ideologically and taken into account when theorizing methods of literary interpretation or strategies for political action. Intellectuals and activists who use these methods and strategies must figure out how to participate in reform struggles while simultaneously attempting to surpass the political restraints of reformism, or how to make use of liberal discourses such as multiculturalism and borderlands theory in such a way as to overcome the limits of liberalism.

The third problem with borderlands theory has to do with the ideological contradictions of theorizing cultural identity nondialectically as a condition of perpetual liminality. Conversely, I argue for a dialectical understanding of identity. As Saldívar points out, "many scholars and critics trained to read texts within the Anglocentric tradition have yet to learn to think dialectically" (*Dialectics* 26). His observation comes at a time that bears witness to a widespread discrediting of the basic principles of Marxist dialectics, including the concept of "contradiction." As an alternative to nondialectical thinking, Saldívar raises the following provocative and certainly valid question: "Might not Adorno's aesthetic philosophy of nonidentity and negative dialectics be more appropriate than a 1960s Sartrean philosophy of engagement?" (*Border Matters* 102). In the present context we might frame the same question as follows: What would happen if we placed a dialectical Marxist critique of cultural identity at the center of Chicana/o literary studies? Taking my cue from Saldívar's question, I suggest that Adorno's negative dialectic can indeed offer Chicana/o critics a more "appropriate" way of thinking about identity.[6] I shall now explain, at the risk of digressing too much in the direction of theoretical abstraction, my purpose for analyzing Adorno's negative dialectic and its relation to borderlands theory. But first, I need to distinguish Adorno's negative dialectic from traditional Marxism's dialectical materialism.

To be sure, Adorno's dialectic differs from that of Marx. For Marx, the historical dialectic progresses forward through the increasing antagonism of social class contradictions. As long as class societies exist, class contradictions are never fully resolved. Historical transformations occur when the struggles between social classes result in the rise to power by one social class over another. Roughly speaking, this leads to the replacement of an old qualitative state by a new one, as in the transition (incomplete and uneven as these transitions always are) from one mode of production to another. The process is not linear, predictable, or inevitable, despite the fact that misinformed critics routinely condemn the Marxist dialectic for being teleological. But the critique of teleology—the view that history develops toward an inevitable end by natural design rather than as the result of human agency—often has more to do with condemning Marxism and the possibility of an egalitarian society beyond capitalism than with criticizing the idea of an absolute telos.[7]

Adorno's dialectic evolves out of the Hegelian and Marxist tradition, but it does not necessarily move forward from one historical stage to another. Nor is there a reconciliation of opposites. Adorno describes his dialectic as "negative" because it never produces a "positive" state, as in Hegel's Absolute Spirit. The movement of Adorno's dialectic never ceases to pursue negation, even to the point of abnegation. Thus at the end of *Negative Dialectics*, Adorno argues that the dialectical critic must "extinguish" the claim of an absolute dialectical knowledge through a "negation of the negation that will not become a positing" (406). He asserts, "To this end, dialectics is obliged to make a final move: being at once the impression and the critique of the universal delusive context, it must now turn even against itself" (406). Fredric Jameson responds to this moment of absolute negativity by explaining that Adorno's "negative dialectic" is a "counteraffirmation . . . in which the classical dialectic seeks, by biting its own tail, to deconstruct itself" (*Political Unconscious* 54).[8] As Jameson correctly points out, Adorno's self-deconstructing dialectic is problematic for political projects aimed at instigating historical transformation. But what I find useful in Adorno's negative dialectic is the refusal to negate one entity for the purpose of positing another. On the contrary, he argues vehemently against any kind of positivism—even a dialectical kind. In this respect, borderlands theory differs from Adorno's negative dialectic by seeking exactly what Adorno opposes, or what I refer to as a *negative affirmation*: the formation of a positive entity through the negation of another.

Consider again Pérez-Torres. Utilizing a methodological framework centered on negative affirmation, Pérez-Torres invokes Adorno's "philosophical sundial of history" (264) to argue that Chicana/o literature, and the lyric poem in particular, "create[s] a vision of wholeness as a promise that stands against the reality of fragmentation and dissociation" (264). At the same time, he takes issue with Adorno in arguing that the Chicana lyric complicates this "vision of wholeness" by constructing a "divided and multiplicitous" identity, rather than a collective identity. Moreover, he asserts that the "fragmentation and dissociation" of Chicana/o lived experience *negates* the modernist aspiration for wholeness in order to *affirm* an identity of perpetual difference and betweenness: "The lyric by Chicana poets is often an expression aware of its position in the borderlands, in worlds between worlds. The Chicana lyric questions the complex relationship between the subject's desire for affirmative flight . . . and the realization that there is no escape from the world. . . . The Chicana lyric therefore manifests an incessant movement of capture and escape, of always being in the moment of betweenness . . . this sense of being between as an affirmative position of difference" (264).

The conceptual structure of Pérez-Torres's "moment of betweenness" and his negation of modernist "wholeness" (read "totality")—directed at affirming a postmodernist borderlands subject based on fragmentation and difference—remain far removed from Adorno's negative dialectic in particular and from a traditional Marxist conception of contradiction generally. Let me emphasize that although Adorno rejects the notions of reconciliation and synthesis, he does not abandon the principle of contradiction. His dialectic remains rigorously "persistent," criticizing above all the idea of a "dialectical positivism": the act of affirmation by way of negation. In the preface to *Negative Dialectics*, Adorno states his criticism clearly in describing the purpose of his book: "As early as Plato, dialectics meant to achieve something positive by means of negation; the thought figure of a 'negation of negation' later became the succinct term. This book seeks to free dialectics from such affirmative traits without reducing its determinacy" (xix). Later in the book he reasons, "In criticizing ontology we do not aim at another ontology, not even at one of being nonontological" (136). Following Adorno's lead, we could argue that in criticizing an essentialist explanation of identity we do not aim at another form of reified identity, not even one that replicates the ambivalence and fragmentation of the border.

In arguing that Chicana/o identity is constituted at the "moment of betweenness," Pérez-Torres posits a conception of identity formation that outwardly gives the appearance of being dynamic even though its inner structure remains static and nondialectical. He claims, for example, that Chicano culture and identity "oscillate" between five different worlds: "the postcolonial, the postnational, the premodern, the postmodern, and the multicultural" (270). The political significance of "migrating" constantly between these "worlds," according to Pérez-Torres, lies in the actual movement itself, rather than in any sense of contradiction, much less in the "imagined resolution" of contradictions. Chicano culture "moves across [these] worlds, carrying a contraband of hope from one to another. In motion, the culture can cast a glance along the far horizons of those worlds, guess at what lies just beyond them. The wonder made evident in Chicano culture is not the getting beyond those horizons. The wonder is the movement between" them (271). Pérez-Torres evidently draws from the postmodernist strategy of escape: the practice of constantly moving to escape the alienating effect of social structures—a strategy similar to that of Giles Deleuze and Felix Guattari's "schizoanalysis."[9]

In addition to arguing that border subjects engage in a form of resistance by moving freely between various political "worlds," as if the freedom to move was a real choice for all border subjects, Pérez-Torres puts forth a view of postmodernism that conceptually bears a strong resemblance to the structure of liberal pluralism: "Postmodernism is like a clear night sky, full of twinkling critical positions that seem to form patterns slowly but endlessly spinning and shifting. Each point of light representing a nexus of the postmodern seems to join one constellation. Yet, when viewed from a slightly different angle, another pattern and potential seems [*sic*] to emerge. Against this black night, the stars of the postmodern burn but do not freeze into a fully coherent pattern" (138). Here Pérez-Torres describes how relations between objects (and, by implication, relations between social classes and groups) are conceptualized by postmodernism generally and by borderlands theory in particular. These relations do not resemble contradictions in a dialectical sense, where the tension and unity between opposing entities within a social totality lead to the cancellation of one entity by the other, thus pushing the totality in the direction of a qualitatively new condition. Rather, for the postmodern critic, the entities themselves remain static and immobile, and their movement remains limited to the "oscillation" between the various discrete entities within these relations, just as the myth of pluralism promises unlimited possibilities while delivering a severely limited set of options.

For borderlands theory to be consistent with Adorno's negative dialectic, it would have to negate its own *positive* quality through a rigorous critique of its own internal contradictions—which is the goal of the present essay. Granted, the efforts to expose racism, sexism, and class conflicts at the border remain exceedingly important. But exposing these problems does not mean that we need to close one eye to open the other. That is, we need to be aware of the ideological contradictions of our own projects. As Adorno states, "To the best of his ability the author means to put his cards on the table—which is by no means the same as playing the game" (xix). Adorno's negative dialectic provides the critical tools to allow us to rethink the borderlands trope of identity formation. Consequently, I argue that our understanding of identity might best be explained through the Marxist theory of the commodity exchange abstraction.

Adorno allows for a dialectical and materialist interpretation of cultural identity precisely because his critique of identity is rooted in his analysis of commodity exchange. I acknowledge that the connotation of "identity" as used in Adorno's "critique of identity" differs from that of "cultural identity" as expressed by most contemporary cultural critics. Adorno's "critique of identity" takes issue with philosophies that claim the possibility of an identity between subject and object, between signifier and signified—or, more simply, between consciousness and social reality. "Cultural identity" refers generally to personal consciousness and an individual's awareness of his or her group affiliation. Adorno himself clarifies, however, that these different connotations of identity are not entirely unrelated, recognizing that in "modern philosophy, the word 'identity' has had several meanings," including that of a "personal consciousness" (142). For Adorno, identity as "personal consciousness" differs from the epistemological assertion that "subject and object coincide," but he admonishes, "Not even Kant keeps [these] two layers of meaning strictly apart" (142). This is so because both refer to a process of cognition, to an attempt to know the world (including one's place in the world) by naming it. Adorno postulates that, in a society based on commodity exchange, it is impossible for "subject and object to coincide," even when both subject and object take the form of a "personal consciousness."

Adorno's negative dialectic fascinates theorists of literature and culture but poses significant problems for Marxism. His work has been described as idealist, pessimist, and proto-postmodernist, although these charges have been disputed. And though he solves one problem by ridding his dialectic of a telos, he implies another—namely, a conception of historical development at a standstill. I would not go as far as Jameson does in claiming that Adorno is "one of the greatest of twentieth-century Marxist philosophers" (*Late Marxism* 4). Yet it seems possible to read him as both a dialectician and a materialist. For Adorno, the non-identity of subject and object is not an eternal condition. On the contrary, identity thinking emerges historically from a capitalist system based on commodity exchange, as explained in the following crucial passage from *Negative Dialectics*:

> If mankind is to get rid of the coercion to which the form of identification really subjects it, it must attain identity with its concept at the same time. . . . The barter principle, *the reduction of human labor to the abstract universal concept of average working hours* [emphasis added], is fundamentally akin to the principle of identification. Barter is the social model of the principle, and without the principle there would be no barter; it is through barter that non-identical individuals and performances become commensurable and identical. (146)

In this passage Adorno argues that the principle of identity originates in the process of commodity exchange. Even though the term "barter" usually refers to a system of trade that precedes commodity exchange, Adorno's qualification of the term—"the reduction of human labor to the abstract universal of average working hours"—describes a process that occurs only with the development of commodity exchange.[10] I am not alone in reading Adorno's critique of identity in this way. In arguing to debunk "post-Marxist" interpretations of Adorno's critique of identity, Jameson comments: "Of identity we have seen that it is in fact Adorno's word for the Marxian concept of exchange relationship (a term he also frequently uses)" (*Late Marxism* 26). Jameson adds that in discussing Adorno's critique of "identity, the abstraction itself—very much including its most sophisticated philosophical equivalent in logic and in the form of universals—is revealed at another level to be at one with the logic of equivalence and exchange; that is to say, with the logic of capital" (28). From this basic materialist view, Adorno does not rule out the possibility of a historical moment when the "coercion" of identity no longer exists, which implicitly makes the identity of subject and object—thought and reality—historically conceivable. Since identity "is fundamentally akin" to commodity exchange, eradicating the "coercion" of identity would require the destruction of capitalism: "From olden times, the main characteristic of the exchange of equivalents has been that unequal things would be exchanged in its name, that the surplus value of labor would be appropriated. If comparability as a category of measure were simply annulled, the rationality which is inherent in the barter principle—as ideology of course, but also as a promise—would give way to direct appropriation, to force, and nowadays to the naked privilege of monopolies and cliques" (146–47).

Adorno explains that in the process of commodity exchange, unequal things get exchanged as if they were equal, hence, the accumulation of surplus value. To make exchange appear equal when it is really not, a deception must take place in the form of ideology: where the nonequality of equivalents in commodity exchange translates directly into the nonidentity of subject and object in abstract thinking. These abstractions—of commodity exchange and cognition—serve also as the social synthesis, or the glue, that keeps the system functional. Without the deception that takes place as a result of these abstractions—that is, if workers were to become aware of the hidden secret in commodity exchange—ideology would self-destruct and "monopolies" and "cliques" would be forced to use brute force to keep the system running. Again, Adorno states:

> When we criticize the barter principle as the identifying principle of thought, we want to realize the ideal of free and just barter. To date, this ideal is only a pretext. Its realization alone would transcend barter. Once critical theory has shown it up for what it is—an exchange of things that are equal and yet unequal—our critique of the inequality within equality aims at equality too, for all our skepticism of the rancor involved in the bourgeois egalitarian ideal that tolerates no qualitative difference. *If no man had part of his labor withheld from him any more, rational identity would be a fact* [emphasis added], and society would have transcended the identifying mode of thinking. (147)

One need not stretch the imagination to realize that here Adorno alludes to a communist society. Call it something else, if you must, but essentially he describes an egalitarian society without commodity exchange, without the exploitation of labor, and without ideology.[11] Additionally, these passages call into question the postmodernist conception of Adorno's negative dialectic as the absence of historical development. To achieve the kind of society Adorno describes here would require the abolition of social classes. More importantly, he argues that the mystification that takes place in commodity exchange, the obfuscation of unequal social relations embedded in the very structure of the commodity, reproduces itself identically in the abstract thinking of human subjects. With this analysis in mind, we might begin to understand how postmodernism as a form of abstract thinking logically favors a model of society and history structured, in the manner of democratic liberalism, as a constellation of discrete entities, reflecting postmodernism's conception of social relations: class collaboration, pluralism, the mystification of borders, the naturalization of class antagonisms, and the irrational denial of social transformation. By contrast, Marxism conceptualizes society as a totality marked by social class contradictions—and it views history as the never-ending sharpening and unraveling of these contradictions.

Rather than consider cultural identity as oscillating between worlds or stuck in the interstices of the borderlands trope, we should think of cultural identity as intricately linked to the abstraction of commodity exchange where nonequivalence gets mistaken for equivalence—where what you see is not exactly what you get, even in terms of "personal consciousness" or cultural identity. Whereas the abstraction that takes place in the exchange of commodities obfuscates the accumulation of surplus value, the abstraction at work in cultural identity results in the emergence of a reified consciousness unable to conceptualize its own complicity in reproducing certain hegemonic relations of production. Thus the goal for Chicana/o cultural criticism should not be to embrace ideological ambivalence, but to demystify its inner content by uncovering its social origins and its historical development. Stated differently, racial and ethnic subjects must become conscious of themselves as a historically situated cultural group but primarily for the purpose of abolishing all divisions based on racial or ethnic difference, including those constructed through the formation of their own cultural identity.

Before closing, let us return to the central issues at hand. Methodologically, I have worked toward a series of dialectical disclosures to show the following: borderlands theory has become the central trope of identity in the criticism of Chicana/o literature and culture, offering many advantages for deconstructing boundaries and barriers of various kinds, both real and symbolic. This theory, however, also poses significant problems for scholarship and activism alike. Borderlands theory tends to romanticize the real border, sometimes minimizing the severity of conditions faced by immigrants in crossing the border. Through the process of making these disclosures, I have argued, implicitly if not forthrightly, that a concept of identity based on postmodernist fragmentation, as in borderlands theory, functions to mystify social contradictions instead of revealing the concealed social causes of their concrete forms. For this reason, postmodernist theory hinders rather than enhances the possibility for emancipatory political projects. Further, postmodernism functions as ideology not because it produces a faulty consciousness, but because it produces a consciousness that takes the form of an abstraction of a real social object, emerging historically as a replication of the abstraction that takes place in commodity exchange as argued by Adorno in his critique of identity.

Finally, I want to make absolutely clear that I am not opposed to studies of the border or to literary representations of life on the border. On the contrary, these kinds of writing are important and necessary. I hold, however, that the social contradictions of class exploitation, racism, and sexism cannot be solved by constructing a cultural identity in the image of the most repressive and racist symbol of demarcation and exclusion produced by capitalism, nationalism, and imperialism—namely, the border. Ideological ambivalence becomes significant only through the meticulous critique of the social and historical determinants of that ambivalence, and only through a praxis aimed at undoing the very structures of power that lie at the root of ambivalence. Thus we find ourselves in a peculiar but nonetheless refreshing position of once again discovering the importance of exhorting vociferously that seemingly obsolete—but in reality more urgently needed now than ever—slogan of the traditional Left, repeated here by way of a conclusion but also as an urgent call to action: "Smash All Borders!"

Notes

1. "La India María" is the name of a character played by María Elena Velasco in various Mexican films. Velasco directed and starred in the 1987 film, *Ni de aquí, ni de allá* (From neither here nor there).

2. A *coyote* is a Spanish slang term used to refer to a person who smuggles undocumented workers from Mexico into the United States.

3. For two good sources on the politics of the border and the economics of immigration, see Chavez and Oscar Martínez.

4. Anti-immigrant sentiment has not been limited to right-wing groups. David Gutiérrez points out that in the early 1970s Cesar Chavez "was among the most vocal critics of illegal immigration. The UFW constantly maintained this position in the early years, going so far as to report undocumented Mexican farm workers to the INS" (197).

5. For a similar argument, but from a Marxist perspective, see Ebert, esp. Chapter Three: "Feminism and Resistant Postmodernism." Ebert identifies two kinds of postmodernism: resistant and ludic.

6. Some readers may complain about my use of a German philosopher to analyze Chicana/o cultural criticism. Nationalists and proponents of identity politics, in particular, have traditionally attacked Marxism for its "Eurocentrism,"

but their criticisms are not well founded. Chicana/o culture is not free from the influence of European culture and history. The fact that most Chicanas/os write in English or Spanish pointedly illuminates the fact that Chicana/o culture is already intricately connected to European culture. Further, I do not consider Marxism to be "Eurocentric." It is the one genuine international philosophy.

7. Jameson argues that the "poststructuralist attack on 'historicism,' which emerges from a no less problematic affirmation of the priority of 'synchronic' thought" can be understood as a repudiation of teleological forms of narrative, which amounts to a "repudiation of the idea of 'progress'" (*Ideologies of Theory* 153). He adds that "[a]s desirable as it may be to rid Marxism of any vestiges of a properly bourgeois notion of 'progress,' it would seem a good deal less desirable nervously to abandon any Marxian vision of the future altogether (an operation in which Marxism itself is generally abandoned in the process)" (154).

8. For an analysis of Adorno's deconstructing dialectic, see Larsen.

9. See Deleuze and Guattari, where they argue: "There is a whole world of difference between the schizo and the revolutionary: the difference between the one who escapes, and the one who knows how to make what he is escaping escape. . . . The schizo is not revolutionary, but the schizophrenic process—in terms of which the schizo is merely the interruption, or the continuation in the void—is the potential for revolution. To those who say that escaping is not courageous, we answer: what is not escape *and social investment at the same time?* [original emphasis]" (341).

10. Jameson (*Late Marxism*) complains about the poor translations of Adorno's books, including *Negative Dialectics*, the volume from which I have taken the passages for this essay. Jameson points out that readers "should make a note of the most urgent howlers," among them, "*Tauschverhaltnis* [which] is in particular not 'barter' but simply 'exchange system' (very much as in 'exchange value')" (x).

11. I realize that in my reading of Adorno I run the risk of being accused of choosing selective passages to make a specific argument in a way that misrepresents a broader understanding of Adorno's work in general and of negative dialectics in particular. But in reading these passages from the perspective I have chosen, I make no claim that they represent the "totality" of Adorno's critical theory. Also, I have already stated that Adorno is a problematical theorist, not easily pigeonholed into an identifiable theoretical project. His critique of identity implies that he would himself resist a categorization of any kind that would "posit" his work ontologically.

Works Cited

Adorno, Theodor. *Negative Dialectics*. New York: Seabury, 1973.

Alarcón, Francisco X. *Snake Poems: An Aztec Invocation*. San Francisco: Chronicle Books, 1992.

Anzaldúa, Gloria. *Borderlands/la frontera: The New Mestiza*. San Francisco: Aunt Lute Books, 1987.

Cantú, Norma. *Canícula: Snapshots of a Girlhood in la Frontera*. Albuquerque: University of New Mexico Press, 1995.

Chavez, Leo R. *Shadowed Lives: Undocumented Immigrants in American Society*. Fort Worth, Tex.: Harcourt Brace College Publishers, 1992.

Deleuze, Giles, and Felix Guattari. *Anti-Oedipus: Capitalism and Schizophrenia.* Minneapolis: University of Minnesota Press, 1983.

Ebert, Teresa L. *Ludic Feminism and After: Postmodernism, Desire, and Labor in Late Capitalism.* Ann Arbor: University of Michigan Press, 1996.

Gutiérrez, David. *Walls and Mirrors: Mexican Americans, Mexican Immigrants, and the Politics of Ethnicity.* Berkeley: University of California Press, 1995.

Gutiérrez-Jones, Carl. *Rethinking the Borderlands: Between Chicano Culture and Legal Discourse.* Berkeley: University of California Press, 1995.

Jameson, Fredric. *The Political Unconscious: Narrative as a Socially Symbolic Act.* Ithaca, N.Y.: Cornell University Press, 1981.

———. *The Ideologies of Theory: Essays, 1971–1986.* Vol. 2 of *The Syntax of History.* Minneapolis: University of Minnesota Press, 1988.

———. *Late Marxism: Adorno, or the Persistence of the Dialectic.* London: Verso, 1990.

Larsen, Neil. "Negation of the Abnegation: Dialectical Criticism in the 1990s." *Rethinking Marxism* 5.2 (1992): 109–17.

Martínez, Oscar J. Ed. *U.S.-Mexico Borderlands: Historical and Contemporary Perspectives.* Wilmington, Del.: SR Books, 1996.

Martínez, Rubén. "Culture, Migration, and Madness: On Both Sides of the Rio Bravo." *El Andar: The Latino Magazine for the New Millenium* (Winter 1998): 21–23.

Moraga, Cherríe. *Loving in the War Years: Lo que nunca pasó por sus labios.* Expanded ed. Cambridge, Mass.: South End Press, 2000.

Pérez-Torres, Rafael. *Movements in Chicano Poetry: Against Myths, against Margins.* Cambridge: Cambridge University Press, 1995.

Pratt, Mary Louise. *Imperial Eyes: Travel Writing and Transculturation.* London: Routledge, 1992.

Rosaldo, Renato. *Culture and Truth: The Remaking of Social Analysis.* Boston: Beacon, 1989.

Rouse, Roger. "Mexican Migration and the Social Space of Postmodernism." David Gutiérrez, ed., *Between Worlds: Mexican Immigrants in the United States.* Wilmington: SR Books, 1996. 247–63.

Saldívar, José David. *The Dialectics of Our America: Genealogy, Cultural Critique, and Literary History.* Durham, N.C.: Duke University Press, 1991.

———. *Border Matters: Remapping American Cultural Studies.* Berkeley: University of California Press, 1997.

Cary Nelson

The Letters the Presidents Did Not Release: Radical Scholarship and the Legacy of the American Volunteers in Spain

In the winter of 1938–39 the Spanish Republic was barely hanging by a thread. Cut in two by a fascist offensive, underarmed, its international volunteers on their way home, it was massively outgunned and undersupplied. Short of a political miracle, a fascist victory was a certainty. But those who cared—those who had risked their lives and those who supported them—were working the small patch of political ground still remaining. In Washington, D.C., the League against War and Fascism held a January 5–8, 1939, conference at a cathedral near the White House, in part to press the campaign to lift the U.S./British embargo against the republic and let it buy the arms it needed to survive.

A few months after the outbreak of the 1936–39 Spanish Civil War, the Western nations had signed a nonintervention pact pledging to provide arms to neither side. Hitler and Mussolini promptly violated the treaty and began to arm the military officers who had staged a revolt against the democratically elected government. In response, Mexico offered the Spanish Republic a small shipment of rifles, and the Soviet Union agreed to sell it weapons. For a time, France permitted the arms shipments to cross its borders. But these limited arrangements never matched in quality and reliability the men and weapons supplied by Germany and Italy. Throughout the war Spain's allies and sympathizers unsuccessfully pressured the United States and Britain to lift the embargo against selling arms to this nation under siege.

So it was that Oliver Loud, a young teacher at Sarah Lawrence College (later a professor of physics at Antioch College, where I was an undergraduate from 1963 to 1967), was at the Washington Cathedral in 1939 and remembered the delegation that the League against War and Fascism sent to the White House for a meeting with Franklin Delano Roosevelt (FDR). On their triumphant return to the cathedral, the league representatives announced that the president had agreed to sign a letter lifting the embargo. The conference thus had achieved its most urgent objective; the participants sang Spanish Civil War songs, as some of us—veterans and their admirers—still do, and then everyone joined in a snake dance through the cathedral isles. The details come from a diary Loud kept at the time. In April 1996 he wrote me his subsequent reflections on the events of 1939:

> Twenty days after our snake dance, Barcelona fell. "Lifting the embargo" would perhaps have been too late—but it would have had other highly significant consequences. (My diary is filled with jottings, as early as in 1937, that record our persistent attempt to get "the embargo lifted.") Indeed Frances [Loud's wife] was in a political theatrical skit, providing a melodramatic scream when Gypsy Rose Lee, before an audience of several thousand, began lifting her skirt—and then explaining: I don't know what you are thinking but I am thinking about "lifting the embargo!"

The conference completed its agenda, which ended with a session on the militant labor movement of the time. For Loud's generation, the struggles against fascism and for workers' rights in the United States were part of one story. Yet hindsight provides some ironies about those on stage in 1939. The speakers included radical artist Rockwell Kent, who later suffered under McCarthyism, and Bella Dodd, a figure in the New York College and Universities Teachers Union, who, conversely, cooperated with the American inquisition as a "reconvert" to Catholicism and an informer.

A week went by, then two, but no letter came from the White House. The embargo persisted. The rumor that circulated through the league was unambiguous: the Catholic hierarchy had gotten to Roosevelt. If he signed the letter to lift the embargo, it had warned him, he was dead in the next election. Whether or not that part of the story is true, the president undoubtedly made the necessary political calculation and decided that his progressive instincts could not be honored.[1] If the U.S. role throughout the war was a scandal, that calculation, I would argue, can hardly be counted one. Most politicians make these sorts of judgment calls every day.

That does not mean that letters of unflinching principle are not signed, and sent, and delivered. Some 2,800 Americans in Spain wrote such letters and signed some of them with their blood. There are places to look for such documents, but the annals of Congress and the White House are not among them. We must look to ourselves to recover those letters and preserve the traditions they embody. And we must look to stories like this to establish the past and future grounds of an imperiled, contested agency for members of the American Left, an agency often not historically decisive but nonetheless historically meaningful.

Both at the time and since, the status of whatever agency the volunteers had—whether individually or collectively—has been both celebrated and assaulted. It is the basis of a continuing debate that evolves but never loses its intensity. In the case of Spain in 1939, the U.S. government maintained a policy of nonintervention on the one hand while nearly three thousand Americans citizens intervened most determinedly on the other. If the International Brigades was organized by the Comintern at Joseph Stalin's behest and for his own reasons, its ranks were filled by a series of individuals who acted out of their own sense of historical necessity. Thus those who volunteered on behalf of a losing cause —the defense of the Spanish Republic—have left a legacy of activism and commitment that has provided an inspiration for the Left ever since.

Condemned as Stalin's dupes by the Right, many of the volunteers in fact understood the threat fascism posed to the world and underwent intensely personal decisions to put their own lives at risk. Their letters—published decades later in a volume entitled *Madrid 1937* (1996)—show how a political movement is inflected in the voice, class, race, ethnicity, and individual experience of each writer. An excerpt of a letter from Canute Frankson, an African American volunteer from Detroit, to his wife reads:

Albacete, Spain
July 6, 1937

My Dear Friend:

I'm sure that by this time you are still waiting for a detailed explanation of what has this international struggle to do with my being here. Since this is a war between whites who for centuries have held us in slavery, and have heaped every kind of insult and abuse upon us, segregated and jim-crowed us; why I, a Negro who have fought through these years for the rights of my people, am here in Spain today?

Because we are no longer an isolated minority group fighting hopelessly against an immense giant. Because, my dear, we have joined with, and become an active part of, a great progressive force, on whose shoulders rests the responsibility of saving human civilization from the planned destruction of a small group of degenerates gone mad in their lust for power. Because if we crush Fascism here we'll save our people in America, and in other parts of the world from the vicious persecution, wholesale imprisonment, and slaughter which the Jewish people suffered and are suffering under Hitler's Fascist heels.

All we have to do is to think of the lynching of our people. We can but look back at the pages of American history stained with the blood of Negroes; stink with the burning bodies of our people hanging from trees; bitter with the groans of our tortured loved ones from whose living bodies ears, fingers, toes have been cut for souvenirs—living bodies into which red-hot pokers have been thrust. All because of a hate created in the minds of men and women by their masters. . . . Must we keep the flame which these masters kindled constantly fed? . . . I think not. . . . Soon, many Angelo Herndons will rise from among them, and from among us, and will lead us both against those who live by the stench of our burnt flesh. We will crush them. We will build us a new society—a society of peace and plenty. There will be no color line, no jim-crow trains, no lynching. That is why, my dear, I'm here in Spain.[2]

When Stalin lost interest in the Spanish Civil War, having decided that it would not become the occasion for an antifascist alliance with the Western democracies, the volunteers fought on and died. Yet Stalin's military advisers in Spain continued to press for victory. Events there suggest that individuals acting through political movements can gain meaningful agency and historical standing despite the differing aims of nation-states and world leaders. Moreover, the meaning that flows from such contextualized agency lives on in new contexts. Without carving out such a relational basis for agency, the Left really has no effective traditions in cultures where it is marginalized. With such a sense of history, on the other hand, it has the necessary basis for understanding and negotiating its present options. The play of similarity and difference apparent when past struggles are compared with present ones sets the proper horizon for progressive activism. And Spain itself, it turns out, has had its full share of recurrent historical moments.

I tell this anecdote of the Spanish Civil War now in part because sixty years later American history brought us to another Democratic White House, another president with good instincts, and another historical context in which those instincts were politically difficult or impossible to follow with any consistency. The title of this essay is "The Letters the Presidents Did Not Release: Radical Scholarship and the Legacy of the American Volunteers in Spain"; in fact, there are two letters and two presidents at stake, with nearly sixty years separating them. It is time to commemorate Franklin Delano Roosevelt's reluctance to sign with William Jefferson Clinton's.

Early in 1996 some board members of the Abraham Lincoln Brigade Archives and their friends spoke with members of the Democratic National Committee (DNC) about the possibility of the White House issuing a letter recognizing the unique contribution the Lincoln Brigade had made to the historic struggle against fascism. The effort started in Hollywood among members of the Screen Actors Guild and their colleagues in the film industry. They had supported Clinton during his first campaign and were well on the way to contributing heavily to his bid for reelection. They thus had good access to the White House and the DNC.

A letter, amounting to a proclamation, was drafted in California and sent to Washington for consideration. I did not participate in the negotiations but was scheduled to receive an advance copy of the letter if it was issued, in part because I had permission to print it as the frontispiece to a publication I had completed, entitled *Shouts from the Wall: Posters and Photographs Brought Home from the Spanish Civil War by American Volunteers* (1996).[3] The plan was to publicize Clinton's letter in conjunction with the sixtieth anniversary of the start of the Spanish Civil War, at which time the book would be published. In April 1996 the veterans of the Abraham Lincoln Brigade and the Abraham Lincoln Brigade Archives (on whose board I serve) would jointly sponsor a major event in New York, where the letter would be read in public for the first time.

Suffice it to say that some White House officials were inclined to issue such a letter and some disinclined. How high the substantive discussions went we will never know for certain, and it really does not matter. What is notable is that we got a hearing when every other White House of the previous sixty years would have thrown us out the door. What is, unfortunately, also notable is that we failed once again.

For a moment, however, it seemed otherwise. I received a call from Washington informing me that President Clinton had signed two copies of the letter. One would be kept in the White House; the other would come to me by express mail the next day. I was, to say the least, excited. I got up early the next morning, wondering whether the White House would opt for morning or afternoon delivery. Unable to concentrate on anything else, I spent a good part of the day looking out the window and waiting for the delivery van. By 5:00 P.M. it was clear that the letter was not coming that day. I made a few phone calls and eventually learned that the president's letter would not be released.

During the course of negotiations the Veterans Administration got wind of the impending proclamation and raised objections. In the end the calculation that supporting the Lincoln Brigade was too risky won out. It may well have been the right political decision in an election year. "Soft on Communism" seemed a relatively empty slogan half a decade after the fall of the Soviet Union, but the elections in Russia might change things. In any case, the Lincolns clearly remained partially tarred with anticommunism, just as they have been for more than half a century. As I said, they wrote their own letters; there are historical alternatives to official Washington.

What else is notable about this inadvertent White House commemoration of FDR's failure to sign is that it produced a remarkable draft letter, a document that exists only because a meaningful dialogue was possible with Clinton's aides. No similar text would have resulted from interaction with a Dole White House, had he won the next election, and Ronald Reagan, of course, thought that the Lincolns should have fought on the other side. George W. Bush will not be holding discussions on this matter.

Thus the draft, negotiated and supposedly signed but unreleased, is itself a significant achievement and one worth disseminating. It can only circulate now if I act against the wishes of my friends and publish it. I volunteered to do so at the time, but my Hollywood contacts were horrified at the prospect. They considered my offer a violation of their confidence. Moreover, they were certain that they would immediately and permanently lose the White House access they had worked so hard to establish if I embarrassed the president. Finally, however, they made one argument I had to accept: If Clinton were reelected in 1996, he might sign the proclamation during his second term. So we would wait; I agreed not to publish the letter during Clinton's term in office. We would wait for other things as well, like a pardon for Leonard Peltier, hanging on for the last minute to see whether political calculation would prevail. I was expecting the Lincoln Brigade to receive nothing whatever from Clinton, which is just what it did receive. Meanwhile, the prospect of embarrassing Clinton eventually seemed quite beside the point. He did that decisively himself. Here is the letter:

> To the Veterans of the Abraham Lincoln Brigade:
>
> Time and distance often provide the perspective necessary to understand historical events in context. That is why "Shouts from the Wall," the exhibition of posters you brought home from the Spanish Civil War, is so important.
>
> This year, the sixtieth anniversary of the Spanish Civil War, seems the perfect moment to remind Americans that your selfless response to the rise of fascism in Spain was exemplary of the best in the American spirit. It speaks of a willingness to sacrifice on behalf of justice and freedom, even in the face of misunderstanding and condemnation here at home.
>
> Many of your young friends and compatriots lost their lives in Spain, a fate they preferred to the alternative of doing nothing. You, who survived, joined our fighting forces in World War II and have lived your entire lives with that same need to commit and to act. Commitment to an ideal, action in the face of ignorance—these are examples which are sorely needed in today's America and are at the heart of good citizenship.
>
> Recently you, the members of the Abraham Lincoln Brigade, were honored by Spain, but here at home you are best recalled for being humiliated during the McCarthy era as Communist sympathizers. Now, sixty years after the onset of the Spanish Civil War, the time has come for Americans to recognize the important contribution the Lincolns made in the decade-long battle against fascism in Europe, and to applaud your continuing devotion to the fight for all human rights and freedoms at home and abroad.
>
> Today, we honor the courage of your youth and the wisdom of your age.[4]

Had the president's advisers all lined up behind this letter and the president released it, I doubt that those American volunteers who still have nightmares about the February 1937 battle of Jarama would sleep any easier. Still, in this their last hurrah a healing gesture from the White House would have had a certain resonance for the few thousand Americans who still care about the Lincoln Brigade legacy. But perhaps the official seal is not essential. Perhaps the words themselves, negotiated with a White House anxious about its image in an election year but nonetheless sympathetic to the brigade, once publicized will have some of the effect they were intended to have.

Though no one in the White House may have been aware of it, Clinton would not have been the first American politician to have honored the American volunteers. Chicago mayor Harold Washington issued a proclamation honoring black American volunteer Oliver Law, who died in Spain, shortly before his own death. The governor of Florida recognized the International Brigades at the time of the *Shouts from the Wall* opening in Tampa in 1997, as did politicians in New York and Washington State.

In any case, the struggle over the legacy of the Lincoln Brigade continues. These presidential letters, it is worth noting, were more than acts of witness. They were political acts with both immediate and long-term impact. Roosevelt's letter, moreover, would have had military and historical consequences. Some still feel that the will to arm Spain would have enabled the republic to win the war and give a signal defeat to European fascism. Had we stood up to fascism in Spain, we might well have found the spine to stand up to Hitler at Munich in 1938. Then perhaps modern history would have taken a different turn.

The public failure to remember and recognize the implications of this watershed moment in 1930s history continues to reverberate in our national imagination and in our political life. By the time the Clinton administration wavered in its decision to honor the Americans who joined the fight against fascism, there were, one may note, a substantial number of public monuments honoring the International Brigades elsewhere. In Spain, of course, there was to be no public honor for the volunteers until after Franco died in 1975. Within twenty years, however, the Spaniards had reconstructed the International Brigades cemetery at Fuencarral north of Madrid and had built a monument in Barcelona. Great Britain was the site of more than forty monuments, from Ireland and England to Scotland and Wales.

In the United States, until the end of the twentieth century, there was but one memorial to our "premature antifascists," a plaque at the City College of New York (CCNY) honoring those of the CCNY community who fought and died in Spain. Finally, a beautiful bronze plaque was set in a massive piece of granite in front of the student union building on the University of Washington campus in Seattle in 1999. The same design was adopted in Madison, Wisconsin, the following year—both mo… …heir friends. Key fi… …roff and Madison … been approved for

…d to be dedicated in a …shire, were taken down. …essful campaign to honor …nd twelve New Hampshire …cated the Seattle design, and … volunteers. After approval by …ittee, the two plaques were in- st… …se awaiting official unveiling until the noto… …per, the *Union Leader*, editorialized against the mon… …uld Cohen—or any other freedom-loving American—want… …e a dog in a fight between fascism and communism?" the newspaper asked on February 12.

This portrayal of the war—as a struggle between fascism and communism—wholly erases the fact that a democratically elected Popular Front government in Spain was under assault simultaneously by its own army and by foreign troops from Germany and Italy. Franco himself liked to define the conflict as one between Christianity and communism, a characterization the Catholic Church widely adopted, hence its opposition to lifting the embargo against selling arms to Spain. Yet at the outbreak of the war the Communists had little influence on the Spanish government; that changed in part because the United States and Britain refused to help the republic, while the Soviet Union did. Then the Spanish Communist Party played a key role in organizing the defense of Madrid, and the Comintern, or Communist International, organized the International Brigades. But the values of the participants defined the struggle as one between democracy and fascism. And certainly antifascism was what motivated most of the international volunteers.

This is the disputed terrain radical scholars enter when they write about the war. To write a book about Spain's struggle is to help shape, albeit at a distance, the possibilities for public memory and commemoration of the most notable international progressive cause of the first half of the twentieth century. And it is thus as well a judgment about a whole history of regularly thwarted or co-opted left-wing social agendas. Any publication about the Spanish Civil War is inherently more than a work of scholarship. It is inescapably a contribution to more than sixty years of political and cultural debate. Further, it either facilitates or inhibits contemporary activism in the same tradition.

Although nations do not necessarily fall in sequence like dominoes, it seems that the ideological consequences of political witness and memory can operate in much that fashion. After the voluntary international participation in the Spanish Civil War was Red-baited, a whole series of progressive beliefs and initiatives became available for Red-baiting in the United States. In the 1950s the union movement would be branded Communist, as the civil rights and antiwar movements would be in the next decade. Indeed, the veterans of the Spanish Civil War were active in all of these causes. These veterans were in the South at the height of the civil rights movement, and they were marching beneath the Abraham Lincoln Brigade banner in demonstrations opposing the Vietnam War. To honor them, to grant them public commemoration, is to recognize lifelong radical commitments.

Even apparently more neutral research traverses this national political terrain. When Jefferson Hendricks and I published letters from American volunteers who had been killed in Spain, we certainly knew that we were doing more than just putting historical documents in print for the first time. These volunteers literally had their voices silenced. The only presence they had in the historical record was the existence of their names on various lists. Now they would contribute their individual letters to personal and institutional libraries across the world. They would, in a sense, acquire a living voice decades after their deaths. That posthumous presence would inevitably humanize their legacy. It is far easier to Red-bait a name on a list than a young man or woman writing to friends and family. It is far easier to dismiss as pawns people whose acts and decisions have no depth and texture than it is people who explain themselves to us in detail across the decades. Of course, we had no interest in pretending that our scholarship had no political implications. We were deeply moved to be able to recover the voices of the largely forgotten dead and hoped they would help energize contemporary political action.

At some level, Left scholarship is always committed scholarship, scholarship with a partisan edge. To do research as part of a political commitment does not mean that one is uninterested in establishing facts and providing accurate accounts of events, though facts are often notoriously elusive in historical research. But as one probes motivations for actions and accounts for their consequences, judgments may be appropriate. I know of no truly disinterested accounts of the Spanish Civil War, though there are certainly scholars who try to recover the self-understanding of all parties to the conflict. In the end, however, just as with scholarship on

World War II or the Holocaust, most writers display a preference for one side or the other. I chose to recover letters from the Lincoln battalion, not letters from Hitler's Condor Legion, the latter notorious for the 1937 bombing of the Basque holy city of Guernica. That choice alone made clear whose legacy I wished to enrich.

Nothing in Left history, moreover, is wholly isolated. However embattled, however frequently suppressed or forgotten, the Left is a tradition. It has a long history for which individual episodes are also part of a larger story. To research and recover one part of that narrative is to strengthen the ground beneath all of its other segments, to see it as an ongoing combat with power and privilege in which losses and gains, discourses promoted, and strategies chosen are lessons at once for current and future generations. By filling out the story of labor struggles in earlier decades, we enrich and amplify the inheritances of those taking up similar battles later. By complicating the character of a commitment to international socialism in Spain, we open possibilities for a better understanding of such commitments in other historical moments. It is not only scholars but also Left activists who sometimes see the present struggles as palimpsests layered with echoes of the past.

Inevitably, then, historical research also resonates among the choices available to us in the present day. There is no alternative. To pretend that one is not alive in the present, that the present makes no demands on scholarly and political commitments lodged in another decade or another century, is to deny responsibility for the contemporary effects your work may already be having. Traditionally, some scholars have avoided contemporary political commitments out of fear that they would compromise the reception of their research. But there is no avoiding the dissemination and multiplication of meanings from scholarly texts. They raise implications for current practice regardless of our intentions. Thus the line between scholarship and political activity is inherently unstable.

The stories about Roosevelt and Clinton that open this essay have never been told. Am I engaged in scholarly activity or political action by telling them here? Are these events, despite their similarity, to be placed in substantially different categories because of when they took place, 1938 versus 1996? To be sure, if I had told the Clinton anecdote in 1996 it would have been received as a political rather than a scholarly act. Indeed, at the time I had in mind not an essay in a university press book but rather a much shorter op-ed piece tentatively entitled "Waiting for Bill." Has the passage of half a decade and the choice of a very different venue freed my account from political implications? Clinton is now out of office, but he is still very much part of the national scene. And certainly both FDR's final refusal to help Spain and Clinton's refusal to honor the Lincoln Brigade join the long story of the dominant culture's relations with the American Left. The lesson they teach us about the limits of American liberalism is one we are apparently compelled to relearn decade after decade. As Loud wrote to me about FDR in 1996, the year of Clinton's own unsent letter, "FDR's subsequent decision *not* to lift the embargo is just one illustration of the failure of the great 'New Deal Coalition' to provide for *accountability* in a 'charismatic leader' who can take for granted the support of the constituencies who press from below and select the advisors he chooses to find persuasive—especially in political compromising."[5]

If Left scholarship inevitably joins Left politics, then the idea that one can withhold one's self from contemporaneity is at best seriously flawed. Left scholarship, moreover, joins the history of Left discourses and discourses about the Left. The differential tradition of manifestos, letters, poems, songs, announcements, editorials, and polemical or scholarly essays is finally one tradition only, rife with disputation and fraternity to be sure, but one tradition nonetheless.

Yet the move from research to activism is one that many scholars cannot make gracefully. We watched labor scholars at Yale University become union busters, Leftists at Columbia cross picket lines. As Jonathan Hunt wrote to me about his experiences as a graduate student union activist:

> I joined the small TA union when I arrived at Santa Cruz in 1989 and walked picket lines and protests for eleven years, first as an underemployed graduate student, then as an underemployed part-time lecturer. The struggle at Santa Cruz was relatively unsung, overshadowed as we were by the proximity of Berkeley and the national prominence of Yale, but it was often bitter. The most bitter pill of all was the behavior, when push came to shove, of our faculty. We were shocked at how quickly the veneer of the teacher and mentor could be discarded to reveal the supervisor underneath. At solidarity meetings with faculty, we watched in disbelief as the faculty members who taught us to read Marx and labor history told us "now is not the time" and "this is not a real political struggle." On a rainy night in the middle of a bitter six-week strike, these "sympathetic" faculty members taught us—inadvertently—an unforgettable lesson in the power structures of the university.[6]

In the end, "now is not the time" means nothing more than "not on my watch, not while my privileges are at stake." "This is not a real political struggle" presumably reflects the mixture of denial and otherworldliness and guilt that permits faculty members to claim that the campus is not the real world. I find that graduate employees or part-timers without health care who become seriously ill feel that they are living in a world that is far too real. Obviously, some Left scholars understand exactly the relationship between past struggles, current ones, and their own benefits and place in a structure of power. But why do so many others not share awareness of their place in a heritage of Left activism?

Several factors converge on academic subject positions to help people avoid seeing who they are. Start with a statistic. Over a thirty-year period membership in the American Association of University Professors has declined by nearly two-thirds—from 120,000 to 45,000. Part of the decline represents a protest against the association's decision to help faculty on individual campuses to unionize if they choose to do so. The other losses have come from the combined result of faculty retirements and the failure of new faculty members to join in sufficient numbers.

Many scholars used to have loyalties to their institution and to the profession as a whole. Those loyalties tend now to be lodged in the individual academic discipline. But the older model was to a significant degree a collective one; it emphasized group identity and mission rather than individual gain. The rise of the entrepreneurial faculty member, however, helped craft disciplinary identities that are primarily self-interested, that see English or philosophy or history less as ongoing traditions than as fields for self-advancement.

When an unreflective community investment in research meets this careerist model of disciplinarity, the result is a faculty member who sees self-advancement and careerism as transcendent virtues. Disciplines then reward and celebrate Left scholars without regard to their practices as teachers, as colleagues, as citizens, or even as human beings. The individual scholar, who may consistently mistreat the people in his or her life, nonetheless thinks of himself or herself as heroic.

It is clear that many accomplished scholars actually have no interest in the future of their disciplines. The history of sociology or political science effectively ends with the close of their own careers. A serious and ethically reflective disciplinary identity would make faculty concerned about the exploitation of contingent teachers because it undermines the discipline's capacity to renew and advance itself. For a Left faculty member, sensitivity to the history of labor injustice should combine with disciplinary loyalty to make reform imperative. But Left faculty who see the campus and the discipline primarily as potential claques, sources of applause and rewards, do not make those connections. Meanwhile, abstract advocacy for victims elsewhere in time or space places self-interested scoundrels on a professional pedestal.

The most well-publicized display of these elitist values among faculty confronted with workplace injustices was, of course, during the graduate student grade strike at Yale University from December 1995 to January 1996. There numerous nationally known scholars with a history of progressive scholarship on issues of race, gender, colonization, or unionization not only rejected the union's strategy but also turned in their teaching assistants for disciplinary action. Yet a core of scholars on the Left—most notably Hazel Carby, Michael Denning, and David Montgomery—stood with the union and were among its most eloquent advocates. These faculty members joined with younger graduate student scholars and campus workers to create alliances that overturned conventional academic hierarchies.

In the process they signaled a powerful interchange between their scholarship and their activism. Carby is the author of groundbreaking studies of race and literature in the 1920s and 1930s, Denning has written an influential work on the Popular Front culture of the 1930s; and Montgomery is a distinguished scholar of labor history. Their scholarship and their activism reinforce one another, flow from the same underlying values, and do comparable work in the culture at large. For them, as for other scholars across the world, student mentoring is activist mentoring that fosters a coherent and unified praxis. One might argue that the African American students who were among the leaders at Yale during the critical days of the grade strike had inherited the legacy not only of the black union and civil rights activists of earlier decades but also of the eighty African Americans who volunteered for service in Spain.

Academics are uniquely well positioned to combine historical research with contemporary activism. Indeed, the practice of joining the two activities is one model of politics that academics can help promote by their example. Interestingly, the veterans of the Spanish Civil War have had a long debate on exactly this issue, with some urging their comrades to abandon historical commemoration and education in favor of contemporary political action and others seeing the possibility of maintaining both commitments. The debate itself, notably, has sustained both traditions. And the combined tradition has evolved, and sometimes, paradoxically, prospered, amid assault from the Right. Just as the veterans and their allies raised money for ambulances in Spain, so did they fund ambulances in Nicaragua decades later. Yet they also established the

Abraham Lincoln Brigade Archives to promote public education about their own Left history.

Whether in the 1930s or the present day, it is always easier to account for inaction than for the decision to take on personal risk and uncertainty. Though the general cultural and political reasons for action are clear enough—from the rise of fascism in the 1930s to the rise of exploitive global corporatization in the 1990s—most people remain passive. Yet sometimes multiple forces combine to make activism a generational option. It becomes an available choice, a place one may go to physically and psychologically, individually and collectively. So it was for the 1930s generation, enough so that failure to act required reflection and self-justification. Inaction seemed not the absence of commitment but its refusal. On American campuses today, as on so many campuses where students volunteered to fight for Spain more than sixty years ago, moral and political values are coalescing in such a way as to place the option of activism before every individual. From unionization drives to No Sweat and Living Wage campaigns, the same values and the same oppositional reading of profit are interpolating people into collective action. The effort to reform a single industry—higher education—may in the process become a model for comparable efforts in other workplaces. In the 1930s capitalism succumbed to a worldwide depression; now its ravages instead accompany triumphalist rhetoric. But an unjust hourglass economy heralded both developments. The legacy of Spain, after all, is to apply principles of justice to the contexts in which you live.

I cannot help but repeatedly recognize how much my friends among the surviving veterans of the Abraham Lincoln Brigade and their families identify themselves with current labor struggles. They left the City College of New York or the University of Wisconsin or Berkeley more than sixty years ago to put their lives on the line for people and principle in Spain. It is they, eighty or ninety years old now, more often than tenured faculty, who contacted me up over the last decade to talk about the latest campus union struggles. "Did you see the story in today's *Times* about Yale?" they would ask, and it always seemed that they had read it before me. These embattled old men and women of the Left understand the traditions to which they belong. And it is they especially who have helped me see my life as whole, who recognize that historiography and commitment are incomplete unless they are partners, who have reinforced my sense that a 1938 letter lifting the embargo on Spain means something today and makes a claim on present action.

Notes

1. Toward the end of *My Mission to Spain: Watching the Rehearsal for World War II* (New York: Simon and Schuster, 1954), Claude Bowers, U.S. ambassador to the Spanish Republic during the war, reports that FDR expressed his regret over his failure to lift the embargo: "I wrote personally to Roosevelt that however good our intentions may have been at first, it had become quite clear that actually our embargo was operating powerfully for the benefit of the Axis. . . . I found President Roosevelt seated at his desk in the White House residence, more serious and graver than I had ever seen him before. I got the impression that he was not happy over the course we had followed. Before I could sit down or utter a word he said: 'We have made a mistake; you have been right all along'" (p. 418). In an April 24–25, 1938, letter to Eleanor Roosevelt from Barcelona, Martha Gellhorn depicts a sympathetic FDR, but one who was willing to accept Spain's sacrifice as part of his domestic calculations: "What goes on here seems to me very much the affair of all of us, who do not want a world whose bible is 'Mein Kampf.' I believe now as much as ever that Spain is fighting our battle, and will not forget that night when we brought the film [*Spanish Earth*] to the White House, and the President said: Spain is a vicarious sacrifice for all of us. . . . But I think Spain is maybe not a sacrifice, but a champion; and hope to God that America at least will not go on letting this country down." Franklin D. Roosevelt Presidential Library, Hyde Park, N.Y.

2. Cary Nelson and Jefferson Hendricks, eds., *Madrid 1937: Letters of the Abraham Lincoln Brigade from the Spanish Civil War* (New York: Routledge, 1996), 33–34. The book includes a number of Frankson's letters.

3. Cary Nelson, *Shouts from the Wall: Posters and Photographs Brought Home from the Spanish Civil War by American Volunteers: A Catalogue to Accompany the Exhibit Curated by Peter Carroll and Cary Nelson for the Abraham Lincoln Brigade Archives* (Waltham, Mass.: Abraham Lincoln Brigade Archives, distributed by University of Illinois Press, 1996).

4. I reproduce the entire text verbatim from my photocopy of the letter provided to the White House.

5. Oliver Loud to the author, April 1996.

6. Hunt also wrote: "The left faculty members closest to me at UC Santa Cruz were very supportive of unionization. When the 1992 strike vote was taken, I told my faculty supervisor, Richard Terdiman (who later served on my dissertation committee) that I would not be able to do any more work as his TA (in an upper-division literature course of 65 students), he told me, 'Jon, I'd be ashamed of you if you did otherwise.' But this was a very rare response. One faculty member teaching a lecture course in German cinema announced to his class (without consulting the TAs) that his two TAs would not strike, because of their commitment to the left politics of the class and of avant-garde German cinema. The two TAs stood up and walked out without a word (if the professor had inquired, he would have known that they were shop stewards in their departments)." Hunt to the author, February 16, 2001; used with permission.

Contributors

Anthony Dawahare is an associate professor of English at California State University, Northridge. He has published articles on the depression-era writings of Langston Hughes, Tillie Olsen, and Meridel Le Sueur. He is the author of *Nationalism, Marxism, and African American Literature between the Wars: A New Pandora's Box.*

Barbara Foley is a professor of English at Rutgers University, Newark. She is the author of *Telling the Truth: The Theory and Practice of Documentary Fiction* and *Radical Representations: Politics and Form in U.S. Proletarian Fiction, 1929–1941*. Her most recent projects are *Georgia on My Mind: Jean Toomer, History, and the Politics of Modernism* and *Ralph Ellison and the Cold War.*

Marcial González is an assistant professor of English at the University of California at Berkeley. His research interests include Chicana/o literature and Marxist literary theory. He was a farm worker, labor organizer, and political activist for fifteen years prior to entering graduate school in 1994.

Fred Ho is a professional musician, composer, and bandleader in New York City. He is the editor of *From Legacy to Liberation: Politics and Culture of Revolutionary Asian Pacific America*, and his articles on jazz and Afro-Asian culture have appeared in *African American Review* and other journals. The recipient of the 1988 Duke Ellington Distinguished Artist Lifetime Achievement Award from the Seventeenth Annual Black Musicians' Conference, he is the leader of the Afro-Asian Music Ensemble and has recorded many albums.

William J. Maxwell is an associate professor of English and an affiliate of the Afro-American Studies and Research Program at the University of Illinois. He is the author of *New Negro, Old Left: African-American Writing and Communism between the Wars* and of numerous articles on black popular music, multiculturalism in the university, working-class culture, and the Harlem Renaissance. He is currently working on an edition of the collected poems of Claude McKay and a republication of Willard Motley's 1951 naturalistic novel *We Fished All Night.*

Bill V. Mullen is an associate professor of English at the University of Texas–San Antonio. He is the author of *Popular Fronts: Chicago and African American Cultural Politics, 1935-1946*. He is the editor of *Revolutionary Tales: Short Stories by African-American Women from the First Story to the Present* and coeditor, with Sherry Linkon, of *Radical Revisions: Rereading 1930s Culture.*

Cary Nelson is a professor of English at the University of Illinois at Champaign-Urbana. He is the author of numerous books on literature, the Left, and academia, including *Repression and Recovery: Modern American Poetry and the Politics of Cultural Memory, 1910–1945* and *Revolutionary Memory: Recovering the Poetry of the American Left*. He is also the editor of the Oxford *Anthology of Modern American Poetry*.

B. V. Olguín is an assistant professor of English at the University of Texas–San Antonio. He has published essays on Chicano literature and is completing a book on Chicana and Chicano Prison Culture, *La Pinta: History, Culture, and Ideology in Chicana and Chicano Convict Discourses*. He has taught writing and literature workshops in prisons throughout upstate New York and in underprivileged communities in Texas and California.

Rachel Rubin is an associate professor of American studies at the University of Massachusetts–Boston. She is the author of *Jewish Gangsters of Modern Literature* and co-editor of *American Popular Music: New Approaches to the Twentieth Century*.

Eric Schocket is an assistant professor of American literature at Hampshire College in Amherst, Massachusetts. His publications have appeared in *Representations*, *PMLA*, and *American Quarterly*. He is currently working on a book on the relationship between culture and class in the United States.

James Smethurst is an assistant professor in the Department of Afro-American Studies at the University of Massachusetts. He is the author of *The New Red Negro: The Literary Left and African American Poetry, 1930–1946*. He is currently at work on *Ethnic Dreams*, a project examining the rise of the Black Arts Movement.

Michelle Stephens is an assistant professor of English at Mount Holyoke College, teaching courses in American, African American, and Caribbean studies. She is currently working on a book on Marcus Garvey, Claude McKay, and C. L. R. James entitled *Black Empire: The New World Negro and the Re-routing of America*, which explores New World internationalist discourse as it engages with different forms of internationalist thought—Bolshevist, Americanist, Pan-Africanist.

Alan Wald is a professor of English and American Culture at the University of Michigan. He is the author of five books on the U.S. literary Left—among them, *Exiles from a Future Time: The Forging of the Mid-Twentieth-Century Literary Left* and *The New York Intellectuals: The Rise and Decline of the Anti-Stalinist Left from the 1930s to the 1980s*.

Mary Helen Washington is a professor of English at the University of Maryland, College Park, where she teaches African American and African Diasporan literary and cultural studies. She is the editor of *Black-Eyed Susans/Midnight Birds: Stories of Contemporary Black Women Writers*, *Invented Lives: Narratives of Black Women, 1860–1960*, and *Memory of Kin: Stories of Family by Black Writers*. She is currently working on a study of black writing and culture of the 1950s entitled *Recovering Black Radicalism(s): Black Writers, Civil Rights, and the Cold War.*

Index